ISSUES &
CONTROVERSIES
IN
AMERICAN HISTORY

SLAVERY IN THE UNITED STATES

ISSUES &
CONTROVERSIES
■■■ IN ■■■
AMERICAN HISTORY

SLAVERY IN THE UNITED STATES

JEFF FORRET, PH.D.
BALLARD C. CAMPBELL, PH.D., SERIES EDITOR

Facts On File

Issues and Controversies in American History: Slavery in the United States

Copyright © 2012 by Infobase Learning

Facts On File, Inc.
An imprint of Infobase Publishing
132 West 31st Street
New York NY 10001

Library of Congress Cataloging-in-Publication Data

Forret, Jeff, 1972–
    Slavery in the United States / Jeff Forret.
        p. cm.—(Issues and controversies in American history)
    Includes bibliographical references and index.
    ISBN 978-0-8160-8115-8 (alk. paper)
    1. Slavery—United States—History. 2. Slavery—United States—History—
Sources. 3. Slavery—Law and legislation—United States—History. 4. Slaves—Legal
status, laws, etc.—United States—History. I. Title.
    E441.F67 2011
    306.3'620973—dc22   2011009090

Facts On File books are available at special discounts when purchased in bulk quantities for businesses, associations, institutions, or sales promotions. Please call our Special Sales Department in New York at (212) 967-8800 or (800) 322-8755.

You can find Facts On File on the World Wide Web at http://www.infobaselearning.com

Text design by Kerry Casey
Composition by Hermitage Publishing Services
Cover printed by Yurchak Printing, Landisville, Pa.
Book printed and bound by Yurchak Printing, Landisville, Pa.
Date printed: September 2012
Printed in the United States of America

This book is printed on acid-free paper.

CONTENTS

List of Documents   vii

About the Author   xi

Preface   xii

Introduction   xiv

1   Slavery and the American Revolution: 1
*Did the American Revolution Significantly Change
the Condition and Status of Black Americans?*

2   Slavery and the U.S. Constitution: 44
Was the U.S. Constitution a Proslavery Document?

3   The Transatlantic Slave Trade: 77
*Should Congress Impose a Tax on Slaves Imported
into the United States?*

4   Colonization: 113
*Was Colonization Outside the United States by
Black Americans a Good Idea?*

5   Slavery and Westward Expansion: 154
Should Slavery Be Restricted in Missouri?

6   Slave Resistance: 193
*Should Virginia Abolish Slavery in Light of the
Nat Turner Revolt?*

7   Slavery and Religion: 235
Was the Bible Proslavery?

8   Fugitive Slaves: 271
Should Congress Pass the Fugitive Slave Bill of 1850?

9 The Kansas-Nebraska Bill: 312
*Should the Missouri Compromise Line of 1820
Be Repealed?*

10 Slavery and the Courts: 354
Was the Dred Scott *Decision of 1857 Legally Sound?*

11 Slavery and the Civil War: 396
*Should Northern Military Forces Accept Fugitive
Slaves Who Flee to Union Lines?*

Index 431

⁓LIST OF DOCUMENTS⁓

Chapter 1   Slavery and the American Revolution: Did the American Revolution Significantly Change the Condition and Status of Black Americans?

1. Clause Purged from the Declaration of Independence, 1776
2. Vermont Declaration of Rights, 1777
3. Gradual Emancipation Laws, 1780, 1784
4. Petitions of Black Americans to State Legislatures, 1779, 1791
5. Letter, Benjamin Banneker to Thomas Jefferson, 1791
6. Thomas Jefferson, *Notes on the State of Virginia*, 1784

Chapter 2   Slavery and the U.S. Constitution: Was the U.S. Constitution a Proslavery Document?

1. Excerpt from Debates at the Constitutional Convention, 1787
2. Excerpts from the U.S. Constitution, 1787
3. Excerpt from Debates at the Constitutional Convention, 1787
4. Federalist 42, 1788
5. Debate over Ratification in South Carolina, 1788
6. Federalist 54, 1788

Chapter 3   The Transatlantic Slave Trade: Should Congress Impose a Tax on Slaves Imported into the United States?

1. Speech of Representative John Baptiste Charles Lucas, 1804
2. Speech of Representative James Madison Broom, 1806
3. Speech of Representative David Bard, 1804
4. Speech of Representative John Baptiste Charles Lucas, 1804
5. Speech of Representative James Madison Broom, 1806
6. Speech of Representative Benjamin Huger, 1804
7. Speech of Representative Thomas Lowndes, 1804
8. Speech of Representative Andrew Gregg, 1804
9. Speech of Representative Nathaniel Macon, 1804
10. Speech of Representative Benjamin Huger, 1804

Chapter 4   Colonization: Was Colonization Outside the United States by Black Americans a Good Idea?
1. Letter, James Madison to Robert J. Evans, 1819
2. Letter, Robert Goodloe Harper to Elias B. Caldwell, 1817
3. Speech of Ebenezer Burgess, 1818
4. Letter, Robert Goodloe Harper to Elias B. Caldwell, 1817
5. Speech of Samuel Hopkins, 1793
6. Speech of Henry Clay, 1816
7. Speech of Ebenezer Burgess, 1818
8. Address of James Forten, 1817
9. William Jay, *An Inquiry into the Character and Tendency of the American Colonization, and American Anti-Slavery Societies,* 1834
10. Speech of Senator Robert Y. Hayne, 1827

Chapter 5   Slavery and Westward Expansion: Should Slavery Be Restricted in Missouri?
1. Tallmadge Amendments, 1819
2. Excerpts from the U.S. Constitution, 1787
3. Speech of Representative John W. Taylor, 1819
4. Speech of Senator Rufus King, 1819
5. Speech of Representative Timothy Fuller, 1819
6. Speech of Representative Alexander Smyth, 1820
7. Speech of Representative Robert W. Reid, 1820
8. Thomas Amendment, 1820
9. Letter, Thomas Jefferson to John Holmes, 1820
10. Speech of Senator James Barbour, 1820

Chapter 6   Slave Resistance: Should Virginia Abolish Slavery in Light of the Nat Turner Revolt?
1. Articles, *Richmond Enquirer,* 1831
2. Letter, Virginia Governor John Floyd to South Carolina Governor James Hamilton, Jr., 1831
3. Petition from the "Females of the County of Augusta," 1832
4. Speech of Samuel Moore, 1832
5. Resolution and Amendment of William O. Goode, 1832
6. Letter, James Goodwyn to Virginia Governor John Floyd, 1832
7. Speech of James McDowell, Jr., 1832

8. Speech of William H. Brodnax, 1832

9. Speech of William H. Brodnax, 1832

10. Speech of Alexander Knox, 1832

Chapter 7   Slavery and Religion: Was the Bible Proslavery?

1. Thornton Stringfellow, *Slavery: Its Origin, Nature, and History*, 1861

2. Letter, Richard Fuller to Francis Wayland, 1840s

3. Charles Hodge, "The Bible Argument on Slavery," 1860

4. Thornton Stringfellow, The New Testament on Polygamy, Divorce, and Slavery, 1860

5. James Henry Hammond, "Slavery in the Light of Political Science," 1860

6. Albert Barnes, *An Inquiry into the Scriptural Views of Slavery*, 1846

7. Letter, Francis Wayland to Richard Fuller, 1845

8. Albert Barnes on Slavery and Polygamy, 1846

9. LaRoy Sunderland, *The Testimony of God Against Slavery*, 1835

10. Albert Barnes on Equality, 1846

Chapter 8   Fugitive Slaves: Should Congress Pass the Fugitive Slave Bill of 1850?

1. Fugitive Slave Act of 1793

2. Excerpts from *Prigg v. Pennsylvania*, 1842

3. Speech of Senator Joseph R. Underwood, 1850

4. Speech of Senator Roger Baldwin, 1850

5. Speech of Representative George W. Julian, 1850

6. Speech of Senator William H. Seward, 1850

7. Northern Ministers Expound upon the Fugitive Slave Act, 1851

8. Speech of Senator Robert Barnwell Rhett, 1851

9. Petition Against the Fugitive Slave Act, 1850

10. Harriet Beecher Stowe, *Uncle Tom's Cabin*, 1852

Chapter 9   The Kansas-Nebraska Bill: Should the Missouri Compromise Line of 1820 Be Repealed?

1. Kansas-Nebraska Bill, 1854

2. Speech of Senator Stephen Douglas on the Necessity of the Nebraska Bill, 1854

3. Speech of Senator Stephen Douglas on the Principle of the Kansas-Nebraska Bill, 1854
4. Speech of Representative William Cullom, 1854
5. "Appeal of the Independent Democrats in Congress to the People of the United States," 1854
6. Speech of Senator Sam Houston, 1854
7. Speech of Abraham Lincoln, 1854
8. Speech of Senator Benjamin Wade, 1854
9. Letter from the Chicago Clergymen, 1854
10. Senator Charles Sumner, "The Crime Against Kansas" Speech, 1856

Chapter 10   Slavery and the Courts: Was the *Dred Scott* Decision of 1857 Legally Sound?
1. Inaugural Address of President James Buchanan, 1857
2. Chief Justice Roger B. Taney on Black Citizenship, 1857
3. Justice Peter V. Daniel on Property Rights, 1857
4. Justice Benjamin R. Curtis on Black Citizenship, 1857
5. Justice Benjamin R. Curtis on Congressional Power over the Territories, 1857
6. Horace Greeley on the *Dred Scott* Decision, 1857
7. Speech of Frederick Douglass, 1857
8. Speech of Senator Stephen Douglas, 1858
9. Speech of Abraham Lincoln, 1857
10. Third Annual Message of President Buchanan, 1859

Chapter 11   Slavery and the Civil War: Should Northern Military Forces Accept Fugitive Slaves Who Flee to Union Lines?
1. Letter, Benjamin F. Butler to Winfield Scott, 1861
2. Letter, E. P. Halsted to John D. Shaul, 1862
3. Letter, George E. Waring, Jr., to Alexander Asboth, 1861
4. Letter of Thomas W. Sherman, 1861
5. Letter, Henry W. Halleck to Alexander Asboth, 1861
6. Letter, John A. Dix to George B. McClellan, 1861
7. Letter, George B. McClellan to D. C. Buell, 1861
8. Letter, Abraham Lincoln to Orville H. Browning, 1861
9. Second Confiscation Act, 1862
10. Speech of Frederick Douglass, 1876

≋ABOUT THE AUTHOR≋

Jeff Forret, Ph.D., is Associate Professor of History at Lamar University in Beaumont, Texas. An expert on slavery and pre–Civil War American history, he is the author of *Race Relations at the Margins: Slaves and Poor Whites in the Antebellum Southern Countryside* and the forthcoming *Conflict in the Community: "Black-on-Black Violence" in the Slave South*. He has written articles on slavery in several journals and anthologies, including the *Journal of Southern History*; *Slavery & Abolition*; and *Fathers, Preachers, Rebels, Men: Black Masculinity in U.S. History and Literature, 1820-1845*. In addition, he is the author of numerous encyclopedia entries on topics relating to slavery for such references as *The New Encyclopedia of Southern Culture*, *Oxford Handbook of Slavery in the Americas*, and *Gale Library of Daily Life: Slavery in America*.

PREFACE

From a distance we tend to see history as a continuous narrative that flows from one period to another. When the largest building blocks of history are considered, such as the American Revolution, slavery, the Civil War, industrialization, the role of women, and the degradation of the environment, history indeed can be viewed as a nearly seamless web of events, with only an occasional sharp shift in direction. On closer inspection, however, we see that historical development entailed numerous conflicts, controversies, and choices. And at virtually every crossroad in American history the future hung in the balance until the key issues were confronted and resolved. It was at these times that individuals debated the central issues at stake. History didn't just happen. Individuals made it happen.

The *Issues and Controversies in American History* series focuses on these critical disputes. The authors believe that historical understanding is furthered by studying the choices that contemporaries debated, how they envisioned these options, and how their decisions influenced the way history unfolded. This approach to history helps us to see the contingency in historical causation – that the directions that individuals, groups, and society took depended in large measure on the outcome of debates at critical junctures in the nation's history. When studied closely, history reveals a landscape of controversies. Some of these issues remained subjects of dispute decades after their initial resolution. Yet every major debate shaped the future course of the nation's history.

The *Issues and Controversies* series is constructed to illuminate the great debates in American history and to illustrate the contingency by which it unfolded. Each volume focuses on an important topic in American history and is composed of chapters, usually arranged chronologically, that address major controversies about the subject. Every chapter opens with a summary of the issue and the debate about it, and then lays out the historical background of the chapter's subject. Two short essays in each chapter provide fuller glimpses of selected subjects. The heart of each chapter contains a summary of the debate on the controversy. Theses discourses are illustrated by primary sources, which present the opposing arguments of the two sides. These documents also offer a sampling of the tone, flavor, and logic of the participants. The conclusion to each chapter examines the impact of the debate and offers thoughts on how different decisions could have produced different outcomes. These "What If?" sections are intended to illustrate contingency and dependency in history—that history isn't inevitable but is shaped by the decisions people make. A list of discussion questions in each chapter is designed to provoke reflection about the issues that contemporaries faced. The bibliography and list of websites for each chapter will help students locate additional resources about each controversy.

Slavery in the United States certainly qualifies as a controversial issue in American history. In terms of its influence on the character and course of the nation, the "peculiar institution" arguably was *the* most critical issue in the antebellum United States. As Jeff Forret's volume vividly demonstrates, slavery was linked to every major turning point in the history of the United States from the American Revolution to the Civil War. Along the way, numerous controversies provoked conflict and debate, from the place of slavery in the U.S. Constitution and whether the slave trade should continue to the settlement of the West, fugitives who escaped from bondage, and the roles of Congress, the Supreme Court, and presidents in fashioning national policy during the 1850s. Forret's volume leads the reader through these and other controversies with background, analysis, primary source documents, and images, which together chart the depth and breadth of debates over slaves and the institution of slavery. His book confirms the interactions between conflicts over slavery and moments of decision in American history. Simply put, slavery was intimately connected to every major aspect of American society from its colonial founding to the Civil War. The conflict between North and South ended formal slavery in 1865, yet reverberations from this great upheaval continue to be felt.

Ballard C. Campbell
Series Editor

⧼⧼⧼INTRODUCTION⧽⧽⧽

In the early 16th century, shortly after Europeans' "discovery" of the Western Hemisphere, they began conveying African slaves across the Atlantic Ocean to work in the Americas. Widespread racial assumptions predisposed Europeans to enslave Africans, and the Portuguese, British, French, Spanish, and Dutch all employed African labor in their American colonies. The overwhelming majority of all captive Africans were enslaved in Brazil or the Caribbean, forced to mine valuable ores or condemned to cultivate sugar. Of the roughly 11 million Africans forcibly seized for labor in the Americas, not even 4 percent were carried to the British North American mainland colonies that would eventually form the United States.

African slaves had toiled for Europeans in the Americas for a century before the founding of the English settlement at Jamestown, Virginia, in 1607. The first blacks to arrive at Jamestown—a cargo of 20—were offloaded from a Dutch sailing vessel more than a decade later, in 1619. By that time, English colonists in Jamestown had begun to cultivate the cash crop of tobacco, but in the early decades of Virginia settlement, it made little economic sense to work African slaves in the tobacco fields. Disease, Indian attacks, and harsh living conditions combined to produce astoundingly high mortality rates among the early settlers in Virginia whether white or black. African slaves were costly, and rational, calculating masters understood the financial risks of purchasing such expensive human property. At midcentury, therefore, only a few hundred slaves worked in Virginia. Altogether, they composed only about 3 percent of the Chesapeake population in 1650. Virginia's black inhabitants numbered a still modest 2,000 or 2,500 by 1676, just 4 percent of the entire population.

Rather than slaves, Chesapeake landholders relied on unfree, white indentured servants—contract laborers—culled from England's surplus population of the poor and unemployed. In payment for the cost of their passage to America, they worked the tobacco fields of the Chesapeake for a finite period, typically four or five years, before gaining their freedom. Because they were not held in permanent bondage, indentured servants cost roughly half as much as African slaves. For the first three-fourths of the 17th century, then, most of the laborers in Virginia's tobacco fields were white, temporarily unfree indentured servants.

Only in the last quarter of the 17th century did African slaves supplant indentured servants as the primary source of labor in the Chesapeake region. One reason was that, for elite landholders, indentured servitude became less attractive over time. As conditions in the Chesapeake improved and society stabilized, mortality rates declined and increasing numbers of indentured servants outlived their terms of service. When former indentured servants acquired their own land, they planted tobacco, contributing to the overproduction of the crop and driving down its price. Competition, in short, cut into the profits of their onetime masters. In response, colonial lawmakers made indentures longer as the 17th century progressed. Statutes increased the required minimum length of servitude in the 1650s and 1660s and tacked additional time onto the term of service should an indentured servant commit a crime or other wrongdoing, such as running away. Both tactics sought to delay the day a servant gained freedom.

Just as colonial elites grew less enamored with contract labor, indentured servitude provided Englishmen much less opportunity than it once had. The prospects for acquiring an independent landholding diminished with time. Lower tobacco prices depressed wages for those former indentured servants who had yet to purchase land, making it more difficult for them to accumulate the funds necessary to buy a plot for themselves. Former indentured servants fortunate enough to gather up the resources to purchase land found that the best lands nearby were already claimed, so they had to go to the frontier, where they were vulnerable to Indian attacks. To promote the safety of English settlers on the frontier, in 1676, Nathaniel Bacon led a band of landless, disaffected former servants in an unauthorized assault upon the native population of colonial Virginia. The frustrated masses then redirected their hostility to the colonial establishment, whose appropriation of the land had limited their economic opportunity. Resenting the concentration of wealth in the hands of a relative few, Bacon's followers marched to the colonial capital of Jamestown and set it ablaze, reinforcing elite anxieties over the system of indentured servitude.

If the factors pulling Englishmen to Virginia waned, so did the push factors driving them out of England. The first generations of indentured servants to the Chesapeake relieved much of England's overpopulation problem. The country's falling birthrate also alleviated its labor surplus, allowing England to put its poor to work at home for increased wages. A devastating fire that broke out in London in 1666 ensured the availability of work in the mother country. With declining birthrates and a revived economy in England contributing to the scarcity of white indentured servants, Virginia's landholders turned to another form of laborer, the African slave compelled to a lifetime of service. By the late 17th century, slave labor represented a more economically viable investment than it had in the past. Improving mortality rates increased the likelihood that slaves would survive long enough to work off their higher purchase price and produce a profit for the master.

Colonial legislatures in Virginia and Maryland passed a series of laws beginning in the 1660s designed to forge racial difference. Slavery as an institution had not been legally defined in the colonies. In Virginia, no law distinguished in any way between blacks and whites until 1640, when some blacks (but not all) were prevented from carrying firearms. Although the status of Africans in the Chesapeake slowly deteriorated during the 1640s and 1650s, the defining decade in the codification of slavery into law was the 1660s. In 1662, a Virginia law stipulated that a child's status followed that of the mother. Any child born to a slave mother would also be enslaved. This marked a legal innovation, reversing the position of English common law, which held that a child inherited the father's condition. The 1662 law virtually guaranteed an ongoing supply of enslaved laborers for future generations of Virginia landowners. Another 1662 law imposed fines for interracial fornication. In 1664, the colony of Maryland defined slavery as a permanent lifelong condition and banned interracial marriage. Any free woman who married a slave was herself enslaved until the death of her husband, and their children would be held in bondage. Other statutes determined who qualified for enslavement and what treatment they could receive. In Virginia, a 1667 law closed a loophole that permitted slaves to convert to Christianity as a means of escaping slavery. Conversion no longer represented an avenue to freedom as it had in previous years. Beginning in 1669, Virginia law excused masters if a slave happened to die during "correction." Since African slavery was a permanent condition, bondpeople could not be punished by tacking time onto their length of service. Therefore, the Virginia legislature considered corporal punishment appropriate for disciplining slaves, and it offered masters legal protection should aggressive whipping result in a slave's death. By the end of the 1660s, the process of creating African slavery in Virginia and Maryland was well under way, through the passage of laws intended to codify racial difference. Over the next several decades, the elaboration of discriminatory legislation continued to weave African slavery into the social fabric of the colonial Chesapeake.

By the late 17th century, elite landholders in the Chesapeake increasingly relied on enslaved Africans to cultivate their tobacco fields, and the black population grew rapidly. African slaves poured into the colony by the thousands per year in the 1680s and 1690s. The pronounced transition to African labor in the last two decades of the 17th century resulted in a dramatic demographic shift by 1700. Whereas white indentured servants outnumbered African slaves in the 1670s by a ratio of 4 to 1, in the 1690s, the number of black slaves exceeded that of white indentured servants. The ratio of servants to slaves eventually reversed, to 1 to 4. By 1700, more than 20,000 African slaves labored in England's colonial mainland colonies. Permanent and hereditary enslavement had become the typical fate of blacks in the Chesapeake region.

African slavery took hold elsewhere in England's American colonies as well. Soon after Chesapeake planters began to rely on enslaved Africans to work their tobacco fields, masters in the South Carolina Lowcountry employed them in the cultivation of rice. Slave labor thus dominated the production of cash crops throughout the southern colonies. By comparison, only a smattering of slaves were carried to the North. There, bond people were not subjected to the harsh plantation regimes common farther to the south and instead engaged in a variety of different tasks, working on small farms, as domestic servants, or in the maritime and other trades. Slavery as an institution was vastly more important to the South than to the North. Yet despite slaves' imbalanced distribution and varying economic significance from one colony to the next, by the outbreak of the American Revolution in 1775, slavery was an established fact in all of Great Britain's mainland North American colonies.

Many slaves challenged the terms and conditions of their bondage. They utilized the various techniques of day-to-day resistance, feigning illness, breaking or "losing" tools, working slowly when unsupervised, or stealing from the master. Some ran away from their owners, at times forming maroon communities in swamps and remote woods away from white settlements. Rarely, but most seriously, slaves engaged in violent revolts. A slave uprising in New York City in 1712 resulted in the execution of more than 20 blacks. In colonial South Carolina, where blacks outnumbered whites, as many as 100 slaves rose up against their masters in the Stono Rebellion of 1739. Neither insurrection freed any slaves. To the contrary, each uprising prompted the passage of repressive slave codes.

The institution of American slavery was largely unquestioned among whites in colonial America. A few Quakers excepted, most white colonists did not agitate against slavery but instead accepted bondage as a normal feature of their society. The American Revolution, however, with its rhetoric of liberty, freedom, and equality, demanded a fresh look at African slavery as an institution. Some of the colonists who embarked upon the task of forging a new nation recognized slavery as remarkably incongruous with their principles. After the United States declared its independence in 1776, the new state governments in the North immediately or gradually eliminated slavery either by law or in their state constitutions. Farther south, in Delaware, Maryland, and Virginia, especially, many masters' consciences compelled them to emancipate their bond people. Slaves also took advantage of the Revolutionary War to run away in individual bids for freedom. Although slavery itself survived the Revolutionary-era attack upon it, it was momentarily weakened and increasingly confined to the southern states. Chapter 1 examines an ongoing debate among scholars over the meaning of the American Revolution for slaves, exploring arguments both for and against understanding the War of Independence as a watershed event in the history of black Americans. The remaining 10 chapters, arranged chronologically, pursue specific debates among contemporary historical actors over a variety of specific issues pertaining to American slavery.

Chapter 2 focuses on the U.S. Constitution. In 1787, the document's framers made multiple compromises with slavery. The second chapter recounts their disputes, cataloging the clauses in the Constitution dealing with slavery and asking the central question, Was the U.S. Constitution a proslavery document? Several subsequent chapters recount the political struggles in Congress over the Constitution's slavery provisions. Soon after ratification, for example, and again in 1804, the House of Representatives pondered the imposition of a $10 tax on slave imports. No congressman doubted the constitutionality of the tax; the debate centered only on the propriety of levying it. Representatives' arguments for and against the proposed duty on the transatlantic slave trade form the heart of chapter 3.

Other chapters chronicle American statesmen's conflicting interpretations of the Constitution's slavery clauses. Most confounding was the question of slavery's expansion westward into the territories. Detailed in chapter 5, Missouri's application for statehood exposed starkly different understandings of Congress's power to restrict slavery in the territories. With the future of slavery in the West hanging in the balance, the Missouri Compromise of 1820 reached an accommodation that tamped down passions in the short term, but the issues raised by the Missouri controversy would plague the nation for decades. The dispute over the Missouri Compromise reignited in 1854, when Senator Stephen A. Douglas of Illinois introduced his Nebraska bill to organize territory in the Great Plains. As chapter 9 shows, competing factions in Congress rehashed the Missouri debate and creatively reimagined the past 30 years of American history to suit their distinct political agendas. The Kansas-Nebraska Act (1854) ultimately overturned a portion of the Missouri Compromise, and the Supreme Court decision of *Dred Scott v. Sandford* (1857) declared it unconstitutional. Chapter 10 discusses the constitutional arguments employed in the majority and minority opinions of the Court.

American slaves were no mere objects of congressional laws and court decisions, however. Their own actions as runaways and rebels frequently inspired the debates about them. Slaves fled their masters by the thousands during the American Revolution, and the U.S. Constitution assured slaveholders that their human property would be returned to them by law. The Fugitive Slave Act of 1793 afforded a mechanism through which to enforce the constitutional provision, but slaveholders complained for decades of the law's ineffectiveness. The Fugitive Slave Act of 1850, the most controversial component of the Compromise of 1850, was intended to repair the flaws of the 1793 law. Chapter 8 examines the debate over its passage. Little more than a decade later, slaves began running to Union troops in search of refuge even before shots fired at Fort Sumter began the Civil War between North and South. As shown in chapter 11, their presence inherently thrust slavery onto the agenda, forcing a debate among Northern military leaders. In his role as commander in chief, President Abraham Lincoln had to deal with fugitive slaves escaping to Union lines as a matter of military necessity. Slaves who fled to Northern armies thus helped to guide the administration slowly and haltingly down the path toward emancipation.

The slave rebel Nat Turner provided a glimpse into another potential route to freedom. In 1831, he and his followers launched a devastating attack in Southampton County, Virginia, that killed approximately 60 whites. Although the revolt failed to secure the slaves their liberty, it triggered a serious debate in the Virginia state legislature—the subject of chapter 6—over the abolition of slavery in the Old Dominion. The abolition proposal suffered a narrow defeat, very nearly exceeding Turner's dreams not through violence but through legislative means.

Any emancipation of slaves meant a rise in America's free black population. A number of chapters address free people of color, the prejudice and discrimination they confronted, and their inferior social position within the United States. As noted in chapter 1, the free black population grew noticeably as a result of the runaways and manumissions of the revolutionary era. Pervasive racism and white hostility, however, denied people of color an equal place in society. The Missouri constitution submitted to Congress in application for statehood restricted free blacks from even entering the state. Given the seemingly insurmountable chasm between the races, many prominent figures in American history—most famously, Thomas Jefferson—advocated black Americans' expulsion outside the United States. Chapter 4 explores the major pro- and anti-colonization arguments common in the 1810s and 1820s. Although serious discussions of colonization schemes generally waned thereafter, in Virginia the Turner revolt revived interest in the removal of black Americans. Even in the North, free blacks' place in society was tenuous, their bodies unsafe. With the passage of the Fugitive Slave Act in 1850, people of color faced an increased threat of kidnapping and sale into slavery. And by 1857, a majority of justices on the Supreme Court declared that black Americans were not citizens of the United States.

Many modern-day readers may observe while browsing the primary sources included in this volume that only a small number of documents express moral outrage toward the institution of slavery and white society's treatment of blacks. To the contrary, they will find a host of sources that are offensive by today's standards, even when produced by individuals sympathetic to those in bondage. In many of the debates over slavery that took place between the American Revolution and the Civil War, political, economic, or racial interests subsumed concerns about morality. But the radical abolitionist movement that emerged by the 1830s propelled the immorality of slavery onto center stage, only to be rebutted by proslavery forces rallying in defense of the peculiar institution. Religious arguments stood at the center of this dispute. Chapter 7 examines the ways in which proslavery and antislavery theologians harnessed the power of the Bible in support of their positions.

No state justified and defended the institution of slavery more readily or more vociferously than South Carolina. Its members of Congress consistently proved among the shrewdest, most clever interpreters of the Constitution, and for good reason. Along with delegates from Georgia, those from the Palmetto State threatened to storm out of the Constitutional Convention in 1787 unless slavery was granted special protections. In the early 19th century, South Carolina was unique among the states in resuscitating its participation in the transatlantic slave trade prior to its constitutionally authorized closure in 1808. Feeling unfairly maligned by congressional efforts to terminate the traffic in slaves, the state hinted at disunion early in the nation's history. On several occasions, South Carolina's allegiance to the Union appeared suspect. Native son John C. Calhoun articulated a theory of nullification and secession that the state acted upon in the tariff controversy of 1832. South Carolina also sent an enthusiastic contingent to the Nashville Convention in 1850, prepared to bolt from the Union. That South Carolina became the first state to secede after the election of Abraham Lincoln as president in 1860 should be no surprise. Had the other slaveholding states shared South Carolina's radicalism, secession and war might have occurred much sooner than they did.

Voices from Virginia, the cradle of slavery in the British colonial mainland, ring across many of the following chapters as well, occasionally rising above the din emanating from South Carolina. Virginia was a state with surplus slaves. As a result, Virginia's congressional delegation favored keeping Missouri open to slavery, thereby giving masters in the Old Dominion the opportunity to sell their excess slaves to the

West. Virginia's close proximity to the North made its representatives in Congress some of the most enthusiastic backers of the Fugitive Slave Act of 1850. In contrast, South Carolina, relatively more immune to the plague of runaway slaves, offered only lukewarm support for the measure. The South, in short, was not a monolithic bloc always acting in unison; rather, slaveholding states responded differently to specific debates over slavery on the basis of their own unique circumstances and relationships to the institution.

Nevertheless, as a whole, the following chapters reveal the depth of southern commitment to slavery, a devotion that ultimately helped fuel the slow and tortuous journey toward the tragedy of civil war. Emancipation in the American South was unusual in at least three important ways. First, it took a violent conflict to force slavery's destruction. In other slave societies, peaceful legislative decrees were the norm. Second, southern masters received no compensation for the loss of their bond people, whether in the form of cash, bonds, or a limited period of service from those freed. And finally, the abolition of slavery occurred later in the South than in most societies in the Western Hemisphere. Only Puerto Rico (1873), Cuba (1886), and Brazil (1888) maintained their systems of slavery later into the 19th century.

To this day, the trauma of civil war remains prominent in the collective national consciousness, and slavery a source of national shame. Enslavement marked the profoundest sort of subjugation of one race to another, and the ratification of the Thirteenth Amendment abolishing slavery in 1865 did little to change the hearts of most white Americans. Already in 1865, former Confederates regained public office in the South and imposed Black Codes that established segregation, prevented blacks from testifying against whites, prohibited interracial marriage, and restricted black rights in countless other ways. The onset of Radical Reconstruction in 1867 forced the creation of new governments in the former Confederate states that overturned the Black Codes and guaranteed black civil rights, but the freedoms that blacks enjoyed were only fleeting, as Radical Republican control of southern state governments slipped away, state by state, the last in 1877.

With the demise of Reconstruction, the situation deteriorated for southern blacks. Politically, their voice was gradually taken away through intimidation, racial violence, and various techniques of disfranchisement—property qualifications, poll taxes, and literacy tests, among them. State governments imposed new segregation laws to divide the races socially, and the Supreme Court decision of *Plessy v. Ferguson* (1896) affirmed the "separate but equal" doctrine. Economically, the masses of southern blacks failed to achieve the dream of land-ownership. Through the sharecropping system, they instead labored for whites, sometimes on the same lands they had cultivated during slavery. In many respects, the institution of slavery persisted in diluted, modified, and carefully disguised forms well beyond the 19th century.

The tragic legacy of slavery in the nation's history was thus difficult to outrun. The failures of Reconstruction necessitated the Civil Rights movement that at last bore fruit decades later, in the 1950s and 1960s. Even today, the ugly history of race relations in the United States informs ongoing debates over reparations for slavery. This volume of the *Issues and Controversies in American History* series is designed to help us understand contemporary historical actors' views of slavery and come to terms with this unfortunate chapter of our past.

Slavery and the American Revolution:
Did the American Revolution Significantly Change the Condition and Status of Black Americans?

—ɱ—

THE CONTROVERSY

The Issue

During the American Revolution, the United States achieved its independence from Great Britain. But did the Revolution significantly change the condition and status of black Americans?

- ♦ *Arguments that the American Revolution did significantly change the condition and status of black Americans:* The American Revolution presented many challenges to the institution of slavery in the new nation of the United States. It was philosophically inconsistent for the rebellious Americans to hold slaves in a republic founded upon principles of liberty and equality. Cognizant of the contradiction between liberty and slavery, northern states passed immediate or gradual emancipation laws. Many individual masters in the Revolutionary era freed their slaves, while other bond people took advantage of wartime opportunities to run away or join the military. The Revolution produced a rising population of free blacks, especially in urban centers of the North. The condition and status of many black Americans changed as a result of the Revolution.

- ♦ *Arguments that the American Revolution did not significantly change the condition and status of black Americans:* Much remained the same for black Americans after the Revolution. The founding generation missed several opportunities to purge slavery from American shores and instead permitted the institution to grow and expand in the South. In the North, emancipation proceeded at a painfully slow rate. Freed slaves discovered that most white Americans were unwilling to accept them as equal members of society. They continued to encounter prejudiced attitudes and discrimination in their daily lives.

The Revolution marked a tremendous lost opportunity to change the history of black Americans.

—៳៴—

INTRODUCTION

Among the "self-evident" truths Thomas Jefferson identified in the Declaration of Independence was that "all men are created equal." Presented to the public on July 4, 1776, the declaration formally announced the American colonies' separation from Great Britain and the formation of an independent United States. The United States was founded on a unique set of principles. Unlike the kings and queens in the monarchies of Europe, America's founders emphasized notions of liberty, freedom, and equality. But how well did the young nation uphold the virtues it claimed for itself? Slavery was a long-established institution throughout the United States at the outbreak of the American Revolution. What did the Revolution and its high-minded ideals mean for black Americans?

Some argue that the Revolution was a particularly momentous event for black Americans. Northern states abolished slavery, and some masters surrendered to their consciences and made individual decisions to free their bond people. Many slaves seized upon the opportunities the Revolution provided to escape bondage, sometimes by running to British lines or enlisting in the U.S. military. Revolutionary-era manumissions and runaways led to an explosion of America's free black population in urban port cities such as Philadelphia.

Others suggest that the American Revolution changed little for black Americans. Slavery persisted for decades in much of the North and flourished across the South. Blacks who achieved their freedom during the Revolution met with prejudice and discrimination in white society. Despite some advances made during the Revolution, most black Americans found that the new nation failed to live up to the principles it claimed to espouse because the founders could not envision a truly multiracial society.

BACKGROUND

In the 1750s, Great Britain was engaged in the process of building an overseas empire. In North America, it fought an alliance of French and

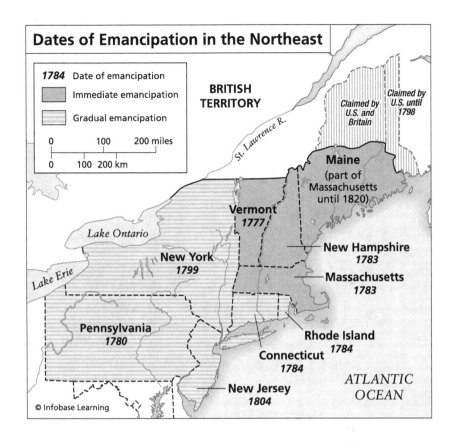

Indians for control of the interior of the continent and emerged victorious. The French and Indian War concluded with the signing of the Treaty of Paris (1763), which expelled the French from mainland colonial North America and secured for Britain lands east of the Mississippi River and north into Canada.

As the French and Indian War was winding down, King George III ascended to the throne in Britain in 1760. Unlike his two royal predecessors, who had ruled since 1714, George III took a much more active role in governing Britain's American colonies. One of the most pressing issues the new king had to contend with was his country's depleted finances. Thanks to prolonged warfare, Britain had incurred massive debts, and now it needed to pay for thousands of soldiers to defend its colonial American holdings. It seemed reasonable to George III to have the colonists help pay for the recent war and their own continued protection.

King George III implemented measures designed to benefit the British treasury, but at the cost of disaffecting his subjects in the American colonies. To prevent conflict with Native Americans in the trans-Appalachian West and reduce the need to construct and staff forts in the region, the king imposed the Proclamation Line of 1763. The proclamation drew an imaginary line down the spine of the Appalachian Mountains and prohibited colonial settlement beyond it to the west. Britain also instituted a series of taxes upon the colonists, the most onerous the Stamp Act of 1765, which taxed virtually anything printed, whether newspapers, almanacs, diplomas, or legal documents. To the colonists, the new taxes imposed by Parliament seemed rather blatant attempts to extort money from them. For the previous several decades prior to the reign of King George III, the colonies had grown accustomed to taxing themselves through their own assemblies. Suddenly in the 1760s, the British Parliament was becoming increasingly intrusive, taxing colonists who had no power to elect a single representative to that legislative body. "No taxation without representation" became a rallying cry for the disenchanted colonists.

As the colonists participated in boycotts and popular protests, they also began reassessing their relationship to the mother country. Colonial American thinkers found the writings of English political philosopher John Locke particularly relevant to their situation. Locke had penned *Two Treatises on Government* many decades before, in 1690, to justify William and Mary's overthrow of England's King James II in the Glorious Revolution. Locke's work presented the social contract theory of government. Locke argued in that theory that human beings had "natural rights," including the rights to life, liberty, and property. The express purpose of government, he asserted, was to protect those rights. When government failed in its responsibility by infringing upon or abusing the rights of the people, those living under that government reserved the right to overthrow their corrupt government and create a new one.

Locke's social contract theory held revolutionary implications for the colonists in their dispute with Great Britain. In the Declaration of Independence, the document through which the colonists severed their political ties to Great Britain and created the United States of America, author Thomas Jefferson drew heavily upon Locke's ideas. When Jefferson wrote in the declaration's second paragraph that "all men" held "certain unalienable rights, that among these are Life, Liberty, and the pursuit of Happiness," he was restating Locke. Jefferson quickly summarized the social contract theory when he wrote, "That to secure these rights, Governments are instituted among Men, deriving their just powers from the consent of the governed. That whenever any Form of Government becomes destructive of these ends, it is the Right of the People to alter or to abolish it, and to institute new Government ... likely to effect their Safety and Happiness."

For Jefferson to proclaim in the Declaration of Independence that "all men are created equal," he either had to have been blind to the institution of slavery or referring to a subset of the overall population of the United States.

In Great Britain, the seal of the Society for Effecting the Abolition of the Slave Trade featured a shackled slave asking the question "Am I not a man and a brother?" In the United States, the image appeared in the 1837 broadside publication of John Greenleaf Whittier's antislavery poem "Our Countrymen in Chains." (Library of Congress)

Jefferson was himself a slaveholder, and slavery had flourished in the colonies for more than a century before he wrote those famous words. In asserting the equality of all, Jefferson discounted the roughly half a million Africans and African Americans living in the newly formed United States. A glaring omission by modern standards, excluding blacks from the polity in his own time would not have made Jefferson exceptional. The Revolutionary War, however, fought to secure and affirm American independence, interjected slavery into the political debates of the period. The colonists' talk of natural rights, liberty, freedom, and equality held special interest for black Americans. Like whites, Africans and African Americans made sacrifices during the revolutionary era. Most famously, Crispus Attucks, purportedly an escaped mulatto slave who worked in the maritime trades, was counted among the five Americans killed by British soldiers in the Boston Massacre of March 1770. But did the American Revolution substantially alter the condition and status of black Americans?

THE DEBATE

The Case that the American Revolution Significantly Changed the Condition and Status of Black Americans

The American Revolution proved a watershed event in the history of slavery in the United States. State legislatures passed a number of antislavery laws, and masters inspired by revolutionary rhetoric sometimes freed their slaves in a process known as manumission. The language the American colonists used to rationalize their uprising against Great Britain held particular resonance for black Americans and imbued the Revolution with special meaning for them. The disruptions of wartime provided opportunities for African and African-American slaves to escape bondage either by lending their services to the fight or by running away. The combination of fugitives who fled to freedom and those granted it by their owners led to the rise of the first significant population of free blacks in the United States. In many ways, black Americans indeed experienced a revolution within the Revolution.

The American Revolution revealed troubling inconsistencies between the rhetoric of the founders and the reality of the society in which they lived. In their disputes with the Crown, the American colonists frequently complained of British attempts to "enslave" them, to take away their liberties and impose their will upon them. Pamphlets and other colonial-era literature repeatedly invoked the notion of slavery as political metaphor, noting slavery's incompatibility with a natural rights doctrine that stressed the freedom of the individual. The language employed by the American patriots highlighted the contradiction between liberty, on one hand, and slavery, on the other.

The words the colonists used for polemical purposes in condemning British oppression—their comments expressing fear of their own political enslavement—could not help but call attention to the literal enslavement of Africans and African Americans living in the colonies. Contemporary observers were aware of the irony. The British writer Samuel Johnson, loyal to his king, scoffed, "How is it that we hear the loudest *yelps* for liberty among the drivers of negroes?"[1] The Revolution thus presented an ideological challenge to slavery and forced the

---

[1] Quoted in David Brion Davis, *Inhuman Bondage: The Rise and Fall of Slavery in the New World* (New York: Oxford University Press, 2006), 144.

rebellious colonists to attempt to reconcile Revolutionary principles of liberty, freedom, and equality with the social fact of bondage.

The Revolutionary era witnessed the first major challenges to American slavery as, first, the colonies, then the states, took steps to confront the glaring contradiction. In 1774, the First Continental Congress ended the colonies' participation in the transatlantic slave trade. No new slaves could legally be imported from Africa or the West Indies, and any discovered to have been smuggled in would be freed. In his original draft of the Declaration of Independence, Thomas Jefferson condemned King George III for foisting slavery upon the colonists, encouraging the African slave trade, and urging slaves to defect to the British to take up arms against Americans. (See "Clause Purged from the Declaration of Independence, 1776," on page 27 in the Primary Sources section.) Though forced to purge this language from the final document, Jefferson still maintained that "all men are created equal." Such prominent figures as Jefferson, Benjamin Franklin, and George Washington—all of whom owned slaves—publicly condemned the institution of slavery. The Northwest Ordinance, passed by the Confederation Congress in July 1787, prohibited slavery in the Northwest Territory, consisting of the modern-day states of Ohio, Indiana, Illinois, Michigan, Wisconsin, and part of Minnesota.

After the United States declared its independence, individual states implemented various antislavery measures, either in their state constitutions or by law. Each one, North and South, outlawed the international slave trade by 1798, and at least in the North, slavery itself came under attack. Fewer slaves lived in the North than in the South, and they were less crucial to the functioning of the northern economy. Each of the northern states abolished slavery either immediately or gradually during or within a generation after the Revolution. Massachusetts and New Hampshire both provided for the immediate emancipation of slaves in 1783. Six years earlier and long before statehood in 1791, the independent republic of Vermont abolished slavery in its constitution of 1777. (See "Vermont Declaration of Rights, 1777," on page 28 in the Primary Sources section.) Northern state legislatures were more likely to abolish slavery gradually than immediately. Pennsylvania, Rhode Island, Connecticut, New York, and New Jersey all passed gradual abolition laws that freed future generations of slaves once they reached adulthood. (See "Gradual Emancipation Laws, 1780, 1784," on page 29 in the Primary Sources section.) Pennsylvania passed the first of the five gradual emancipation laws in 1780. That legislation also freed any slave carried into the state after six months. By 1804, every single state north of Maryland and Delaware had implemented either an immediate or a gradual emancipation measure. In addition, prior to the formal abolition of slavery in 1865, all states north of the Ohio River, Iowa, Minnesota, and the western states of California and Oregon forbade slavery in their constitutions.

Many individual masters could not reconcile slaveholding with revolutionary principles and therefore elected privately to manumit, or free, their slaves during the war or shortly afterward. Before the Revolution, laws in the southern colonies forbade or limited slaveholders' ability to emancipate their slaves, even if so inclined. In many colonies, if masters desired to free a slave, they were legally obligated to post prohibitively expensive bonds ensuring the freed person's good behavior. During the Revolution, however, states began passing legislation to encourage private manumissions. State laws decreased the amount of money that masters were required to post as bond or eliminated it altogether. In 1782, Virginia repealed a 1723 act that entirely prevented masters from freeing their slaves. By 1790, masters in every southern state except North Carolina could liberate their slaves if they so chose. Private acts of manumission during the Revolutionary era were most numerous in Maryland and Virginia, the two states in which half of the United States' black population resided in 1776. In the Upper South, the quantity of private manumissions threatened the very survival of slavery as an institution in Maryland and Delaware.

Like their Revolutionary-era masters, slaves imbibed the philosophy of natural rights. As they watched white colonists protest British taxes, slaves appropriated the language of liberty for themselves and attached their own unique meaning to it. Enslavement framed a distinctive understanding of the Revolution that emphasized personal freedom. As a result, if a master reneged on promises of freedom, slaves might file freedom suits in court to gain their liberty. They sometimes sued for freedom by claiming descent from a white or Indian woman, for a child's status as slave or free legally followed that of the mother. Tracing their ancestry in this way allowed them to show wrongful enslavement and thereby gain their liberty. Slaves in the Revolutionary period sought redress not only through the judicial system but also through petitions to colonial and state legislatures. Very much aware of Revolutionary rhetoric, blacks commonly petitioned on behalf of their own rights in the 1770s and 1780s. (See "Petitions of Black Americans to State Legislatures, 1779, 1791," on page 32 in the Primary Sources section.)

If some slaves benefited from acts of private manumission, others took matters upon themselves during the Revolution by running away. Tens of thousands of slaves took advantage of wartime disruptions to abscond from their masters. Slaves fled to the northern states, to secluded southern swamps, to remote regions of the backcountry, to various Indian tribes such as the Cherokee or Creek, to the Spanish in Florida, or aboard seagoing vessels. As many as 20,000 runaways escaped to British lines. In November 1775, Lord Dunmore, the royal governor of Virginia, promised freedom to any slaves who fled their masters, joined the British, and took up arms against the American rebels. With the siege and surrender of Charleston, South Carolina, in 1780, British general Sir Henry Clinton echoed Dunmore's pledge. Nearly 1,000 blacks flocked to Dunmore's ranks, and thousands of others escaped to British forces in Virginia, South Carolina, and elsewhere, assuming that they would be free at the conclusion of the war. According to Thomas Jefferson, there were 30,000 runaways in Virginia alone. South Carolina lost about one-quarter of its enslaved population amid the chaos of the Revolution, Georgia about two-thirds. Altogether, masters lost perhaps 100,000 slaves as a result of war, whether through escapes or death.

Slaves who absconded to the British met a variety of fates. Many who fled to the British died of illness, poor nutrition, or war injuries. Survivors were not always granted their freedom as promised. Some were reenslaved in the Bahamas and parts of the British Caribbean. The British sent others to Spanish Florida and some 3,000 to the Canadian maritime province of Nova Scotia. From there, British abolitionists helped relocate 1,000 former slaves to the African nation of Sierra Leone. Others migrated to London. Because most of the slaves who fled to British lines were young adult men, the enslaved population remaining in the United States included greater percentages of women, older slaves, and enslaved children than existed before the Revolution.

The lure of freedom meant that blacks who participated directly in the American Revolution more frequently fought for the British than on the American side of the conflict. Many slaves believed a British victory would produce emancipation for all bond people. Thus, when British forces occupied Philadelphia, slaves reported to the British, eager to gain their freedom. A smaller number of slaves cast their lot with the patriot forces, but American military leaders initially resisted allowing slaves or free blacks to serve. Many commanding officers were large slaveholders themselves and feared the prospect of the Revolution's unleashing a slave insurrection. Early on in the war, blacks most commonly aided the American cause as mariners on the high seas. They served in state militias only rarely and were barred from serving in the Continental army. A patriot manpower shortage already evident by 1777, however, forced the Americans to reevaluate their policies. Patriot forces began accepting black enlistments, but initially only in Maryland and the northern states. Prince, a slave belonging to a New Hampshire master, helped clandestinely to row George Washington across the Delaware River under the cover of darkness Christmas night 1776, contributing directly to the patriot cause in the Battle of Trenton. Rhode Island promised freedom to 250 slaves for their participation in the war effort. Connecticut and Rhode Island both created all-black regiments, but throughout the American Revolution, most blacks served in integrated units, usually laboring at menial tasks such as drumming or cooking rather than fighting on the battlefield. The U.S. Congress approved arming some 3,000 black troops in South Carolina and Georgia, offering to compensate masters and liberate slaves upon completion of their service. South Carolina rejected the plan, however, fearful it would undermine the institution of slavery. Ultimately, approximately 5,000 slaves served in the Continental army. With the conclusion of hostilities, state legislatures took steps to liberate individual black soldiers who fought in the war and prevent their reenslavement.

The combination of manumissions and runaways during the Revolution led to a striking demographic development: the staggering growth of a free black population in the United States. The number of free blacks—statistically insignificant before the Revolution—rose to 60,000 across the country by 1790. Free blacks counted as only 1.6 percent of the total population but almost 8 percent of the black population. Their numbers increased most dramatically in the Upper South and middle states, regions where private manumissions were more prevalent. Neither Delaware nor Maryland passed an immediate or gradual emancipation law; nevertheless, privately manumitted slaves contributed to the swelling of the free black population in those states. By 1790, Delaware boasted almost 3,900 free blacks, Maryland 8,000. Another 13,000 free blacks resided in Virginia, up from 1,800 just eight years earlier.

In the 1780s, Philadelphia emerged as the most important urban center for the nation's free blacks. Thousands of freed slaves from the nearby Upper South states of Delaware, Maryland, and Virginia made their way north to Pennsylvania's largest city. Migration from the countryside to urban areas made sense for free blacks. In cities, especially port towns such as Philadelphia, New York, or Boston, work was more plentiful. The maritime trades provided employment to black men, while black women labored as domestics, laundresses, and seamstresses. In addition to finding economic opportunities, free blacks who congregated in the nation's cities developed a social and communal life. They could more readily find a spouse, construct families and households, and establish institutions such as churches and mutual aid societies to help ease the transition to freedom. (See the sidebar "Absalom Jones" on page 14.)

Adopting new names marked a personal sort of liberation and a statement of political assertion for the nation's rising free black population. Whereas the relatively small numbers of free blacks in the Lower South kept the name of their former master to reap the benefits of a connection to an influential family, in the North and Upper South, former slaves chose new names for themselves as they cast off their enslaved past. Naming patterns proved revealing. In deciding their own names, free blacks typically chose full English or biblical names. They avoided diminutive English names such as *Bob* for *Robert* or *Bill* for *William*, classical names such as *Pompey* or *Caesar*, as well as distinctly African names such as *Cudjo*. In selecting last names of their own, free blacks in the North and Upper South opted for common English surnames such as *Smith*, *Brown*, and *Johnson*. In Philadelphia and other northern locales, some free blacks chose the family names *Freeman* and *Newman* to symbolically sever their ties to slavery.

Many early American free blacks achieved success and fame. Benjamin Banneker, a free black from Maryland, was the mixed-race grandson of a white woman who liberated one of her slaves and married him. Banneker had a distinguished career as a mathematician and astronomer, publishing several almanacs in the 1790s. (See "Letter, Benjamin Banneker to Thomas Jefferson, 1791," on page 36 in the Primary Sources section.) In Philadelphia, the free black sailmaker James Forten became one of the wealthiest black men in America. He used his fortune to advance equal rights for blacks and other social causes. When white churches in Philadelphia ignored blacks' needs and discriminated

Richard Allen was one of the leading figures in the thriving free black community of Philadelphia in the late 18th and early 19th centuries. (© The Art Archive)

against black congregants, two former slaves, Richard Allen and Absalom Jones, spearheaded the formation of an independent black church in that city. Farther north, in Massachusetts, sailor Paul Cuffee amassed a fortune in the shipping business and supported a plan for black colonization in Sierra Leone.

African-American historian Benjamin Quarles called the Revolutionary War "a black declaration of independence." Many subsequent scholars have agreed. Gary Nash referred to the American Revolution

Jones also spearheaded an effort to create a black ecumenical church—the African Church of Philadelphia—for the promotion of black unity and well-being. Philadelphia blacks lacked the economic means to finance the construction of a church on their own. To raise the needed funds, Jones cultivated relationships with the white community and with the famous Philadelphia physician Benjamin Rush in particular. Although they received donations from such high-profile Americans as George Washington and Thomas Jefferson, most whites did not display much generosity. Leading white churchmen in Philadelphia, though often sympathetic to blacks' postwar plight, feared losing control of the city's black population should an independent black church be formed. Although it was a struggle to solicit the necessary monies, the subscription drive eventually met with success. Construction on a new church building began in 1793. It opened the following year and was renamed the African Episcopal Church of St. Thomas. That first year, almost 250 members made up the congregation, a number that blossomed to more than 400 in the second. Black churchgoers gathered to hear the sermons of one their own, their minister Absalom Jones, who journeyed from slavery to lead an independent black church.

Absalom Jones (The Granger Collection, New York)

in the North and in Delaware, it expanded dramatically in southern states such as Virginia. The nearly 293,000 slaves in Virginia in 1790 marked an increase of one-third in only eight years. The loss of tens of thousands of slaves during the Revolutionary War heightened the resolve of southern states to preserve the bond people who remained. To compensate for wartime reductions, Georgia kept open the transatlantic slave trade until 1798, and South Carolina reopened it in 1803 after having closed it a decade earlier. According to the historian David Brion Davis, "Between 1790 and 1807 the United States imported more African slaves than during any twenty-year period of the colonial era."[3] Almost 40,000 new arrivals were more than enough to compensate for wartime losses of human chattel. Through a combination of slave imports and natural reproduction, slavery became more entrenched in the South than ever. More human beings were forced into slavery during the revolutionary era than escaped it.

As the institution of slavery gained strength in the South, congressional delegates missed several opportunities to abolish slavery or stem its expansion. Under the Articles of Confederation, Congress received Quaker antislavery petitions in 1783 and 1785 requesting the termination of the international slave trade and the abolition of slavery itself, but it refused to act. After independence from Great Britain was gained through the Treaty of Paris (1783), British imperial policies that had inhibited westward migration, such as the Proclamation Line of 1763, no longer applied. The Indian lands in the Ohio and Tennessee River valleys that the United States acquired were laid open to slavery. Thomas Jefferson submitted a proposal to exclude slavery from the trans-Appalachian West, both north and south of the Ohio River, but it fell one vote short of passage in 1784. By the Northwest Ordinance of 1787, the Confederation Congress did prohibit slavery from the area north of the Ohio, but it freed no slaves already living there and did not contain any enforcement mechanism to prevent slaveholders from filtering in with their bond people. Despite the restriction on slavery in the Northwest Territory, hundreds of slaves lived in Illinois and Indiana for decades after the ordinance was enacted. Moreover, by excluding slavery north of the Ohio, the ordinance implied the legitimacy of slavery in the region to the south, in Kentucky, Tennessee, Alabama, and Mississippi.

The contradiction of slaveholding in the American republic was perhaps best personified in Thomas Jefferson, the slaveholder who wrote in the Declaration of Independence that "all men are created equal." In Virginia, Jefferson proposed a bill in 1776 to emancipate slaves born in his state after passage of the act, and, in 1783, he drafted a law

---

[3] David Brion Davis, "American Slavery and the American Revolution," in *Slavery and Freedom in the Age of the American Revolution* (New York: Oxford University Press, 2006), 265.

to prevent the introduction of new slaves into Virginia and free all of those born after December 31, 1800. Neither measure passed, but both added to Jefferson's antislavery bona fides. Simultaneously, however, over the course of his lifetime, hundreds of slaves called Jefferson "master." Despite Revolutionary-era condemnations of slavery and a rising number of private manumissions, Jefferson liberated only eight slaves in total (including five in his will), all relatives of Sally Hemings, the bondwoman with whom Jefferson carried on a long-term relationship. Like other masters across the South, Jefferson built his lifestyle on the backs of his slaves. Jefferson entertained extravagantly at Monticello; the finest French wines graced his table. The income Jefferson's slaves generated only partly financed his lavish ways and profligate spending. To pay debts totaling in the millions in modern-day dollars at the time of his death, Jefferson's will authorized the sale of 200 slaves at auction. That Jefferson's public proclamations about slavery contradicted his own actions as a master did not set him apart from many of his slaveholding contemporaries.

The Revolutionary-era fervor to manumit slaves proved fleeting, even among northern slaveholders. North or South, many masters relied economically on their slaves and resisted emancipating valuable bond people, and white Americans respected masters' property rights in their slaves. As a result, emancipation was out of the question in the slave-rich South. Like other state assemblies in the South, the Virginia legislature in 1806 tightened its manumission policy, reversing the revolutionary trend toward liberalizing emancipation laws. Throughout most of the North, emancipation could proceed only gradually. Gradual emancipation laws in Pennsylvania, Connecticut, Rhode Island, New York, and New Jersey freed no slaves at the time of passage and only emancipated enslaved children once they reached adulthood. Pennsylvania, which in 1780 enacted the first gradual emancipation statute, required the registration of existing slaves and liberated the children born to them upon attaining the age of 28. Any enslaved infant born in Pennsylvania before March 1, 1780, however, still faced a lifetime of servitude. Rhode Island freed children born to slaves after March 1, 1784, but bound them until the age of 21 if male, 18 if female. Such gradual emancipation schemes lessened the economic impact of losing a slave. Laws that bound slaves until their late teens or twenties permitted masters the right to extract labor from their bond people for several productive years. That appropriation of slaves' time served to compensate masters for the impending loss of their labor.

In 1804, New Jersey became the last of the northern states to pass a gradual emancipation law, but it took several more decades to make freedom a reality for thousands. Combined, New York and New Jersey— the two northern states with the largest slave populations—held 33,000 bond people in 1800. By 1820, this figure was reduced by almost half, but 17,000 slaves still lived there. As late as 1840, more than 1,100 slaves resided in the northern states, almost 60 percent of them in New Jersey. Even in the North, liberation for slaves unfolded slowly and unevenly.

Most white Americans were unprepared to welcome emancipated slaves into free society. They viewed blacks as inherently inferior and could not accept them as equals. In his *Notes on the State of Virginia*, published in 1784, Thomas Jefferson gave voice to the widespread racial stereotypes that he shared with many of his contemporaries. (See "Thomas Jefferson, *Notes on the State of Virginia*, 1784," on page 39 in the Primary Sources section.) Jefferson described blacks as, by nature, both physically and mentally inferior to whites. The racial differences between blacks and whites he found so evident precluded the possibility of harmonious coexistence. Jefferson furthermore considered free blacks a dangerous element within society. He feared that emancipated slaves, filled with fresh memories of the horrors of bondage, might seek vengeance upon whites and ignite a race war. In the 1790s, Jefferson's nightmare of black insurrection became reality on the French Caribbean island of Saint-Domingue. There, a slave uprising culminated in the overthrow of the European colonizers and the creation of Haiti, the first independent black republic in the Western Hemisphere. Pervasive fears of such a rebellion in the United States prompted some negrophobic whites to question whether freed slaves should be allowed to live in their midst. They preferred expelling blacks to living in proximity to them. In 1776, Thomas Jefferson's proposal to emancipate Virginia's slaves included provisions for their removal from the state. Jefferson clearly did not want free blacks residing in Virginia, but the state's Revolutionary-era manumission law allowed them to stay. In 1806, however, the law changed, requiring Virginia's emancipated slaves to leave the state within a year. Only with special legislative permission could they be allowed to remain. Anxieties over the presence of freed blacks also inspired various proposals for colonization abroad, most often in Africa. Commonly held white racial attitudes prevented the assimilation of blacks and the formation of a genuinely biracial society in early America.

Early American blacks experienced discriminatory treatment in many facets of their lives—social, economic, and political. The American Revolution inspired some degree of racial goodwill, but white racial attitudes hardened after the 1780s. In the North, hostilities toward free blacks increased. Excluded from white institutions, emancipated slaves established their own churches, schools, and mutual aid societies. Many northern whites also feared that a flood of free blacks would inundate urban areas such as Philadelphia in search of work. They denied free blacks many employment opportunities and typically relegated them to menial jobs. Economically strapped free black parents in Philadelphia frequently indentured their children to more affluent white families, often until the age of 28. These indentured free blacks experienced a lack of freedom that resembled slavery. Barred from many occupations, free blacks were also frequently excluded from the body politic. Most states in the North and South passed legislation denying them suffrage. Free blacks could vote in only five of the original 13 states: New York, Pennsylvania, Delaware, Maryland, and North Carolina. Other laws prevented free blacks from sitting on juries or testifying against whites. Free blacks also had to register in their county of residence and were restricted in their ability to travel. Even in the North, unwary free blacks risked kidnapping by unscrupulous whites who sold them into slavery. Although they were free, emancipated slaves did not share full citizenship rights with white Americans. (See the sidebar "Phillis Wheatley" on page 22.)

The American Revolution briefly called slavery into question but ultimately left much unchanged for black Americans. Slavery continued to flourish as even the country's founders with seeming antislavery credentials such as Thomas Jefferson failed in practice to live up to revolutionary ideals. No immediate or gradual emancipation laws passed in southern legislatures, and in most of the North, manumission proceeded at a snail's pace. Moreover, the growing free black population of the United States that emerged in the wake of the Revolution achieved quasi-freedom without gaining all the rights white Americans enjoyed. The American Revolution marked a missed opportunity in the history of race relations in the United States. When Jefferson wrote in the Declaration of Independence that all men are created equal, he was referring only to whites, as blacks did not become equal citizens of the American republic in that era.

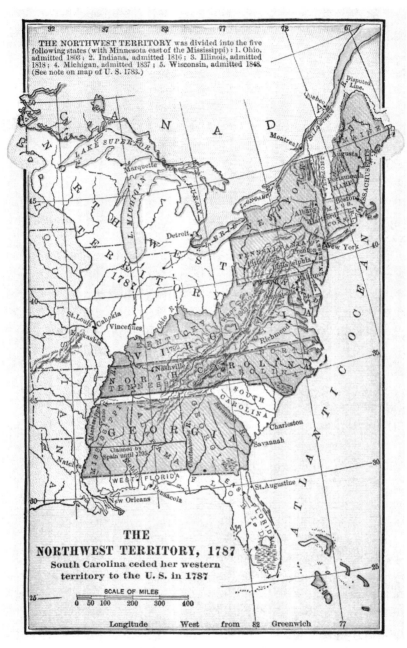

The Northwest Ordinance of 1787 prohibited slavery in the Northwest Territory, encompassing the modern-day states of Ohio, Indiana, Illinois, Michigan, Wisconsin, and a portion of Minnesota. (© North Wind Picture Archives/Alamy)

OUTCOME AND IMPACT

General George Washington's defeat of Great Britain's Lord Cornwallis at the Battle of Yorktown in 1781 marked the last major engagement of the American Revolution. It was the victory the United States needed to drive Britain to the bargaining table and draw the war to a close. By the Treaty of Paris (1783), the American Revolution formally concluded, Britain recognized American independence, and the United States acquired land from the Appalachian Mountains to the Mississippi River. America's expanding boundaries made additional room for slavery. Although the Northwest Ordinance of 1787 prohibited slavery north of the Ohio River, it suggested that the region to the south was ripe for settlement by masters and their slaves. In the 1790s, with the advent of Eli Whitney's cotton gin, a mechanical contraption that simplified the process of extracting the seed from the cotton fiber, the cotton frontier was able to spread from east to west across the Deep South states of Alabama, Mississippi, and beyond over the next several decades. The American Revolution dealt slavery a glancing blow but in actuality paved the way for the expansion of the institution.

WHAT IF?

What would have become of slavery if the American Revolution had not occurred or if Britain had defeated the rebellious colonists?

The Revolution inspired a range of antislavery statutes. Absent the ideological conundrum slavery posed to liberty-loving Americans in the revolutionary context, the northern states might not—or might not as quickly—have passed the immediate or gradual emancipation laws they did. The American Revolution lent philosophical impetus to the antislavery cause. Before the independence of the United States, Great Britain might have overturned any manumission laws passed by colonial legislatures. With its interest in the Royal African Company, the British government in the colonial era had indeed negated attempts to stem the transatlantic slave trade. The profits gleaned from slavery and the slave trade proved too dear to abandon easily.

Had Britain defeated the rebellious colonists, the fate of slavery would have been uncertain. British imperial policies had the effect of retarding the westward

PHILLIS WHEATLEY

Phillis Wheatley was the first black American female poet and the first black American to publish a book. Born in West Africa in the early 1750s, she was kidnapped and enslaved as a child of seven or eight. After undergoing the dreaded Middle Passage across the Atlantic Ocean, she was sold in 1761 to a Boston tailor named John Wheatley, who wanted a house servant for his wife, Susanna. The Wheatleys treated their young slave girl as a member of the family and raised her along with their other children. Unlike most slaves, Phillis Wheatley received an education. She quickly learned to read and write English. A precocious child, she could also read Latin and Greek by the age of 12. Wheatley began writing poems early in her teenage years, and her master's family encouraged her efforts.

Wheatley composed many verses on religious themes. Her elegy to the evangelical Methodist minister and Great Awakening preacher George Whitefield catapulted her to fame in the Boston area in the latter 1760s. A publisher in London, England, printed a collection of 39 of her poems in 1773, making her the first published black American. That same year, her master also liberated her from slavery. As the United States struggled in its fight for independence, Wheatley wrote patriotic poems in support of the Revolution. One of them celebrated General George Washington, whom she once met.

Wheatley's personal experiences as a slave did not pervade her poetry, but she occasionally put her past to poignant use in her rhyming couplets. In explaining her "love of Freedom," she wrote:

expansion of American colonists, confining them to the strip of land east of the Appalachian Mountains. King George III opposed incurring the additional expenses of constructing western garrisons and staffing the forts with soldiers. Masters might have been unable or unwilling to carry their slaves into a dangerous, unprotected frontier region, and slavery might have stagnated along the eastern seaboard.

Eventually, Great Britain made the institution of slavery illegal throughout its empire in 1834, more than three decades before the Thirteenth Amendment to the Constitution freed those blacks still enslaved in the American South. At first glance, it seems obvious that American slaves would have gained their freedom much more quickly had they remained under the British imperial umbrella. But could the British Parliament have passed the Emancipation Act of 1833 if the

I, young in life, by seeming cruel fate
Was snatched from Afric's fancied happy seat:
What pangs excruciating must molest,
What sorrows labour in my parent's breast!
Steeled was that soul, and by no misery moved,
That from a father seized his babe beloved:
Such, such my case. And can I then but pray
Others may never feel tyrannic sway?

In another poem, Wheatley expressed gratitude for her exposure to Protestant religion yet scolded fellow Christians with uncharitable racial sensibilities:

'Twas mercy brought me from my pagan land,
Taught my benighted soul to understand
That there's a God—that there's a Saviour too:
Once I redemption neither sought nor knew.
Some view our sable race with scornful eye—
"Their color is a diabolic dye."
Remember, Christians, Negroes black as Cain
May be refined, and join the angelic train.

However powerful, Wheatley's poetry never gained her financial success. She died in 1784 of complications in childbirth. For more of Phillis Wheatley's poetry, visit http://docsouth.unc.edu/neh/wheatley/wheatley.html.

American colonies had remained within its empire? Britain successfully enacted its emancipation program because the funds were available to compensate masters deprived of their slaves under the law. The government paid masters a fair value for the slaves they freed, sparing slaveholders economic hardship due to liberating their bond people. With approximately 2 million additional slaves to pay for in the American South, Britain's compensated emancipation program might very well have been prohibitively costly. Had southern slaves also been included in Britain's emancipation policy, expenses would probably have risen 150 percent, from 20 million to roughly 50 million pounds.

A similar program of compensated emancipation seemed not to occur to Revolutionary-era legislators in the United States. Many masters voluntarily manumitted their slaves during the Revolution, but a compensation program would certainly have increased the tally. Providing masters compensation for liberating their slaves would have been the only way to preclude violating sacrosanct principles of private property. Any such governmental program, however, would have been economically devastating to an infant nation already in dire financial straits. The historian Gary Nash calculated that if 600,000 slaves were emancipated at an average cost of $150 each, the $90 million expense (more than $2 billion in today's dollars) would have placed an incredible economic strain on the country. Sales of the valuable lands in the trans-Appalachian West the United States acquired after the Revolution might have compensated masters who freed their bond people. Yet without their slaves, masters would have considered western lands less valuable since they had no one to work them. With no compensated emancipation plan in the United States, slavery continued to grow and expand despite the momentary possibilities of the revolutionary period.

CHRONOLOGY

1760   King George III accedes to the British throne.

1763   The Peace of Paris concludes the French and Indian War.
The Proclamation Line is imposed.

1774   First Continental Congress forbids American participation in the transatlantic slave trade.

1775   Fighting erupts at Lexington and Concord, Massachusetts.
Lord Dunmore promises freedom to slaves who take up arms against the colonists.

1776   The United States declares independence.

1777   Vermont's constitution frees its slaves.

1780   Pennsylvania's legislature passes the first gradual emancipation law.

1781   Lord Cornwallis surrenders at Yorktown.

1782   The Virginia legislature passes a law permitting private manumissions.

1783   Massachusetts frees its slaves.
New Hampshire frees its slaves.
The Treaty of Paris formally ends the Revolutionary War.

1784   Rhode Island passes a gradual emancipation law.

Connecticut passes a gradual emancipation law.

1787   The Northwest Ordinance prohibits slavery in the Northwest Territory.

The Constitutional Convention meets.

1789   George Washington is elected the first president of the United States.

1790   The first federal census records 60,000 free blacks in the United States.

1798   Georgia becomes the last state to outlaw the transatlantic slave trade.

1799   New York passes a gradual emancipation law.

1803   South Carolina renews its participation in the transatlantic slave trade.

1804   New Jersey passes a gradual emancipation law.

1806   Virginia law requires free blacks to leave the state within a year.

1808   The United States ends the legal importation of slaves through the transatlantic slave trade.

1827   New York emancipates its last remaining slaves.

1840s   Small numbers of slaves can still be found in New Jersey and other northern states.

DISCUSSION QUESTIONS

1. How accurate is the claim that the American Revolution was a war of independence for black Americans?

2. If you had been a slave during the American Revolution, would you have cast your lot with the rebel colonists, the British, or neither? Why?

3. After the Revolution, how "free" was the growing free black population? How accurate is it to describe the northern states in the 1780s and 1790s as "free"?

4. Solely on the basis of his words and actions regarding slavery, how should Americans remember Thomas Jefferson?

5. How were the founders able to reconcile their belief in liberty with the institution of slavery?

WEB SITES

Massachusetts Historical Society. "African Americans and the End of Slavery in Massachusetts." Available online. URL: http://www.mass hist.org/endofslavery/?queryID=61. Accessed October 2, 2009.

National Humanities Center. "Equality," Toolbox Library: Primary Resources in U.S. History & Literature. Available online. URL: http://nationalhumanitiescenter.org/pds/livingrev/equality/equality.htm. Accessed April 24, 2009.

Slavery in the North. Available online. URL: http://www.slavenorth.com/slavenorth.htm. Accessed August 18, 2010.

United States Department of the Interior. "The American Revolution: Lighting Freedom's Flame," National Park Service. Available online. URL: http://www.nps.gov/revwar/about_the_revolution/african_americans.html. Accessed April 24, 2009.

BIBLIOGRAPHY

Berlin, Ira. *Many Thousands Gone: The First Two Centuries of Slavery in North America.* Cambridge, Mass.: Belknap Press of Harvard University Press, 1998. One of the major works on the history of slavery in early America. Part 3 examines slaves and free blacks in the Revolutionary era.

———, and Ronald Hoffman, eds. *Slavery and Freedom in the Age of the American Revolution.* Charlottesville: University Press of Virginia, 1983. A brilliant collection of essays from many of the leading scholars of Africans and African Americans in the Revolutionary era.

Davis, David Brion. *Inhuman Bondage: The Rise and Fall of Slavery in the New World.* New York: Oxford University Press, 2006. Chapter 7, "The Problem of Slavery in the American Revolution," offers perhaps the most concise, informative account available on the subject.

———. *The Problem of Slavery in the Age of Revolution, 1770–1823.* Ithaca, N.Y.: Cornell University Press, 1975. Examines the antislavery movement during and after the American Revolution in Atlantic perspective.

Finkelman, Paul. *Slavery and the Founders: Race and Liberty in the Age of Jefferson.* Armonk, N.Y.: M. E. Sharpe, 1996. The fifth and sixth chapters, on Thomas Jefferson, supply a pointed critique of those scholars who tout the sage of Monticello's antislavery credentials.

Frey, Sylvia R. *Water from the Rock: Black Resistance in a Revolutionary Age.* Princeton, N.J.: Princeton University Press, 1991. Examines relations among masters, slaves, and the British in the Revolutionary South.

MacLeod, Duncan J. *Slavery, Race and the American Revolution.* London: Cambridge University Press, 1974. One of the earlier book-length accounts of the failure of the American Revolution to live up to its rhetoric.

Nash, Gary B. *Forging Freedom: The Formation of Philadelphia's Black Community, 1720–1840.* Cambridge, Mass.: Harvard University Press, 1988. A detailed look at the development of a free black community in a city that straddled the North and the South.

———. *Race and Revolution.* Madison, Wis.: Madison House, 1990. A collection of three essays written for the Merrill Jensen Lectures in Constitutional Studies at the University of Wisconsin, one of which criticizes the North for failing to do more to eradicate slavery. Includes 19 primary source documents.

Quarles, Benjamin. *The Negro in the American Revolution.* Chapel Hill: University of North Carolina Press, 1961. The pioneering book on African Americans in the Revolution.

White, Shane. *Somewhat More Independent: The End of Slavery in New York City, 1770–1810.* Athens: University of Georgia Press, 1991. An excellent case study of emancipation in a major northern city.

PRIMARY SOURCES

1. Clause Purged from the Declaration of Independence, 1776

Thomas Jefferson included the following clause in his original draft of the Declaration of Independence. To the litany of abuses committed by King George III, Jefferson added the continuation of the African slave trade and British efforts to foment insurrection among the slaves against the rebellious colonists. Jefferson's language ignored the fact that it was American colonists who held the slaves in bondage. The objections of the southern slaveholding colonies of South Carolina and Georgia, as well as those of northern colonies whose ships conducted the transatlantic traffic, forced Jefferson to delete the passage from the final document.

> He has waged cruel war against human nature itself, violating its most sacred rights of life and liberty in the persons of a distant people who never offended him, captivating & carrying them into slavery in another hemisphere, or to incur miserable death in their transportation thither. This piratical warfare, the opprobrium of INFIDEL powers, is the warfare of the CHRISTIAN king of Great Britain. Determined to keep open a market where MEN should be bought & sold, he has prostituted his negative for suppressing every legislative attempt to prohibit or to restrain this execrable commerce. And that this assemblage of horrors might want no fact of distinguished die, he is now exciting those very people to rise in arms among us, and to purchase that liberty of which he has deprived them by murdering the people on whom he also obtruded them: thus paying off former crimes committed against the LIBERTIES of one people, with crimes which he urges them to commit against the LIVES of another.

Source: John P. Kaminski, ed., *A Necessary Evil? Slavery and the Debate over the Constitution* (Madison, Wis.: Madison House, 1995), 7.

—m—

2. Vermont Declaration of Rights, 1777

After the Declaration of Independence proclaimed that "all men are created equal," several states passed statements affirming the Revolutionary principle of equality and the natural rights of man. On July 8, 1777, Vermont—an independent republic at the time—placed the following proclamation in its constitution attacking the institution of slavery.

> THAT all men are born equally free and independent, and have certain natural, inherent and unalienable rights, amongst which are the enjoying and defending life and liberty; acquiring, possessing and protecting property, and pursuing and obtaining happiness and safety. Therefore, no male person, born in this country, or brought from over sea, ought to be holden by law, to serve any person, as a servant, slave or apprentice, after he arrives to the age of twenty-one Years, nor female, in like manner, after she arrives to the age of eighteen years, unless they are bound

by their own consent, after they arrive to such age, or bound by law, for the payment of debts, damages, fines, costs, or the like.

Source: http://avalon.law.yale.edu/18th_century/vt01.asp.

—ɷ—

3. Gradual Emancipation Laws, 1780, 1784

Of all the new American states, Pennsylvania in 1780 passed the first yet most restrictive gradual abolition law. Compare it to the more liberal gradual emancipation law passed by Rhode Island in 1784.

PENNSYLVANIA

Act for the Gradual Abolition of Slavery (1780)

SECTION 1. WHEN we contemplate our abhorrence of that condition to which the arms and tyranny of Great-Britain were exerted to reduce us; when we look back on the variety of dangers to which we have been exposed, and how miraculously our wants in many instances have been supplied, and our deliverances wrought, when even hope and human fortitude have become unequal to the conflict; we are unavoidably led to a serious and grateful sence of the manifold blessings which we have undeservedly received from the hand of that Being from whom every good and perfect gift cometh. Impressed with these ideas, we conceive that it is our duty, and we rejoice that it is in our power to extend a portion of that freedom to others, which hath been extended to us; and a release from that state of thraldom to which we ourselves were tyrannically doomed, and from which we have now every prospect of being delivered. It is not for us to enquire why, in the creation of mankind, the inhabitants of the several parts of the earth were distinguished by a difference in feature or complexion. It is sufficient to know that all are the work of an Almighty Hand. We find in the distribution of the human species, that the most fertile as well as the most barren parts of the earth are inhabited by men of complexions different from ours, and from each other; from whence we may reasonably, as well as religiously, infer, that He who placed them in their various situations, hath extended equally his care and protection to all, and that it becometh not us to counteract his mercies. We esteem it a peculiar blessing granted to us, that we are enabled this day to add one more step to universal civilization, by removing as much as possible the sorrows of those who have lived in undeserved bondage, and from which, by the assumed authority of the kings of Great Britain, no effectual, legal relief could be obtained. Weaned by a long course of experience from those narrower prejudices and partialities we had imbibed, we find our hearts enlarged with kindness and benevolence towards men of all conditions and nations; and we conceive ourselves at this particular period extraordinarily called upon, by the blessings which we have received, to manifest the sincerity of our profession, and to give a Substantial proof of our gratitude.

SECT. 2. And whereas the condition of those persons who have heretofore been denominated Negro and Mulatto slaves, has been attended with circumstances which not only deprived them of the common blessings that they were by nature entitled to, but has cast them into the deepest afflictions, by an unnatural separation and sale of husband and wife from each other and from their children; an injury, the greatness of which can only be conceived by supposing that we were in the same unhappy case. In justice therefore to persons So unhappily circumstanced, and who, having no prospect before them whereon they may rest their sorrows and their hopes, have no reasonable inducement to render their service to society, which they otherwise might; and also in grateful commemoration of our own happy deliverance from that state of unconditional submission to which we were doomed by the tyranny of Britain.

SECT. 3. Be it enacted, and it is hereby enacted, by the representatives of the freemen of the commonwealth of Pennsylvania, in general assembly met, and by the authority of the same, That all persons, as well Negroes and Mulattoes as others, who shall be born within this state from and after the passing of this act, shall not be deemed and considered as servants for life, or slaves; and that all servitude for life, or slavery of children, in consequence of the slavery of their mothers, in the case of all children born within this state, from and after the passing of this act as aforesaid, shall be, and hereby is utterly taken away, extinguished and for ever abolished.

SECT. 4. Provided always, and be it further enacted by the authority aforesaid, That every Negro and Mulatto child born within this state after the passing of this act as aforesaid (who would, in case this act had not been made, have been born a servant for years, or life, or a slave) shall be deemed to be and shall be by virtue of this act the servant of such person or his or her assigns, who would in such case have been entitled to the service of such child, until such child shall attain unto the age of twenty eight years, in the manner and on the conditions whereon servants bound by indenture for four years are or may be retained and holden; and shall be liable to like correction and punishment, and entitled to like relief in case he or she be evilly treated by his or her master or mistress, and to like freedom dues and other privileges as servants bound by indenture for four years are or may be entitled, unless the person to whom the service of any such child shall belong shall abandon his or her claim to the same; in which case the overseers of the poor of the city, township or district respectively, where such child shall be So abandoned, shall by indenture bind out every child so abandoned, as an apprentice for a time not exceeding the age herein before limited for the service of such children. . . .

SECT. 7. And be it further enacted by the authority aforesaid, That the offences and crimes of Negroes and Mulattoes, as well slaves and servants as freemen, shall be enquired of, adjudged, corrected and punished in like manner as the offences and crimes of the other inhabitants of this state are and shall be enquired of, adjudged, corrected and punished, and not otherwise; except that a slave shall not be admitted to bear witness against a freeman.

RHODE ISLAND

An ACT authorizing the manumission of Negroes, Mulattos and others, and for the gradual abolition of slavery.

Whereas all men are entitled to life, liberty and the pursuit of happiness, and the holding mankind in a state of slavery, as private property, which has gradually obtained by unrestrained custom and the permission of the laws, is repugnant to this principle, and subversive of the happiness of mankind, the great end of all civil government:

Be it therefore enacted by this General Assembly, and by the authority thereof it is enacted, That no person or persons, whether Negroes, Mulattos or others who shall be born within the limits of this State, on or after the first day of March, A.D. 1784, shall be deemed or considered as servants for life, or slaves; and that all servitude for life, or slavery of children, to be born as aforesaid, in consequence of the condition of their mothers, be and the same is hereby taken away, extinguished and forever abolished.

And whereas humanity requires, that children declared free as afore-said remain with their mothers a convenient time from and after their birth; to enable therefore those who claim the services of such mothers to maintain and support such children in a becoming manner, *It is fur-ther enacted by the authority aforesaid,* That such support and mainte-nance be at the expence of the respective towns where those reside and are settled: *Provided however,* That the respective Town-Councils may bind out such children as apprentices, or otherwise provide for their support and maintenance, at any time after they arrive to the age of one year, and before they arrive to their respective ages of twenty-one, if males, and eighteen, if females.

And whereas it is the earnest desire of this Assembly, that such children be educated in the principles of morality and religion, and instructed in reading, writing and arithmetic: *Be it further enacted by the authority aforesaid,* That due and adequate satisfaction be made as aforesaid for such education and instruction. And for ascertaining the allowance for such support, maintenance, education and instruction, the respective Town-Councils are hereby required to adjust and settle the accounts in this behalf from time to time, as the same shall be exhib-ited to them: Which settlement so made shall be final; and the respec-tive towns by virtue thereof shall become liable to pay the sums therein specified and allowed.

And be it further enacted by the authority aforesaid, That all per-sons held in servitude or slavery, who shall be hereafter emancipated by those who claim them, shall be supported as other paupers, and not at the separate expence of the claimants, if they become chargeable; pro-vided they shall be between the ages of twenty and forty years, and are of sound body and mind; which shall be judged of and determined by the Town-Councils aforesaid.

Sources: http://avalon.law.yale.edu/18th_century/pennst01.asp; John P. Kamin-ski, ed., *A Necessary Evil? Slavery and the Debate over the Constitution* (Madi-son, Wis.: Madison House, 1995), 28–29.

—⚭—

4. Petitions of Black Americans to State Legislatures, 1779, 1791

The rhetoric of the American Revolution inspired white patriots as well as enslaved and free blacks. The following documents are two examples of petitions seeking racial justice submitted to state legislatures during the Revolutionary era. One was sent by slaves requesting liberty to the assembly of Connecticut in 1779, the other by free blacks asking for expanded rights to the South Carolina legislature in 1791.

To the Honbl. General Assembly of the State of Connecticut to be held at Hartford on the Second Thursday of Instant May [1779]—The Petition of the Negroes in the Towns of Stratford and Fairfield in the County of Fairfield who are held in a State of Slavery humbly sheweth—

That many of your Petitioners, were (as they verily believe) most unjustly torn, from the Bosom of their dear Parents, and Friends, and without any Crime, by them committed, doomed, and bound down, to perpetual Slavery; and as if the Perpetrators of this horrid Wickedness, were conscious (that we poor Ignorant Africans, upon the least Glim[m]ering Sight, derived from a Knowledge of the Sense and Practice of civilized Nations) should Convince them of their Sin, they have added another dreadful Evil, that of holding us in gross Ignorance, so as to render Our Subjection more easy and tolerable, may it please your Honours, we are most grievously affected, under the Consideration of the flagrant Injustice; Your Honours who are nobly contending, in the Cause of Liberty, whose Conduct excites the Admiration, and Reverence, of all the great Empires of the World; will not resent, our thus freely animadverting, on this detestable Practice; altho our Skins are different in Colour, from those whom we serve, Yet Reason & Revelation join to declare, that we are the Creatures of that God, who made of one Blood, and Kindred, all the Nations of the Earth; we perceive by our own Reflection, that we are endowed with the same Faculties with our masters, and there is nothing that leads us to a Belief, or Suspicion, that we are any more obliged to serve them, than they us, and the more we Consider of this matter, the more we are Convinced of our Right (by the Laws of Nature and by the whole Tenor of the Christian Religion, so far as we have been taught) to be free; we have endeavoured rightly to understand what is our Right, and what is our Duty, and can never be convinced that we were made to be Slaves. Altho God almighty may justly lay this, and more upon us, yet we deserve it not, from the hands of Men. We are impatient under the grievous Yoke, but our Reason teaches us that it is not best for us to use violent measures, to cast it off; we are also convinced, that we are unable to extricate ourselves from our abject State; but we think we may with the greatest Propriety look up to your Honours, (who are the fathers of the People) for Relief. And we not only groan under our own burden, but with concern, & Horror, look forward, & contemplate, the miserable Condition of our Children, who are training up, and kept in Preparation, for a like State of Bondage, and Servitude. We beg leave to submit, to your Honours serious Consideration, whether it is consistent with the present Claims, of the united States, to hold so many Thousands, of the Race of Adam, our Common Father, in perpetual Slavery. Can human Nature endure the Shocking Idea? Can your Honours any longer Suffer this great Evil to prevail under your Government: we entreat your Honours, let no considerations of Publick Inconvenience deter your Honours from interposing in behalf of your Petitioners; we ask for nothing, but what we are fully persuaded is ours to Claim. We beseech your Honours to weigh this matter in the Scale of Justice, and in your great Wisdom and goodness, apply such Remedy as the Evil does require; and let your Petitioners rejoice with your Honours in the Participation with your Honours of that inestimable Blessing, *Freedom* and your Humble Petitioners, as in Duty bound shall ever pray &c.

> dated in Fairfield the 11th Day of May A.D. 1779—
> prime a Negro man
> servant to Mr.
> Vam A. Sturge
> of Fairfield
> his
> Prince X a Negro man
> [His] Mark
> servant of Capt. Stephen Jenings
> of Fairfield—
> in Behalf of themselves and
> the other Petitioners

To the Honorable David Ramsay Esquire President and to the rest of the Honorable New Members of the Senate of the State of South Carolina The Memorial of Thomas Cole Bricklayer P. B. Mathews and Mathew Webb Butchers on behalf of themselves & others Free-Men of Colour. Humbly Sheweth

That in the Enumeration of Free Citizens by the Constitution of the United States for the purpose of Representation of the Southern States in

Congress Your Memorialists have been considered under that description as part of the Citizens of this State. Although by the Fourteenth and Twenty-Ninth clauses in an Act of Assembly made in the Year 1740 and intitled an Act for the better Ordering and Governing Negroes and other Slaves in this Province commonly called The Negro Act now in force Your Memorialists are deprived of the Rights and Privileges of Citizens by not having it in their power to give Testimony on Oath in prosecutions on behalf of the State from which cause many Culprits have escaped the punishment due to their atrocious Crimes, nor can they give their Testimony in recovering Debts due to them, or in establishing Agreements made by them within the meaning of the Statutes of Frauds and Perjuries in force in this State except in cases where Persons of Colour are concerned, whereby they are subject to great Losses and repeated Injuries without any means of redress.

That by the said clauses in the said Act, they are debarred of the Rights of Free Citizens by being subject to a Trial without the benefit of a jury and subject to Prosecution by Testimony of Slaves without Oath by which they are placed on the same footing.

Your Memorialists shew that they have at all times since the Independence of the United States contributed and do now contribute to the support of the Government by cheerfully paying their Taxes proportionable to their Property with others who have been during such period, and now are in full enjoyment of the Rights and Immunities of Citizens Inhabitants of a Free Independent State.

That as your Memorialists have been and are considered as Free-Citizens of this State they hope to be treated as such, they are ready and willing to take and subscribe to such Oath of Allegiance to the States as shall be prescribed by this Honorable House, and are also willing to take upon them any duty for the preservation of the Peace in the City or any other occasion if called on.

Your Memorialists do not presume to hope that they shall be put on an equal footing with the Free white citizens of the State in general they only humbly solicit such indulgence as the Wisdom and Humanity of this Honorable House shall dictate in their favor by repealing the clauses the act aforementioned, and substituting such a clause as will efectually Redress the grievances which your Memorialists humbly submit in this their Memorial but under such restrictions as to your Honorable House shall seem proper.

May it therefore please your Honors to take your Memorialists case into tender consideration, and make such Acts or insert such clauses for the purpose of relieving your Memorialists from the unremitted grievance they now Labour under as in your Wisdom shall seem meet.

And as in duty bound your Memorialists will ever pray

Sources: Gary B. Nash, *Race and Revolution* (Madison, Wis.: Madison House, 1990), 174–176; http://www.pbs.org/wgbh/aia/part2/2h70t.html.

—⚏—

5. Letter, Benjamin Banneker to Thomas Jefferson, 1791

The free black astronomer, mathematician, and surveyor Benjamin Banneker sent Thomas Jefferson a memorable letter in 1791 in which he appealed to Jefferson to use his clout in the fight for civil rights for those of African ancestry. Banneker flattered Jefferson yet also condemned his hypocrisy in continuing to hold slaves despite having railed against British "enslavement" of the colonies during the Revolution. Banneker bestowed upon Jefferson the gift of an almanac he had produced as evidence of black accomplishment. Jefferson's reply to Banneker raised the possibility that blacks' condition—enslavement—was more responsible than nature for their perceived inferiority, but he apparently told Banneker what he wanted to hear. Jefferson later confided to his friend Joel Barlow his belief that Banneker's intellect and accomplishments had been overestimated.

SIR,

I AM fully sensible of the greatness of that freedom, which I take with you on the present occasion; a liberty which seemed to me scarcely allowable, when I reflected on that distinguished and dignified station in which you stand, and the almost general prejudice and prepossession, which is so prevalent in the world against those of my complexion.

I suppose it is a truth too well attested to you, to need a proof here, that we are a race of beings, who have long labored under the abuse and censure of the world; that we have long been looked upon with an eye of contempt; and that we have long been considered rather as brutish than human, and scarcely capable of mental endowments.

Sir, I hope I may safely admit, in consequence of that report which hath reached me, that you are a man far less inflexible in sentiments of this nature, than many others; that you are measurably friendly, and well disposed towards us; and that you are willing and ready to lend your aid and assistance to our relief, from those many distresses, and numerous calamities, to which we are reduced. Now Sir, if this is founded in truth, I apprehend you will embrace every opportunity, to eradicate that train of absurd and false ideas and opinions, which so generally prevails with respect to us; and that your sentiments are concurrent with mine, which are, that one universal Father hath given being to us all; and that he hath not only made us all of one flesh, but that he hath also, without partiality, afforded us all the same sensations and endowed us all with the same faculties; and that however variable we may be in society or religion, however diversified in situation or color, we are all of the same family, and stand in the same relation to him.

Sir, if these are sentiments of which you are fully persuaded, I hope you cannot but acknowledge, that it is the indispensible duty of those, who maintain for themselves the rights of human nature, and who possess the obligations of Christianity, to extend their power and influence to the relief of every part of the human race, from whatever burden or oppression they may unjustly labor under; and this, I apprehend, a full conviction of the truth and obligation of these principles should lead all to. Sir, I have long been convinced, that if your love for yourselves, and for those inestimable laws, which preserved to you the rights of human nature, was founded on sincerity, you could not but be solicitous, that every individual, of whatever rank or distinction, might with you equally enjoy the blessings thereof; neither could you rest satisfied short of the most active effusion of your exertions, in order to their promotion from any state of degradation, to which the unjustifiable cruelty and barbarism of men may have reduced them.

Sir, I freely and cheerfully acknowledge, that I am of the African race, and in that color which is natural to them of the deepest dye; and it is under a sense of the most profound gratitude to the Supreme Ruler of the Universe, that I now confess to you, that I am not under that state of tyrannical thraldom, and inhuman captivity, to which too many of my brethren are doomed, but that I have abundantly tasted of the fruition of those blessings, which proceed from that free and unequalled liberty with which you are favored; and which, I hope, you will willingly allow you have mercifully received, from the immediate hand of that Being, from whom proceedeth every good and perfect Gift.

Sir, suffer me to recal to your mind that time, in which the arms and tyranny of the British crown were exerted, with every powerful effort, in order to reduce you to a state of servitude: look back, I entreat you, on the variety of dangers to which you were exposed; reflect on that time, in which every human aid appeared unavailable, and in which even hope and fortitude wore the aspect of inability to the conflict, and you cannot but be led to a serious and grateful sense of your miraculous and providential preservation; you cannot but acknowledge, that the present freedom and tranquility which you enjoy you have mercifully received, and that it is the peculiar blessing of Heaven.

This, Sir, was a time when you clearly saw into the injustice of a state of slavery, and in which you had just apprehensions of the horrors of its condition. It was now that your abhorrence thereof was so excited, that you publicly held forth this true and invaluable doctrine, which is worthy to be recorded and remembered in all succeeding ages: "We hold these truths to be self-evident, that all men are created equal; that they are endowed by their Creator with certain unalienable rights, and that among these are, life, liberty, and the pursuit of happiness." Here was a time, in which your tender feelings for yourselves had engaged you thus to declare, you were then impressed with proper ideas of the great violation of liberty, and the free possession of those blessings, to which you were entitled by nature; but, Sir, how pitiable is it to reflect, that although you were so fully convinced of the benevolence of the Father of Mankind, and of his equal and impartial distribution of these rights and privileges, which he hath conferred upon them, that you should at the same time counteract his mercies, in detaining by fraud and violence so numerous a part of my brethren, under groaning captivity and cruel oppression, that you should at the same time be found guilty of that most criminal act, which you professedly detested in others, with respect to yourselves.

I suppose that your knowledge of the situation of my brethren, is too extensive to need a recital here; neither shall I presume to prescribe methods by which they may be relieved, otherwise than by recommending to you and all others, to wean yourselves from those narrow prejudices which you have imbibed with respect to them, and as Job proposed to his friends, "put your soul in their souls' stead;" thus shall your hearts be enlarged with kindness and benevolence towards them; and thus shall you need neither the direction of myself or others, in what manner to proceed herein. And now, Sir, although my sympathy and affection for my brethren hath caused my enlargement thus far, I ardently hope, that your candor and generosity will plead with you in my behalf, when I make known to you, that it was not originally my design; but having taken up my pen in order to direct to you, as a present, a copy of an Almanac, which I have calculated for the succeeding year, I was unexpectedly and unavoidably led thereto.

This calculation is the production of my arduous study, in this my advanced stage of life; for having long had unbounded desires to become acquainted with the secrets of nature, I have had to gratify my curiosity herein, through my own assiduous application to Astronomical Study, in which I need not recount to you the many difficulties and disadvantages, which I have had to encounter.

And although I had almost declined to make my calculation for the ensuing year, in consequence of that time which I had allotted therefor, being taken up at the Federal Territory, by the request of Mr. Andrew Ellicott, yet finding myself under several engagements to Printers of this state, to whom I had communicated my design, on my return to my place of residence, I industriously applied myself thereto, which I hope I have accomplished with correctness and accuracy; a copy of which I have taken the liberty to direct to you, and which I humbly request you will favorably receive; and although you may have the opportunity of perusing it after its publication, yet I choose to send it to you in manuscript previous thereto, that thereby you might not only have an earlier inspection, but that you might also view it in my own hand writing.

And now, Sir, I shall conclude, and subscribe myself, with the most profound respect, Your most obedient humble servant,

BENJAMIN BANNEKER.
University of Virginia

Source: http://www.pbs.org/wgbh/aia/part2/2h71t.html.

—⁂—

6. Thomas Jefferson, *Notes on the State of Virginia,* 1784

In 1780, a Frenchman named François de Barbé Marbois sent a series of questions to American officials to learn more about the new United States. His queries eventually made their way to the Virginia governor, Thomas Jefferson, who responded in cursory fashion in 1781. Unhappy

with the quality of his responses, Jefferson continued working on his replies over the next few years. He eventually privately published his responses in book form as Notes on the State of Virginia *in 1784, and several different editions appeared over the next two decades. Printed here are excerpts from Jefferson's reply to Query XIV, in which he shares his thoughts on race and racial differences. His prejudices did not make him unique among white Americans.*

The first difference which strikes us is that of colour. Whether the black of the negro resides in the reticular membrane between the skin and scarf-skin, or in the scarf-skin itself; whether it proceeds from the colour of the blood, the colour of the bile, or from that of some other secretion, the difference is fixed in nature, and is as real as if its seat and cause were better known to us. And is this difference of no importance? Is it not the foundation of a greater or less share of beauty in the two races? Are not the fine mixtures of red and white, the expressions of every passion by greater or less suffusions of colour in the one, preferable to that eternal monotony, which reigns in the countenances, that immoveable veil of black which covers all the emotions of the other race? Add to these, flowing hair, a more elegant symmetry of form, their own judgment in favour of the whites, declared by their preference of them, as uniformly as is the preference of the Oranootan for the black women over those of his own species. The circumstance of superior beauty, is thought worthy attention in the propagation of our horses, dogs, and other domestic animals; why not in that of man? Besides those of colour, figure, and hair, there are other physical distinctions proving a difference of race. They have less hair on the face and body. They secrete less by the kidnies, and more by the glands of the skin, which gives them a very strong and disagreeable odour. This greater degree of transpiration renders them more tolerant of heat, and less so of cold, than the whites. . . . They seem to require less sleep. A black, after hard labour through the day, will be induced by the slightest amusements to sit up till midnight, or later, though knowing he must be out with the first dawn of the morning. They are at least as brave, and more adventuresome. But this may perhaps proceed from a want of forethought, which prevents their seeing a danger till it be present. When present, they do not go through it with more coolness or steadiness than the whites. They are more ardent after their female: but love seems with them to be more an eager desire, than a tender delicate mixture of sentiment and sensation. Their griefs are transient. Those numberless afflictions, which render it doubtful whether heaven has given life to us in mercy or in wrath, are less felt, and sooner forgotten with them. In general, their existence appears to participate more of sensation than reflection. To this must be ascribed their disposition to sleep when abstracted from their diversions, and unemployed in labour. An animal whose body is at rest, and who does not reflect, must be disposed to sleep of course. Comparing them by their faculties of memory, reason, and imagination, it appears to me, that in memory they are equal to the whites; in reason much inferior, as I think one could scarcely be found capable of tracing and comprehending the investigations of Euclid; and that in imagination they are dull, tasteless, and anomalous. It would be unfair to follow them to Africa for this investigation. We will consider them here, on the same stage with the whites, and where the facts are not apocryphal on which a judgment is to be formed. It will be right to make great allowances for the difference of condition, of education, of conversation, of the sphere in which they move. Many millions of them have been brought to, and born in America. Most of them indeed have been confined to tillage, to their own homes, and their own society: yet many have been so situated, that they might have availed themselves of the conversation of their masters; many have been brought up to the handicraft arts, and from that circumstance have always been associated with the whites. Some have been liberally educated, and all have lived in countries where the arts and sciences are cultivated to a considerable degree, and have had before their eyes samples of the best works from abroad. The Indians, with no advantages of this kind, will often carve figures on their pipes not destitute of design and merit. They will crayon out an animal, a plant, or a country, so as to prove the existence of a germ in their minds which only wants cultivation. They astonish you with strokes of the most sublime oratory; such as prove their reason and sentiment strong, their imagination glowing and elevated. But never yet could I find that a black had uttered a thought above the level of plain narration; never see even an elementary trait of painting or sculpture. In music they are more generally gifted than the whites with accurate ears for tune and time, and they have been found capable of imagining a small catch. Whether they will be equal to the composition of a more extensive run of melody, or of complicated harmony, is yet to be proved. Misery is often the parent of the most affecting touches in poetry.—Among the blacks is misery enough, God knows, but no poetry. . . . Their love is ardent, but it kindles the senses only, not the imagination. Religion indeed has produced a Phyllis Whately [Phillis Wheatley]; but it could not produce a poet. The compositions published under her name are below the dignity of criticism. . . . The improvement of the blacks in body and mind, in the first instance of their mixture with the whites, has been observed by every one, and proves that their inferiority is not the effect merely of their condition of life. . . .

It is not their condition then, but nature, which has produced the distinction.—Whether further observation will or will not verify the conjecture, that nature has been less bountiful to them in the endowments of the head, I believe that in those of the heart she will be found to have done them justice. That disposition to theft with which they have been branded, must be ascribed to their situation, and not to any depravity of the moral sense. The man, in whose favour no laws of property exist, probably feels himself less bound to respect those made in favour of others. When arguing for ourselves, we lay it down as a fundamental, that laws, to be just, must give a reciprocation of right: that, without this, they are mere arbitrary rules of conduct, founded in force, and not in conscience: and it is a problem which I give to the master to solve, whether the religious precepts against the violation of property were not framed for him as well as his slave? And whether the slave may not as justifiably take a little from one, who has taken all from him, as he may slay one who would slay him? That a change in the relations in which a man is placed should change his ideas of moral right and wrong, is neither new, nor peculiar to the colour of the blacks.

Notwithstanding these considerations which must weaken their respect for the laws of property, we find among them numerous instances of the most rigid integrity, and as many as among their better instructed masters, of benevolence, gratitude, and unshaken fidelity.—The opinion, that they are inferior in the faculties of reason and imagination, must be hazarded with great diffidence. To justify a general conclusion, requires many observations. . . . Let me add too, as a circumstance of great tenderness, where our conclusion would degrade a whole race of men from the rank in the scale of beings which their Creator may perhaps have given them. To our reproach it must be said, that though for a century and a half we have had under our eyes the races of black and of red men, they have never yet been viewed by us as subjects of natural history. I advance it therefore as a suspicion only, that the blacks, whether originally a distinct race, or made distinct by time and circumstances, are inferior to the whites in the endowments both of body and mind. It is not against experience to suppose, that different species of the same genus, or varieties of the same species, may possess different qualifications. Will not a lover of natural history then, one who views the gradations in all the races of animals with the eye of philosophy, excuse an effort to keep those in the department of man as distinct as nature has formed them? This unfortunate difference of colour, and perhaps of faculty, is a powerful obstacle to the emancipation of these people.

Source: http://xroads.virginia.edu/~HYPER/JEFFERSON/ch14.html.

SLAVERY AND THE U.S. CONSTITUTION:

Was the U.S. Constitution a Proslavery Document?

—⁂—

THE CONTROVERSY

The Issue

Several clauses of the U.S. Constitution drafted in 1787 dealt with the institution of slavery in the United States. Was the Constitution proslavery or antislavery?

♦ *Arguments that the U.S. Constitution was a proslavery document:* Some contemporaries considered the U.S. Constitution, written in 1787 and ratified by all of the original 13 states between 1787 and 1790, a proslavery document. It counted slaves as three-fifths of a person for purposes of both taxation and representation, permitted the importation into the United States of new slaves from abroad, and included a fugitive slave clause for the return of runaways to their masters. The Constitution freed no slaves but rather provided certain assurances that slaveholders' peculiar property in human beings would be preserved.

♦ *Arguments that the U.S. Constitution was not a proslavery document:* Others saw the Constitution as an antislavery document. The three-fifths clause denied slaveholding states recognition of 40 percent of all bond people, laid the groundwork for the termination of the transatlantic slave trade, and contained mechanisms through which Congress could legislate against slavery. In addition, the framers never explicitly acknowledged the institution of slavery by name in the text of the Constitution. In spirit, the Constitution reflected many signers' discomfort with slavery and their desire to see the institution's demise.

—⁂—

INTRODUCTION

In the 1780s, the infant United States teetered on the brink. Recent years had exposed the deficiencies in the U.S. government under the Articles of Confederation. Confidence in America's future was at an ebb. In this context, more than 50 delegates met in Philadelphia at the Constitutional

Convention in 1787. Casting the Articles of Confederation aside, they agreed to create a new and improved government for the nation. Slavery quickly emerged as a point of conflict in the debates over what this government should entail. The Constitution the delegates were crafting had implications for the fate of slavery in the United States.

Some observers believed that the U.S. Constitution protected slavery within the borders of the United States. It counted three-fifths of all slaves for purposes of taxation and representation, it made no effort to immediately sever America's ties to the transatlantic slave trade, and it required Americans to deliver captured fugitive slaves to their masters. Such provisions made the Constitution appear to be a proslavery document.

Others disagreed. The Constitution was antislavery in that its three-fifths clause did not count slaves as full persons. It created an opportunity for the United States to end its participation in the international slave trade and possibly even the internal, domestic slave trade. Furthermore, the language of the Constitution conscientiously avoided any direct acknowledgment of slaves or slavery. The framers' uneasiness with slavery was evident in the document they crafted.

BACKGROUND

The United States publicly declared its independence from Great Britain on July 4, 1776. The Constitution that governs us today was not the country's first national government, however. The Continental Congress, which functioned as the U.S. government immediately after independence, adopted the Articles of Confederation and Perpetual Union in November 1777, pending ratification, or approval, by each of the 13 original states. All of the states except Maryland quickly ratified the Articles of Confederation. Concerned about various states' claims to western land, Maryland withheld ratification until 1781.

The Articles of Confederation, finally implemented in March 1781, outlined an intentionally weak national government. Having just overthrown the British monarchy, the founders were in no mood to create another powerful, possibly tyrannical government capable of infringing upon states' rights. Their distrust and fear of centralized authority resulted in a government whose structure vested most powers at the state level rather than at the national. The new government boasted neither an executive nor a judicial branch. The infant nation had no king, president, or governor; no series of federal courts to try cases. Government consisted of a unicameral, or one-house, Congress, and even its powers were limited. Under the Articles, Congress could conduct foreign affairs, wage war, coin money, oversee the territories, and deal with Native Americans, but it lacked the important power to levy taxes directly on the American people, thus denying the government an important source of revenue. In addition, any amendments or changes to the Articles required the unanimous consent of all 13 states. Though weak, the Articles of Confederation as a frame of government proved entirely consistent with the philosophy behind the American Revolution (1775–83) itself, which was still being waged as the Articles went into effect.

Despite some successes under the government established by the Articles of Confederation, including the negotiation of the Treaty of Paris (1783), which formally ended the war with Great Britain, and the resolution of questions surrounding the settlement of lands in the trans-Appalachian West, the 1780s has sometimes been referred to as the "critical period," a label that speaks to the seriousness of the issues plaguing the United States during that decade. Diplomatically, even after the conclusion of the revolution, Great Britain lingered as a threatening presence in Canada and portions of the Northwest Territory, the region north of the Ohio River and east of the Mississippi. In 1784, Spain forbade American access to the Mississippi River itself. Spain controlled the land on each side of the Mississippi's southernmost reaches as well as the port city of New Orleans. Its strategic position at the mouth of the river allowed it to close the river to American commerce and thereby jeopardize the dreams of Americans hoping to settle and farm west of the Appalachians. Farmers and planters in the West understood that access to the river was the only profitable way to get their crops to market. Economically, a postwar depression, a worthless continental currency, rampant inflation caused by the reckless printing of paper money, a Congress impotent to compel the states to contribute funds to the national treasury, and restrictions the British imposed on American trade all combined to throw the nation's finances into turmoil. To help pay off its wartime debts, the state of Massachusetts passed new taxes on land, which naturally burdened the state's farmers most. When the farmers' petitions for relief went unheeded, they rose up in rebellion under the leadership of one of their own, a Revolutionary War veteran named Daniel Shays. Shays's Rebellion of 1786–87 reinforced the belief already growing among the nation's founders that a stronger central government was necessary. Without it, the infant nation risked premature death.

At the Constitutional Convention convened in Philadelphia in May 1787, slavery emerged as arguably the single most contentious issue. Despite heated debates over the best means of determining representation in Congress, Virginia delegate and "Father of the Constitution" James Madison insisted that the divide between North and South outweighed the tensions between the states large and small in population. (See "Excerpt from Debates at the Constitutional Convention, 1787," on page 69 in the Primary Sources section.) The sharp dichotomy he drew between North and South obscures the fact that slavery could still be found in much of the North in 1787 and for subsequent decades. Nevertheless, slavery was a dead or dying institution in all but two northern states (New York and New Jersey) by the time of the convention. Slaves made up less than 3 percent of the population in the North but more than 35 percent in the South. By 1787, slavery was thoroughly entrenched in the states from Maryland to Georgia. Not surprisingly, the convention's southern delegates sought to defend their increasingly "peculiar institution."

Delegates to the Constitutional Convention wrangled over two primary issues related to slavery: how to count slaves in terms of representation and taxation and what to do about the transatlantic slave trade. If, as the Great Compromise held, representation in the lower house of Congress was determined on the basis of population, it mattered greatly how slaves were counted. Southern states, containing a disproportionate share of all bond people, insisted that slaves be included in their respective populations when apportioning seats in the House of Representatives. At a distinct legislative disadvantage should slaves be counted, northern states disagreed. Their delegates readily accepted the idea, however, of taxing slaves equally with free people, a point on which the South took umbrage. To resolve this pair of disputes, northern and southern delegates reached the three-fifths compromise, whereby for purposes of representation and taxation, each slave would count as three-fifths of a free person. Put another way, five slaves were the equivalent of three free white citizens. Three-fifths became the "federal number," or "federal ratio."

Delegates in Philadelphia did not conjure the three-fifths fraction out of thin air; rather, the three-fifths compromise had a history that pre-dated the convention by a full four years. The federal number originated in 1783 with a proposed amendment, under the Confederation Congress, to transition the apportionment of taxes away from land values and to population. During that debate, northern states campaigned hard to use population as the basis of taxation and to count slaves as people. The northerners' position made sense for them because, at the time, a slight majority of all Americans (including slaves) lived in the South. By contrast, southern states argued for the continuation of taxation based on land values. The problem with that proposal was that state governments assessed the values of their own land and notoriously underval-ued their property in an attempt to escape the full brunt of taxation.

If population was to play any role in computing taxes, the Confederation Congress had to confront the issue of how to count slaves. Northern delegates favored counting slaves as persons for the sake of apportioning taxes, thereby increasing the share of taxes owed by the southern states. There seemed little question, North or South, that a slave did not constitute a full person, but there were differences over what fraction of a person a slave was. Delegates from Massachusetts and Connecticut argued for a ratio of 4 to 3—four slaves would count as three people. For their part, southern delegates argued that slaves were hardly persons, and if counted at all, should be counted by a ratio of perhaps 3 to 1 or 4 to 1. James Madison offered the compromise position of 5 to 3—every five slaves would count as three free people. Madison's federal ratio was not implemented in 1783. Although 11 of the 13 states approved it, the proposal to make population the basis for taxation failed because all amendments to the Articles of Confederation required unanimous ratification to take effect. Nevertheless, Madison established the three-fifths principle for taxation, setting the precedent for its reintroduction four years later.

By the time of the Constitutional Convention, delegates generally agreed that slaves were taxable, and the debate over how to calculate slaves for purposes of taxation was not very contentious. Likewise, the federal ratio in and of itself did not provoke prolonged discussion. When Pennsylvania's James Wilson suggested it, the delegates recalled the familiar fraction from four years before and felt no compelling need to rehash an old debate. Members of the Constitutional Convention proved more innovative, however, in applying the federal ratio not only to taxation, as in the 1783 proposal, but also to representation. On this score, northern delegates opposed counting slaves, while southern delegates clamored to count them more fully. If representation was based only on the free population, the North would have the edge in the House of Representatives. If slaves counted as the equals of free people, southern representatives would outnumber northern. Invoking the three-fifths principle for both taxation and representation promised to resolve dual dilemmas over slavery that exacerbated sectional tensions between northern and southern delegates. Although not agreed upon unanimously, the three-fifths compromise measure passed, making its way into the Constitution in Article I, Section 2, Clause 3: "Representatives and direct taxes . . . shall be determined by adding to the whole number of free persons, . . . three-fifths of all other persons." Three-fifths of a state's slave population would be counted under the new government for purposes of both representation and taxation. All southern states except one agreed to the three-fifths clause; for its part, South Carolina, which had taken the lead in arguing that slavery ought to be explicitly linked to representation, held out for a full accounting of slaves in determining the size of its membership in the House. (See "Excerpts from the U.S. Constitution, 1787," on page 69 in the Primary Sources section.)

In late July 1787, two weeks after delegates to the Constitutional Convention reached the three-fifths compromise concerning slavery's relationship to taxation and representation, they launched into heated arguments over America's participation in the international slave trade. (See "Excerpt from Debates at the Constitutional Convention, 1787," on page 71 in the Primary Sources section.) Slave imports into the United States from Africa and the West Indies had halted during the Revolutionary War, and by 1787, all state governments except that of Georgia had passed some limitation on the introduction of new slaves from abroad. Some at the convention thought 1787 an opportune time to formally prohibit the introduction of new slaves from abroad into the United States. William Paterson of New Jersey, Gouverneur Morris of Pennsylvania, and other delegates to the Constitutional Convention observed that counting even three-fifths of all slaves for representation might reverse the downward trend in the slave trade by providing an incentive for the South to import additional bond people. Under the three-fifths rule, purchasing vast quantities of slaves from Africa or the West Indies could dramatically strengthen the South's political power.

Discussions of the possible termination of American involvement in the transatlantic slave trade did not divide neatly along sectional lines. Dissent was evident among the slaveholding states of the South. The Virginia and Maryland delegations spearheaded the movement to put a stop to the traffic in slaves. (See the sidebar "Luther Martin" on page 52.) Although those states' delegates never admitted it, they were motivated more by economic considerations than by interests of humanity. As the states with the longest histories of slavery, Virginia and Maryland had an overabundance of bond people, with more slaves than work for them to do. If the international slave trade were closed and access to fresh arrivals from abroad cut off, the only source of bond people would be domestic. Masters desiring slaves would have to purchase them via an internal domestic slave trade. Virginia and Maryland masters could then sell their surplus slaves at inflated prices to buyers in other states and realize enormous profits. South Carolina and Georgia, two slave states without similar excess populations of bond people, objected to any prohibitions on the transatlantic trade. The Revolutionary War had devastated those two states. Farms were destroyed, and runaways depleted their slave populations. In replenishing their enslaved workforces, they did not want to be held hostage to the high prices Virginia and Maryland masters would charge. Moreover, South Carolina and Georgia understood that they could enlarge their slave populations more quickly by purchasing them from abroad than by waiting for natural reproduction to take its course. Once they had enough slaves to meet their labor needs, they claimed, they could always end importation on their own.

In the debate over the transatlantic slave trade, the Deep South states found some seemingly unlikely allies in the North. The New England states were well known for their shipbuilding and maritime interests. Yankee captains piloted Yankee ships owned by Yankee merchants—ships sometimes used to carry slaves from Africa or the West Indies to destinations in the South. South Carolina delegate John Rutledge indicated to his northern colleagues the benefits to New England shipping interests if the international slave trade continued. South Carolina delegates and cousins Charles Pinckney and Charles Cotesworth Pinckney threatened to pull out of the Constitutional Convention if the slave trade

One of South Carolina's delegates to the Constitutional Convention, John Rutledge staunchly defended the interests of slaveholders. (Library of Congress)

issue was not satisfactorily decided. To prevent South Carolina's premature departure, delegates proposed delaying any possible action against the transatlantic trade until 1800. Charles Cotesworth Pinckney's rejoinder was to suggest 1808, 20 years from the date of the ratification of the Constitution. The founders accepted Pinckney's recommendation, including it in the Constitution as Article I, Section 9, Clause 1: "The Migration or Importation of such Persons as any of the States now existing shall think proper to admit, shall not be prohibited by the Congress

LUTHER MARTIN

Born in New Jersey in 1748, Luther Martin earned a degree in 1766 from what would become Princeton University. After graduation, he moved to Maryland, taught, and studied law. He was admitted to the bar in 1771. An enthusiastic patriot during the American Revolution, Martin served as Maryland's attorney general, prosecuting the state's Tories—those loyal to Great Britain—during the conflict. He briefly fought in the Revolutionary War under the leadership of France's Marquis de Lafayette, who lent his services and military expertise to the American cause.

Martin, a successful lawyer in the 1780s, represented Maryland at the Constitutional Convention. He counted among the many delegates who filtered slowly into Philadelphia, arriving more than two weeks after proceedings had officially begun. During the convention, he consistently reflected the opinion of Maryland and other states small in population that the central government created under the Constitution was too powerful. His was also one of the few scattered voices at the convention that expressed moral opposition to slavery, along with Pennsylvania's Gouverneur Morris and a handful of other antislavery delegates. Martin objected to the inclusion of slaves in determining a state's representation, as he feared that the three-fifths principle encouraged the importation of additional slaves from Africa and the Caribbean. Martin considered "the privilege of importing" slaves

prior to the Year one thousand eight hundred and eight." Although several other provisions in the Constitution related directly or indirectly to the subject of slavery, the three-fifths clause and the transatlantic slave trade discussions proved the most noteworthy and contentious.

In late August 1787, southern delegates raised one last issue related to slavery. Pierce Butler and Charles Cotesworth Pinckney of South Carolina noted a lack of provision in the Constitution for the return of runaway slaves. Butler introduced a proposal requiring that captured escaped slaves be restored to their masters. With little debate, the states unanimously adopted the fugitive slave clause and included it in Article IV, Section 2.

The meetings of the Constitutional Convention during summer 1787 were held in secret, doors and windows closed, to prevent eavesdroppers completely "unreasonable" and found it abhorrent that the Constitution could countenance the international traffic in human cargoes. According to Martin, the transatlantic slave trade was "inconsistent with the principles of the revolution and dishonorable to the American character." He proposed "a prohibition or tax on the importation of slaves" to mitigate the effects of the three-fifths clause.

Only 39 of the 55 delegates who attended the proceedings in Philadelphia committed their signatures to paper. Upset with several features of the Constitution, Martin and 15 other delegates, including a fellow member of the Maryland contingent named John Francis Mercer, either walked out of the convention early or refused to sign the finished document. Martin emerged as a staunch Anti-Federalist, lobbying unsuccessfully against the ratification of the Constitution.

Martin boasted a long and distinguished career in law. He served as Maryland's attorney general for more than three decades and as defense counsel in the impeachment trial of Supreme Court justice Samuel Chase and in the treason trial of former vice president Aaron Burr. He also labored on behalf of his state in the Supreme Court case of *McCulloch v. Maryland* (1819). Martin's health began to deteriorate in 1819, and his penchant for excessive drinking caught up with him. He died impoverished in 1826 in the home of Aaron Burr and was buried in an unmarked grave.

from overhearing fragments of conversations and spreading rumors of the proceedings. (See the sidebar "George Washington" on page 62.) James Madison's notes on the convention were published only posthumously, in 1840, more than 50 years after the meeting. Only then could the literate masses of Americans gain some sense of the discussions, disputes, and negotiations that took place inside the Philadelphia State House. Immediately those who hoped to abolish slavery sought to discern the framers' original intent regarding slavery. Some abolitionists interpreted the Constitution as antislavery in spirit, a document that contained the seeds of slavery's destruction. They maintained that slavery could be outlawed from within the existing framework the Constitution provided. For others, Madison's notes reinforced suspicions that the Constitution was a corrupt document, blatantly proslavery in its leanings. The abolitionist William Lloyd Garrison contemptuously referred to the Constitution as "a covenant with death and an agreement with hell." The split between the two different camps of abolitionists kept alive the debate: Was the U.S. Constitution a proslavery document?

THE DEBATE

The Argument that the Constitution Was a Proslavery Document

Some delegates to the Constitutional Convention, as well as the Garrisonian wing of the abolitionist movement, considered the Constitution a proslavery document. They argued that the Constitution contained a series of provisions for slavery not found in the Articles of Confederation. The three-fifths compromise on taxation and representation, the refusal to put an immediate end to the transatlantic slave trade, and the fugitive slave clause all combined to support the institution of slavery. Other, more minor passages in the Constitution further reinforced the document's proslavery message.

Article I, Section 2, of the Constitution read: "Representatives and direct Taxes shall be apportioned among the several States which may be included within this Union, according to their respective Numbers, which shall be determined by adding to the whole Number of free Persons, including those bound to Service for a Term of Years, and excluding Indians not taxed, three fifths of all other Persons." This three-fifths clause enhanced southern slave states' voting power in the U.S. House of Representatives. Only 5 of the 13 original states—Maryland, Virginia, North Carolina, South Carolina, and Georgia—maintained substantial slave populations in 1787. Even though these 5 states represented only 38 percent of all states and contained 41 percent of America's free population, by virtue of the privilege under the three-fifths clause to include 60 percent of their slaves for purposes of representation, the southern voice in the House was magnified to almost 50 percent. Augmenting southern states' delegations to the House had effects on the crafting of legislation for decades. Less obvious, the three-fifths clause also had ramifications in the selection of presidents of the United States. According to Article II, Section 1, the Electoral College, which ultimately chooses the president of the United States, consists of "a

Number of Electors, equal to the whole Number of Senators and Representatives to which the State may be entitled in the Congress." A southern state whose number of representatives in the House was increased by counting three-fifths of that state's slaves therefore gained additional clout in its ability to select the president.

In addition to increasing slave-state representation in the House, the federal ratio counted only three-fifths of a master's slaves for taxation. The three-fifths principle thus gave the South an economic bonus—a tax exemption—on 40 percent of those held in bondage. Additional provisions in the Constitution dealt specifically with the economics of slaveholding. Article I, Section 9, prohibited Congress from passing a head tax or other direct tax on slaves that would increase the costs associated with slaveholding and thereby encourage masters to emancipate their bond people. No amendment could change this provision until 1808 at the earliest. Article I, Section 9, further held that "No Tax or Duty shall be laid on Articles exported from any State," and Article I, Section 10, added that "No State shall, without the Consent of the Congress, lay any Imposts or Duties on . . . Exports." In other words, neither the national nor the state governments could tax American goods intended for sale abroad. Tobacco, rice, or other commodities produced by slave labor for sale on international markets were not subject to export duties. The exemption of slave-produced goods prevented the passage of any indirect tax designed to undermine the institution of slavery itself.

In the 1840s, Garrison and his camp of abolitionists also decried the message the three-fifths compromise implied. Garrison touted the equality of all human beings, regardless of race or color. He saw the compromise as a devaluation of the slave to something less than a full human being. Legally, slaves were worth less than white people. For anyone like Garrison who upheld the principle of human equality—and there were not many in the decades before the Civil War—the Constitution's three-fifths clause was inhumane and insulting.

Another proslavery feature of the Constitution was the framers' decision not to tamper with American participation in the transatlantic slave trade. Article I, Section 9, permitted the continued importation of slaves into the United States through at least 1808 and possibly longer. The Constitution set no definitive cutoff date for the termination of the trade and, at the insistence of John Rutledge of South Carolina, even added a redundant statement in Article V to guarantee no congressional interference with the slave trade until 1808. Under the Constitution, the U.S. Congress enjoyed power over virtually all international commerce with the conspicuous exception of the transatlantic slave trade. Perfectly consistent with Article I, Section 9, the state of South Carolina reopened the international traffic in slaves during a four-year window from 1803 to 1807, importing almost 40,000 new slaves during that time. The Constitution capped the possible tax on each newly imported slave at a maximum of $10, which, adjusted for inflation, amounts to roughly $233 in today's dollars—a very modest sum compared to duties on other imported goods.

The Constitution included in Article IV, Section 2, a clause that protected masters' investment in human property: "No Person held to Service or Labour in one State, under the Laws thereof, escaping into another, shall, in Consequence of any Law or Regulation therein, be discharged from such Service or Labour, but shall be delivered up on Claim of the Party to whom such Service or Labour may be due." Runaway slaves or indentured servants who were apprehended could not be freed but rather had to be returned at the order of the master. Such a clause marked a constitutional innovation in favor of slave owners and holders of indenture contracts by making residents of free states police institutions of bound labor. The Articles of Confederation had contained no similar provision mandating the return of fugitive slaves or servants. The Constitution afforded additional security for southern slaveholders in Article I, Section 8, and in Article IV, Section 4. The former vested in Congress the power to summon state militias to "suppress Insurrections," while the latter reinforced the government's message that states would be protected from "domestic Violence." By these provisions, the government promised to quell all categories of internal rebellion, including slave revolts.

All of these proslavery aspects of the Constitution were designed to placate anxious southern states. Southern delegates at the convention understood that they would hold an initial minority in the Senate, where northern states outnumbered southern. Six states in the North had already passed either a gradual or an immediate emancipation law prior to the meeting of the Constitutional Convention. The Revolutionary generation had successfully attacked slavery where it was weakest and less crucial to the functioning of the economy. Moreover, the Northwest Ordinance of 1787, passed by Congress as the Constitutional Convention was still in session, forbade slavery in the Northwest

Territory. The South felt isolated and besieged, already a beleaguered minority within the union in 1787, and craved some security for the institution of slavery. Without protections for slavery, South Carolina and Georgia delegates threatened to walk out of the convention; their states would refuse to ratify the Constitution. Slaveholding delegates arrived at the convention with a clear agenda to protect slavery and the wealth it generated. Their commitment and resolve to maintain the institution overwhelmed the mild antislavery convictions or indifference of delegates from farther north. If the framers had not crafted a proslavery Constitution, they would have had no constitution at all. A Constitution that was proslavery was the necessary price of national harmony and national union. Pragmatic accommodations with slavery made the Constitution possible.

The Argument that the Constitution Was Not a Proslavery Document

However many bargains the founders struck regarding slavery, it is still possible to make a case that the Constitution was an antislavery document. The three-fifths compromise and the slave importation agreement can both be interpreted as antislavery features of the Constitution. The very language of the Constitution betrayed many of the framers' discomfort with slavery, and developments in the early decades of the republic revealed other antislavery aspects of the Constitution that seemingly did not occur to the founders themselves.

In debates at the Constitutional Convention, southern delegates considered the three-fifths compromise a concession on their part. The three-fifths principle penalized the South by denying it representation for 40 percent of the region's slaves. Some abolitionists repeated this point in the years before the Civil War as evidence of the Constitution's antislavery leanings.

Article I, Section 9, authorized the closing of the transatlantic slave trade as soon as 1808, only two decades after the ratification of the Constitution. South Carolina regarded this provision as a concession because it limited the window during which masters could import slaves from overseas to as little as 20 years. James Madison of Virginia attempted to allay concerns about increased African imports in the intervening time. Slaveholding states, Madison assured, would not try to import new slaves because doing so would increase not only their representation in

Congress but also their tax burden. The clever linkage of representation and taxation in the three-fifths clause, he wrote, was enough to lay those fears to rest. "It ought to be considered as a great point gained in favor of humanity," Madison wrote, "that a period of twenty years may terminate forever" the transatlantic slave trade to the United States.

Article I, Section 9, postponed congressional action on the slave trade for a generation. In the meantime, most individual states shunned the transatlantic traffic, and as Madison observed, the possible constitutional "duty of ten dollars per head" served "as a discouragement to such importations." (See "Federalist 42, 1788," on page 71 in the Primary Sources section.) In addition, the Constitution allowed the importation of slaves only into the "States now existing." Congress maintained the authority to exclude slave imports from the territories. Under its constitutionally derived power, Congress prohibited the introduction of newly arrived slaves in the Mississippi Territory in 1798 and the Louisiana Territory in 1804. The founders did not intend for the transatlantic slave trade to populate areas outside the original 13 states. In 1807, in accordance with Article I, Section 9, Congress passed a bill outlawing American participation in the international slave trade effective January 1, 1808, the earliest date permitted by the Constitution. The slaveholding president Thomas Jefferson of Virginia signed the bill into law.

The closing of the transatlantic slave trade in 1808 could not prevent all smuggling, and illegal slave importations continued. Nevertheless, the prohibition of the international trade reoriented attention to the internal, domestic slave trade, the forced migration of slaves from one state to another. The framers could not have predicted the importance of the interstate slave trade in the 19th century. The internal migration of slaves was insignificant in 1787, and many founders believed slavery a dying institution. But with the invention of the cotton gin, the acquisition of new territory, and the rise and spread of cotton culture in the 1790s and early 1800s, masters moved with their slaves or sold their slaves away to states of the Old Southwest such as Alabama and Mississippi.

Antislavery forces argued that the Constitution permitted Congress to restrict or abolish the interstate slave trade, just as it had the international slave trade. Article I, Section 9, gave Congress the authority to prohibit "migration or importation" beginning in 1808. If "migration" implied the freedom to move at will, slaves could not be said to migrate. Only free people migrated, and only slaves were imported. According to some abolitionists, however, *migration* referred to the domestic slave trade, *importation* to the transatlantic. Article I, Section 8, Clause 3, of the Constitution gave Congress the power to regulate commerce not only with "foreign Nations" but also "among the several States." Some abolitionists therefore contended that Congress held power to prohibit both the international and interstate slave trades starting in 1808. The commerce clause gave abolitionists a constitutional loophole.

The language used in the Constitution offers one last piece of evidence testifying to the document's antislavery intent. Reviewing their handiwork in September 1787, northern delegates balked at using the word *slavery* in the Constitution. They proved hesitant to convey the impression that the Constitution explicitly endorsed slavery, bestowed upon it legal sanction, or validated the belief that human beings could be held as property. As a result, the framers purged any references to "slaves" or "slavery" from the finished document. "Slavery" was not mentioned by name in the Constitution until the Thirteenth Amendment abolished the institution in 1865. The Constitution instead euphemistically referred to "Person[s] held to Service or Labour" or to "free Persons" and "all other Persons," that is, the unfree, or slaves. Although a circuitous way of concealing slavery, the linguistic dance appeased northern delegates squeamish over the institution. Moreover, all of the euphemisms used to disguise slavery in the Constitution referred to slaves as "persons" rather than property.

Northern scruples against slavery wove their way into the particular phrasing of certain passages. The fugitive slave clause, for instance, stated, "No Person held to Service or Labour in one State, under the Laws thereof, escaping into another, shall, in Consequence of any Law or Regulation therein, be discharged from such Service or Labour, but shall be delivered up on Claim of the Party to whom such Service or Labour may be due." In debates over this clause, the founders struck the word *legally* from before the word *held* and substituted "under the Laws thereof." The framers transitioned away from a legal acknowledgment of slavery to concede only that some states permitted it. Likewise, "the Party to whom such Service or Labour may be due" replaced "the person justly claiming their service or labour." The founders denied that someone may "justly" claim another's labor. Such language massaged away the shame over slavery some delegates to the Constitutional Convention felt.

The Constitution embraced an antislavery spirit. It created a government designed to oppose tyranny and oppression. Its preamble spoke of "a more perfect Union," "Justice," "the general Welfare," and "the Blessings of Liberty." Slavery was antithetical to those values. When the founders denied southern states representation based on their entire slave populations, paved the way for restrictions on the slave trade, and carefully worded the Constitution to prevent any legitimization of slavery as an institution, they displayed their antislavery credentials.

OUTCOME AND IMPACT

The delegates meeting in Philadelphia concluded their work in September 1787 after a full summer of deliberation. The document they created—the Constitution—could not go into effect without the ratification, or approval, of nine states. (See "Debate over Ratification in South Carolina, 1788," on page 72 in the Primary Sources section.) During the ratification process, two camps quickly emerged: the Federalists, who favored the adoption of the Constitution, and the Anti-Federalists, who opposed it. Arguments during the ratification process mentioned slavery infrequently. The Anti-Federalist critique of the Constitution focused more on the powerful central government it created, its failure to protect individual rights, and other related concerns. Federalists James Madison, Alexander Hamilton, and John Jay together authored a series of 85 persuasive essays known collectively as *The Federalist Papers,* designed to convince the state conventions to ratify. In *The Federalist Papers,* they confronted the various objections to the Constitution voiced during the convention. They addressed the subject of slavery extensively in only two essays. Writing under the pseudonym *Publius,* Madison defended the slave importation decision in Federalist 42. Either he or Hamilton then justified the three-fifths clause in Federalist 54. Slavery's conspicuous absence during the ratification debates testifies to the founders' ability to hammer out a middle ground on the issue acceptable to the nation's white majority. (See "Federalist 54, 1788," on page 73 in the Primary Sources section.)

Federalist 54 in particular illustrates the compromises made at the convention to reconcile North and South. Northern delegates in Philadelphia questioned why slaves, unlike cattle, horses, or other forms

"Father of the Constitution" and coauthor of *The Federalist Papers,* James Madison defended the Constitution's handling of slavery. (©GL Archive/Alamy)

of property, merited representation. If only property, slaves should be taxed but given no representation at all. Federalist 54 made clear that slaves constituted a very peculiar form of property: "We must deny the fact that slaves are considered merely as property, and in no respect whatever as persons," its author wrote. "The true state of the case is, that they partake of both these qualities; being considered by our laws, in some respects, as persons, and in other respects, as property." Through the three-fifths clause, the Constitution implicitly acknowledged the reality of slaves' dual status as both persons *and* property: "In being compelled to labor, not for himself, but for a master; in being vendible by one master to another master; and in being subject at all times to be restrained in his liberty and chastised in his body, by the capricious

GEORGE WASHINGTON

One of the most famous figures in all of American history, George Washington was born in Virginia in 1732. As a young man, he worked as a surveyor before participating in the French and Indian War. He put his military experience to use as commander of the Continental army during the American Revolution. Despite his initial recruits' lack of military training and chronic shortages of essential supplies, Washington skillfully managed the war for six years, forcing the surrender of Great Britain's Lord Cornwallis at Yorktown in 1781. With the conclusion of the revolution, Washington retired to his beloved estate at Mount Vernon, Virginia, overlooking the Potomac River, to live the life of the gentleman farmer.

Like many observers in the 1780s, Washington realized the inadequacies of the government that had been established under the Articles of Confederation. After the alarming events of Shays's Rebellion in Massachusetts, he agreed to attend the Constitutional Convention in Philadelphia. Delegates quickly named him president of the convention, for good reason. More than anyone else, Washington was the one true national hero the United States had in 1787. He enjoyed respect and admiration throughout the country. A man with his reputation served as a unifying force during the contentious debates of the convention. His mere presence in Philadelphia added greatly to the credibility and legitimacy of the proceedings.

Those whom Washington presided over at the convention included most of the greatest men and political minds of the day, especially James Madison. About the only notable figures absent from the convention were Thomas Jefferson of Virginia and John Adams of Massachusetts, both away on diplomatic assignments in Europe. The typical delegate was an elite landed gentleman with experience in government. Approximately one-third held college degrees. Around 20 of the 55 owned human property,

will of another—the slave may appear to be degraded from the human rank, and classed with those irrational animals which fall under the legal denomination of property." But, Federalist 54 continued, slaves were not property in that they had the right to protection of life and limb. Furthermore, "in being punishable . . . for all violence committed against others—the slave is no less evidently regarded by the law as a member of from small slaveholders like Madison to large planters like John Rutledge of South Carolina, master of well more than 200 bond people, or Washington himself.

As president of the convention, Washington famously sat in a high-backed chair. Above his head, carved into the wood of the chair's back, was a half-sun. Salty Pennsylvania octogenarian Benjamin Franklin, the oldest delegate present at the convention, observed that he could not tell whether the wooden sun perched above Washington's head was rising or setting. His remarks captured the uncertainty of all the delegates assembled in Philadelphia about the mission they had undertaken. Crafting the Constitution generated new hopes as well as new fears. Ultimately, however, Franklin discerned that the sun was rising over Washington and the United States as a whole. Under the provisions outlined in the Constitution, the Electoral College unanimously elected Washington the first president of the United States in 1789.

Washington served two terms as president before retiring to Mount Vernon in 1797. He died two years later. In his will, he betrayed the internal conflicts over slavery with which a number of the framers struggled. Though a slaveholder in life, Washington ordered that his slaves be freed upon the death of his wife, Martha. He strictly forbade the breakup of enslaved families or the sale of any of his bond people, made provisions for his elderly and infirm slaves to be looked after by relatives, and instructed the Virginia court to bind out orphaned slave infants until the age of 25. He ordered that the young slaves be taught to read and write and learn a trade in preparation for their freedom. Last, Washington offered immediate emancipation as well as an annual payment of $30 to his slave William Lee as a reward for his loyal service during the Revolution. For the full text of Washington's will, visit http://nationalhumanitiescenter.org/pds/livingrev/equality/text2/washingtonwill.pdf.

the society, not as a part of the irrational creation; as a moral person, not as a mere article of property. The federal Constitution, therefore, decides with great propriety on the case of our slaves, when it views them in the mixed character of persons and of property. This is in fact their true character." Federalist 54 thus stumbled into the fundamental contradiction inherent in the institution of American slavery.

More practically, Federalist 54 argued that it would be unfair to reject slaves for purposes of representation but to include them for purposes of taxation: "Could it be reasonably expected, that the Southern States would concur in a system, which considered their slaves in some degree as men, when burdens were to be imposed, but refused to consider them in the same light, when advantages were to be conferred?" Publius conceded that the rationale behind the three-fifths compromise "may appear to be a little strained in some points, yet, on the whole, I must confess that it fully reconciles me to the scale of representation which the convention have established." "Let the case of the slaves be considered, as it is in truth, a peculiar one," he implored. "Let the compromising expedient of the Constitution be mutually adopted, which regards them as inhabitants, but as debased by servitude below the equal level of free inhabitants, which regards the *slave* as divested of two fifths of the *man*."

Despite the mental gymnastics required to rationalize slaveholding in a land where "all men are created equal," the Federalists carried the day. Between 1787 and 1790, each of the 13 states ratified the Constitution. With only 27 amendments to date, the Constitution remains the supreme law of the land in the United States today, more than 220 years later. Subtract the first 10 amendments—the Bill of Rights—ratified in 1791 at the insistence of the Anti-Federalists, and the Constitution has been modified only 17 additional times in all of U.S. history. Since the Twenty-first Amendment (1933) repealed the Eighteenth Amendment (1919), which established Prohibition, technically the Constitution has been permanently changed only 15 times since 1791. The durability of the document would almost certainly surprise its creators.

From a modern perspective, it appears that the framers botched an incredible opportunity to eradicate slavery. The founders met at a peculiar moment when the Revolutionary-era rhetoric of liberty, freedom, and equality still had resonance. Slavery was under legal assault in many states, and the cotton boom had yet to strike. If anything was to be done about slavery, 1787 was the time. Nevertheless, moral outrage against slavery was remarkably muted at the Constitutional Convention. Pragmatism overwhelmed troubling issues of ethics and justice. Even those objections to slavery voiced at the convention were more political or economic than moral. The delegates who opposed slavery were not adamant enough in their beliefs to pursue slavery's destruction.

As practical men of politics, the founders prioritized union over moral principle and abolition. In their drive to reconcile sectional differences and competing interests, they approved concessions that safeguarded slavery. Motivated by a desire to craft a working government, committed to the preservation of private property, and shaped by the prevailing racial attitudes of their day, the founders sidestepped a direct confrontation with slavery. As a result, slavery in the United States survived and even expanded during the next seven decades.

WHAT IF?

What if the framers had not compromised on the issue of slavery?

However imperfect, the compromises the framers hammered out at the Constitutional Convention laid to rest the most pressing questions concerning slavery for roughly a generation. Constitutional provisions went largely unchallenged until the Missouri crisis of 1819. By that time, American settlement westward had progressed beyond the Mississippi River. When the territory of Missouri applied for admission to the Union in 1819, a dispute erupted over the permissibility of slavery there. Migrating masters had already carried slaves into Missouri, but attempts to prohibit the introduction of additional slaves and to free those already living there reignited the sectional controversy over slavery the Constitutional Convention had tamped down more than 30 years earlier. Although a compromise involving the admission of Missouri as a slave state and Maine as a free state defused the situation, it was not the last time tempers flared over the fate of slavery in the territories.

If the framers had tackled slavery as a moral issue, the story of America's past might have been markedly different. Deep South delegates to the Constitutional Convention had threatened to walk out if their northern counterparts pressed for the abolition of slavery, yet no one called what might have been a bluff. Georgia, in particular, needed a strong central government. It is not certain that Georgia would have sacrificed the military protection of the U.S. government considering the nearby presence of both the Creek Indians and the Spanish. If Georgia, South Carolina, and other states more wedded to slaveholding carried out their threats and bolted from the union, the remaining delegates to the convention would have had to decide how committed they were to a single national government for all the states. To preserve the United States as it existed, the delegates might have agreed to soldier on under the weak government established by the Articles of Confederation. In light of the "critical period," there is no guarantee that government would have survived very long. Alternatively, the remaining delegates might have decided to forge ahead with the Constitution despite the absence of their southern colleagues. Under that scenario, a truly antislavery Constitution that abolished slavery peacefully could have been ratified. That imaginary Constitution would have governed a truncated nation, however, without Georgia and South Carolina at the very least. Those states might have formed a separate, independent country—a small, proslavery southern confederacy. Or they might have allied themselves with the Spanish, who still countenanced slaveholding. As it was, the founders made compromises with slavery. It took the Civil War and the deaths of some 700,000 Americans to abolish the South's peculiar institution.

CHRONOLOGY

1776	*July 4:* The United States declares its independence.
	July 12: John Dickinson heads the committee that drafts a new constitution for the United States, the Articles of Confederation.
1777	Congress adopts the Articles of Confederation; all states must ratify them before they go into effect.
1781	Maryland's ratification makes the Articles of Confederation the United States' first constitution.
mid-1780s	Calls emerge to strengthen the U.S. government.
1786–1787	Shays's Rebellion erupts in Massachusetts.
1787	*May 25:* The Constitutional Convention convenes.
	July 5: Delegates propose the Great Compromise, which includes the three-fifths proposal.
	July 12: Delegates adopt three-fifths compromise.
	Aug. 24: Delegates adopt the 1808 clause.
	Sept. 17: The Constitutional Convention ends.
	Dec. 7: Delaware becomes the first state to ratify the Constitution.
1788	*June 21:* New Hampshire becomes the ninth state to ratify the Constitution and put it into effect, but Virginia and New York have yet to ratify.
	June 25: Virginia ratifies the Constitution.
	July 26: New York ratifies the Constitution.

1789	George Washington is elected the first president of the United States.
1790	Rhode Island becomes the last of the original 13 states to ratify the Constitution.
1808	The United States ends the legal importation of slaves through the transatlantic slave trade.
1865	The Thirteenth Amendment to the Constitution abolishes slavery.

DISCUSSION QUESTIONS

1. Did the Constitutional Convention afford the founders a genuine opportunity to limit slavery? Why or why not?
2. How important were economic considerations in determining the fate of slavery at the Constitutional Convention?
3. How significant was a delegate's geographic location within the United States—his home state—as a predictor of his views on slavery-related issues?
4. Is it most accurate to describe the Constitution as endorsing slavery, preserving slavery, or undermining slavery? Why?
5. How well did the Constitution live up to Thomas Jefferson's assertion in the Declaration of Independence that all men are created equal?

WEB SITES

Gordon Lloyd. "Introduction to the Constitutional Convention," Ashbrook Center for Public Affairs. Available online. URL: http://www.teachingamericanhistory.org/convention/intro.html. Accessed February 15, 2009.

Library of Congress. "Documents from the Continental Congress and the Constitutional Convention, 1774–1789," American Memory. Available online. URL: http://memory.loc.gov/ammem/collections/continental/constit.html. Accessed February 15, 2009.

Library of Congress. "The Federalist Papers," American Memory. Available online. URL: http://thomas.loc.gov/home/histdox/fedpapers.html. Accessed February 15, 2009.

Library of Congress. "The Records of the Federal Convention of 1787," American Memory. Available online. URL: http://memory.loc.gov/ammem/amlaw/lwfr.html. Accessed August 18, 2010.

Yale Law School, Lillian Goldman Law Library. "Notes on the Debates in the Federal Convention," Avalon Project. Available online. URL: http://avalon.law.yale.edu/subject_menus/debcont.asp. Accessed February 15, 2009.

BIBLIOGRAPHY

Finkelman, Paul. *Slavery and the Founders: Race and Liberty in the Age of Jefferson.* Armonk, N.Y.: M. E. Sharpe, 1996. A collection of essays on the framers and slavery, from the leading scholar of slave law.

Goldwin, Robert A., and Art Kaufman, eds. *Slavery and Its Consequences: The Constitution, Equality, and Race.* Washington, D.C.: American Enterprise Institute for Public Policy Research, 1988. An edited collection that includes noteworthy essays from Don E. Fehrenbacher, William M. Wiecek, Herbert J. Storing, and W. B. Allen.

Kaminski, John P., ed. *A Necessary Evil? Slavery and the Debate over the Constitution.* Madison, Wis.: Madison House, 1995. A valuable collection of primary source documents on slavery in the early republic.

Lightner, David L. *Slavery and the Commerce Power: How the Struggle Against the Interstate Slave Trade Led to the Civil War.* New Haven, Conn.: Yale University Press, 2006. The second chapter examines the confusion over the slave trade and the Constitution's commerce clause.

Lynd, Staughton. *Class Conflict, Slavery, and the United States Constitution: Ten Essays.* Indianapolis: Bobbs-Merrill, 1967. Chapters 7 and 8 examine the founders' compromises with the institution of slavery.

Phillips, Wendell. *The Constitution a Pro-Slavery Compact: Selections from the Madison Papers, &c.* 1844. Reprint, New York: Negro Universities Press, 1969. A collection of primary source documents from the Constitutional Convention and the state ratification conventions, assembled by an abolitionist.

Waldstreicher, David. *Slavery's Constitution: From Revolution to Ratification.* New York: Hill and Wang, 2009. Examines the centrality of slavery to the U.S. Constitution.

Wiecek, William M. *The Sources of Antislavery Constitutionalism in America, 1760–1848*. Ithaca, N.Y.: Cornell University Press, 1977. Chapter 3 chronicles the ways slavery informed the making of the Constitution.

PRIMARY SOURCES

1. Excerpt from Debates at the Constitutional Convention, 1787

At the Constitutional Convention on June 30, 1787, Virginia's James Madison recorded where the fissures dividing the delegates lay.

He (Mr. Madison) . . . contended that the States were divided into different interests, not by their difference of size, but by other circumstances; the most material of which resulted partly from climate, but principally from the effects of their having or not having slaves. These two causes concurred in forming the great division of interests in the United States. It did not lie between the large and small States. IT LAY BETWEEN THE NORTHERN AND SOUTHERN.

Source: Wendell Phillips, *The Constitution a Pro-Slavery Compact: Selections from the Madison Papers, &c.* (1844; reprint, New York: Negro Universities Press, 1969), 14–15.

—⁓—

2. Excerpts from the U.S. Constitution, 1787

The following selections from the Constitution of 1787 are the passages with the most direct bearing on slavery.

Preamble: "We the People of the United States, in order to form a more perfect Union, establish Justice, . . . promote the general Welfare, and secure the Blessings of Liberty to ourselves and our Posterity, do ordain and establish this Constitution for the United States of America."

Article I, Section 2: "Representatives and direct Taxes shall be apportioned among the several States which may be included within this Union, according to their respective Numbers, which shall be determined by adding to the whole Number of free Persons, including those bound to Service for a Term of Years, and excluding Indians not taxed, three fifths of all other Persons."

Article I, Section 8: "Congress shall have Power . . . To regulate Commerce with foreign Nations, and among the several States, and with the Indian Tribes. . . ."

Article I, Section 8: "Congress shall have Power . . . To provide for calling forth the Militia to execute the Laws of the Union, suppress Insurrections and repel Invasions. . . ."

Article I, Section 9: "The Migration or Importation of such Persons as any of the States now existing shall think proper to admit, shall not be prohibited by the Congress prior to the Year one thousand eight hundred and eight, but a Tax or duty may be imposed on such Importation, not exceeding ten dollars for each Person."

Article I, Section 9: "No Capitation, or other direct, Tax shall be laid, unless in Proportion to the Census or Enumeration herein before directed to be taken."

Article I, Section 9: "No Tax or Duty shall be laid on Articles exported from any State."

Article I, Section 10: "No State shall, without the Consent of the Congress, lay any Imposts or Duties on Imports or Exports, except what may be absolutely necessary for executing its inspection Laws: and the net Produce of all Duties and Imposts, laid by any State on Imports or Exports, shall be for the Use of the Treasury of the United States; and all such Laws shall be subject to the Revision and Controul of the Congress."

Article II, Section 1: "Each State shall appoint, in such Manner as the Legislature thereof may direct, a Number of Electors, equal to the whole Number of Senators and Representatives to which the State may be entitled in the Congress."

Article IV, Section 2: "No Person held to Service or Labour in one State, under the Laws thereof, escaping into another, shall, in Consequence of any Law or Regulation therein, be discharged from such Service or Labour, but shall be delivered up on Claim of the Party to whom such Service or Labour may be due."

Article IV, Section 4: "The United States shall guarantee to every State in this Union a Republican Form of Government, and shall protect each of them against Invasion; and on Application of the Legislature, or of the Executive (when the Legislature cannot be convened) against domestic Violence."

Article V: "No Amendment which may be made prior to the Year One thousand eight hundred and eight shall in any Manner affect the first and fourth Clauses in the Ninth Section of the first Article. . . ."

—⟋⟍—

3. Excerpt from Debates at the Constitutional Convention, 1787

At the Constitutional Convention on August 21, 1787, Luther Martin of Maryland and John Rutledge of South Carolina debated Article I, Section 9, of the Constitution, dealing with the importation of slaves from the transatlantic trade.

Mr. L. Martin proposed . . . to allow a prohibition or tax on the importation of slaves. In the first place, as five slaves are to be counted as three freemen, in the apportionment of Representatives, such a clause would leave an encouragement to this traffic. In the second place, slaves weakened one part of the Union, which the other parts were bound to protect; the privilege of importing them was therefore unreasonable. And in the third place, it was inconsistent with the principles of the Revolution, and dishonorable to the American character, to have such a feature in the Constitution.

Mr. Rutledge did not see how the importation of slaves could be encouraged by this section. He was not apprehensive of insurrections, and would readily exempt the other States from the obligation to protect the Southern against them. Religion and humanity had nothing to do with this question. Interest alone is the governing principle with nations. The true question at present is, whether the Southern States shall or shall not be parties to the Union. If the Northern States consult their interest, they will not oppose the increase of slaves, which will increase the commodities of which they will become the carriers.

Source: Wendell Phillips, *The Constitution a Pro-Slavery Compact: Selections from the Madison Papers, &c.* (1844; reprint, New York: Negro Universities Press, 1969), 25.

—⟋⟍—

4. Federalist 42, 1788

Writing in 1788 under the name Publius, *in Federalist 42, James Madison defended the Constitution's provisions dealing with slave importations.*

JANUARY 22, 1788

To the People of the State of New York:

THE SECOND class of powers, lodged in the general government, . . . includ[es] a power to prohibit, after the year 1808, the importation of slaves, and to lay an intermediate duty of ten dollars per head, as a discouragement to such importations. . . .

It were doubtless to be wished, that the power of prohibiting the importation of slaves had not been postponed until the year 1808, or rather that it had been suffered to have immediate operation. But it is not difficult to account, either for this restriction on the general government, or for the manner in which the whole clause is expressed. It ought to be considered as a great point gained in favor of humanity, that a period of twenty years may terminate forever, within these States, a traffic which has so long and so loudly upbraided the barbarism of modern policy; that within that period, it will receive a considerable discouragement from the federal government, and may be totally abolished, by a concurrence of the few States which continue the unnatural traffic, in the prohibitory example which has been given by so great a majority of the Union. Happy would it be for the unfortunate Africans, if an equal prospect lay before them of being redeemed from the oppressions of their European brethren!

Attempts have been made to pervert this clause into an objection against the Constitution, by representing it on one side as a criminal toleration of an illicit practice, and on another as calculated to prevent voluntary and beneficial emigrations from Europe to America. I mention these misconstructions, not with a view to give them an answer, for they deserve none, but as specimens of the manner and spirit in which some have thought fit to conduct their opposition to the proposed government.—PUBLIUS.

Source: http://www.law.emory.edu/law-library/research/ready-reference/us-federal-law-and-documents/ historical-documents-the-federalist-papers/the-federalist-no-42.html.

—⁓—

5. Debate over Ratification in South Carolina, 1788

After delegates concluded work on the Constitution, each state legislature held a convention to debate the proposed new government. A native of Charleston, South Carolina, unreconciled to the Constitution, Rawlins Lowndes criticized the document in the South Carolina state House of Representatives on January 16, 1788.

In the first place, what cause was there for jealousy of our importing negroes? Why confine us to twenty years, or rather why limit us at all? For his part he thought this trade could be justified on the principles of religion, humanity and justice; for certainly to translate a set of human beings from a bad country to a better, was fulfilling every part of those principles. But they don't like our slaves, because they have none themselves, and therefore want to exclude us from this great advantage; why should the southern states allow this without the consent of nine States? . . . Without negroes this state would degenerate into one of the most contemptible in the union . . . whilst there remained one acre of swamp land in South Carolina, he should raise his voice against restricting the importation of negroes. Even in granting the importation for 20 years, care had been taken to make us pay for this indulgence, each negro being liable on importation to pay a duty not exceeding ten dollars, and in addition to this were liable to a capitation tax. Negroes were our wealth, our only natural resource, yet behold how our kind friends in the North were determined soon to tie up our hands, and drain us of what we had.

Source: John P. Kaminski, ed., *A Necessary Evil? Slavery and the Debate over the Constitution* (Madison, Wis.: Madison House, 1995), 167–168.

—ᴡᴡ—

6. Federalist 54, 1788

Authored by either James Madison or Alexander Hamilton in 1788, Federalist 54 defended the Constitution's three-fifths clause.

FEBRUARY 12, 1788

To the People of the State of New York:

Does it follow, from an admission of numbers for the measure of representation, or of slaves combined with free citizens as a ratio of taxation, that slaves ought to be included in the numerical rule of representation? Slaves are considered as property, not as persons. They ought therefore to be comprehended in estimates of taxation which are founded on property, and to be excluded from representation which is regulated by a census of persons. This is the objection, as I understand it, stated in its full force. I shall be equally candid in stating the reasoning which may be offered on the opposite side.

"We subscribe to the doctrine," might one of our Southern brethren observe, "that representation relates more immediately to persons, and taxation more immediately to property, and we join in the application of this distinction to the case of our slaves. But we must deny the fact, that slaves are considered merely as property, and in no respect whatever as persons." The true state of the case is, that they partake of both these qualities: being considered by our laws, in some respects, as persons, and in other respects as property. In being compelled to labor, not for himself, but for a master; in being vendible by one master to another master; and in being subject at all times to be restrained in his liberty and chastised in his body, by the capricious will of his owner, the slave may appear to be degraded from the human rank, and classed with those irrational animals which fall under the legal denomination of property. In being protected, on the other hand, in his life and in his limbs, against the violence of all others, even the master of his labor and his liberty; and in being punishable himself for all violence committed against others; the slave is no less evidently regarded by the law as a member of the society, not as a part of the irrational creation; as a moral person, not as a mere article of property. The federal Constitution, therefore, decides with great propriety on the case of our slaves, when it views them in the mixed character of persons and of property. This is in fact their true character. It is the character bestowed on them by the laws under which they live; and it will not be denied, that these are the proper criterion; because it is only under the pretext that the laws have transformed the negroes into subjects of property, that a place is disputed them in the computation of numbers; and it is admitted, that if the laws were to restore the rights which have been taken away, the negroes could no longer be refused an equal share of representation with the other inhabitants.

This question may be placed in another light. It is agreed on all sides, that numbers are the best scale of wealth and taxation, as they are the only proper scale of representation. Would the convention have been impartial or consistent, if they had rejected the slaves from the list of inhabitants, when the shares of representation were to be calculated, and inserted them on the lists when the tariff of contributions was to be adjusted? Could it be reasonably expected, that the Southern States would concur in a system, which considered their slaves in some degree as men, when burdens were to be imposed, but refused to consider them in the same light, when advantages were to be conferred? Might not some surprise also be expressed, that those who reproach the Southern States with the barbarous policy of considering as property a part of their human brethren, should themselves contend, that the government to which all the States are to be parties, ought to consider this unfortunate race more completely in the unnatural light of property, than the very laws of which they complain?

It may be replied, perhaps, that slaves are not included in the estimate of representatives in any of the States possessing them. They neither vote themselves nor increase the votes of their masters. Upon what principle, then, ought they to be taken into the federal estimate of representation? In rejecting them altogether, the Constitution would, in this respect, have followed the very laws which have been appealed to as the proper guide.

This objection is repelled by a single observation. It is a fundamental principle of the proposed Constitution, that as the aggregate number of representatives allotted to the several States is to be determined by a federal rule, founded on the aggregate number of inhabitants, so the right of choosing this allotted number in each State is to be exercised by such part of the inhabitants as the State itself may designate. The qualifications on which the right of suffrage depend are not, perhaps, the same in any two States. In some of the States the difference is very material. In every State, a certain proportion of inhabitants are deprived of this right by the constitution of the State, who will be included in the census by which the federal Constitution apportions the representatives. In this point of view the Southern States might retort the complaint, by insisting that the principle laid down by the convention required that no regard should be had to the policy of particular States towards their own inhabitants; and consequently, that the slaves, as inhabitants, should have been admitted into the census according to their full number, in like manner with other inhabitants, who, by the policy of other States, are not admitted to all the rights of citizens. A rigorous adherence, however, to this principle, is waived by those who would be gainers by it. All that they ask is that equal moderation be shown on the other side. Let the case of the slaves be considered, as it is in truth, a peculiar one. Let the compromising expedient of the Constitution be mutually adopted, which regards them as inhabitants, but as debased by servitude below the equal level of free inhabitants, which regards the SLAVE as divested of two fifths of the MAN. . . . Although it may appear to be a little strained in some points, yet, on the whole, I must confess that it fully reconciles me to the scale of representation which the convention have established.—PUBLIUS.

Source: http://www.law.emory.edu/law-library/research/ready-reference/us-federal-law-and-documents/ historical-documents-the-federalist-papers/the-federalist-no-54.html.

THE TRANSATLANTIC SLAVE TRADE:
Should Congress Impose a Tax on Slaves Imported into the United States?

—⁂—

THE CONTROVERSY

The Issue

In the U.S. Constitution, the founders established no definitive date for the termination of U.S. participation in the transatlantic slave trade. In the first years of the 19th century, Congress debated a proposal to impose a tax on slaves imported into the United States. Should such a tax be imposed?

- ◆ *Arguments in favor of taxing slave imports:* In the first decade of the 1800s, congressional proponents of levying a $10 tax on each slave imported into the United States argued that it was a constitutionally permissible measure that did not legitimize the slave trade itself. The proposed tax would be applied equally to all the states and have the effect of discouraging the traffic in human cargoes. Although the tax would generate revenue for the U.S. Treasury, it would more importantly demonstrate American opposition to the transatlantic slave trade. In deterring traders from introducing new Africans into the United States, the $10 duty would also contribute to the prevention of slave revolts.

- ◆ *Arguments against taxing slave imports:* Those opposed to the $10 tax on slave imports maintained that the imposition of a tax lent governmental sanction to the slave trade. Such a small duty would have no effect in suppressing the traffic. To the contrary, taxing the trade would only burden the U.S. government with the obligation to protect slaving vessels. Furthermore, since South Carolina was the only state that lawfully permitted the slave trade, the importation tax would unfairly target that one state and serve to censure it. Foes of the slave importation tax recommended that South Carolina be given time to correct its own law or that Congress wait until it could constitutionally end the slave trade completely in 1808.

—⁂—

INTRODUCTION

Drafted in 1787, the new U.S. Constitution guaranteed American slaveholders the right to import slaves from abroad through at least 1808. At the end of the American Revolution, however, the transatlantic slave trade to the United States was under assault. Many state legislatures had prohibited the importation of foreign slaves, and, by 1798, all states had banned the traffic. Then, in 1803, South Carolina reversed course and opted to reinstate the African slave trade. The state's decision met widespread condemnation. Within weeks, in 1804, the U.S. House of Representatives began discussing a possible tax on slave imports, the only constitutional means then available to Congress to express its disapprobation of the trade. The resulting debate was less about political party than section, marking a turning point in the relationship between South and North. The alliance between the Deep South and the New England states evident during the Constitutional Convention of 1787 had dissolved. The controversy exposed sectional hostility and portended the division between North and South that dominated antebellum politics and culminated in the Civil War.

Proponents of the tax on slave imports noted its constitutionality and denied that it sanctioned the transatlantic slave trade. The tax would be imposed fairly on all of the states as a means of diminishing the number of slaves entering the country. As it generated income for the U.S. government, the proposed tax would also signal to the world Congress's disapproval of the slave trade. As an additional benefit of the tax, potentially dangerous African slaves would be kept out of the country, lessening the chance of slave rebellion.

Noting the failure of existing laws to quell the transatlantic slave trade, opponents of the tax on slave imports argued that imposing a duty validated the trade and offered no legitimate discouragement to it. If taxed by Congress, slavers would request protection from the U.S. government and negate any possible financial benefit of the tax. The tax would serve only to censure and anger South Carolinians. The South Carolina legislature merely needed time to repair its error. Failing that, Congress would probably close the transatlantic slave trade in 1808 anyway, so the House of Representatives need not bother pursuing the tax on slave imports.

BACKGROUND

The first Africans to the British North American mainland arrived in Virginia's Jamestown colony in 1619, but it was not until the end of the 17th century that African slaves composed the major source of labor in Virginia's tobacco fields. African laborers arrived in Virginia and other English colonies via a transatlantic slave trade that had its origins in the early 1500s. Soon after the European encounter with the Americas, the Spanish and Portuguese turned to Africa as a valuable source of labor for the sugar cane fields and mines of the Western Hemisphere. Captives endured the horrors of the Middle Passage as they crossed the Atlantic to begin work for their new masters. African slavery was thus an established institution in the Americas by the time England settled its colony at Jamestown in 1607. Altogether, in its more than 300 years in existence, the transatlantic slave trade carried almost 11 million African slaves to the Americas, most to the Caribbean and Brazil. Less than 4 percent of all captive Africans landed in the colonies that would later become the United States.

British vessels laden with cargoes of African slaves docked in American port cities such as Charleston, South Carolina, throughout much of the colonial period. During the American Revolution, however, the colonies banned the slave trade as part of a broader economic boycott against Great Britain. Once independence was declared in 1776, most of the new state governments imposed some ban on slave importation. The transatlantic slave trade fell under scrutiny at the Constitutional Convention of 1787 as well. Confronting a shortage of slave labor, largely the product of Revolutionary-era runaways, the Deep South states of South Carolina and Georgia were adamant that the trade remain open. Their alliance with the New England states—suppliers of the ships, captains, and crews that conducted the trade and transported the products of slave labor—forced an accommodation to slavery. Article I, Section 9, of the Constitution forbade Congress to tamper with the transatlantic slave trade prior to 1808, or 20 years from the ratification of the document. At that time, Congress would have the option to end American participation in the African slave trade, but its termination was not guaranteed. The constitutional ban on congressional interference in the slave trade for at least two decades provided the Deep South states a generous window in which to recoup wartime losses of slave labor by importing new slaves from abroad. Moreover, as it was widely assumed at the time that the southern states would grow more rapidly than the northern, South Carolina and Georgia may have anticipated having enough legislative clout by 1808 to keep the slave trade open.

The constitutional protections granted to the transatlantic slave trade sparked a controversy that erupted during the First Congress of the United States. On February 11, 1790, Representative Thomas Fitzsimons of Pennsylvania presented to the U.S. House of Representatives an address from the Yearly Meeting of Quakers in Pennsylvania, New Jersey, Delaware, and western Maryland and Virginia, held the previous autumn. Active in its opposition to slavery since before the American Revolution, the Society of Friends urged Congress to give "serious christian attention, to . . . the gross national iniquity of trafficking in the persons of fellow-men." Out of a sense of religious duty, the Quakers requested "the abolition of the slave trade." Theirs was just one of several petitions to Congress in the 1790s against the traffic in slaves.[1]

Reaction to the Quaker memorial divided largely along sectional lines. Representatives from northern states upheld the Quakers' right, as citizens, to petition their government, but many southern representatives, including James Jackson of Georgia, Michael J. Stone of Maryland, and Aedanus Burke, William L. Smith, and Thomas T. Tucker, all of South Carolina, opposed committing the Quaker petition. They charged that, since the Constitution prohibited the abolition of the slave trade until 1808 at the earliest, the Quaker request for congressional intervention was unconstitutional. Southern states would never have ratified the Constitution if they had anticipated any threat to the security of masters' property rights in their slaves, they claimed, and since they entered the Union with their slaves, any effort to curtail the slave trade would amount to an ex post facto law, forbidden by the Constitution. Since the Quakers had no direct interest in slaveholding, southern representatives explained, they were clearly meddling, attempting to impose their morality on others. Indignant southern congressmen cautioned that committing the Quaker memorial "will create jealousies and alarm in the Southern States," "blow the trumpet of sedition," and "light up the flame of civil discord."[2]

---

[1] *Annals of Congress of the United States,* 1st Cong., 2d sess. (Washington, D.C.: Gales & Seaton, 1834), 1224, 1225.
[2] *Annals of Congress,* 1st Cong., 2d sess., 1244, 1241, 1242.

In the midst of the uproar over the Quaker petition, Representative Josiah Parker of Virginia, sympathetic to the Quakers' cause, introduced a proposal to levy a tax on slave imports as a means of decreasing the African slave trade. Immediately after barring congressional interference in the African slave trade until 1808, Article I, Section 9, of the Constitution allowed that "a Tax or duty may be imposed on such Importation, not exceeding ten dollars for each Person." Obviously constitutional, Parker's proposal appealed to many of his colleagues in the House seeking a lawful way to discourage the slave trade. Since constitutional limitations upon Congress prevented the complete termination of the slave trade, taxing the traffic seemed the next best alternative. Nothing resulted from Parker's proposal during the First Congress, but it did anticipate a more extensive debate some 14 years later on taxing the African slave trade.

Although for the time being constitutionally powerless to abolish the trade, Congress still pursued legislation designed to regulate it and curtail American involvement in it. With petitions continuing to pour into the House and Senate from Quakers and various abolitionist societies, Congress enacted important pieces of slave-trade legislation in 1794 and 1800. The 1794 law made it illegal for any vessel sailing from a U.S. port to engage in the slave trade, while the act of 1800 forbade citizens or residents of the United States to hold a stake in or serve aboard any ship that conveyed slaves from one foreign port to another. Through these measures, Congress undermined the transatlantic slave trade without violating the Constitution. The trade might legally continue, but Americans' lawful role in it would be dramatically reduced.

At the beginning of the 19th century, then, the United States seemed on the verge of extracting itself entirely from the transatlantic slave trade. In addition to the congressional acts of 1794 and 1800, in 1798, Georgia became the last of the original 13 states to prohibit the African slave trade. No states were now actively, legally importing slaves. And soon, Congress would be constitutionally empowered to prohibit the African slave trade, as most contemporaries assumed it would.

In this context, South Carolina's decision to reopen the slave trade in 1803 appeared a stunning reversal. The Palmetto State had closed the trade in 1787, but the ban lapsed in 1790. The next year, however, a slave revolt erupted in the French Caribbean colony of Saint-Domingue, launching the Haitian Revolution. Fears of slave insurrections in a state with a majority black population prompted South Carolina lawmakers to rethink the wisdom of slave importation, and in 1792 they unanimously passed a measure that temporarily outlawed the trade once again. This ban commenced in 1793 and, through a series of renewals, remained in effect until 1803.

South Carolinians did not remain united behind the ban, however. Sectional division was evident within the state. In the slave-rich coastal region known as the South Carolina Lowcountry, whites feared African influences in spawning slave unrest and threatening whites' safety. The recent example of Saint-Domingue as well as the bloody Stono Rebellion of 1739, in which native Africans rose up to attack South Carolina whites, illustrated the dangers posed by African slaves. In the South Carolina interior, by contrast, where fewer slaves lived and demand for slave labor was high, backcountry planters chafed under the restriction against importation. They no longer wanted to be held economic hostage to the higher prices Lowcountry slaveholders could command for their surplus chattel if alternate sources of slave labor remained closed. Consequently, Lowcountry legislators were substantially more enthusiastic than their backcountry counterparts in maintaining the ban on the slave trade. A malapportioned legislature weighted in favor of the Lowcountry kept the prohibition in place.

In 1803, however, the United States' acquisition of the Louisiana Purchase from France altered the dynamic within the South Carolina assembly. The addition of the Louisiana Territory opened a prospective new market for slaves. Slaveholders across South Carolina hoped to realize almost unimaginable profits by securing a virtual monopoly on the slave trade to Louisiana. Large-scale importation would be required for South Carolina planters to acquire slaves for subsequent export and sale. Setting concerns over safety aside, half of the Lowcountry legislators joined their colleagues from the backcountry to reinstate the transatlantic slave trade in December 1803. Within a mere five hours, two British ships laden with enslaved cargoes glided into Charleston harbor.

South Carolina's repeal of its prohibition on the African slave trade sparked outrage in Congress. For the first time in five years, since Georgia's termination of the trade in 1798, a state could legally import slaves from abroad. Constitutionally, Congress could not express its disapproval by outlawing the trade, but it could revisit the idea of taxing slave imports, introduced by Josiah Parker in 1790. No one disputed Congress's constitutional authority to levy a tax up to $10 on slave imports; Congress had never imposed such a tax because the individual states had

Roughly 11 million captive Africans crossed the Atlantic Ocean in the dreaded Middle Passage. They endured unspeakable horrors aboard the slave ships. Below deck, the heat and stench were unbearable. (The Art Archive)

ended their legal participation in the slave trade themselves. (Ironically, three times in the colonial period—1717, 1740, and 1764—the South Carolina assembly had imposed special duties on the slave trade to discourage imports and check the rapid growth of the African population in the colony.) Moved to act by South Carolina's reopening of the slave trade, in January 1804, Republican David Bard of Pennsylvania proposed a resolution in the House of Representatives that would impose a $10 tax on slave imports. For almost two years, the House debated the question, Should Congress levy a tax on slaves imported into the United States?

THE DEBATE

The Argument that Congress Should Impose a Tax on Imported Slaves

Proponents of the $10 tax on slave imports conceded that South Carolina operated within its lawful rights when it reopened the African slave trade in 1803. Likewise, they understood that Congress could not legally intervene to end importation altogether until 1808. But that did not mean Congress was completely powerless to act. The constitutional provision for a $10 slave importation tax held forth a number of benefits that members of the House of Representatives identified in the Eighth and Ninth Congresses. The tax not only was constitutional and fair but also promised to discourage the transatlantic slave trade, increase revenue for the U.S. Treasury, testify to the national character of the United States, and contribute to the safety of American citizens from possible slave revolts. In the House, Pennsylvania Republicans David Bard, William Findley, John Baptiste Charles Lucas, and John Smilie led the fight in favor of the tax, along with Republican Samuel Latham Mitchill of New York and Federalist James Madison Broom of Delaware. Supporters of the tax hailed from both major political parties of the time but only from states with little or no commitment to slavery.

Slave imports seemed a fitting subject for taxation to many in the House. Other imported goods were taxed; why should slaves be excepted? "As a profitable article of commerce," remarked Representative Findley, slavery "appeared as eligible a subject of taxation as could be found, and as justly liable to taxation as any other." Representatives Lucas and Republican Ebenezer Elmer of New Jersey thought slave imports especially worthy of taxation because "the trade is odious" and "injurious . . . to society." Lucas noted as well that the trade "affords a great profit to those who carry it on," and since "no article imported into the United States gives a greater profit, so no article can better bear a tax." Furthermore, Lucas, Findley, and Bard each stressed that the proposed tax on slave imports was a measly $10, just 2.5 percent of the value of a typical $400 slave. Customary duties on imported goods, Findley reported, averaged around 20 percent. In relative terms, then, the tax on slave imports would hardly be oppressive.[3]

Representatives Bard, Mitchill, Lucas, and Broom all emphasized the constitutionality of the proposed $10 tax on slave imports. Article I, Section 9, of the Constitution clearly authorized the duty. Consequently, Mitchill announced in 1804, "There could be no doubt of the power of Congress to declare and levy such an impost on imported slaves for four years to come." Lucas denied that implementing the tax implied that the U.S. government either legalized or validated the transatlantic slave trade in any way. The trade, he argued, was currently lawful only through a statute of South Carolina, not by any congressional measure.

---

[3] *Annals of Congress*, 8th Cong., 1st sess., 999, 1008, 1034, 1008–1009.

The $10 tax marked the only legal way (for the time being, at least) for Congress to assert its disapprobation of the trade. (See "Speech of Representative John Baptiste Charles Lucas, 1804," on page 105 in the Primary Sources section.) The founders had inserted a clause into the Constitution that allowed for the $10 tax, Representative Broom observed, so presumably they believed it could go into effect. Thus, if South Carolina's citizens so strenuously objected to the tax, the state ought not to have ratified the Constitution: "Why did South Carolina submit to the Constitution, and thereby pledge herself to pay this tax, if she is now unwilling to submit to it?" Broom asked. The attitude of South Carolina's congressional delegation struck the representative from Delaware as singularly and unreasonably defiant.[4]

Merely taxing slave imports did not require the U.S. government to protect the transatlantic slave trade, a prospect that struck many members of the House as morally repugnant and economically objectionable. The U.S. Navy was under no obligation to guard slaving vessels, however, because other laws already in effect applied. Representatives Mitchill and Broom reminded their colleagues in the House that Congress had passed legislation in 1794 and 1800 prohibiting American ships or American citizens from participating directly in the slave trade. It would be absurd to suggest that the navy protect foreign vessels engaged in trafficking slaves. The Constitution authorized the taxation of slave imports, but taxation entailed no further commitment of the U.S. government. (See "Speech of Representative James Madison Broom, 1806," on page 106 in the Primary Sources section.)

The proposed tax on slave imports was not only constitutional but also perfectly fair. Congressmen from South Carolina protested that the tax targeted their state alone, but Representative Bard observed that the tax would apply uniformly throughout the country. Any state that imported slaves would be equally subject to its provisions. (See "Speech of Representative David Bard, 1804," on page 106 in the Primary Sources section.) Thus, the $10 tax on slave imports neither insulted, dishonored, nor disgraced the state of South Carolina. "It does not follow," argued Representative Findley, "that, because we lay a particular tax, we censure those who pay it." It was "principle" rather than a desire to punish South Carolina that motivated the proposed tax, asserted New Jersey representative

---

[4] *Annals of Congress,* 8th Cong., 1st sess., 1001; *Annals of Congress of the United States,* 9th Cong., 1st sess., 367.

Henry Southard, although, he added, if "the people of South Carolina feel the weight of it[,] it is right they should." Representative Lucas and many other members of the House noted that if South Carolina resented the tax, the state legislature need only repeal its law legalizing slave importation to escape it.[5] (See "Speech of Representative John Baptiste Charles Lucas, 1804," on page 107 in the Primary Sources section.)

Several representatives hoped that the proposed tax on slave imports would discourage the African slave trade. Most, however, believed that a meager $10 tax would at best retard the traffic only slightly. Nevertheless, the ability to tax slave imports was the only power Congress presently wielded over the trade. Representative Findley did not stand alone when he encouraged the House to take advantage of the means at Congress's disposal to "discountenanc[e] the importation of slaves." Any impediment to the transatlantic slave trade was desirable. Although optimistic that the tax could significantly reduce the importation of slaves, Representative Southard maintained that even if the proposed tax prevented only "a single one of these miserable creatures from being torn from the bosom of their family and country, in violation of the ties of nature and the principles of justice," Congress would have spent its time wisely in imposing it. Representative Mitchill and other members of the House were entirely comfortable using taxation to punish those who purchased African slaves from abroad.[6] (See the sidebar "Forfeiture" on page 88.)

Whereas the proposed tax lightly penalized masters who imported slaves, another group of whites—poor whites—stood to benefit from the duty. Two representatives, Lucas and Broom, argued that continued slave importations were detrimental to lower-class whites "who draw their subsistence from labor." According to Lucas, the increase in African slaves devalued the labor of whites and made it difficult for them to find gainful employment. "The rich part of the community," Lucas explained, preferred using slaves, whom they could more readily coerce and control, to hiring free white laborers. Poor whites would therefore suffer when confronted with increased competition for work from imported slaves.[7] To Representative Broom, moreover, it made little sense for Congress to

---

[5] *Annals of Congress,* 8th Cong., 1st sess., 999; *Annals of Congress,* 9th Cong., 1st sess., 349.

[6] *Annals of Congress,* 8th Cong., 1st sess., 999; *Annals of Congress,* 9th Cong., 1st sess., 349.

[7] *Annals of Congress,* 8th Cong., 1st sess., 1009.

impose duties on necessities that common people used on a daily basis, such as salt or sugar, but refuse to tax slaves, an item of luxury purchased only by the wealthy. Justice demanded that the segment of society with the greatest ability to pay should not escape taxation on a commodity that they alone could afford. If Congress approved a tax on slave imports, taxes on goods consumed by the masses could be eliminated. (See "Speech of Representative James Madison Broom, 1806," on page 108 in the Primary Sources section.)

Proponents of the $10 tax anticipated welcome revenue from it. Although the duty itself would be small, when multiplied by each slave taken into the country, tax monies would flow into the public coffers by the thousands. The precise amount was the subject of speculation. Representative Mitchill estimated that some 20,000 slaves would enter South Carolina annually. Assuming that Congress imposed the maximal tax permitted by the Constitution, the slave trade would produce yearly revenue of $200,000 for the next four years. If Mitchill's arithmetic came to pass, the country stood to make a total of $800,000 from the African slave trade prior to 1808. Rhode Island representative Joseph Stanton IV advanced more aggressive calculations. He reckoned that South Carolina would import 100,000 slaves per year until 1808, yielding an impressive $4 million for the U.S. Treasury. Regardless of which congressman proved the more astute accountant, profits from the tax on slave imports could be put to use in any number of valuable ways. Mitchill and Stanton, for example, both recommended paying the claims of Revolutionary War veterans in compensation for their service to the country. Mitchill also suggested constructing roads, completing the erection of public buildings in Washington, D.C., and exploring lands in the recently acquired Louisiana Purchase as other programs worthy of financial support. Thus, Mitchill proclaimed, "By laying the tax, he would imitate the ways of Divine Providence, and endeavor to extract good out of evil." For members of Congress morally squeamish about benefiting from the transatlantic slave trade, Representative Findley suggested that the funds produced from the $10 tax be applied to "special objects—to ameliorate the state of slavery."[8]

Less important than the revenue it generated, however, the $10 tax would send a message that Congress disapproved of the transatlantic

(continues on page 90)

---

[8] *Annals of Congress*, 8th Cong., 1st sess., 1002, 999.

FORFEITURE

If a slave ship was intercepted while attempting to smuggle its human cargo into the United States, what should happen to those captive Africans onboard? What should be done with slaves imported illegally into the country? In December 1806, as Congress debated the bill that would eventually outlaw American participation in the Atlantic slave trade, these questions proved divisive.

In extant records from the House, southern representatives as a rule favored confiscation and forfeiture to the United States, whereby the African captives would be transferred or surrendered to the U.S. government and sold as slaves. Other members of Congress rejected forfeiture and suggested their own solutions to the problem of captured slaves. Quaker and New Jersey Republican representative James Sloan and Barnabas Bidwell, a Republican representative from Massachusetts, abhorred the thought of the U.S. government's turning slave trader and profiting from their sale. They instead recommended that any forfeited slaves be emancipated in the United States. Southern representatives were horrified. Since the overwhelming majority of illegal slave imports would be apprehended in the South, manumitted Africans allegedly ill suited for freedom would overrun the region. "What is to become of the cargoes of those persons, when thus turned loose in any State?" asked pro-forfeiture Speaker of the House Nathaniel Macon of North Carolina. "By what means are they, understanding nothing about the country, to be supported? Not even speaking the language of the country, what is to become of them?" Macon not only questioned liberated Africans' ability to survive in a strange land, but also expressed alarm at their presence among southern whites. He believed them a danger to white safety, fearing that "these creatures" would "cut our throats." Representative Peter Early of Georgia echoed Macon's concerns, describing free blacks as "instruments of murder, theft, and conflagration." With the prospect of black rebellion and the slaughter of whites before them, Early warned, no southern whites would inform federal agents of slave smuggling operations because they would not want free Africans living among them. As Early explained, "the principle of self-preservation, and . . . the love of family" militated against it. Macon and Early also found an ally in the executive mansion. President Thomas Jefferson had long expressed his hostility to the presence of free blacks within the United States. His animosity ran deep enough for him to ponder schemes of black colonization outside the country.*

Pennsylvania representative John Smilie, opposed to forfeiture and U.S. government sales of African captives, proffered the idea of returning them to Africa. Deporting them would prove costly, however, and as Speaker Macon observed, it would be virtually impossible to restore many of them to their actual homes, especially if they originated in the interior of Africa. Macon went further, prophesying that if the United States sent the smuggled slaves back to Africa, they would only be reseized, reenslaved, and shipped somewhere else.

Representative Timothy Pitkin, a Federalist from Connecticut, proposed a system of indentured servitude for captured slaves in which they would labor for someone else for perhaps seven to 10 years, until they acquired the skills to support themselves. At that time, they would gain their freedom. House colleagues William Findley of Pennsylvania and Josiah Quincy of Massachusetts expressed support for Pitkin's apprenticeship idea. "These Africans," Quincy declared, "are helpless, ignorant of our laws, and of our language and manners," and "incompetent as . . . children." Binding them out until they were able to take care of themselves seemed to him the only humanitarian option.†

In the final act of 1807 that would end U.S. involvement in the transatlantic slave trade, federal agents who apprehended smuggled slaves were to turn the Africans over to the state in which they were captured to be treated in accordance with the laws of that state. Thus, slaves illegally introduced to the South and apprehended there would, despite the overall intent of the 1807 law, be sold and remain in bondage. If it took place in the South, then, their discovery could hardly be described as a rescue. Legislation in 1819 later mandated slaves' return to Africa; however, regardless of the location of their original home on the continent, captured bond people would be funneled to Liberia, the American colony for emancipated slaves.

---

* *Annals of Congress*, 9th Cong., 2d sess., 173, 225, 174.
† *Annals of Congress*, 9th Cong., 2d sess., 183, 224.

(continued from page 87)
slave trade. Some members of Congress did indeed consider slavery an immoral institution, but they conscientiously steered away from the contentious issue of slavery as a moral question and instead framed the debate over the proposed tax in terms of national character. The presence of slavery in a country that cherished liberty and freedom impugned the nation's reputation. "The Americans boast of being the most enlightened people in the world. . . . They have denounced tyranny and oppression," Representative Bard observed. "But will foreigners concede this high character to us, when they examine our census and find that we hold a million of men in the most degraded slavery?" Imposing the $10 duty on imported slaves would demonstrate the U.S. government's opposition to slavery and cultivate the United States' image before a global audience. "We owe it indispensably to ourselves and to the world, whose eyes are on our Government," Bard insisted, "to maintain its republican character." Representatives Smilie and Southard agreed that the proposed tax's expression of noble principle vastly outweighed in importance any revenue it might produce.[9]

Bard, Smilie, and Broom also raised the specter of slave revolt during their speeches supporting the $10 importation tax. To them, each slave taken into the country represented "an imported enemy." According to Bard, "the importation of slaves is hostile to the United States: to import slaves is to import enemies into our country; it is to import men who must be our natural enemies, if such there can be. Their circumstances, their barbarism, their reflections, their hopes and fears, render them an enemy of the worst description." Bard invoked the deadly slave uprising in Saint-Domingue to illustrate the danger to public safety that slaves posed. Slave revolts similarly threatened the domestic tranquility of the United States. The importation of slaves into South Carolina therefore concerned "the whole Union," Representative Broom noted, and all states had a vested interest in suppressing it.[10] (See the sidebar "The Death Penalty and the Transatlantic Slave Trade" on page 100.)

---

[9] *Annals of Congress,* 8th Cong., 1st sess., 996, 994–995.
[10] *Annals of Congress,* 8th Cong., 1st sess., 1015, 995; *Annals of Congress,* 9th Cong., 1st sess., 371.

The Argument that Congress Should Not Impose a Tax on Imported Slaves

Although widely criticized in the North and in the states of the Upper South, South Carolina's decision to reopen the transatlantic slave trade did not provoke a unanimous desire among House members to impose a $10 tax on slave imports. Regardless of party affiliation, South Carolina's representatives in Congress, especially Benjamin Huger, Thomas Lowndes, and Thomas Moore, lobbied against the tax. But they were not alone. House members from other southern states, such as Nathaniel Macon of North Carolina and Peter Early of Georgia, as well as a few northern representatives, joined their South Carolina colleagues in denouncing the tax. Together they argued that South Carolina's law forbidding the African slave trade had failed miserably. Smugglers had disregarded the law and taken slaves into the state in spite of it. Taxing the slave trade would only recognize and sanction it. Although it might produce some desirable revenues, the trivial $10 tax would not discourage masters from acquiring slaves from overseas. Ironically, taxing slave imports could cost the U.S. government money because the navy would be required to protect slave-trading vessels. In addition, it would be inappropriate for the government to discipline or penalize an individual state for exercising a power it retained in the Constitution. Doing so would only stigmatize South Carolina and generate resentment. Imposing the tax might even encourage unrest among the slaves. The tax's opponents urged patience. Rather than antagonize, pressure, or coerce South Carolina, actions that could easily backfire, they recommended either giving the South Carolina state legislature time to correct its course or waiting for Congress to terminate the trade in 1808, as allowed by the Constitution.

Lowndes and Huger both criticized the transatlantic slave trade but nevertheless defended the right of South Carolina—the state they represented—to reopen it. As they explained, South Carolina had been profoundly unsuccessful in enforcing the state's prohibition against the slave trade. Smuggling proved impossible to prevent. "The law was completely evaded," Lowndes confessed, "and, for the last year or two, Africans were introduced into the country in numbers little short, I believe, of what they would have been had the trade been a legal one." Since the state legislature had passed a law that was widely disregarded anyway, Lowndes thought it fit to "remove from the eyes of the people the spectacle of its authority being daily violated."[11] Huger echoed the sentiments of his South Carolina colleague. Since the statute was ineffective, repeal spared the legislature the mockery that illicit traders made of its laws. (See "Speech of Representative Benjamin Huger, 1804," on page 108 in the Primary Sources section.)

Several members of the House expressed concerns that taxing slave imports legitimated the transatlantic trade. Thomas Moore of South Carolina, Peter Early of Georgia, and Andrew Gregg of Pennsylvania, all Republicans, believed it improper for the U.S. government to derive revenue from the sordid traffic in human beings. It would be not only inconsistent with the American character, they said, but hypocritical for Congress to tax an activity it despised. "I am astonished to hear gentlemen, who advocate the resolution now under consideration, reprobate a traffic as horrid and infamous, and yet wish to draw a revenue from infamy," Moore declared, adding, "if it is an infamy." He characterized profits acquired through the African slave trade as shameful, ill-gotten gains. "I flatter myself," Moore continued, "this House will never legalize an act by which our national coffers will be stained with the price of liberty." Representative George M. Bedinger of Kentucky agreed. Although he thought "the slave trade . . . little better than murder," he nevertheless "felt a difficulty in his mind as to the propriety of admitting one shilling of it into the Treasury of the United States."[12]

Opponents differed in their understanding of the economic impact of the proposed tax. Representative Lowndes of South Carolina argued that if the government passed the $10 tax on slave imports, it would not want to surrender the income it generated, even after Congress gained the constitutional authority to prohibit it. The African slave trade would thus become more difficult to end. (See "Speech of Representative Thomas Lowndes, 1804," on page 109 in the Primary Sources section.) But whereas Lowndes predicted that taxing slave imports would produce welcome revenue, many more members of Congress noted that the money raised would be negligible and not worth the irritation it would cause to South Carolina.

Opponents of the tax could agree, however, that the constitutionally permitted tax of $10 was too minuscule to deter the purchase of

---

[11] *Annals of Congress*, 8th Cong., 1st sess., 992.
[12] *Annals of Congress*, 8th Cong., 1st sess., 1003, 1004, 1027.

newly arrived slaves. Representative Gregg explained that the $10 duty might have been effective in retarding the trade had it been passed soon after the Constitution was ratified, but the invention of the cotton gin in the 1790s heightened the demand for slaves and pushed their prices out of all proportion to the meager $10 tax. (See "Speech of Representative Andrew Gregg, 1804," on page 110 in the Primary Sources section.) Gregg, Lowndes, and many others in the House doubted that such a slight tax would place any check whatsoever on the transatlantic slave trade. As Lowndes proclaimed, "I am convinced that the tax of ten dollars will not prevent the introduction into the country of a single slave."[13] .

Some foes of the measure believed that the tax on slave imports would obligate the U.S. government to protect the African slave trade. "Sanction the trade by imposing the tax," cautioned Representative Gregg, "and soon the traders will demand your protection."[14] Gregg, Early, and North Carolina representative James Holland all expounded on this theme, but none more than Republican Speaker of the House Nathaniel Macon of North Carolina. The U.S. Navy protected American shipping, he explained, so if the tax on slave imports passed, thereby condoning the slave trade, slave ships would be rightfully entitled to U.S. government protection. The cost of protection, in turn, would negate any economic benefit of the tax. (See "Speech of Representative Nathaniel Macon, 1804," on page 110 in the Primary Sources section.)

Several southern representatives charged that the proposed tax treated South Carolina unfairly. Representatives Huger, Lowndes, and Robert Marion of South Carolina and their fellow lawmakers from the neighboring states of North Carolina and Georgia objected that the $10 tax singled out the Palmetto State for censure. (See "Speech of Representative Benjamin Huger, 1804," on page 111 in the Primary Sources section.) Like any other state, they observed, South Carolina already paid its fair share in taxes. Cognizant that only South Carolina persisted in the importation of slaves from abroad, Congress was considering a tax that would not operate equally upon all the states, instead affecting South Carolina alone. "The tax, if imposed," complained Representative Lowndes, "will be partial, and therefore unjust. . . . It is a tax exclusively falling on the State where the importation is admitted." The people of his state, he

---

[13] *Annals of Congress,* 8th Cong., 1st sess., 992.
[14] *Annals of Congress,* 8th Cong., 1st sess., 1014.

warned, would refuse "to be subjected to a tax which will fall exclusively on her while the rest of the community will bear no part of it." Representative Early of Georgia sympathized with his colleague. Principles of fair taxation demanded that the people of South Carolina not be subjected to a "double tax" as a penalty for acting within their constitutional rights.[15]

Representatives from slaveholding states identified other dangers of the proposed $10 tax. For one, the southern economy was dependent upon slave labor. Absent a sufficient quantity of labor, agriculture would suffer in South Carolina. At least two congressmen also suggested that imposition of the tax would poison the master-slave relationship. Representative Huger asserted that "any interference between a master and his slave induces the former to be more severe" but offered no rationale for linking the potential tax on slave imports to masters' increased brutality. Speaking immediately after Huger, North Carolina representative Holland lent clarity to Huger's remarks. He hinted that the resolution in favor of the $10 tax would somehow "induce the slaves to rise against their masters." "Might it not tend to make the slaves more refractory; might it not tend to make them rise and commit crimes too horrid to name?" he asked. According to Holland, then, masters might exercise harsher discipline to control unruly slaves. Neither Holland nor Huger made explicit, however, precisely how the importation tax could make slaves more ungovernable in the first place.[16]

Many enemies of the slave importation tax urged their colleagues in the House not to antagonize the South Carolina state legislature. They believed that when the legislature convened again, it would repeal the "obnoxious law" itself. A majority of South Carolina's citizens reportedly opposed it, and having witnessed the uproar over the reinstitution of the African slave trade, South Carolina lawmakers simply needed the opportunity to meet and correct the error. Representative Gregg believed that if South Carolina were left "undisturbed by any act of ours, she may, on cool reflection, and in conformity to the wishes of her own citizens, be induced to repeal." If Congress interfered, however, South Carolina might prove recalcitrant. According to Representative Huger, concerted action against South Carolina by Congress "must excite

---

[15] *Annals of Congress*, 8th Cong., 1st sess., 1026; *Annals of Congress*, 9th Cong., 1st sess., 364.

[16] *Annals of Congress*, 8th Cong., 1st sess., 1007.

jealousy and a spirit of resistance," thereby undermining the broad goal of ending the transatlantic slave trade.[17]

It was widely assumed among members of Congress that the United States' legal participation in the transatlantic slave trade would soon end. If Congress prohibited slave importation as soon as constitutionally permissible, in 1808, South Carolina had only four remaining years in which to import slaves. Since Congress would shortly terminate the trade altogether, explained Speaker Macon in February 1804, "There does not appear to me to be any necessity for our interposition."[18]

OUTCOME AND IMPACT

The proposed $10 tax on slave imports languished in Congress for two years. In mid-February 1804, the House of Representatives passed a resolution to impose the tax but then postponed discussion on the matter to give the South Carolina legislature time to repeal the statute itself. Some representatives detected in the delay a ploy designed to give South Carolinians more time to import all the slaves they wanted. As they feared, the South Carolina assembly failed to rescind its offensive law, albeit by only a single vote in the state senate. Undeterred, Representative Henry Southard of New Jersey reintroduced the resolution in February 1805, but the process repeated itself. The House granted a postponement, but again the South Carolina legislature kept the slave trade open. On the motion of Representative James Sloan, a Republican from New Jersey, the House took up the proposed $10 tax yet again on December 11. Representative David Rogerson Williams, a Republican from South Carolina, called for another postponement, with the prediction—once again—that his state's legislature would outlaw the slave trade. By now, declared Representative Southard, South Carolina had enjoyed ample opportunity to repeal. It was time to act.

Meanwhile, in the Senate, the debate over the African slave trade charted a different course. On December 12, 1805, the day after Sloan revisited the idea of a $10 tax, Stephen Row Bradley, a Republican senator from Vermont, announced his intention to introduce a bill outlawing the transatlantic slave trade altogether as of January 1, 1808. This

---

[17] *Annals of Congress,* 8th Cong., 1st sess., 1016, 1013, 1006.
[18] *Annals of Congress,* 8th Cong., 1st sess., 998.

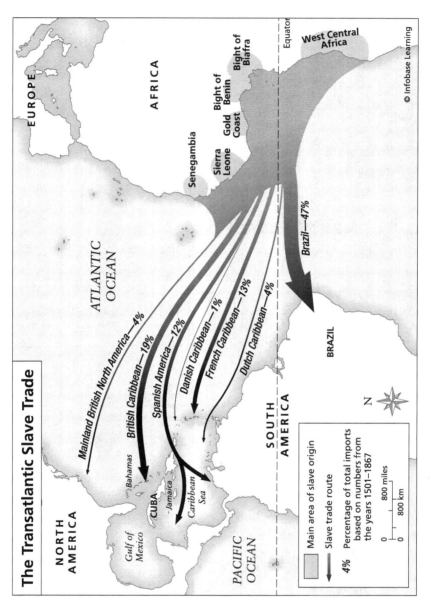

The Transatlantic Slave Trade

Mainland British North America—4%
British Caribbean—19%
Spanish America—12%
Danish Caribbean—1%
French Caribbean—13%
Dutch Caribbean—4%
Brazil—47%

EUROPE

AFRICA

Senegambia
Sierra Leone
Gold Coast
Bight of Benin
Bight of Biafra
West Central Africa

Equator

ATLANTIC OCEAN

NORTH AMERICA

Gulf of Mexico
Bahamas
CUBA
Jamaica
Caribbean Sea

SOUTH AMERICA

BRAZIL

PACIFIC OCEAN

N

Main area of slave origin
Slave trade route
4% Percentage of total imports based on numbers from the years 1501–1867

0   800 miles
0   800 km

© Infobase Learning

Fewer than 4 percent of all slaves carried to the Americas arrived in what became the United States.

marked the first effort in Congress to exercise its constitutional prerogative to ban the slave trade. Bradley followed through on his promise on December 16, but after a second reading, the bill was postponed until December 1806.

The House of Representatives continued debating the $10 tax on slave imports in January and February 1806. On February 4, however, that discussion merged with a proposal to end the slave trade. Representative Barnabus Bidwell of Massachusetts advanced an amendment to impose the tax on importations only until 1808, when the slave trade would end, thanks to a new section he proposed adding to the same bill. Bidwell insisted on the propriety of passing the prohibition on the slave trade now, even though it would not take effect until the constitutionally prescribed date of 1808. Representative Joseph Clay, a Republican from Pennsylvania, objected, doubting that Congress could constitutionally discuss the matter until 1808. The 142-seat House voted down Bidwell's amendment with only 17 yeas. All attempts to include an amendment prohibiting the slave trade in the bill taxing slave imports failed.

In his annual message to Congress, on December 2, 1806, President Thomas Jefferson encouraged Congress to pass legislation outlawing the slave trade. Eliminating any doubt over whether or not Congress could constitutionally legislate against it prior to 1808, he urged immediate action against the slave trade so that the ban might take effect at the earliest possible date. The following day, Bradley announced his intention to reintroduce the ban in the Senate. Before the month was out, the House was also considering "A Bill to prohibit the importation or bringing of slaves into the United States, or the territories thereof, after the thirty-first day of December, 1807." Thus, Congress never levied the $10 tax on slave imports, as the proposal was subsumed by legislation banning the transatlantic slave trade.

Members of Congress agreed on the end—the destruction of the slave trade—but not the means. No one in Congress spoke in favor of the perpetuation of the trade. As Representative Sloan observed, "It appeared to be the universal wish of every member . . . to put an entire stop to this inhuman traffic." Yet crafting the actual legislation proved challenging. According to Connecticut's Benjamin Tallmadge, "I can scarcely recollect an instance in which the members seem so generally to agree in the principles of a bill, and yet differ so widely as to its details." Congressmen debated the future fate of slaves found to have been smuggled into the United States as well as the appropriate punishment for those convicted of illicit trading. After a remarkable amount of wrangling given the widespread support of the legislation's ultimate goal, the House of Representatives passed the bill outlawing the slave trade by a narrow margin of 63 to 49. Of the 63 yeas, 51 were from northern representatives, 12 from southern. Republicans cast 51 votes in favor of the measure; Federalists, 12. Among the 49 nay voters, 11 were from the North, 38 from the South. Eight Federalists and 41 Republicans opposed the bill as written.[19]

President Jefferson signed the bill into law the first week of March 1807, giving slave traders a nine-month window in which to draw their operations to a close before the act's provisions took effect on January 1, 1808. The law imposed exorbitant individual fines of up to $20,000 for constructing or outfitting a slaving vessel and up to $10,000 for captaining a ship or taking slaves aboard for sale. Anyone who purchased or sold slaves taken illicitly into the country forfeited them and was fined $800 per bond person. Commanders of ships were subject to prison sentences of 2 to 4 years; others involved might serve 5 to 10 years in jail. Congressional acts of 1818, 1819, and 1820 later amended provisions of the 1807 law.

Although the white American public paid remarkably little attention to the debate, entranced instead by news of the unraveling Aaron Burr conspiracy as well as Napoleon's exploits in Europe, African Americans took notice. They applauded the 1807 act ending U.S. participation in the transatlantic slave trade. On January 1, 1808, Peter Williams, Jr., and Absalom Jones delivered memorable sermons in African Episcopal churches in New York City and Philadelphia, respectively, celebrating the momentous day. The two ministers' orations pursued common themes. Both rejoiced and expressed gratitude for the law but also offered sober notes of caution. The racial magnanimity of the Revolutionary era was waning rapidly in the first decade of the 19th century. With white hostility toward blacks on the rise, Williams and Jones each advised African Americans to comport themselves with propriety, to obey and respect the law, and to provide no occasion for regret among the whites who had helped terminate the African slave trade.

The act of 1807 brought to a close the most active 20 years of the transatlantic slave trade in colonial and early U.S. history. Almost 40,000 slaves entered South Carolina from 1803 to the end of 1807, more than

---

[19] *Annals of Congress*, 9th Cong., 2d sess., 170, 232.

enough to satisfy masters' demand for labor in the state. Excess imports were sold to markets in the Southwest, such as those in New Orleans or Natchez, Mississippi. But if the act of 1807 was intended to eliminate the African slave trade, it proved an imperfect means. Some southern whites refused to cooperate with the law. The nature of smuggling makes it impossible to determine the precise magnitude of the illegal slave trade over the next half-century, but scholars affix the number at around 50,000, including imports from both Africa and the Caribbean. Whatever the true figure, smugglers flouted the act of 1807 to convey thousands upon thousands of new slaves into the country between 1808 and the Civil War.

The structure of the 1807 statute was at times self-defeating. When slaves carried clandestinely into the United States were discovered, state law governed their dispensation. Thus, if captured in the slaveholding states of the South, they were still sold as slaves in utter violation of the spirit of the law. The closure of the transatlantic trade also had the effect of spurring the rise of a domestic slave trade. Masters with surplus slaves sold them farther south and west to the cotton frontier, where demand for slaves exceeded supply. This internal trade devastated enslaved families, separating husbands from wives and parents from children. Despite the domestic slave trade, by the 1850s, demand for labor continued to outstrip the supply of slaves on the burgeoning cotton lands of the Southwest, prompting calls to revive the African slave trade. Nevertheless, the act of 1807 remained in effect until the institution of slavery was abolished in 1865.

WHAT IF?

What if Congress had imposed a tax on slaves imported to the United States?

Congress never levied such a tax. As lawmakers debated the measure, postponed their discussions, and debated it again, it was overtaken and superseded in importance by the proposal to end American involvement in the transatlantic slave trade altogether. Had the proposed $10 tax on imported slaves passed, it would have been in effect for only a few short years before the African slave trade ended by law on January 1, 1808. A tax so small probably would not have discouraged the trade much if at all. Since approximately 38,000 slaves entered South Carolina

(continues on page 102)

THE DEATH PENALTY AND THE TRANSATLANTIC SLAVE TRADE

While debating the proposed $10 tax on slave imports in February 1804, Republican representative James Holland of North Carolina told the House that he "trusted" Congress would soon prohibit the transatlantic slave trade by making it a "capital offence" to participate in it. A punishment as severe and irreversible as execution, he believed, would surely serve as an effective deterrent to the traffic in human beings.[*] Holland's remark, glanced over at the time, presaged a more intensive debate from late 1806 to early 1807 over the most appropriate punishment for those convicted of smuggling slaves into the United States once American participation in the trade was outlawed.

In crafting the bill that declared the slave trade illegal, some members of the House of Representatives thought hanging a perfectly suitable punishment for the crime of slave smuggling. Pennsylvania Republican John Smilie averred that "a captain of a ship engaged in this traffic was guilty of murder," and since execution was the common punishment for murder, any person who transported or attempted to sell another human being should likewise "suffer death." Moreover, many crimes far less serious than slave trading were also capitally punished. Massachusetts Federalist William Ely assumed that, "If the punishment of death was inflicted, . . . no persons would venture to engage in the trade." His fellow Federalist Benjamin Tallmadge of Connecticut invoked the biblical injunction of Exodus 21:16: "And he that stealeth a man and selleth him, or if he be found in his hand, he shall surely be put to death." The crime of man stealing, he argued, was as heinous today as in biblical times and merited the same punishment.[†]

Other representatives opposed the death penalty for trafficking in slaves. Republican Edward Lloyd of Maryland noted that biblical punishments were not always appropriate in modern times. Death was "not proportional to the crime" of slave smuggling, he explained, especially when many captives had previously been enslaved in Africa anyway. New Jersey Republican Ebenezer Elmer thought the death penalty improper because slave trading was not analogous to murder; rather, it was more akin to a property crime, "committed merely out of a love of gain." Republican Joseph Stanton IV of Rhode

---

[*] *Annals of Congress,* 8th Cong., 1st sess., 1008.

[†] *Annals of Congress,* 9th Cong., 2d sess., 89–190, 232, 233.

Island took yet another approach. "Those who buy, are as bad as those who import them, and deserve hanging quite as much." James Holland predicted that when placed on trial, slave traders would argue precisely that—that masters of slaves were far more morally culpable for owning slaves than traders were for merely moving them from one place to another. Such an argument might prove persuasive enough to a jury to prevent conviction of the trader. Georgia Republican Peter Early went even further. Slave trading was not worthy of capital punishment, he said, and with a penalty as severe as death, no southerner would be willing to report the smugglers because "[t]hey do not consider it as a crime." According to Early, "A large majority of people in the Southern States do not consider slavery as even an evil."[*]

Representative Jonathan Ogden Moseley, a Federalist from Connecticut, countered the arguments of the anti–death penalty contingent in the House. Moseley dismissed the notion that imposing capital punishment would undermine the enforcement of the law by making people reluctant to report those guilty of smuggling. He contended, rather, that the certainty of punishment was more important than its severity. Moreover, he continued, if southerners were sincere in their denunciations of the transatlantic slave trade, "they will cheerfully and cordially co-operate" in enforcing the law, regardless of the penalty. Moseley added that southerners need not fear northern rebuke. Although southern politicians frequently deflected the blame for slavery onto the northern ship owners and sailors who engaged in the "nefarious" business of importing slaves, Moseley assured the South that northerners, "so far from charging their Southern brethren with cruelty or severity in hanging them, . . . would acknowledge the favor with gratitude." Only death, Moseley insisted, would deter the "hardened and abandoned" characters who participated in the African slave trade.[†]

Efforts to affix the death penalty to the transatlantic slave trade failed. A majority of the House did not consider trafficking in slaves a crime that deserved capital punishment. Instead, the act of 1807 made participation in the transatlantic slave trade a misdemeanor punishable by thousands of dollars in fines, depending on the particular offense or offenses committed, and a prison sentence not to exceed 10 years. Only after congressional legislation in 1820 redefined slave trading as a form of piracy did it become a capital crime.

---

[*] *Annals of Congress*, 9th Cong., 2d sess., 235, 240, 238.

[†] *Annals of Congress*, 9th Cong., 2d sess., 234.

(continued from page 99)
between 1803 and 1807, Congress's refusal to pass a slave importation tax cost the government at least $380,000 in revenue.

During debates over the $10 duty, members of the U.S. House of Representatives suggested various proposals as alternatives to the tax. Thomas Moore of South Carolina urged his colleagues to pass a resolution to condemn all state laws permitting the importation of slaves "and to totally disapprove every measure which attempts to draw revenue from an act that rivets the chains of slavery on any of the human race." His proposed resolution read: "this House receive[s] with painful sensibility information that one of the Southern States, by a repeal of certain prohibitory laws, have permitted a traffic unjust in its nature, and highly impolitic in free Governments."[20] His motion was out of order, however, and not taken up for consideration. Shamed by the prospect of the U.S. Treasury's profiting by the slave trade, Pennsylvania's Andrew Gregg regretted that constitutionally he was unable to vote for a prohibitively costly duty of $500 per slave, a much more substantial sum that he predicted would have the salutary effect of shutting down the African slave trade. Several state legislatures recommended a constitutional amendment authorizing Congress to ban the international slave trade immediately. Even without pursuing that cumbersome remedy, the United States terminated its legal participation in the transatlantic slave trade on the earliest possible date allowed by the Constitution.

CHRONOLOGY

1619 The first Africans to England's North American mainland colonies arrive at Jamestown.

1676 Bacon's Rebellion erupts in Virginia, increasing landholders' interest in African slaves.

1739 The Stono Rebellion erupts in colonial South Carolina.

1776 The United States declares independence.

1787 The founders at the Constitutional Convention permit the continuation of the transatlantic slave trade but authorize a $10 tax on slave imports.

1790 Petitions against the transatlantic slave trade reach the new U.S. Congress.

Josiah Parker proposes taxing slave imports.

---

[20] *Annals of Congress*, 8th Cong., 1st sess., 1004.

1791   A slave revolt erupts on Saint-Domingue.

1794   Congress passes "An Act to prohibit the carrying on of the slave-trade from the United States to any foreign place or country."

1798   Georgia becomes the last state to outlaw the transatlantic slave trade.

1800   Congress passes "An Act in addition to the act, entitled 'An act to prohibit the carrying on of the slave-trade from the United States to any foreign place or country.'"

The Gabriel slave conspiracy is exposed.

1803   The United States purchases Louisiana from France.

South Carolina reopens the African slave trade.

1804   The House of Representatives considers a tax on slave imports.

1807   Congress passes a law ending U.S. participation in the transatlantic slave trade.

A British law banning the slave trade passes and goes into effect.

1808   The United States ends the legal importation of slaves through the transatlantic slave trade.

1820   Congress defines slave trading as piracy and makes it punishable by death.

DISCUSSION QUESTIONS

1. In your estimation, would levying a tax on slave imports have implied approval of the African slave trade? Why or why not?

2. How "fair" was the proposed tax on slave imports? Were congressmen from South Carolina justly offended by it? Why or why not?

3. How important was the possible revenue raised by the proposed $10 tax on slave imports to the debate over the tax?

4. In your opinion, would it have been proper for the U.S. government to profit from the transatlantic slave trade by levying a tax on slave imports? Why or why not?

5. How effective do you think a $10 tax levied on each imported slave would have been in reducing the slave trade? Why?

WEB SITES

Emory University. "Voyages: The Trans-Atlantic Slave Trade Database." Available online. URL: http://www.slavevoyages.org/. Accessed August 31, 2010.

Schomburg Center for Research in Black Culture. "The Abolition of the Slave Trade." Available online. URL: http://abolition.nypl.org/home/. Accessed August 31, 2010.

Schomburg Center for Research in Black Culture. "The Abolition of the Slave Trade." Available online. URL: http://abolition.nypl.org/print/us_constitution/. Accessed October 1, 2010.

Schomburg Center for Research in Black Culture. "In Motion: The African-American Migration Experience." Available online. URL: http://www.inmotionaame.org/home.cfm. Accessed August 31, 2010.

Schomburg Center for Research in Black Culture. "The Transatlantic Slave Trade." Available online. URL: http://digital.nypl.org/lwf/english/site/flash.html. Accessed August 31, 2010.

Yale Law School, Lillian Goldman Law Library. "Documents on Slavery," Avalon Project. Available online. URL: http://avalon.law.yale.edu/subject_menus/slavery.asp. Accessed October 1, 2010.

BIBLIOGRAPHY

Einhorn, Robin L. *American Taxation, American Slavery.* Chicago: University of Chicago Press, 2006. Discusses the relationship between slavery and taxation in American history, emphasizing planters' desire to protect their enslaved property from taxation.

Ford, Lacy K. *Deliver Us from Evil: The Slavery Question in the Old South.* New York: Oxford University Press, 2009. Traces the growing commitment of southern whites to slavery from the post-Revolutionary era to about 1840. Chapter 3 examines South Carolina and the slave trade on both the state and national levels.

Klein, Rachel N. *Unification of a Slave State: The Rise of the Planter Class in the South Carolina Backcountry, 1760–1808.* Chapel Hill: University of North Carolina Press, 1990. Shows how Lowcountry and backcountry slaveholders in South Carolina overcame their differences to become a unified ruling class.

Lindsay, Lisa A. *Captives as Commodities: The Transatlantic Slave Trade.* Upper Saddle River, N.J.: Pearson Prentice Hall, 2008. A brief history of the transatlantic slave trade designed for classroom use.

Mason, Matthew. *Slavery and Politics in the Early American Republic.* Chapel Hill: University of North Carolina Press, 2006. The first chapter examines slavery's role in early American politics to 1808.

Obadele-Starks, Ernest. *Freebooters and Smugglers: The Foreign Slave Trade in the United States after 1808.* Fayetteville: University of Arkansas Press, 2007. Studies the illicit slave trade in the United States after legal participation in the transatlantic slave trade ended.

Rawley, James A. *The Transatlantic Slave Trade: A History.* Rev. ed. Lincoln: University of Nebraska Press, 2005. A broad survey of the transatlantic slave trade, originally published in 1981.

Rediker, Marcus. *The Slave Ship: A Human History.* New York: Viking, 2007. A study of the transatlantic slave trade through the lens of those aboard slaving vessels, including captains, crews, and captives.

Smallwood, Stephanie E. *Saltwater Slavery: A Middle Passage from Africa to American Diaspora.* Cambridge, Mass.: Harvard University Press, 2007. A cultural analysis of the experiences of slaves taken from Africa, carried through the Middle Passage, and sold in British North America in the late 17th and early 18th centuries.

PRIMARY SOURCES

1. Speech of Representative John Baptiste Charles Lucas, 1804

Republican John Baptiste Charles Lucas of Pennsylvania served in the House of Representatives from 1803 to 1805. Although brief, his time in the House coincided precisely with discussions of the $10 tax on slave imports. In the following excerpt from a speech he delivered on February 14, 1804, Lucas denied that taxing slave imports lent governmental sanction to the African slave trade.

The importation is not legalized by the Union, but by the act of South Carolina; and, legalized by her, it is out of our power to illegalize it. In laying this tax we are only exercising that power which the Constitution confers.... Deeming the importation an evil, we shall, by laying this tax, do all in our power to diminish it, and, to the extent of our ability, extract the little good it is capable of producing.

Source: Annals of Congress of the United States, 8th Cong., 1st sess. (Washington, D.C.: Gales & Seaton, 1852), 1010.

—⚬⚬—

2. Speech of Representative James Madison Broom, 1806

A Federalist, James Madison Broom was born in 1776, the year the United States declared independence. He represented Delaware in the House of Representatives in the 9th and 10th Congresses, from 1805 to 1809, and supported the $10 tax on slave imports. In an oration on January 21, 1806, he denied that taxing the slave trade obligated the U.S. government to protect it.

We can never be bound to protect this trade, because the United States have solemnly declared that it shall never be carried on in any of our vessels, or by any of our citizens. How, then, protect it? In French, Spanish, or English vessels? Does not the common sense of every man revolt at the idea? By the laws of the land, our own citizens cannot carry on the trade; surely, then, we cannot be called on to protect foreign vessels in practices disallowed to our own citizens. We have, therefore, no reason on earth to fear that our armed vessels will be degraded by convoying a parcel of slaves to this boasted land of liberty.

Source: Annals of Congress of the United States, 9th Cong., 1st sess. (Washington, D.C.: Gales & Seaton, 1852), 368.

—⚬⚬—

3. Speech of Representative David Bard, 1804

Republican David Bard of Pennsylvania introduced a resolution to the House of Representatives in January 1804 that opened the debate over the proposed tax on slave imports. On February 14, he denied allegations that the tax would function unfairly against South Carolina. First elected in 1795, Bard served nine terms in the House.

The tax is a general one; no State in the Union is exempted; it will operate wherever its object can be found. It may be that some States will pay more and some less, but it will be at the option of any State how much, or whether it will pay any of this tax; for it will be just as the State shall please to deal in this article of commerce. And, on the score of uniformity, no objections can lie against the tax—the slaves have already been the object of direct taxation, and Vermont paid none of that tax, because she had none of that kind of taxable property.

Source: *Annals of Congress of the United States,* 8th Cong., 1st sess. (Washington, D.C.: Gales & Seaton, 1852), 994.

—⚬⚬—

4. Speech of Representative John Baptiste Charles Lucas, 1804

In the following excerpt of a speech he delivered in the House of Representatives on February 14, 1804, John Baptiste Charles Lucas of Pennsylvania explained why the proposed tax on slave imports did not punish or censure the state of South Carolina.

But when we lay a tax on the importation of slaves, it is a sufficient reply to such remarks to say that the tax is not laid exclusively on slaves admitted into South Carolina. It does not therefore apply to South Carolina alone. That State has an undoubted right to admit the importation; but Congress have also an undoubted right of taxing them. The resolution, therefore, does not encroach on the rights of that State. The United States and South Carolina form two bodies politic, both of which are possessed of Constitutional rights. To the one belongs the right of importing, to the other, the right of taxation; and this last right may be exercised without involving any censure of the State of South Carolina. . . . It cannot, I think, be justly said, by imposing this tax we single out the State of South Carolina with a view to punishing her. . . . The resolution does not . . . single out South Carolina; there is, in fact, not one word respecting South Carolina in it. It is not said the tax shall be laid upon slaves coming from Africa or going to South Carolina, but on slaves imported into the United States. If the tax shall operate more on South Carolina than on any other State, it will not be our fault. It will remain at her option at any moment to put herself into such a situation as to avoid it. The remedy is in her hands; she can when she pleases prohibit the importation of slaves, and the tax, so far as it falls on her, will immediately cease. And if other States admit the importation of slaves the tax will equally apply to them.

Source: *Annals of Congress of the United States,* 8th Cong., 1st sess. (Washington, D.C.: Gales & Seaton, 1852), 1009–1010.

—⚬⚬—

5. Speech of Representative James Madison Broom, 1806

Federalist representative James Madison Broom of Delaware believed it was unjust for the wealthy to escape taxes on slave imports while the poor masses paid duties on basic, essential commodities. In his speech in the House of Representatives on January 21, 1806, Broom urged the redistribution of the tax burden.

Upon salt, sugar, and other articles of the first necessity, we have laid high and oppressive duties. We have laid a duty of twenty cents on every bushel of salt, and correspondent duties on tea, coffee, sugar, and molasses. I ask, then, when it is considered that these articles are extensively consumed by the poor of our country, do we not take from labor the price of its industry, while we omit to lay any duty on slaves, who, so far from being owned by the poor, are the exclusive property of the rich?—thus exempting this article of luxury, while others of the first necessity, which are consumed by the poor, in common with all descriptions of citizens, are burdened with a heavy duty. While articles allowed to be beneficial to all classes pay high duties, articles which are injurious, used by the rich to pamper their luxury, remain free from duty, and all the efforts of the nation cannot obtain the imposition of even a slight duty on them. How inconsistent is this with the pompous profession of relieving the poor, so long sounded in our ears! . . . I do not know why we should trample on the poor in order to privilege the rich. . . . Viewed in the aspect of revenue, is the duty so small as to be unworthy of notice? If the tax produce only $20,000, it will enable us to take off the tax on pepper; and should it produce only $10,000, we may take off the tax on medicines and a variety of other articles consumed by all classes of our citizens.

Source: Annals of Congress of the United States, 9th Cong., 1st sess. (Washington, D.C.: Gales & Seaton, 1852), 369–370.

―∞―

6. Speech of Representative Benjamin Huger, 1804

Rice planter Benjamin Huger of South Carolina served in the House of Representatives as a Federalist from 1799 to 1805 and again from 1815 to 1817. On February 14, 1804, he explained to the House that the wide-

spread violation of South Carolina's law forbidding the African slave trade justified his state's decision to reopen the traffic.

We do not pretend to advocate the act, but the right of our State to pass this law. It is not to be inferred that we are friendly to the importation. I believe, on the contrary, every Representative of the State on this floor is hostile to it. But how can gentlemen expect that we will disregard the voice of our own State, and especially when the measure may have been dictated by good and substantial reasons. One good reason may be that the importation could not be prevented, and that the restraining law was extensively broken. This we know was the fact. If so, may it not have been sound policy in the State to repeal it? . . . It may have been conceived to have been better to import slaves directly from Africa than to be indebted for them to New York and other States in which they may have been surreptitiously introduced.

Source: Annals of Congress of the United States, 8th Cong., 1st sess. (Washington, D.C.: Gales & Seaton, 1852), 1006.

—⁂—

7. Speech of Representative Thomas Lowndes, 1804

A Federalist, Thomas Lowndes of South Carolina served in the House of Representatives in the 7th and 8th Congresses, from 1801 to 1805. Lowndes stated on February 14, 1804, that he opposed the slave trade and hoped to end it but simultaneously objected to the proposed tax on slave importations. He feared that the revenue generated by the tax would give the U.S. government a vested interest in the trade and make it more difficult to terminate.

I can regard the Government deriving a revenue from it in no other light than a sanction. . . . It appears to me to be directly calculated to defeat their own object—to give to what they wish to discountenance a legislative sanction; and, further, an interest to the Government in permitting the trade after the period when it might constitutionally terminate it. . . . The tax, if imposed, will undoubtedly produce a revenue, and in proportion to the amount of this revenue will be the interest of the Government in the trade. . . . It will not be a discouragement to the trade, nor will the introduction of a single African into the country be prevented.

The only result will be, that it will produce a revenue to the Government. I trust that no gentleman is desirous of establishing this tax with a view to revenue.

Source: *Annals of Congress of the United States,* 8th Cong., 1st sess. (Washington, D.C.: Gales & Seaton, 1852), 993.

—⁓—

8. Speech of Representative Andrew Gregg, 1804

A longtime Republican representative from Pennsylvania, Andrew Gregg saw the $10 tax on slave imports as no deterrent to the trade. In a speech in the House of Representatives on February 15, 1804, he explained how the tax was no longer proportional to the market price of slaves.

[The constitutional provision that allowed a $10 tax on slave imports] was given . . . for the purpose of being used as a check to the trade, and at the time the Constitution was adopted, the exercise of that power might have contributed to produce such effect. The price of slaves was then low; their labor was not so productive to their owners, and, of course, ten dollars in addition to the then current price might, in some measure, have checked the spirit of purchasing. But soon after that period, by the introduction of the cultivation of cotton, the labor of slaves became more valuable, and their price enhanced in proportion. Ten dollars then bore some proportion to the price of a slave, but at this time it is comparatively as a cipher. . . . I take it the proposed tax cannot effect the object contemplated by the mover of the resolution—it can neither prevent nor remedy the evil; and as it has the appearance of giving legal sanction to the trade, and may have an influence on the Legislature of South Carolina, inasmuch as it is an implied attack on their sovereignty, and a censure on them for passing an act.

Source: *Annals of Congress of the United States,* 8th Cong., 1st sess. (Washington, D.C.: Gales & Seaton, 1852), 1014.

—⁓—

9. Speech of Representative Nathaniel Macon, 1804

Republican Nathaniel Macon of North Carolina was a fixture in Congress from 1791 to 1829. He served as Speaker of the House from 1801 to 1806, during the debate over the $10 tax on slave imports. In a speech on

February 14, 1804, Macon warned that taxing the African slave trade would require the protection of slaving vessels by the U.S. government.

The avowed object of the proposed tax was to show the hostility of Congress to the principle of importing slaves. How would this opposition of Congress be manifested, when it would become the duty of the armed ships of the United States, as soon as the tax was imposed, to protect this trade, as well as all other trade on which taxes were laid? He asked whether vessels engaged in this trade would not, under such circumstances, possess the same right to the protection of the Government as any other vessels engaged in any other kind of trade? Can this House tax this trade, and refuse it the same protection that is extended to all other trade? The question is not whether we shall prohibit the slave trade, but simply whether we shall tax it. . . . And the simple question now is, whether, for a trifling revenue, we will undertake to protect this trade. My idea is, that those who at present go into the traffic, have no right to claim your protection; but once legalize it by taxing it, and they will acquire the right thereto, and will demand it.

Source: Annals of Congress of the United States, 8th Cong., 1st sess. (Washington, D.C.: Gales & Seaton, 1852), 998.

—∞—

10. Speech of Representative Benjamin Huger, 1804

In the following excerpt from a speech he delivered in the House of Representatives on February 14, 1804, Benjamin Huger, a Federalist from South Carolina, complained that the proposed tax on slave imports unfairly singled out South Carolina for punishment.

When the Southern States were admitted into the Union they were in the habit of carrying on this species of trade, and they, by the express language of the Constitution, retained the right of continuing it until the year 1808. Under this Constitution the State of South Carolina enjoyed the exclusive right of judging of the propriety of allowing the trade or of prohibiting it. . . . After the State had exercised their undoubted right, however he might dislike the measure, it was his duty to defend the right which they had to adopt it. That State had in truth done no more than she possessed a Constitutional right to do. . . . He could not therefore but feel sensibly the attempt to single out this particular State to censure her for doing that which she had an undisputed right to do. . . .

It was a question whether the Government of the Union should come forward and condemn the act of a State, which she was fully authorized to pass. If it is necessary to increase the revenue, let us meet that subject fairly and fully, and not single out a particular resource of a particular State. It is on this ground that I principally object to this measure. . . . The fair principle of taxation is, that every part of the Union should contribute equally. When any branch of trade is profitable in New York, I, though a Southern man, rejoice at it. When the fisheries of the Eastern States prosper, I feel highly gratified—not because those whom I represent are particularly interested in them, but because I consider myself as a part of the whole, and that whatever advances the interests of any part of this Union must promote the interests of every part of it.

With regard to the moral principle involved in the slave trade, we have nothing to do with it. On this point the Union ought to be silent.

Source: Annals of Congress of the United States, 8th Cong., 1st sess. (Washington, D.C.: Gales & Seaton, 1852), 1004–1005.

COLONIZATION:

Was Colonization Outside the United States by Black Americans a Good Idea?

—ɯɯ—

THE CONTROVERSY

The Issue

Beginning in the late 18th century, various proposals were advanced to transport and colonize black Americans abroad. Was the colonization of black Americans outside the United States a good idea?

♦ **Arguments in favor of colonization:** In the early republic, various proposals were put forth to colonize free people of color outside the United States, most commonly in Africa. Supporters of colonization included far more whites than blacks. Many whites feared racial intermixing and race war if emancipated slaves and free blacks were allowed to remain in the United States. Ubiquitous, ingrained racial prejudice among whites made life difficult for free black Americans. Proponents of colonization argued that free blacks, if relocated abroad, would enjoy greater rights and opportunities than in the United States. In addition, some slaveholders feared the bad example that free people of color set for their slaves. At the same time, deporting emancipated slaves would persuade masters to liberate more slaves than they otherwise would without transportation. Slaves eager to return to Africa would comport themselves according to masters' expectations, so colonization would actually promote good behavior on the plantation. Once in Africa, relocated free blacks could introduce "civilization" and Christianity to that continent. Such a benevolent outcome, argued some colonizationists, recast the enslavement of Africans and African Americans as a crucial step in God's divine plan to uplift their native land. Moreover, from their African outpost, free black Americans could then suppress the international slave trade and institute a profitable commerce with the United States. In this view, colonization was a noble undertaking.

♦ *Arguments opposed to colonization:* Contemporaries often dismissed colonization as wildly impractical. The associated costs and the numbers of emigrants involved made colonization abroad impossible. The vast majority of free blacks did not believe colonizationists had their best interests in mind anyway and resented their efforts to exile them from their own home in the United States. They pledged not to emigrate and desert their brothers and sisters in bondage. By the 1830s, radical abolitionists in the North grew critical of colonization as well. Rejecting pro-colonizationist arguments as disingenuous, they thought the scheme shameful. Radical abolitionists favored the immediate abolition of slavery and the introduction of slaves into American society on terms of equality. To them, colonizationists avoided the difficult work of forging racial equality at home and surrendered any hope for free black uplift within the United States. In addition to free blacks and abolitionists, the third major group to oppose colonization was a subset of southern masters, mostly from the Deep South. They argued that colonization schemes rendered erstwhile happy slaves discontented. Possible federal involvement in colonization also established what they considered a dangerous precedent for governmental interference in the master-slave relationship.

—⁂—

INTRODUCTION

In the first decades of the United States, many different proposals were advanced to colonize America's rapidly expanding free black population away from white society. Some plans recommended domestic asylum for free people of color in a remote corner of the United States. Others looked to Africa. In the 1780s, the British established a black colony in West Africa called Sierra Leone. The American Colonization Society considered Sierra Leone an example for their own colonization venture in neighboring Liberia. But colonization proved a controversial idea.

Colonizationists counted among their numbers many whites afraid of racial amalgamation or race war. They found free blacks a repulsive and expendable segment of American society. Slaveholding colonizationists charged that free blacks fomented unrest among their slaves and thus threatened whites' safety. For them, colonization appeared a safe way to dispose of the country's purportedly dangerous surplus black population. Given whites' nearly unanimous belief in black inferiority, relocation offered black Americans an escape from rampant racial prejudice and the chance to enjoy rights and freedoms denied them in the United States. Colonization reportedly benefited slaves as well. According to antislavery forces, masters would more willingly manumit their slaves if they knew emancipated slaves would be relocated. Clergymen posited that black Americans restored to Africa could share the blessings of Christianity and "civilization" with heathen and "primitive" peoples. Slavery served as a school for Africans and their descendants; enslaved pupils exposed to Christianity and bettered through interactions with whites, once liberated and colonized, were positioned to enlighten the "dark continent." They could also place a check on the transatlantic slave trade. Under this view, the horror of slavery was suddenly revealed as part of God's plan for the spiritual, cultural, and intellectual uplift of African peoples.

Colonization also had its enemies. Many thought it too costly and impractical, considering the size of the population to be deported. Free blacks opposed colonization as a callous attempt to expel them from their American home and feared for their counterparts in slavery should they depart. With their rise in the early 1830s, radical abolitionists argued that colonization missed the point. Whereas justice demanded the immediate abolition of slavery, colonizationists catered to immoral principles and sin. The product of prejudice, abolitionists charged, colonization was a racist plan to oust people of color from American soil. Abolitionists seriously doubted colonization could possibly accomplish their ultimate goal, the eradication of slavery. Some slaveholders feared colonization plans would generate discontent among their chattel and provoke U.S. government intervention on the slavery issue, interference masters desperately wished to prevent. Although very different groups of people with conflicting agendas, free blacks, radical abolitionists, and some slaveholders all labored in opposition to colonization.

BACKGROUND

After the American Revolution ended in 1783, the final extinction of slavery seemed within reach. Northern states passed either immediate or gradual emancipation laws. Inspired by the rhetoric of the war, many masters in the North and Upper South privately manumitted their slaves.

Other bond people fled to the British or took to the woods during the revolution as fugitives, seizing their own freedom. By 1790, the nation's free black population had skyrocketed to almost 60,000. But whether in the North or the South, free people of color did not enjoy all the rights of whites. Most states denied black men the vote. Free blacks struggled to acquire an education or find profitable employment. Poverty, discrimination, and the threat of kidnapping and sale into slavery were harsh realities of life. And conditions for free blacks only worsened over time as the Revolutionary impulse waned. As the 18th century yielded to the 19th, manumission laws tightened. Five years after the 1800 Gabriel slave conspiracy in Virginia, for example, the Old Dominion passed a law requiring emancipated slaves to leave the state within a year or forfeit their freedom. Where to go was a complicated matter, however, because some state legislatures forbade the entry of free blacks from other states. South Carolina law appropriated the power to manumit slaves from individual masters altogether, stipulating that only the state legislature exercised that authority. Legal prohibitions against masters' freeing their slaves, or freeing them without removal, curtailed manumissions in the early 19th century. Though reduced in numbers, emancipations combined with natural increase (and some successful escapes by runaway slaves) to increase the free black population by almost 66,000 in the first decade of the 19th century and another 56,000 in the second. By 1820, 229,000 free blacks called the United States home. From 1790 to 1820, between 33 and 37 percent of all free black Americans lived in the two Upper South states of Maryland and Virginia.

The idea to colonize black Americans had emerged even before the American Revolution. Samuel Hopkins, for instance, minister of the First Congregational Church in Newport, Rhode Island, formulated plans for colonization as early as 1773 as a means of attacking the slave trade. The Revolution itself placed such ideas temporarily on hold, but its effects lent immediacy to the discussions of colonization that reemerged in the 1780s. In 1785, Dr. William Thornton, a Quaker, inherited slaves in the West Indies but wanted to surrender his ownership of them. Since his interests intersected with those of Hopkins, he consulted Reverend Hopkins to devise a plan for colonization. In 1787, Thornton announced a proposal to colonize black Americans on the west coast of Africa, but a dearth of funds led to his plan's failure. Cautious, savvy people of color generally remained suspicious of whites eager to help them, but talk of colonization also percolated in northern black circles in the 1780s. Free blacks in northern cities such as Boston, Newport, and Providence hatched plans to emigrate. A number of black Americans in the 1780s were native to Africa and happy to return home. Some saw colonization as a solution to the inequalities they faced daily or as a means to uplift Africa. As with Thornton, however, funding presented a major obstacle to their plans.

Colonization proposals proliferated in the late 18th and early 19th centuries. Some plans called for black removal to Spanish Florida or to some location in the American West. Plans for colonization within the United States gained little traction, however. Remote settlements of black Americans would infringe upon Indian lands and require the protection of American troops. Moreover, in their inexorable march across the American landscape, white settlers would eventually collide with any domestic black colony, however distant or secluded originally. Colonizationists instead preferred relocation abroad, possibly in the West Indies but more likely in Africa.

By 1787, Great Britain offered Americans in favor of colonization in Africa a precedent by establishing the colony of Sierra Leone on the West African coast. In 1786, British philanthropists under the leadership of Granville Sharp determined to cleanse the London slums. They targeted the city's poor blacks, many of whom were former American slaves whose loyalty to the British Crown during the Revolution had earned them their freedom. Though liberated from bondage, many now lived in urban squalor. Motivated by a combination of humanitarian goals and the more selfish desire to rid the city streets of black loyalists, Sharp and his fellow philanthropists gathered some 350 or 400 of London's poor blacks (as well as several dozen white prostitutes) on a ship and deposited them in Sierra Leone in 1787. Five years later, in 1792, Britain helped transport another 1,100 former American slaves who had relocated to Nova Scotia after the Revolution. Sierra Leone experienced tremendous difficulties in becoming established. Quarrels among the colonists, attacks by the native peoples, disease, and death prompted the colony's takeover by a British trading company. After a destructive raid by the French in 1794, the company turned over the settlement to the British government, transforming Sierra Leone into a colony of the Crown.

Despite Sierra Leone's troubled beginnings, American colonizationists upheld the colony as a positive example of the possibilities for relocation to Africa. Free black mariner Paul Cuffee's successful transport of 38 free black Americans to Sierra Leone in 1816 further energized the colonization movement. (See the sidebar "Paul Cuffee" on page 119.) Later that year, Virginia politician Charles Fenton Mercer

From a Drawing by JOHN POLE, M. D. of Bristol, Eng.

Paul Cuffee was one of the few free black Americans who favored colonization abroad by African Americans. He used his own money to finance a voyage to Sierra Leone. (Library of Congress)

PAUL CUFFEE

A leading proponent of colonization in the early republic, Paul Cuffee was born in Massachusetts in 1759 to an enslaved African father and a Native American mother. A devout Quaker, Cuffee rose from humble beginnings to amass a fortune whaling, smuggling, and shipping in the pirate-infested waters of the Atlantic. Over the course of his lifetime, he graduated from novice sailor to ship captain to owner of a fleet of vessels, reportedly becoming the wealthiest free black man in the United States.

Always concerned with the condition of America's free people of color, Cuffee petitioned to protest the fact that free blacks in Massachusetts paid taxes but lacked the right to vote. He also opened a school that children of any race or color could attend. Most famously, however, he championed the cause of African colonization. Acutely aware that the Revolution failed to achieve the promise of equality for black Americans, Cuffee believed in colonization's power to help liberate slaves and to regenerate the African continent. In 1811, he visited Sierra Leone, Great Britain's colony for free blacks on the west coast of Africa, and struck an agreement to deliver respectable black American settlers in exchange for trading privileges there. Upon his return to the United States, he publicized his proposed venture and lobbied both black and white audiences to support his colonization project. His campaign took him to the major urban areas of the East Coast, such as New York and Baltimore. In Philadelphia, Cuffee persuaded free black sailmaker James Forten and other prominent persons of color to back colonization, at least for a time. He also met President James Madison in 1812 to inform him of conditions in Sierra Leone and to discuss his colonizationist ideas, but the commencement of war with Great Britain that year interrupted his colonization plans.

With the conclusion of the War of 1812, Cuffee resumed his efforts. Financing a voyage of colonization with thousands of dollars of his own money, he departed in late 1815 to repatriate 38 black Americans to Sierra Leone. Landing in the capital of Freetown safely early the next year, his emigrants were welcomed, but his business arrangement was not honored, outlawed by the terms of peace between the United States and Great Britain. Cuffee departed hastily before the British seized his vessel. His well-intentioned plan cost him some $4,000 out of his own pocket. He died the following year, in 1817, one of the relatively few free blacks who still touted the benefits of African colonization.

and New Jersey Presbyterian minister Robert Finley played crucial roles in the formation of a private organization, the American Society for Colonizing the Free People of Color of the United States, commonly known as the American Colonization Society (ACS). The more cumbersome moniker explicitly stated the official goal of the organization: to colonize free black Americans. From its founding in December 1816, the ACS denied any intention to abolish slavery or effect a general emancipation. It thus attracted many slaveholding members interested in the deportation of free blacks. The South—and the Upper South in particular—contributed not only a preponderance of ACS members but also a clear majority of its officeholders. As the ACS told masters that colonization could expel troublesome free blacks from southern communities, however, it portrayed colonization to northern audiences as a gradual means to abolish slavery and the transatlantic slave trade. The ACS did not mandate that members adhere to a single, uniform understanding of colonization. As a result of its flexible marketing strategy and purposefully murky aims, the ACS ultimately attracted support from northerners and southerners, nonslaveholders and slaveholders, those opposed to slavery and those in favor. Petitions supporting colonization poured into Congress in the late 1810s and 1820s from states both North and South.

Many prominent Americans attached their support to the American Colonization Society. Bushrod Washington, first president of the ACS, was a Supreme Court justice and nephew of the first president of the United States. James Madison, U.S. president when the ACS was founded, belonged to the organization. So did his successor to the presidency, James Monroe; his fellow Virginian John Randolph of Roanoke; "Star-Spangled Banner" composer Francis Scott Key; and distinguished Kentucky statesman Henry Clay. Politically, Clay advocated the "American system," an expansive economic program that embraced protective tariffs, a national bank, and federally funded internal improvements. Clay also proposed using national funds to finance colonization. Since free blacks could be found throughout the Union, he believed it appropriate for the U.S. government to devote a portion of the looming federal budget surplus to the great national purpose of colonization.

Clay thought federal monies were crucial to the success of the ACS. Lobbying efforts won the organization $100,000 from Congress in 1819, but the ACS relied more heavily upon appropriations from state legislatures and private donations. Although constantly struggling to locate funds, the ACS managed to establish the African colony of Liberia. In 1821, ACS agents acquired land from tribal chiefs on the West African coast, just southeast of Sierra Leone, as a refuge for free black Americans. The first free people of color arrived in Liberia in 1822. Two years later, its capital of Christopolis was renamed Monrovia in honor of U.S. president and colonization advocate James Monroe. Even the establishment of an African colony for free black Americans, however, did not conclusively answer the question, Was colonizing black Americans outside the United States a good idea?

THE DEBATE

The Case that Colonization Outside the United States by Black Americans Was a Good Idea

Beginning in the late 18th century, thoughts of colonizing black Americans abroad captured the imagination of a range of Americans. Whites enamored of the idea included antislavery Congregationalist ministers Samuel Hopkins and Ebenezer Burgess, the latter of whom became an agent of the American Colonization Society, as well as such prominent political figures as Thomas Jefferson, James Madison, and Henry Clay. (See the sidebar "Thomas Jefferson" on page 122.) Maryland senators Robert Goodloe Harper and Ezekiel Chambers also lent support to the cause of colonization in the 1810s and 1820s. Although free black seafarer and businessman Paul Cuffee personally delivered almost 40 black Americans to the colony of Sierra Leone on the West African coast, relatively few black leaders in the United States advocated African colonization. Former slave and Baptist minister Lott Cary, John B. Hepburn of Virginia, and Jamaican-born newspaper editor John Brown Russwurm were exceptions. Each counted among the small number of black supporters of the ACS. White and black proponents of colonization argued that removal would benefit free blacks denied the full rights of citizenship in the United States, promote the emancipation of slaves, civilize and uplift Africa, and suppress the African slave trade as it bestowed economic benefits on the United

THOMAS JEFFERSON

For nearly a half-century, Virginia slaveholder and third president of the United States Thomas Jefferson thought and wrote about the colonization of black Americans. His first major commitment of ink to paper on the subject occurred in the 1780s, with his *Notes on the State of Virginia*. In Query 14, he cataloged a list (offensive to modern sensibilities) of both physical and mental distinctions between blacks and whites. Beyond the obvious external differences in skin color and hair, Jefferson posited that blacks emitted a foul odor, tolerated heat better than whites, required less sleep, were more sexually passionate, and felt sorrow only fleetingly. He also criticized blacks' delinquency of thought, highlighting their inability to reason or anticipate. Although musically inclined, he continued, people of color were deficient in the arts, with no literary accomplishments to speak of. According to Jefferson, nature—rather than their condition of enslavement—made blacks physically and mentally inferior to whites. In his mind, the two races were so profoundly and innately different that they could never peacefully coexist as members of a single, unified society. To the contrary, Jefferson predicted, white prejudice and black resentments that accumulated over their years in bondage would culminate in race war. "We have the wolf by the ear," Jefferson ruefully wrote of slavery, "and we can neither hold him, nor safely let him go."

Jefferson's attempt to balance his twin concerns of "justice" for blacks and "self-preservation" for whites led him to the panacea of colonization. Slaves could be emancipated but then promptly deported elsewhere, distant from whites. But, as Jefferson explained in an 1824 letter to the Reverend Jared Sparks, colonizing the entire slave population at once was neither "practicable for us" nor "expedient for them." Jefferson instead recommended a "post-nati" emancipation scheme in which black children born after an appointed date would remain with their parents until adulthood, during which time they would receive education and training commensurate with their talents. Upon reaching the age of 18 if female or 21 if male, they would be expelled to a suitable location, with provisions to help them begin life anew. For Jefferson, the advantages of his plan were numerous. Most basically, he explained to fellow Virginian Edward Coles in 1814, it rid society of people of color, who "are by their habits rendered as incapable as children of taking care of themselves." Second, slaves' labor up until the time of colonization would compensate masters for the cost of raising them, so it honored slaveholders' property rights. Finally, colonization represented a means to effect the gradual abolition of slavery. Jefferson estimated that, under the plan he outlined, it would take 25 years to complete the process of relocation. Jefferson apparently believed that the safest way to release the wolf's ear was slowly.

Jefferson thought through how to finance his plan for colonization. Funding would derive from sales of public lands in the West. In the 1780s, various states had ceded to Congress lands between the Appalachian Mountains and the Mississippi River that they had once claimed as their own. The U.S. government sold plots of western land, now part of the national domain, to eager settlers, whose money filled the national treasury. For Jefferson, Henry Clay, and others, the project of colonization seemed a perfectly suitable use for this public revenue: national funds for a national cause.

Less clear was the appropriate destination for the emancipated slaves. Jefferson and James Madison both pondered some kind of black refuge in the western United States. Canada and Spanish Florida were other possibilities, but Jefferson doubted that either Great Britain, Spain, or the indigenous occupants of the land would relinquish territory as a haven for blacks. He entertained the possibility of resettlement in Africa but deemed that continent "a last and undoubted resort." Jefferson reasoned that the quantity of black emigrants and the prohibitive costs of the Atlantic crossing militated against an African colony, despite the potential benefits to both the United States and Africa itself. Although an advocate of colonization, Jefferson did not support the American Colonization Society and its emphasis on emigration to Liberia. He instead leaned more in favor of an island refuge somewhere in the West Indies, perhaps Saint-Domingue. As Jefferson explained to his friend and Virginia governor James Monroe in 1801, a tropical climate and an established black population made the Indies the ideal "receptacle of the blacks transplanted into this hemisphere."*

---

* Thomas Jefferson, *Notes on the State of Virginia*, Query 14, http://xroads.virginia.edu/~hyper/jefferson/ch14.html; Thomas Jefferson to John Holmes, April 22, 1820, http://www.loc.gov/exhibits/jefferson/159.html; Thomas Jefferson to Jared Sparks, February 4, 1824, in *Speech of Thomas J. Randolph*, 20; Thomas Jefferson to Edward Coles, August 25, 1814, in Frank Donovan, ed., *The Thomas Jefferson Papers* (New York: Dodd, Mead, 1963), 266; Wayne Franklin, ed., *The Selected Writings of Thomas Jefferson* (New York: W. W. Norton, 2010), 287.

States. Occasionally, whites also frankly acknowledged their desire to use relocation to purge the country of the alleged scourge of black Americans. The drive for colonization thus resulted from an eclectic mix of motives: racism, humanitarianism, abolitionism, missionary zeal, and commercial interests.

Racial self-interest prompted some whites' promotion of the colonization of black Americans. Some feared the possibility of racial amalgamation, or race mixing, if free blacks and whites cohabited the same country. In a biracial society, sexual encounters across the color line threatened to erase distinctions between the races. Whites, wrote Robert Goodloe Harper, "recoil with horror from the idea of an intimate union with the free blacks." To many, mixed-race children evidenced, in the words of Quaker abolitionist John Parrish, "debasing sinful conduct." What better way to prevent race mixing than to expel the free black population from the United States?[1]

Whites' distaste for amalgamation was at least equaled if not exceeded by their fear of race war. As victims of injustice and abuse, the argument ran, slaves despised their masters. Their desire to wreak vengeance upon their oppressors jeopardized the domestic tranquility of the United States. No less illustrious an American than Thomas Jefferson, in his *Notes on the State of Virginia*, predicted a future marred by interracial warfare if masters manumitted their slaves without subsequent colonization. The combustible combination, he wrote, of "deep rooted prejudices entertained by the whites" against blacks and "ten thousand recollections, by the blacks, of the injuries they have sustained" during slavery "will divide us into parties, and produce convulsions which will probably never end but in the extermination of the one or the other race." The looming prospect of race war convinced Jefferson that liberated slaves must be colonized to ensure "our happiness and safety." Other socially attuned political contemporaries agreed with Jefferson, including his successor to the presidency, James Madison. (See "Letter, James Madison to Robert J. Evans, 1819," on page 143 in the Primary Sources

---

[1] Robert Goodloe Harper, *A Letter from Gen. Harper, of Maryland, to Elias B. Caldwell, Esq. Secretary of the American Society for Colonizing the Free People of Colour. In the United States. With Their Own Consent* (Baltimore: R. J. Matchett, 1818), 6; John Parrish, *Remarks on the Slavery of Black People* (Philadelphia: Kimber, Conrad, and Company, 1806), 42.

section.) To maintain peace between the races, declared congressman and fellow Virginian Alexander Smyth, "Let an ocean divide them."[2]

Many pro-colonization whites abhorred free blacks and the effect their presence exerted on the slave population. Harper thought it "natural" that whites discerned colonization's "tendency to confer a benefit on ourselves." Colonization, he wrote in 1818, promised to "[rid] us of a population for the most part idle and useless, and too often vicious and mischievous." Emancipation freed slaves but did not make them acceptable or socially desirable to the vast majority of white Americans, Harper observed. In a discriminatory society, African Americans had no motivation to excel. Deprived of realistic dreams for improvement, they lacked "incitements to industry, frugality, good conduct, and honourable exertion." As a result, with only a few exceptions, the free black "lives in idleness, and probably in vice, and obtains a precarious support by begging or theft." In modeling laziness and vice, Harper complained, free blacks corrupted slaves. Senator Ezekiel Chambers of Maryland concurred. Describing free blacks as "a degraded, miserable race of beings," he argued that the "poison of their example, and their habits, has infected our slaves, and made them indolent and immoral." Harper went even further than Chambers, however, noting that free blacks colluded with slaves in clandestine social interactions and crime and fomented unrest in the quarters. Their example demonstrated to those in bondage that people of color need not automatically be enslaved. (See "Letter, Robert Goodloe Harper to Elias B. Caldwell, 1817," on page 144 in the Primary Sources section.) Free blacks, in short, were an inferior, repugnant, and dangerous element in society, and their repatriation in Africa would prove an unmitigated blessing to white Americans.[3]

---

[2] Thomas Jefferson, *Notes on the State of Virginia*, Query 14, http://xroads.virginia.edu/~hyper/jefferson/ch14.html; Thomas Jefferson to Jared Sparks, February 4, 1824, in *The Speech of Thomas J. Randolph, (of Albemarle,) in the House of Delegates of Virginia, on the Abolition of Slavery: Delivered Saturday, Jan. 21, 1832,* 2nd ed. (Richmond, Va.: Thomas W. White, 1832), 20; *Speech of Mr. Smyth, on the Restriction of Slavery in Missouri. Delivered in the House of Representatives of the United States, January 28, 1820* (1820), 32.

[3] Harper, *Letter from Gen. Harper,* 6, 8, 17; *Register of Debates in Congress, Comprising the Leading Debates and Incidents of the Second Session of the Nineteenth Congress: Together with an Appendix, Containing Important State Papers and Public Documents and the Laws Enacted during the Session, with a Copious Index to the Whole,* vol. 3 (Washington, D.C.: Gales & Seaton, 1829), 323.

If colonization offered an appealing remedy for white racial fears, the perceived "nuisance" of America's free black presence, and slave discontent, it also held forth advantages for free blacks themselves. As Henry Clay explained, free people of color were "peculiarly situated" in the United States: "They neither enjoyed the immunities of freemen, nor were they subject to the incapacities of slaves, but partook in some degree of the qualities of both." Legally denied many rights guaranteed to whites, free blacks enjoyed only a truncated sort of citizenship in the United States. A number of religious figures in the early republic lamented the social position occupied by America's free people of color. The Reverend Robert Finley of New Jersey characterized free blacks as "wretched": "Every thing connected with their condition, including their colour, is against them." Likewise, his fellow minister Ebenezer Burgess regretted that free blacks lacked "a fair opportunity" to improve themselves and advance in American society. Entrenched white prejudices were to blame. (See "Speech of Ebenezer Burgess, 1818," on page 145 in the Primary Sources section.) Pastor Samuel Hopkins agreed. "The whites are so habituated, by education and custom, to look upon and treat the blacks as an inferior class of beings," he declared, ". . . that they never can be raised to an equality with the whites, and enjoy all the liberty and rights to which they have a just claim."[4]

Many whites doubted the situation could improve for people of color if they remained in the United States. Reverend Finley saw little "prospect that their state can ever be greatly meliorated, while they shall continue among us." The reason, explained Harper, was that most white Americans reviled free blacks' skin color and associated their race with enslavement. Their insurmountable prejudice toward black Americans condemned people of color "to a state of hopeless inferiority, and consequent degradation" and erected an "impassible barrier" between the races. "This barrier is closed for ever, by our habits and our feelings," Harper declared. "We never could consent, and they never

---

[4] James F. Hopkins, ed., *The Papers of Henry Clay*, vol. 2 (Lexington: University of Kentucky Press, 1961), 263; M. Carey, *Letters on the Colonization Society; and on Its Probable Results* (Philadelphia: L. Johnson, 1833), 7; Samuel Hopkins, *A Discourse upon the Slave-Trade, and the Slave of the Africans Delivered in the Baptist Meeting-House at Providence, before the Providence Society for Abolishing the Slave-Trade, &c. at Their Annual Meeting, on May 17, 1793* (Providence: J. Carter, 1793), unnumbered appendix.

could hope, to see the two races placed on a footing of perfect equality with each other" and become "one people." Clay shared Harper's pessimistic prognostications, arguing that blacks could never overcome "the unconquerable prejudices resulting from their color" to "amalgamate with the free whites of this country." Therefore, Clay concluded, "It was desirable . . . to drain them off." Removal would produce benefits for free black emigrants. In Africa, wrote Samuel Hopkins, "they would enjoy all desirable equality and liberty, and live in a climate which is peculiarly suited to their constitution." "Transplanted to a colony composed of themselves alone," Harper asserted, free people of color could at last experience "real freedom." Free blacks such as John Brown Russwurm shared in this hope. Colonization offered black Americans a haven from deeply ingrained white prejudice and afforded them opportunities to enjoy rights, including the ability to govern themselves, unavailable in the United States.[5]

Just as colonization might improve conditions for free black migrants, so, too, did it promise to benefit those who remained in bondage in the United States. Although the American Colonization Society did not formally embrace the complete eradication of slavery as a goal, former president Madison and other ACS members believed that colonization "merits encouragement from all who regard slavery as an evil" and "who wish to see it diminished and abolished by peaceable & just means." In the early republic, many masters described slavery as a curse inherited from their ancestors. Still, they proved reluctant to manumit their slaves in the absence of a colonization plan. Some states passed laws that expelled emancipated slaves from their borders and cast them out into an unfamiliar world. According to Senator Chambers, emancipation could in truth become an act of cruelty, because to liberate bond people in the racist society of the United States, North or South, was "to doom them to penury and want, to a life of degraded vice and infamy, and very often to an ignominious death as malefactors." Other masters feared the pernicious influences of freed blacks on those still enslaved. Implementing a plan of colonization, however, eliminated these misgivings and encouraged masters to manumit their slaves voluntarily.

---

[5] Carey, *Letters on the Colonization Society*, 7; Harper, *Letter from Gen. Harper*, 6, 7, 17; Hopkins, *Papers of Henry Clay*, 263; Hopkins, *Discourse upon the Slave-Trade*, unnumbered appendix.

Colonization was, in short, a boon to emancipation. The repatriation of free blacks also had the potential to make slaves more tractable. If free blacks were relocated to Africa, Harper observed, they would no longer tempt slaves to misbehavior for which bond people suffered punishment. To the contrary, colonization would promote "good conduct" among slaves eager for emancipation and removal. Thus, colonization allegedly inspired cheerful optimism among the enslaved.[6] (See "Letter, Robert Goodloe Harper to Elias B. Caldwell, 1817," on page 146 in the Primary Sources section.)

Many promoters of colonization expressed a hope that relocated black Americans would introduce "civilization" and Christianity to Africa. Religion infused the colonization movement with missionary zeal, earning it the support of many churches and benevolent societies. Advocates of colonization portrayed Africa as a "stranger" to "arts[,] knowledge and civilization," a land aching for redemption from "ignorance, barbarism and superstition." Colonization, wrote Madison, would bestow "new blessings civil & religious on the quarter of the Globe most in need of them." According to Harper and others, American "blacks already instructed in the arts of civilized life and the truths of the gospel" would exert a positive influence on Africa, sharing their knowledge of agriculture, industry, and culture and spreading the message of Christianity. Africa, Harper confidently asserted, would welcome the "return of her children to her bosom" for such benevolent and philanthropic purposes. The missionary imperative embraced by African colonization inspired Reverend Hopkins and made him one of its earliest proponents. For the antislavery Hopkins, the power of colonization to redeem Africa from heathenism and savagery helped him make sense of bondage. The evil of the transatlantic slave trade to the Americas was now revealed to be part of a divine plan to prepare blacks to proselytize the African continent. As one religious body

---

[6] James Madison to Robert J. Evans, June 15, 1819, in Jack N. Rakove, ed., *James Madison: Writings* (New York: Library of America, 1999), 729; *Register of Debates in Congress, Comprising the Leading Debates and Incidents of the First Session of the Twenty-second Congress: Together with an Appendix, Containing Important State Papers and Public Documents, and the Laws, of a Public Nature, Enacted during the Session: With a Copious Index to the Whole*, vol. 8 (Washington, D.C.: Gales & Seaton, 1833), 645; Harper, *Letter from Gen. Harper*, 18–19.

Thomas Jefferson believed that colonizing black Americans would help prevent race war in the United States. (The Art Archive/Superstock)

averred, "To labour in this work" of colonization "is to co-work with God."[7] (See "Speech of Samuel Hopkins, 1793," on page 147 in the Primary Sources section.)

---

[7] Harper, *Letter from Gen. Harper*, 19, 20; *The Debates and Proceedings in the Congress of the United States; with an Appendix, Containing Important State Papers and Public Documents, and All the Laws of a Public Nature; with a Copious Index. Fifteenth Congress—First Session* (Washington, D.C.: Gales & Seaton, 1854), 1771; James Madison to Robert J. Evans, June 15, 1819, in Rakove, *James Madison: Writings*, 729; Journal of the Convention of the Protestant Episcopal Church of Virginia, May 14, 1819, in *The Second Annual Report of the American Society for Colonizing the Free People of Colour in the United States*, 2nd ed. (Washington, D.C.: Davis and Force, 1819), 103.

Several colonizationists began to regard American slavery as a blessing in disguise. Although not a supporter of colonization *to Africa,* former president Jefferson mused in 1811 that black Americans transplanted there might "carry back to the country of their origin, the seeds of civilization, which might render their sojournment here a blessing." "The establishment of a colony on the coast of Africa, which may introduce among the aborigines the arts of a cultivated life, and the blessings of civilization and science," Jefferson later observed, ". . . may make to them some retribution for the long course of injuries we have been committing on their population." The Reverend Ebenezer Burgess similarly deemed colonization "a work of humanity and retributive justice to the African race," a vehicle to right a wrong. In a speech he delivered at the founding of the American Colonization Society, Henry Clay posited that the return to Africa of former slaves improved through their exposure to civilization and Christianity in the United States expunged to some degree the "moral debt" due that continent. For many white observers, colonization at least partly excused America's culpability for slavery.[8] (See "Speech of Henry Clay, 1816," on page 148 in the Primary Sources section.)

Another advantage of colonization was its potential to suppress the ongoing transatlantic slave trade. Although U.S. participation in the international slave trade ended by law in 1808, the clandestine smuggling of human cargoes from Africa into the South continued. Ships laden with slaves also departed Africa bound for other slaveholding societies, in the West Indies and Latin America. Burgess considered the reduction or abolition of the traffic in slaves one of the greatest possible benefits of the establishment of a free black colony on the African coast. From such an outpost, vigilant patrols could work to exterminate the slave trade. (See "Speech of Ebenezer Burgess, 1818," on page 149 in the Primary Sources section.) The colony could simultaneously become a valuable trading partner of the United States in a more legitimate commerce. "In this benefit our own nation would most largely participate,"

---

[8] Thomas Jefferson to John Lynd, January 21, 1811, in *Second Annual Report,* 107; Thomas Jefferson to Jared Sparks, February 4, 1824, in *Speech of Thomas J. Randolph,* 20; Ebenezer Burgess, *Address to the American Society for Colonizing the Free People of Colour of the United States* (Washington, D.C.: Davis and Force, 1818), 31.

Harper explained, "because we having founded the colony, and giving it constant supplies of new members, as well as its first and principal supply of necessaries and comforts, its first connexions would be formed with us." With time, the economic relationship between the United States and its free black colony "would naturally grow" and "[ripen] into fixed habits of intercourse[,] friendship and attachment."[9]

"THE idea of finding an asylum for an oppressed people in the land of their fathers is humane and . . . noble, commending itself to the sympathy of the philanthropist, and the benevolence of the Christian," Burgess declared.[10] For him and others, humanitarian motives inspired support for the great national project of colonization. Founding a colony in Africa would provide free blacks the right to self-government and other opportunities denied people of color in the United States. By creating a refuge for emancipated slaves, colonization would encourage manumissions, promote the moral improvement of Africa, and suppress the transatlantic slave trade. Proponents of colonization denied accusations that they callously desired only to expel black Americans from the United States, stressing that removal was not compulsory but entirely voluntary. Nevertheless, for many white supporters, racial animosity and fears of free blacks' deleterious influences on slaves factored into their support for colonization.

The Case that Colonization Outside the United States by Black Americans Was Not a Good Idea

Many Americans, both white and black, strongly objected to colonization. They frequently cited practical reasons for their opposition, such as the exorbitant costs of removal and the impossibility of meaningfully reducing the black population. The overwhelming majority of free people of color themselves preferred to remain in their American home, refusing to abandon their enslaved brethren. If free blacks feared that their departure would more firmly entrench the institution of slavery, some southern slaveholders believed the opposite—that colonization was the first step to the complete eradication of slavery. Arrestingly, joining those southern planters in rejecting colonization

---

[9] Harper, *Letter from Gen. Harper*, 19.
[10] Burgess, *Address*, 5.

were northern radical abolitionists, who insisted upon the immediate emancipation of American slaves and their incorporation in society on terms of equality with whites. The anti-colonization movement produced strange bedfellows.

The most basic charge anti-colonizationists levied against plans for removal was that such schemes were "impracticable." Necessary expenses mounted quickly when repatriating free people of color to Africa. The costs of transport were only the beginning; emigrants must also be provisioned for up to a year as they established themselves in their new home. In addition, many masters insisted upon compensated emancipation, in which they were paid the market value of any bond people they manumitted for relocation. The tally quickly ran into the millions of dollars. Demographic realities did nothing to reduce the cost. Birthrates among African Americans exceeded death rates. At most, colonization could reasonably remove only a small fraction of the annual increase of the black population, much less the free black population in its entirety. As one critic put it, "The whole navy and revenue of the United States would not suffice to transport the blacks of this country one half so fast as they increase in the natural way." The vast sums required to effect colonization especially disappointed those who saw removal as a possible means of making inroads against the institution of slavery. Even proponents of colonization such as Daniel Raymond, an antislavery Marylander, cautioned his like-minded allies not to "deceive ourselves" into clinging to the "fallacious hope" that colonization could extirpate "the curse of slavery from our soil." Given the limited financial resources of the American Colonization Society, he wrote, "It is not possible . . . to colonize the whole, or any considerable portion of the black population of this country." The expectation that colonization could produce the gradual abolition of slavery in the United States, he conceded, was "utterly chimerical."[11]

Colonization met with widespread disapproval in the free black community. Some free people of color initially showed interest in colonization, but, by 1817, the vast majority had rejected the idea. Although misinformation led some to fear their compulsory expulsion,

---

[11] Marcus [Joseph J. Blunt], *An Examination of the Expediency and Constitutionality of Prohibiting Slavery in the State of Missouri* (New York: C. Wiley, 1819), 13; Daniel Raymond, *The Missouri Question* (Baltimore: Schaeffer & Maund, 1819), 5, 7.

even voluntary colonization was not an idea that first emanated from the free black community. Like committees of free people of color throughout the North and Upper South, prosperous sailmaker James Forten and other free black Philadelphians voiced strong objections to relocation proposals. Most free blacks had no particular attachment to Africa. They had been born in America; some had even fought for national independence in the American Revolution. For most, colonization unfairly banished black Americans from their home in the United States. To be sure, free blacks did not enjoy

James Forten (The Granger Collection, New York)

all the rights of citizenship in all parts of the country, but they nevertheless preferred to stay rather than to risk the alternative overseas. Many questioned the motives lurking behind plans for removal. They viewed the American Colonization Society with suspicion, as a racist, surreptitiously proslavery organization controlled by southern masters. As the furtive tool of slaveholders, the ACS was not founded for benevolent purposes, many free blacks alleged, but rather for serving whites' selfish ends. Former slave Frederick Douglass described colonization bluntly as "the bastard spawn of prejudice."[12]

Simultaneously, colonization seemed to many free blacks as a slaveholder plot to tighten the shackles of bondage around those who remained enslaved. Masters would compel reduced slave workforces to complete all the tasks once performed by those transported, thus exacerbating the oppression, exploitation, and suffering of bond people left on the plantation. Slaveholders would benefit financially because the economic law of supply and demand dictated that the monetary value of slaves still in bondage would necessarily increase. If there were fewer slaves, each remaining slave would become that much more valuable.

---

[12] Quoted in David A. Copeland, comp., *The Antebellum Era: Primary Documents on Events from 1820 to 1860* (Westport, Conn.: Greenwood Press, 2003), 45.

Forten's committee of free black Philadelphians, however, vowed not to abandon their enslaved brethren. They remained loyal to their family members, friends, and counterparts in slavery and refused to betray them by consenting to colonization schemes. (See "Address of James Forten, 1817," on page 149 in the Primary Sources section.) Early reports that the unhealthful climate of Liberia doomed black emigrants to disease and death further heightened free blacks' resolve in opposition to colonization.

Many white abolitionists in the North initially embraced colonization as a means of gradually eradicating slavery, but, by the 1830s, they determined to reject it. The overwhelming numbers of free blacks who shunned colonization opened white abolitionists' eyes to its impracticality and, more importantly, its immorality. Free black James Forten convinced abolitionist William Lloyd Garrison, a onetime backer of the ACS, to abandon his support for the organization by 1830. Garrison reached the conclusion that slavery was inherently sinful. Nothing, he wrote, "can justly make one individual the slave of another." Hence, the ACS "shamelessly surrenders the claims of justice."[13] To Garrison, colonization tacitly condoned slavery and excused slaveholders for holding people as property. Garrison thus condemned the ACS as an immoral institution. Rather than expel blacks from the United States slowly, over time, why not free them now and uplift them here? Eschewing gradual abolition via colonization, Garrison and the radical abolitionists of the 1830s instead demanded the immediate emancipation of slaves and their welcome as equal members into American society. The free black readers of Garrison's abolitionist newspaper the *Liberator* applauded his public denunciations of colonization as an accurate reflection of their views. Upholding a vision of racial equality in a society freed from the curse of slavery, Garrison and his American Anti-Slavery Society, founded in 1833, adopted an anti-colonizationist stance.

Much of the criticism radical abolitionists of the 1830s levied against the ACS stemmed from the organization's apparent bias against people of

---

[13] William Lloyd Garrison, *Thoughts on African Colonization: or an Impartial Exhibition of the Doctrines, Principles and Purposes of the American Colonization Society. Together with the Resolutions, Addresses and Remonstrances of the Free People of Color* (Boston: Garrison and Knapp, 1832; reprint, New York: Arno Press and the New York Times, 1968), 70.

color. ACS annual reports and the ACS-published *African Repository* frequently described America's free black population as "vicious," "miserable," and "corrupt, depraved and abandoned"; as a "nuisance," a "curse and contagion," and even the "morbid excrescence from the body politic."[14] A British abolitionist writing under the pseudonym *Clericus* pondered how such debased free blacks could be expected to civilize and uplift Africans. It appeared obvious to radical abolitionists that claims of colonization's power to benefit the African continent, exterminate slavery, or suppress the transatlantic slave trade were mere pretense to camouflage a slaveholder plot to expel an undesirable segment of the population from the United States. According to abolitionist Elizur Wright, Jr., "The Colonization Society basely slanders the whole body of the free people of color. It makes them a degraded, vicious, incurably besotted class, who not only never can rise, but never can *be raised,* and are properly to be got rid of." But, Wright countered, "The negroes are none the less men, nor are they the less Americans on account of their color."[15] Radical abolitionists understood racial prejudice as both a cause and an effect of colonization. Prejudice inspired colonization, which in turn perpetuated prejudice. To break the vicious cycle, white antipathy toward black Americans must be overcome. Treating African Americans as equals and not inferiors, revising discriminatory laws, providing access to education, and consulting free blacks and respecting their own wishes and desires for their futures were places to start. Abolitionist William Jay urged his readers to pursue the only truly Christian course by attacking the root causes of racial prejudice. (See "William Jay, *An Inquiry into the Character and Tendency of the American Colonization, and American Anti-Slavery Societies,* 1834," on page 151 in the Primary Sources section.)

For reasons uniquely their own, a portion of southern slaveholders joined free blacks and abolitionists in resisting colonization schemes.

---

[14] William Jay, *Inquiry into the Character and Tendency of the American Colonization, and American Anti-Slavery Societies,* 6th ed. (New York; R. G. Williams, 1838; reprint, Miami: Mnemosyne, 1969), 18; Joseph Cooper, *Strictures on Dr. Hodgkin's Pamphlet on Negro Emancipation and American Colonization. [From "The Imperial Magazine" for July 1833.]* (London: H. Fisher, R. Fisher, and P. Jackson, 1833), 5.

[15] Clericus, *Facts Designed to Exhibit the Real Character and Tendency of the American Colonization Society* (Liverpool: Egerton Smith and Co., 1833), 16; Elizur Wright, Jr., *The Sin of Slavery, and Its Remedy; Containing Some Reflections on the Moral Influence of African Colonization* (New York: Printed for the author, 1833), 32, 25.

Colonization remained on the table for many masters, especially in Upper South states such as Virginia, into the early 1830s and beyond. In the Lower South, however, opposition mounted. South Carolina supplied the most vociferous attacks upon plans for removal. Senator Robert Y. Hayne argued that the American Colonization Society was covertly "hostile" to the South because some of its members favored the eventual abolition of slavery. (See "Speech of Robert Y. Hayne, 1827," on page 152 in the Primary Sources section.) The ACS might begin by transporting free blacks, he feared, but that was only a prelude to the repatriation of southern slaves. Masters committed to slavery had no desire to rid the South of its bond people, and any efforts to colonize slaves infringed on slaveholders' property rights to their chattel. Slave owners were especially threatened by the prospect of federal funding for the ACS. When the ACS petitioned Congress for federal monies in 1827, Senator Hayne leapt to the defense of his planter constituency. Hayne believed colonization the exclusive preserve of the states. The U.S. government, he proclaimed, possessed no constitutional authority to appropriate federal funds for any "wild, impracticable, or mischievous" plan of relocation. His apprehension that the colonization of free blacks paved the way for the removal of southern slaves was evident. It was also an irresponsible use of the public treasury. If the government became a major purchaser of slaves as part of a federal program of compensated emancipation, Hayne continued, it would interfere with the slave market and drive prices lower. Colonization would also exert a detrimental effect on "contented, happy, and useful" southern slaves by "disquieting their minds" and "creating dissatisfaction." The result would bring "ruin on the whole community." Most ominously for Hayne, federal involvement in colonization would set a precedent that permitted the national government to tamper with slavery as an institution. "The only safety of the Southern States," Hayne insisted, "is to be found in the want of power on the part of the Federal Government to touch the subject at all. Thank God, the Constitution gives them no power to engage in the work of colonization, or to interfere with our institutions."[16] Beginning in the 1820s, South Carolina repeatedly threatened to secede from the United States if colonization was implemented with federal dollars. Individually, states lacked the resources

---

[16] *Register of Debates in Congress*, vol. 3, 328, 289.

to relocate their black populations, but federal funding of colonization jeopardized national unity.

The interests of some slaveholders, radical abolitionists, and free blacks peculiarly coincided in their mutual antipathy toward colonization. Not that their rejection of colonization made them allies in any conventional sense. Removal was fraught with very different meanings: To masters, colonization threatened the institution of slavery; to abolitionists, removal condoned and preserved the institution; and to free blacks, it magnified the severity of bondage and increased the suffering of the enslaved. Despite approaching the subject of colonization from vastly different perspectives, the three groups arrived at a common conclusion, their shared hostility to colonization.

OUTCOME AND IMPACT

Colonization did not meet with a great deal of success. In the American Colonization Society's first dozen years of existence, fewer than 3,000 black Americans resettled in Liberia. Among the more famous emigrants was John Brown Russwurm, coeditor of the African-American–owned and –operated abolitionist newspaper *Freedom's Journal*, who gradually warmed to the idea of colonization and departed for Liberia in 1829. Every glowing report of thriving conditions and possibilities on the African coast, however, was countered by stories of pestilence and death. In total, the ACS repatriated only 12,000 or 13,000 people of color to Liberia by 1867. Approximately 6,000 of these were slaves whose emancipations were predicated upon removal. These figures are infinitesimally small considering the 229,000 free blacks and 1.5 million slaves who lived in the United States in 1820. The free black population alone increased by more than 80,000 between 1820 and 1830. By comparison, the ACS repatriated a total of between 15,000 and 17,000 black Americans throughout the entire 19th century. Other colonization societies added a few thousand more emigrants, but no more than 20,000 black Americans reached Liberia by century's end.

By 1830, colonization already appeared an increasingly moribund solution to America's perceived racial dilemma. Funding for removal was always an issue, and with each passing year, the growth of the black population made relocation seem a more unrealistic option. In 1831, however, the rebellion of the slave Nat Turner in Southampton County, Virginia, revived interest in the colonization movement. Many white Virginians believed that for their own safety, they ought to expel free blacks—a population believed to generate unrest among slaves—from the state. In late 1831, 350 blacks from Southampton County relocated to Liberia, but no mass exodus ensued. Thanks to the slave rebel Nat Turner, colonization remained popular among Virginia whites after it fell out of favor elsewhere in the South. Scattered voices from the Upper South states of Virginia, Maryland, and Kentucky continued to press for colonization long after Deep South states had forsaken the idea.

Despite the obstacles any proposal faced, colonization persisted tenaciously in the public imagination. Abraham Lincoln endorsed colonization in speeches he delivered in the 1850s. When Democrats charged Lincoln's Republican Party, which opposed the extension of slavery into the western territories, with supporting racial equality and race mixing, Lincoln responded that "the only perfect preventative of amalgamation" was "separation of the races." Although the Republican Party platform did not formally embrace colonization as a means to achieve segregation, Lincoln considered the removal of blacks the best antidote to the perceived horrors of "amalgamation."[17] Among African Americans, Martin R. Delany emerged midcentury as a major proponent of black emigration and colonization. Hostile to the ACS yet personally aware of the struggles of black Americans, Delany investigated possible locations for blacks to settle in Africa and elsewhere. He himself moved to Canada in the mid-1850s before returning to the United States to participate in the Civil War.

The idea of colonization persevered even after the Union victory over the Confederacy and the Thirteenth Amendment's abolition of slavery in 1865. Although black Americans briefly enjoyed rights and freedoms denied them under slavery, with the conclusion of Radical Reconstruction by 1877, freed people in the United States confronted disfranchisement, growing segregation, economic hardship, and increased dangers of racial violence and lynching at the hands of white mobs. Deteriorating conditions for southern blacks suggested

---

[17] Abraham Lincoln, *Speeches and Writings 1832–1858: Speeches, Letters, and Miscellaneous Writings: The Lincoln-Douglas Debates* (New York: Library of America, 1989), 402.

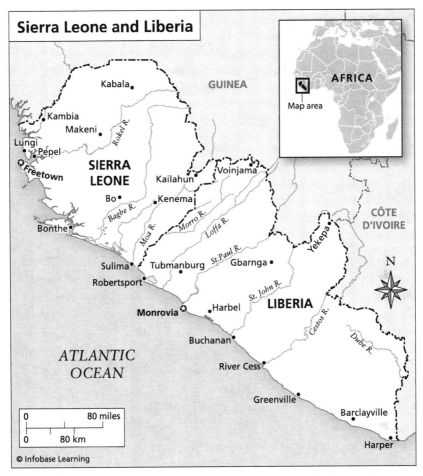

In West Africa, Sierra Leone and Liberia both became colonies for former slaves.

the impossibility of achieving genuine equality in the United States and piqued renewed interest in emigration to Africa. By that time, the independent black nation of Liberia had become a source of racial pride for African Americans, and small numbers proved both willing and able to relocate. Arkansas contributed more black emigrants to Liberia in the late 19th century—600—than any other southern state. Southern black interest in African colonization declined after the 1890s, and, by the early 20th century, the American Colonization Society had essentially dissolved (although not formally until 1963). Nevertheless, the Jamaican-born black nationalist Marcus Garvey continued to champion the back-to-Africa movement in the 1910s and 1920s. Garvey entered the United States in 1916 and three years later founded the Black Star Line of steamships in part to facilitate the transport of emigrants to Liberia. Soon thereafter, he was charged with mail fraud in his efforts to attract investors. Garvey was convicted and imprisoned for almost three years until pardoned by President Calvin Coolidge in 1927 and deported to Jamaica. In total, serious attempts to colonize black Americans in Africa spanned more than one and one-quarter centuries.

WHAT IF?

What if large numbers of black Americans had been colonized outside the United States?

To begin with, the colonization of black Americans abroad faced formidable obstacles. Any attempt to transport free blacks from the United States and establish them in West Africa presented both a fiscal challenge and a logistical nightmare. It is not surprising that the Liberian experiment failed to meet the optimistic expectations of the American Colonization Society (ACS). Had the ACS somehow managed to relocate the entirety of the U.S. free black population—a task that would have required a massive outpouring of federal funds—the demographic landscape of the United States would have changed substantially. Almost 230,000 free people of color lived in the United States in 1820. Their absence would have been most notable in Maryland, Virginia, Pennsylvania, and New York, the four states with the highest free black populations. Generally relegated to the performance of unskilled, menial tasks, free blacks did work that was valuable to the growing nation. In their absence, the country would have relied more heavily on white, working-class immigrants such as the Irish to fill the void. But the "race problem" would not have been resolved. In antebellum America, not all people who appeared physically white, such as the Irish, were automatically granted all the benefits of whiteness. They faced prejudice and discrimination, too. The ongoing presence of slaves in the South would have continued to feed the pervasive antiblack racism among whites as well.

Had antislavery forces somehow seized control of the ACS and miraculously dispatched the entire U.S. black population, slave and free, to Liberia, American history appears almost unimaginably different. Under a scenario without slaves, the Civil War and, consequently, Reconstruction probably could have been averted. In the absence of black Americans, there would have been no Civil Rights movement as we understand it. These were defining events, however, that taught

Americans much about themselves. White Americans' racial thinking might never have evolved if isolated from contact with blacks. Furthermore, a wholesale expulsion of people of color to Liberia in the antebellum decades would have deprived the United States of future generations of black talent and accomplishments.

Greater ACS success might also have proven detrimental to the emigrants to Liberia as well as to the indigenous peoples of the area. Black Americans found hunger, sickness, and death awaiting them in Liberia. Approximately 20 percent of the first emigrants quickly succumbed; mortality rates among emigrant children were even higher. Though aware of the deaths, the ACS continued to funnel emigrants into disease-prone locations. Repatriated blacks fortunate enough to survive clashed with the indigenous peoples of the region, sometimes violently. Ethnic rivalries and tensions between African-American settlers and native Africans ran deep. Coastal tribes resented the loss of their lands to the newcomers, often through coerced purchase. Black emigrants identified themselves as Americans, distinct from the Africans they encountered. They assumed the leadership positions in government, segregated themselves from native groups, and denied the indigenous people citizenship and other rights. Mutual hostility belied the prediction that black colonists would introduce "civilization" and Christianity to Africa. A more massive influx of black emigrants would probably only have magnified the troubles for the colonists and their reluctant hosts.

CHRONOLOGY

1787   Great Britain sends blacks to Sierra Leone in West Africa.

1792   Former slaves freed during the American Revolution arrive in Sierra Leone via Nova Scotia.

1800   Gabriel's conspiracy is discovered in Virginia.

1801   Governor James Madison writes to President Thomas Jefferson about colonization.

1808   The British government makes Sierra Leone a colony.

1816   The American Colonization Society is organized.

1821   American Colonization Society agents acquire land in West Africa.

1822   The first free people of color from the United States arrive in Liberia.

1827   Ezekiel Chambers and Robert Y. Hayne debate colonization in the U.S. Senate.

1831   William Lloyd Garrison publishes the first issue of *The Liberator.*

Nat Turner's slave rebellion erupts in Southampton County, Virginia.

A total of 350 blacks from Southampton County, Virginia, relocate to Liberia.

1832   The Virginia House of Delegates decides against gradually emancipating the state's slaves.

1833   Parliament abolishes slavery in the British Empire through a program of compensated emancipation.

1847   Liberia declares its independence.

1862   The United States grants diplomatic recognition to Liberia.

DISCUSSION QUESTIONS

1. Why might some black Americans in the early republic have favored colonization abroad? Why might some prove reluctant to participate in various colonization schemes?
2. What do you believe most strongly motivated members of the American Colonization Society to send free blacks and emancipated slaves to Africa? Is it more accurate to describe the ACS as antislavery or proslavery? Benevolent or racist? Why?
3. How valid were the reasons for supporting colonization to Africa? How valid were the reasons for opposing it?
4. How "fair" was colonization to free people of color living in the United States? Did it have their best interests in mind?
5. How realistic were proposals for African colonization? Under what circumstances, if any, could colonization have resulted in the ultimate eradication of slavery?

WEB SITES

Burrows, C. Patrick. "African Americans to Liberia, 1820–1904." Available online. URL: http://www.liberianrepatriates.com. Accessed May 25, 2010.

Library of Congress. "The African-American Mosaic," Resource Guide for the Study of Black History & Culture. Available online. URL: http://www.loc.gov/exhibits/african/afam002.html. Accessed April 23, 2010.

Public Broadcasting Service. "American Colonization Society," Africans in America, Resource Bank. Available online. URL: http://www.pbs. org/wgbh/aia/part3/3p1521.html. Accessed April 23, 2010.

BIBLIOGRAPHY

Barnes, Kenneth C. *Journey of Hope: The Back-to-Africa Movement in Arkansas in the Late 1800s.* Chapel Hill: University of North Carolina Press, 2004. A study of black colonization in late 19th-century Arkansas.

Beyan, Amos J. *African American Settlements in West Africa: John Brown Russwurm and the American Civilizing Efforts.* New York: Palgrave Macmillan, 2005. A biographical study of one of the most influential African Americans involved in the colonization movement.

Burin, Eric. *Slavery and the Peculiar Solution: A History of the American Colonization Society.* Gainesville: University Press of Florida, 2005. Explores the leadership of the American Colonization Society, its supporters, and its detractors and profiles individual emigrants to Liberia. Suggests that colonization destabilized slavery on a local basis.

Clegg, Claude A., III. *The Price of Liberty: African Americans and the Making of Liberia.* Chapel Hill: University of North Carolina Press, 2004. Studies more than 2,000 black emigrants from North Carolina to Liberia and the considerable difficulties they encountered there.

Staudenraus, P. J. *The African Colonization Movement, 1816–1865.* New York: Columbia University Press, 1961. The classic monograph on the colonization movement and the American Colonization Society.

Tyler-McGraw, Marie. *An African Republic: Black and White Virginians in the Making of Liberia.* Chapel Hill: University of North Carolina Press, 2007. Examines the important roles played by Virginians in the history of colonization.

PRIMARY SOURCES

1. Letter, James Madison to Robert J. Evans, 1819

Former president James Madison believed that any emancipation of American slaves must be gradual and contingent upon colonization. He favored a program of compensated emancipation, funded through sales of

public lands in the West, to reimburse masters for the value of manumit-
ted slaves. In the following excerpt of a letter he wrote on June 15, 1819,
Madison expressed his opinion that racial animosity between whites and
blacks in American society necessitated the removal of people of color.

To be consistent with existing and probably unalterable prejudices in the
U.S. the freed blacks ought to be permanently removed beyond the region
occupied by or allotted to a White population. The objections to a thorough incorporation of the two people are, with most of the Whites insuperable; and are admitted by all of them to be very powerful. If the blacks,
strongly marked as they are by Physical & lasting peculiarities, be retained
amid the Whites, under the degrading privation of equal rights political
or social, they must be always dissatisfied with their condition as a change
only from one to another species of oppression; always secretly confeder-
ated agst. the ruling & privileged class; and always uncontroulled by some
of the most cogent motives to moral and respectable conduct. The character of the free blacks, even where their legal condition is least affected by
their colour, seems to put these truths beyond question. It is material also
that the removal of the blacks be to a distance precluding the jealousies &
hostilities to be apprehended from a neighboring people stimulated by the
contempt known to be entertained for their peculiar features; to say nothing of their vindictive recollections, or the predatory propensities which
their State of Society might foster. Nor is it fair, in estimating the danger
of Collisions with the Whites, to charge it wholly on the side of the Blacks.
There would be reciprocal antipathies doubling the danger.

Source: Jack N. Rakove, ed., *James Madison: Writings* (New York: Library of
America, 1999), 728–729.

---

2. Letter, Robert Goodloe Harper to Elias B. Caldwell, 1817

Pro-colonization politician Robert Goodloe Harper wrote to Elias B.
Caldwell, secretary of the American Colonization Society, on August 20,
1817. Harper noted the immutable hostility between blacks and whites in
the United States as well as free blacks' corrupting influence upon slaves.

You may manumit the slave, but you cannot make him a white man. He
still remains a negro or a mulatto. The mark and the recollection of his
origin and former state still adhere to him; the feelings produced by that
condition, in his own mind and in the minds of the whites, still exist; he is

associated by his colour, and by these recollections and feelings, with the class of slaves; and a barrier is thus raised between him and the whites, that is between him and the free class, which he can never hope to transcend. . . .

Such a class must evidently be a burden and a nuisance to the community; and every scheme which affords a prospect of removing so great an evil, must deserve to be most favourably considered.

But it is not in themselves merely that the free people of colour are a nuisance and burden. They contribute greatly to the corruption of the slaves, and to aggravate the evils of their condition, by rendering them idle[,] discontented and disobedient. This also arises from the necessity under which the free blacks are, of remaining incorporated with the slaves, of associating habitually with them, and forming part of the same class in society. The slave seeing his free companion live in idleness, or subsist, however scantily or precariously, by occasional desultory employment, is apt to grow discontented with his own condition, and to regard as tyranny and injustice the authority which compels him to labour. Hence he is strongly incited to elude this authority, by neglecting his work as much as possible, to withdraw himself from it altogether by flight, and sometimes to attempt direct resistance. . . . Such is the tendency of that comparison which the slave cannot easily avoid making, between his own situation and that of the free people of his own colour, who are his companions, and in every thing, except exemption from the authority of a master, his equals.

Source: Robert Goodloe Harper, *A Letter from Gen. Harper, of Maryland, to Elias B. Caldwell, Esq. Secretary of the American Society for Colonizing the Free People of Colour. In the United States. With Their Own Consent* (Baltimore: R. J. Matchett, 1818), 8–10.

—៳—

3. Speech of Ebenezer Burgess, 1818

In the following excerpt of an address to the American Colonization Society (ACS) in 1818, Massachusetts clergyman and ACS agent Ebenezer Burgess lamented the widespread white prejudice against black Americans. In his mind, whites' responsibility for blacks' degradation in American society obligated them to aid free people of color.

The elevation of the character of the free people of colour, who are now in this country, is another inducement to their colonization in Africa.—They have not here a fair opportunity to show themselves men. Their minds are, in some degree, shackled from childhood. They have not the same motives to improvement, nor the same encouragement to honourable exertion, as others born in this land. Their debasement and subordination can afford us no pleasure. The principal ground of their inferiority is acknowledged to be a matter of prejudice. But the time when colour will not be a ground of prejudice in this country, is not near. A distinction, then, painful and injurious to them, and no source of pleasure to us, will for a long period be inseparable from their residence with us. Having in some sense been accessory to this state of things, we ought to be willing, and are willing, to assist some of them to change their condition.

Source: Ebenezer Burgess, *Address to the American Society for Colonizing the Free People of Colour of the United States* (Washington: Davis and Force, 1818), 27–28.

—ᴍ—

4. Letter, Robert Goodloe Harper to Elias B. Caldwell, 1817

In the same letter of August 20, 1817, to American Colonization Society secretary Elias B. Caldwell cited previously, Robert Goodloe Harper pointed out the benefits of colonization for slaves who remained in bondage.

To the slaves the advantages, though not so obvious or immediate, are yet certain and great.

In the first place they would be greatly benefited by the removal of the free blacks, who now corrupt them, and render them discontented: thus exposing them to harsher treatment, and greater privations. In the next place, this measure will open the way to their more frequent and easier manumission: for many persons who are now restrained from manumitting their slaves, by the conviction that they generally become a nuisance when manumitted in the country, would gladly give them freedom, if they were to be sent to a place where they might enjoy it, usefully to themselves and to society. And lastly, as this species of manumission, attended by removal to a country where they might obtain all the advantages of freedom, would be a great blessing, and would soon be so considered by the slaves, the hope of deserving and obtaining it would be a great solace to their sufferings, and a powerful incitement to good conduct. It would thus tend to make them happier and better before it came, and to fit them better for usefulness and happiness afterwards.

Source: Robert Goodloe Harper, *A Letter from Gen. Harper, of Maryland, to Elias B. Caldwell, Esq. Secretary of the American Society for Colonizing the Free People of Colour. In the United States. With Their Own Consent* (Baltimore: R. J. Matchett, 1818), 18–19.

—〰—

5. Speech of Samuel Hopkins, 1793

New Englander and Congregationalist minister Samuel Hopkins was counted among the earliest proponents of colonization. The clergyman saw colonization as instrumental to benevolent missionary activity in Africa. In the following selection from a speech he delivered at a Baptist church in Providence, Rhode Island, on May 17, 1793, Hopkins expressed his optimism that freed American slaves could return to Africa to spread Christianity.

We may hope, that all this dark and dreadful scene will not only have an end, but is designed by the Most High to be the mean[s] of Introducing the gospel among the nations in Africa: that those who have embraced the gospel, while among us, with all who have been or may be in some good measure civilized and instructed, will, by our assistance, return to Africa, and spread the light of the gospel in that now dark part of the world; and propagate those arts, and that science, which shall recover them from that ignorance and barbarity which now prevail, to be a civilized, Christian and happy people, making as great improvement in all useful knowledge, and in the practice of righteousness, benevolence and piety, as has yet been done by any people on earth, and much greater. Thus all this past and present evil which the Africans have suffered by the Slave-Trade, and the slavery to which so many of them have been reduced, may be the occasion of an over-balancing good: and it may hereafter appear, as it has in the case of Joseph being sold a slave into Egypt, and the oppression and slavery of the Israelites by the Egyptians, that though the Slave-Traders have really meant and done that which is evil, yet God has designed it all for good, the good of which all this evil shall be the occasion.

OUGHT not this prospect to animate us earnestly to pray for such an happy event, and to exert ourselves to the utmost to promote it? Can we be indifferent and negligent in this matter, without slighting and disobeying the command of Christ, to go into all the world, and preach the gospel to every creature? And will not such an attempt to send the gospel to Africa, being willing to spare no expence or labour thus to spread the knowledge of the Saviour among the nations there, be a proper expression of our love and regard to this benevolent, important injunction?

Source: Samuel Hopkins, *A Discourse upon the Slave-Trade, and the Slave of the Africans Delivered in the Baptist Meeting-House at Providence, Before the Providence Society for Abolishing the Slave-Trade, &c. At Their Annual Meeting, on May 17, 1793* (Providence: J. Carter, 1793), 18–19.

—⁓—

6. Speech of Henry Clay, 1816

Kentucky slaveholder and statesman Henry Clay was instrumental in the organization of the American Colonization Society (ACS). Clay delivered a speech, excerpted here, at the meeting founding the ACS in 1816. In it, he suggested that the benefits accruing to Africa from the colonization of black Americans in some measure expunged the United States' moral responsibility for slavery. At the same time, Clay's hostile sentiments toward free blacks were evident.

Various schemes of colonization had been thought of, and a part of our own continent, it was supposed by some, might furnish a suitable establishment for them. But . . . he had a decided preference for some part of the coast of Africa. There ample provision might be made for the colony itself, and it might be rendered instrumental to the introduction, into that extensive quarter of the globe, of the arts, civilization and Christianity. There was a peculiar, a moral fitness in restoring them to the land of their fathers. And if, instead of the evils and sufferings which we had been the innocent cause of inflicting upon the inhabitants of Africa, we can transmit to her the blessings of our arts, our civilization and our religion, may we not hope that America will extinguish a great portion of that moral debt which she has contracted to that unfortunate continent? . . . Can there be a nobler cause than that which, whilst it proposes to rid our own country of a useless and pernicious, if not dangerous portion of its population, contemplates the spreading of the arts of civilized life, and the possible redemption from ignorance and barbarism of a benighted quarter of the globe!

Source: James F. Hopkins, ed., *The Papers of Henry Clay,* vol. 2 (Lexington: University of Kentucky Press, 1961), 263–264.

—⁓—

7. Speech of Ebenezer Burgess, 1818

The Reverend Ebenezer Burgess supported colonization for religious and humanitarian motives. In the following portion of a speech to the American Colonization Society in 1818, Burgess expressed his hope that the establishment of a free black colony on the African coast would suppress the slave trade's ongoing traffic in human beings.

A colonization of the free people of colour of the United States in Africa will operate, in several ways, directly against this trade. It will take away its grand temptation with the native princes and people by introducing those articles of foreign produce and manufacture, to which they have become accustomed, and have few means of obtaining except by the sale of slaves. It may lead some of our vessels to engage in an honourable trade along the coast. It may be found convenient that some of our armed ships should occasionally visit stations on that continent. The people of colour themselves, taught in the school of experience, will surely exert their influence by persuasion, example and instruction to effect its ruin. Though a single colony could not look far up or down the coast, yet a few colonies like Sierra Leone would do much to guard the coast. Colonization may be regarded as one principal means, by which this scourge of Africa will be destroyed, this blot of humanity washed away, for ever.

Source: Ebenezer Burgess, *Address to the American Society for Colonizing the Free People of Colour of the United States* (Washington, D.C.: Davis and Force, 1818), 27.

―៣៣―

8. Address of James Forten, 1817

Prosperous free black businessman James Forten of Philadelphia briefly supported colonization. But at an 1817 meeting of 3,000 African Americans held at Philadelphia's Bethel Church, Forten and other people of color cataloged their objections to colonization and approved publication of the address excerpted here.

The free people of color, assembled together, under circumstances of deep interest to their happiness and welfare, humbly and respectfully lay before you this expression of their feelings and apprehensions. . . .

It is . . . with painful solicitude, and sorrowing regret, we have seen a plan for colonizing the free people of color of the United States on the coast of Africa, brought forward under the auspices and sanction of gentlemen whose names give value to all they recommend, and who certainly are among the wisest, the best, and the most benevolent of men, in this great nation.

If the plan of colonizing is intended for our benefit; and those who now promote it, will never seek our injury; we humbly and respectfully urge, that it is not asked for by us. . . .

We, therefore, a portion of those who are the objects of this plan, and among those whose happiness, with that of others of our color, it is intended to promote; with humble and grateful acknowledgments to those who have devised it, renounce and disclaim every connexion with it; and respectfully but firmly declare our determination not to participate in any part of it.

If this plan of colonization now proposed, is intended to provide a refuge and a dwelling for a portion of our brethren, who are now held in slavery in the south, we have other and stronger objections to it, and we entreat your consideration of them. . . .

If the emancipation of our kindred shall, when the plan of colonization shall go into effect, be attended with transportation to a distant land, and shall be granted on no other condition; the consolation for our past sufferings and of those of our color who are in slavery, which have hitherto been, and under the present situation of things would continue to be, afforded to us and to them, will cease for ever. The cords, which now connect them with us, will be stretched by the distance to which their ends will be carried, until they break; and all the sources of happiness, which affection and connexion and blood bestow, will be ours and theirs no more. . . .

To those of our brothers, who shall be left behind, there will be assured perpetual slavery and augmented sufferings. Diminished in numbers, the slave population of the southern states, which by its magnitude alarms its proprietors, will be easily secured . . . [Only] the tame and submissive will be retained, and subjected to increased rigor. Year after year will witness these means to assure safety and submission among their slaves, and the southern masters will colonize only those whom it may be dangerous to keep among them. The bondage of a large portion of our brothers will thus be rendered perpetual. . . .

We humbly, respectfully, and fervently entreat and beseech your disapprobation of the plan of colonization now offered by "the American Society for colonizing the free people of color of the United States."

Source: Scott J. Hammond, Kevin R. Hardwick, and Howard Leslie Lubert, eds., *Classics of American Political and Constitutional Thought,* vol. 1 (Indianapolis: Hackett, 2007), 951–953.

—⁊⁊—

9. William Jay, *An Inquiry into the Character and Tendency of the American Colonization, and American Anti-Slavery Societies,* 1834

The son of the statesman and first chief justice of the United States John Jay, William Jay was active in the abolitionist movement. He published a book-length investigation critical of colonization in 1834. In the brief portions reprinted here, Jay attacked colonization on religious grounds.

The tone of these extracts is very different from that used when the speaker desires to excite sympathy for the wretched. We are told that these people are vicious and debased, but no hint is given that their vice and debasement are the result of sinful prejudices and cruel laws.—No appeal is made to the spirit of Christianity to pour oil and wine into the wound of suffering humanity. We are not reminded that these wretches are our brethren for whom Christ died. Nothing is omitted to impress us with a sense of the depth of the misery into which they are plunged; but for what object are these frightful pictures presented to us? Is it to urge us to feed the hungry, to clothe the naked, to instruct the ignorant, and to reform the wicked! No, but to transport them to Africa!

To an unsophisticated Christian it would seem that the true way of relieving the wretchedness and vice of these people would be, first to protest against their unrighteous oppression, and to procure the repeal of those laws which forbid their instruction; and then to make them partakers of the blessings of education and religion. But far from the Colonization Society are all such old fashioned ways of doing good. Instead of protesting against the causes of all this misery, THE SOCIETY EXCUSES AND JUSTIFIES THE OPPRESSION OF THE FREE NEGROES, AND THE PREJUDICES AGAINST THEM. . . .

To the Christian members of the society, we would now address ourselves, and ask, have we not *proved* enough to induce you to pause, to examine, and to pray, before you longer lend your names, and contribute your funds to the purposes of Colonization? Do no secret misgivings of conscience now trouble you; and are you perfectly sure that in supporting the society, you are influenced by the precepts of the Gospel, and not by prejudice against an unhappy portion of the human family? If on a full investigation of the subject, you discover that Colonization is not what you believed and hoped it was, remember that it is your duty to obviate, as far as possible, by a frank and open declaration of your opinion, the evil your example has done. Be not ashamed . . . in entering your protest against the society. If that society leads to the degradation and oppression of the poor colored man—if it resists every effort to free the slave—if it misleads the conscience of the slaveholder, you are bound, your God requires you to oppose it, not in secret, but before the world. Soon will you stand at the judgment seat of Christ; there will you meet the free negro, the slave, and the master—take care lest they all appear as witnesses against you.

Source: William Jay, *An Inquiry into the Character and Tendency of the American Colonization, and American Anti-Slavery Societies,* 6th ed. (New York: R. G. Williams, 1838; reprint, Miami: Mnemosyne, 1969), 19, 124.

—⟨⟨⟨—

10. Speech of Senator Robert Y. Hayne, 1827

The American Colonization Society petitioned Congress in early 1827 for federal funding to aid African colonization. Senator Ezekiel Chambers of Maryland spoke in support of the measure, but South Carolina senator Robert Y. Hayne offered the following rejoinder on February 9.

The gentleman from Maryland has vindicated the object of the Society. . . . He insists, that it is not the wish or intention of the Society to interfere with, or in any way disturb, the policy of the Southern States. So say the Society. But, sir, facts speak stronger than professions. And what are the facts? Are not the members and agents of this Society every where (even while disclaiming all such intentions) making proclamations that the end of their scheme is universal emancipation? Have we not heard their orators, at their meetings here, openly held under the eyes of Congress, asking whether, when all the free People of Color are transported, we are to stop there; and answering their question, by the avowal that the great work will be but then begun? Sir, let any man examine the whole scope and tendency of the reports and speeches made to this Society, nay, of this very manifesto, published by their authority, and he must be dull of apprehension, if he does not perceive that the spirit which lurks beneath their fair professions, is hostile to the peace and best interests of the Southern States; and not the less so, because it comes clothed in the garb of friendship, and with professions of peace and good will. Besides, sir, does not every Southern man know that, wherever the Colonization Society has invaded our country, a spirit of hostility to our institutions has instantly sprung up?

Source: Register of Debates in Congress, Comprising the Leading Debates and Incidents of the Second Session of the Nineteenth Congress: Together with an Appendix, Containing Important State Papers and Public Documents and the Laws Enacted During the Session, with a Copious Index to the Whole, vol. 3 (Washington, D.C.: Gales & Seaton, 1829), 328.

SLAVERY AND WESTWARD EXPANSION:
Should Slavery Be Restricted in Missouri?

———————

THE CONTROVERSY ————————————————————————————

The Issue

When Missouri applied for admission into the Union in 1819, one congressman proposed amendments to the statehood bill that would prohibit the future introduction of slaves into the state and gradually emancipate those born after statehood was achieved. Should slavery be restricted in Missouri?

- ♦ *Arguments for restricting slavery in Missouri:* Representing the northern states, restrictionists favored the Tallmadge amendments of 1819 that would place prohibitions on slavery in Missouri. They believed the Constitution authorized Congress to accept or reject new territories that applied for union and to impose reasonable conditions for admission. Congress had placed restrictions on territories in the past, including prohibitions against slavery. Placing restrictions on slavery and the domestic slave trade to Missouri was therefore consistent with historical precedent. Slavery itself violated cherished republican principles, and its extension into Missouri would perpetuate the institution and discourage northern settlement there. A Missouri filled with slaves was inconsistent with the founders' vision for the United States.

- ♦ *Arguments against restricting slavery in Missouri:* Overwhelmingly from the South, anti-restrictionists opposed any form of federal interference on the slavery question in Missouri. They denied that Congress had the constitutional authority to limit slavery there. Doing so would attack the principles of states' rights by violating Missouri's sovereignty. The United States was also under a contractual obligation to honor the treaty with France that gave Missouri to the United States. Any restriction on slavery also impinged on masters' rights to slave property. If the emancipation of slaves was a commendable goal, the diffusion of slavery into Missouri would help accomplish that end because masters would more likely liberate smaller quantities of slaves than large masses of them.

—ᴠᴠ—

INTRODUCTION

In 1819, Missouri was preparing to join the United States when the Tall-madge amendments, sponsored by Representative James Tallmadge, Jr., of New York, proposed a prohibition on the introduction of additional slaves into Missouri and the gradual emancipation of slaves born after statehood was achieved. The issue of slavery in Missouri forced Congress to reconsider significant issues the founders had struggled with in crafting the Constitution. The Missouri controversy raised questions about whether slavery was compatible with republican government, whether the nation had a proslavery or antislavery past, and whether the United States was destined to be an "empire for liberty" or an "empire for slavery." Northern congressmen invested power in the federal government's ability to restrict slavery in Missouri, while their southern colleagues—the vast majority of all antirestrictionists—upheld the principles of states' rights. The Missouri controversy fundamentally reoriented American politics away from an East-West divide that had been evident as recently as the War of 1812 and made it more appropriate than ever to speak accurately of a free North and a slave South.

Northern restrictionists supported the Tallmadge limits on Missouri slavery. They had every confidence that the Constitution let Congress decide whether or not to admit a territory or to set requirements for admission. Congress had already limited slavery in an entire region of the country, so it must also have the authority to prohibit new slaves from entering Missouri. The prospect of a slaveholding Missouri undermined restrictionists' republican notions of equality and threatened to exclude northern whites, who eschewed settling in the midst of slaveholders and their slaves. Without restrictions, Missouri would open a new market for bond people, encourage the domestic slave trade, and subvert antislavery efforts to secure emancipation. The admission of Missouri presented Congress an opportunity to right the wrongs of the past.

Anti-restrictionists challenged the Tallmadge prohibitions on slavery in Missouri. They expressed a limited interpretation of federal power in which the national government had no right to infringe on the rights of the states to determine their own laws. Congress could not constitutionally legislate for the sovereign state of Missouri. Already, they said, a treaty signed with France obligated admitting Missouri to the Union with rights equal to those of the existing states. The property rights of masters were also at stake. Congress could not deprive them of their property without violating the Constitution. According to the anti-restrictionists, if their opponents truly had slaves' humanitarian interests in mind, the best course was to allow for the diffusion of slavery into Missouri. The reduced concentrations of slaves would allow them to enjoy better material conditions and facilitate emancipation by their masters. For all of these reasons, southerners worked to defeat the Tallmadge restrictions.

BACKGROUND

For more than three decades, the constitutional compromises on slavery endured with remarkably little contention between states where slavery persisted and those where it was a dead or dying institution. The question of Missouri's entrance into the Union, however, unleashed partisan rancor along a predominantly geographic line. Missouri had been carved out of the Louisiana Purchase, a vast, triangular-shaped piece of land in the West, between the Mississippi River and the Rocky Mountains. The United States roughly doubled in size when it purchased Louisiana from France for $15 million in 1803. The Louisiana Territory had a long colonial history, governed alternatively by Spain and France. For centuries, slavery had been legal there, and when the Orleans Territory, the southernmost portion of the Louisiana Purchase, joined the United States in 1812, it became the slave state of Louisiana. Farther north, upstream from Louisiana, lay Missouri. When a northern congressman suggested that slavery be restricted there, he ignited a sectional controversy with potentially catastrophic repercussions. (See the sidebar "The Louisiana Purchase" on page 158.)

During an 1819 discussion in the U.S. House of Representatives over a bill authorizing the people of the Missouri Territory to begin writing a state constitution, James Tallmadge, a one-term Democratic-Republican representative from New York, proposed amendments prohibiting "the further introduction of slavery or involuntary servitude" into Missouri and emancipating at age 25 slaves born after Missouri's admission into the Union. (See "Tallmadge Amendments, 1819," on page 179 in the Primary Sources section.) Tallmadge's recommendations were rather modest in scope, similar to the gradual emancipation plans already implemented in many northern states. Although they barred new slaves from entering Missouri, those currently living there—some 10,000, or 16 percent of the territorial population—could remain enslaved. No slaves born in Missouri before 1820 would be freed, and those born after that date would only be manumitted slowly, over time. Masters would retain the right to sell their slaves prior to emancipation, if they so chose.

What inspired Tallmadge's measures? It might have been his own moral opposition to slavery. Tallmadge had previously opposed Illinois statehood for its constitution's lax antislavery provisions, and he had also labored in support of New York's final emancipation act of 1817. The answer may also be political. Some northerners in the early republic chafed under the constitutional compromise that allotted slaveholding states additional representation in the House for three-fifths of their slaves. The extra representation that slaveholding states gained had important ramifications outside Congress, in the selection of the president. Constitutionally, a state's number of presidential electors was determined by adding together the state's number of senators (in all cases, two) and the state's number of representatives. Slaveholding states claimed disproportionate leverage in choosing presidents because a bonus three-fifths of their slaves counted in determining the size of their delegation in the House. It seemed no accident to many northerners that the slave state of Virginia exerted a stranglehold on the presidency, claiming as native sons four of the first five presidents and holding the office for 32 of the nation's first 36 years. Restricting slavery in Missouri and arranging for the institution's ultimate demise would have the effect of reducing southern political power.

Southerners saw the situation differently. Approximately 2.1 million more free whites lived in the North than in the South in 1820. Despite the additional congressmen the three-fifths compromise bestowed, representatives from slaveholding states composed a minority of all House members, and the disparity was growing. Outnumbered in the House of Representatives, slaveholding states insisted on maintaining political parity with the North in the Senate, where each state had equal

THE LOUISIANA PURCHASE

The Louisiana Purchase of 1803 laid the groundwork for the Missouri controversy. Louisiana, encompassing a vast territory west of the Mississippi River and east of the Rocky Mountains, had a complex colonial history. While England established settlements along the Atlantic seaboard in the 1600s, the French laid claim to the Mississippi River valley and the North American interior. The French and Indian War that erupted in 1754 can be understood in part as an imperial contest between France and Great Britain for control of the North American continent. In 1763, the defeated French surrendered their claims to all of that country's North American mainland possessions. French lands east of the Mississippi transferred to Britain; those west of the Mississippi were ceded to Spain.

With the conclusion of the American Revolution in 1783, the boundary of the United States extended westward to the Mississippi. Spain, controlling the opposite bank of the river, provoked a crisis in the young nation in the 1780s by sealing off the Mississippi and the port of New Orleans to American commerce. Access to river transportation was crucial to the settlement of the trans-Appalachian West. A general lack of infrastructure in the United States required that farmers who settled in the Ohio River valley send crops to market via water rather than by land, over the rugged terrain separating them from coastal ports. With no outlet for their crops, American farmers would have little incentive to settle there. The administration of George Washington negotiated Pinckney's Treaty with Spain in 1795 to ensure free navigation of the Mississippi River and the right to enter New Orleans.

representation. For southerners, this meant admitting a slave state for every free state that entered the Union. At the time the Missouri statehood bill first went before Congress, the United States contained 11 free states and only 10 slave states. The recent addition of Illinois as a free state in 1818 (albeit with protections for the state's existing slaveholders and toleration of various forms of servitude) had tipped the balance in favor of the North. Most southerners naturally assumed that Missouri would enter the Union as a slave state.

By secret treaty in 1800, however, Spain returned the Louisiana Territory to France. Thomas Jefferson, inaugurated president in 1801, was concerned. With France supplanting Spain as the United States' neighbor to the west, Pinckney's Treaty guaranteeing American access to the Mississippi, negotiated with Spain, was moot. Always a friend of the independent American farmer, Jefferson sought an agreement with France that would guarantee continued free navigation of the Mississippi. He dispatched ambassador Robert R. Livingston to France in 1801. Authorized only to buy the city of New Orleans, the gateway to the Mississippi, Livingston was stunned when France offered to sell the United States all of Louisiana.

Ruling France, Napoléon Bonaparte might have had many different reasons for selling Louisiana. He understood the difficulties that accompanied the possession of colonial holdings in the Americas. In the 1790s, black slaves in the French Caribbean colony of Saint-Domingue had risen up in rebellion, overthrown French rule, and eventually created the independent black republic of Haiti. Napoléon's failure in his attempt to retake Haiti might have convinced him of the futility of maintaining an Atlantic empire and caused him to abandon his designs for Louisiana. Napoleon's ambitions focused more on Europe, where he was engaged in intense warfare. France's far-flung military exploits meant that Napoléon was strapped for cash. All of these considerations might have factored into France's unexpectedly generous proposal that would double the size of the United States for $15 million (less than $290 million in today's dollars). Although the precise boundary of the Louisiana Territory was ill defined, the terms agreed upon with France made its purchase a bargain, at roughly three cents per acre. In October 1803, the U.S. Senate voted to ratify the treaty acquiring Louisiana by a margin of 26 to 6.

For the South, a Missouri safe for slavery was not only politically but also economically necessary. More than 1.5 million slaves inhabited the United States in 1820. Growing numbers of them were producing the cash crop of cotton, rapidly becoming the country's single most important export. The rising demand for slave-grown cotton after the War of 1812 roughly doubled the price of enslaved field hands between 1814 and 1819. Depleted lands in the South Atlantic states were becoming gradually less productive, however, and slaveholders looked west for more

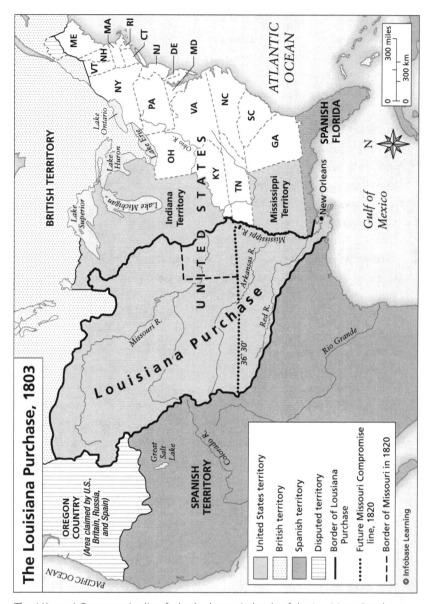

The Louisiana Purchase, 1803

The Missouri Compromise line forbade slavery in lands of the Louisiana Purchase north of the 36°30' line, Missouri excepted.

fertile, virgin soils. Missouri seemed promising. Masters ventured to Missouri with more than 10,000 slaves, anticipating healthy profits.

When Representative Tallmadge proposed restrictions on slavery, then, he ignited a debate more heated and contentious than he probably could have imagined. In both the House and the Senate, restrictionists and antirestrictionists exchanged arguments justifying their positions. Compared to discussions of slavery in later decades, those concerning the Tallmadge amendments proved remarkably substantive, with most grounded firmly in interpretive disagreements over various provisions of the Constitution. (See "Excerpts from the U.S. Constitution, 1787," on page 180 in the Primary Sources section.) Although slavery was already an emotionally laden issue, and passions on the subject were evident, little of the debate revolved around the morality or immorality of slavery. The North took the lead in agitating against slavery, but in 1819, even most southerners continued to speak of bondage as a "necessary evil," an institution regrettably inherited from their ancestors. The presence of slaves, they said, was the unfortunate by-product of past mistakes, but what could they do? To liberate their slaves and send them out into the world would be cruel. It would be best to hold on to their slaves until a safe, effective means of emancipation could be achieved. Not until after the Missouri crisis, in the late 1830s, did southern politicians rally to defend slavery as a "positive good"—a benefit to the nation, the South, and even the slave. The Missouri question nonetheless evinced a southern willingness to defend the institution of slavery more fully than ever. South and North alike formulated multifaceted responses to the central political question the Tallmadge amendments inspired: Should slavery be restricted in Missouri?

THE DEBATE

The Case that Slavery Should Be Restricted in Missouri

Representing northern states, restrictionist forces in Congress hoped to pass the Tallmadge amendments and limit the power of slavery in Missouri. Their leading spokesmen in the House of Representatives included William Plumer of New Hampshire, John W. Taylor of New York, Timothy Fuller of Massachusetts, and both Joseph Hemphill and John Sergeant of Pennsylvania. In the Senate, Rufus King of New York led the restrictionists, joined by Jonathan Roberts of Pennsylvania and others. (See the sidebar "Rufus King" on page 164.) They marshaled an array of arguments in their favor, most of them based directly on the U.S. Constitution. Congress maintained the authority, they said, to impose rules on the territories, set conditions for admission to statehood, and create an environment conducive to settlement by those opposed to slavery. Humanitarian arguments, though present, played a secondary role in restrictionists' appeals. The restrictionists invoked all arguments at their disposal in the prolonged battle over the fate of slavery in Missouri.

Article IV, Section 3, of the U.S. Constitution states that "New States may be admitted by the Congress into this Union." For restrictionists such as Plumer, the key word in that clause was *may*. Congress reserved the exclusive power to admit new states to the Union and could do so at its own discretion. Nothing and no one could compel Congress to admit a state if the House and Senate opposed it. Article IV, Section 3, furthermore bestows upon Congress the power "to make all needful Rules and Regulations" for a U.S. territory. Taylor and King maintained that, constitutionally, Congress exercised unlimited sovereignty over American territories. (See "Speech of Representative John W. Taylor, 1819," and "Speech of Senator Rufus King, 1819," on pages 181 and 183 in the Primary Sources section.) They therefore insisted that Congress had the right to impose reasonable conditions upon a territory for admission to statehood. In fact, during negotiations at the Constitutional Convention in 1787, the founders had struck out a clause stating that new states must be admitted "on the same terms with the original states." Since a given territory was free to accept or reject the terms Congress set, Plumer explained, the process marked no violation of sovereignty. Refusal meant continued territorial status but did not preclude the possibility of statehood at some future date.

Taylor, Fuller, and other restrictionists observed that historical precedent supported conditional admission. When Louisiana—like Missouri, carved out of the Louisiana Purchase—became a state, Congress mandated that the state guarantee religious freedom, establish the writ of habeas corpus, provide trials by jury, and record judicial and legislative proceedings in the English language. That such features were unfamiliar in Spanish and French colonial Louisiana convinced Congress of the need to impose those requirements for statehood. Although Congress made no restriction against slavery in Louisiana, it did so elsewhere. As Taylor, Hemphill, and Sergeant all pointed out, in 1787 the Confederation Congress prohibited slavery in the Northwest Territory, which included the future states of Ohio, Indiana, and Illinois. The first Congress under the Constitution affirmed the

Northwest Ordinance, with the support of slaveholding states such as Virginia. When Ohio entered the Union in 1803, Congress mandated that its constitution uphold the ordinance's antislavery prohibition. It set similar terms for Indiana and Illinois. Thus, argued the restrictionists, by the time Missouri applied for statehood, conditional admission was commonplace. The language of the Tallmadge amendments simply mirrored that which had already restricted slavery in the Old Northwest.

Those seeking to restrict slavery in Missouri pointed to Congress's authority under Article I, Section 9, to prohibit "Migration or Importation" as early as 1808. Fuller was not alone in maintaining that *importation* and *migration* both referred to slaves. Under Article I, Section 9, Congress had already terminated the country's legal *importation* of slaves via the transatlantic slave trade in 1808, the earliest possible date permitted by the Constitution. According to Fuller, the same clause also authorized Congress to end the *migration* of slaves—their movement from one state to another, whether in company with their masters or through the internal, domestic slave trade. Preventing the further introduction of slaves into Missouri was therefore constitutional.

In Article IV, Section 4, the Constitution also "guarantee[s] to every State . . . a Republican Form of Government." Fuller, Roberts, and other restrictionists charged that slavery and republican government were utterly incompatible. No government that permitted slavery could properly be construed as republican, because republican governments granted rights to their citizens. Restrictionists conceded that they could not eradicate slavery where it already existed. They had to tolerate slavery in the South because that concession had been made for the sake of union at the Constitutional Convention, and emancipating slaves now threatened whites' safety in the slaveholding states. But, Fuller argued, slavery should only be permitted in states existing at the time the Constitution was ratified. The further expansion of slavery into new states such as Missouri violated republican principles and should be prohibited.

Permitting slavery in Missouri, restrictionists observed, would deter northerners from settling there. In debating the Tallmadge amendments, Taylor traced the outlines of a free labor ideology. Northern farmers and laborers would avoid a state infested with slaves because slavery degraded labor. No white person would want to work if work

RUFUS KING

Rufus King was a prominent statesman whose distinguished career spanned the late 18th and early 19th centuries. A native of the Massachusetts district of Maine, King served in the Confederation Congress in the 1780s and represented Massachusetts at the Constitutional Convention, signing his name on the resulting document. He relocated to New York City in 1788 and remained active in New York politics throughout the remainder of his life. A member of the Federalist Party, King lost several races for high political office in the early 1800s to the ascendant Jeffersonian Republicans. He was the losing Federalist vice-presidential candidate in 1804 and 1808 and suffered defeat by Virginia Republican James Monroe in the presidential election of 1816. That same year, he also ran an unsuccessful campaign for the governorship of New York. King fared much better in contests for the U.S. Congress, representing his adopted state as senator from 1789 to 1796 and again between 1813 and 1825. In the Senate, he chaired, successively, the Committee on Roads and Canals and the Committee on Foreign Relations.

Even though it was a Democratic-Republican who proposed the Tallmadge amendments, the Federalist King was arguably their most avid supporter in the Senate chamber. He viewed the Constitution's three-fifths compromise as a temporary measure applicable only to the original slave states. Any extension of the agreement to new slave states unfairly bestowed undeserved political power on the South at the expense of northern whites.

Some contemporary political observers alleged that the Missouri controversy was a plot manufactured to install Rufus King as president and revive the fortunes of the moribund Federalist Party to which he belonged.

was associated with slaves. It would be manifestly unfair, Taylor argued, to effectively seal off Missouri to settlement by the masses of honorable, hardworking white northerners. Justice required that Missouri remain free and open to all.

Restrictionists such as Fuller noted that the expansion of slavery also meant the survival of the institution. The extension of slavery into Missouri would open a new market for slaves in the West, thereby substantially increasing the monetary value of slaves. Masters who might otherwise have considered emancipating their slaves would refuse for

The Federalists, concentrated in the New England states, had long opposed westward expansion because western farmers tended to vote for their Democratic-Republican opponents. As a party, Federalists had objected to the Louisiana Purchase, and a few had even suggested secession from the Union to form a northern confederacy. They had also opposed the War of 1812. When the United States claimed victory in that conflict in 1815, King's party was further discredited. In 1820, the Federalist Party effectively ceased to exist, not even advancing a presidential candidate to challenge the reelection of James Monroe. Certainly in 1819, when the Missouri crisis erupted, the Federalists were in severe decline and in need of resuscitation. As a general rule, northern Republicans were the strongest proponents of the Tallmadge amendments. Nevertheless, King lent his Federalist voice to the restrictionist cause and considered the Missouri Compromise a tremendous defeat.

In 1825, shortly before leaving the Senate to retake the post of U.S. minister to Great Britain that he had held between 1796 and 1803, King proposed a plan to divert revenues from the sale of public lands in the West to fund the emancipation and colonization of slaves. King had been a longtime foe of colonization schemes, and his plan had virtually no chance of passing, but it offered him a satisfying parting shot at the South as he ended his senatorial career. King's proposal echoed one presented by Thomas Jefferson, whose name politicians from the South often invoked as the exemplar of the antislavery southern man. In rejecting King's proposal, southerners were forced to rebuke Jefferson, their native son. Satisfied that he had shrewdly embarrassed his southern colleagues, King departed the Senate. He died on Long Island, New York, in 1827, at the age of 72.

reasons of pecuniary gain. Rather than liberate their slaves, they would put them up for sale at auction. Restrictionists cautioned that free blacks might even be abducted and sold into bondage for the sake of profit. Because slavery was not yet deeply entrenched in Missouri, it need not be tolerated there as in the more established states. Now was the time to institute restrictions. As Representative Plumer eloquently explained in support of slavery's restriction, it would be "ungenerous and unjust . . . to extend to our brethren [in Missouri] . . . the bitter ingredients of our own poisoned chalice. . . . Never was hope more fallacious than that of lessening permanently the evils of slavery in the *old* states, by extending them to the *new*."[1]

Although it was not the major focus of the argument against slavery in Missouri, Plumer, his fellow New Hampshire representative Arthur Livermore, Fuller, and other restrictionists did comment on the sinfulness of slavery, its immorality, and its inhumanity. Fuller took the Declaration of Independence at its word that "all men are created equal." (See "Speech of Representative Timothy Fuller, 1819," on page 185 in the Primary Sources section.) Plumer feared that a Missouri opened to slavery would encourage the domestic slave trade, which ruthlessly severed familial ties between enslaved husbands and wives and parents and children. The offensive commerce in bond people would accelerate to fill the lands beyond the Mississippi River. The perceived need for slaves in Missouri might even encourage the illicit smuggling of slaves into the United States from abroad in violation of laws prohibiting the transatlantic slave trade. Restricting slavery in Missouri would reduce the abominable traffic in human flesh, afford politicians the prospect of correcting the mistakes of the past, and strike a blow against slavery. If, as most slaveholding southerners agreed, slavery was a "necessary evil," an unfortunate inheritance from their forefathers, Missouri presented the opportunity to act on those sentiments, to put principles into practice, and to obliterate the greatest stain on the national character.

Some restrictions saw the effort to weaken the institution of slavery in Missouri as a fulfillment of the promises of the preamble to the Constitution. Slavery, Plumer argued, did not "form a more perfect Union, establish Justice, insure domestic Tranquility, provide for the common defence, promote the general Welfare, and secure the Blessings of Liberty." To the contrary, it undermined each of those vaunted goals. Indeed, Plumer observed, slavery created a domestic enemy within the nation's borders and raised the specter of slave insurrection, violating the U.S. government's guarantee in Article IV, Section 4, to protect against "domestic Violence." Restricting slavery in Missouri would make the state, as well as the entire nation, safer than if the peculiar

---

[1] William Plumer, *Speech of Mr. Plumer, of New-Hampshire, on the Missouri Question: Delivered in the House of Representatives of the United States, February 21, 1820* (N.p.: n.p., 1820), 28.

institution persisted there. The greater threat to the country was the continuation of slavery in Missouri, not its limitation.

The Case that Slavery Should Not Be Restricted in Missouri

New York representative James Tallmadge's proposed amendments to the Missouri bill in 1819 unexpectedly placed slaveholding states in a position to defend slavery. Although not alone, a host of Virginians who included Senator James Barbour and Representatives Philip P. Barbour, Alexander Smyth, (the future U.S. president) John Tyler, and the Virginia-born John Scott, the Missouri Territory's delegate to Congress, took up the task. They and other southern politicians had no doubt that the U.S. Constitution protected the peculiar institution. The three-fifths clause, a prohibition against tampering with the international slave trade for 20 years, and a provision for the return of fugitive slaves convinced slaveholding states that the Constitution indeed recognized enslaved property. Southern lawmakers contended that restrictionist arguments resulted from creative, self-serving readings of the Constitution, too clever by half. Slaveholders and their political allies countered with arguments favoring the extension of slavery into Missouri. They scrambled to issue point-by-point rebuttals to the restrictionists' charges. What resulted was not the finely honed proslavery defense that would eventually emerge beginning in the 1830s but a series of arguments that challenged the constitutional authority of Congress to restrict slavery in Missouri.

Some vague wordings in the Constitution invited multiple, conflicting interpretations of several different clauses. Anti-restrictionists clashed with their opponents, for example, over the meaning of the provisions of Article I, Section 9, regarding "Migration or Importation" after 1808. Whereas restrictionists considered the terms *importation* and *migration* roughly synonymous in referring to slaves, anti-restrictionists vested the words with discrete meanings. They agreed with the restrictionists that importation related to slaves and that Congress had constitutionally prohibited American participation in the transatlantic slave trade effective on the first day of 1808. They denied, however, that *migration* applied to the domestic slave trade, because migration implied voluntary action. Slaves did not "migrate," because they were forcibly removed by their masters to new lands. Virginia brothers James Barbour and Philip P. Barbour joined Delaware senator Nicholas Van Dyke in maintaining that the term *migration,* juxtaposed with *importation,* referred to free foreigners or freemen rather than slaves. Because Article I, Section 9, discussed "admitting" persons, anti-restrictionists assumed that the Constitution was discussing people entering the country from abroad, whether slave or free, since it would be strange to speak of someone's being "admitted" into one state from another.

Anti-restrictionists also denied that Congress had any authority to impose conditions as prerequisites for admission into the Union. According to the two Barbour brothers, Missouri territorial delegate John Scott, and others, the constitutional provision in Article IV, Section 3, which explained that "New States may be admitted by the Congress into this Union," sanctioned only an up-or-down vote on statehood. The *may* implied only a yes or no. Adding conditions overstepped the power granted Congress in the Constitution.

Imposing conditions would violate Missouri's sovereignty as a state. According to Article IV, Section 2, of the Constitution, "The Citizens of each State shall be entitled to all Privileges and Immunities of Citizens in the several States." Representative Smyth and other antirestrictionists interpreted these words to mean that new states added to the Union must enjoy exactly the same rights as the existing states. (See "Speech of Representative Alexander Smyth, 1820," on page 186 in the Primary Sources section.) The Tallmadge proposals would permanently restrict slavery in Missouri, robbing current and future generations of citizens of that state of the ability to decide for themselves the fate of slavery within its bounds. As migrants from other parts of the United States, the citizens of Missouri had every right to determine whether slavery would be allowed there. In states where slavery had been eradicated, anti-restrictionists observed, it occurred because state legislatures, not the federal government, passed laws against it. Those same assemblies, they insisted, could legislate slavery back into existence if they chose. In contrast, the Tallmadge amendments deprived Missourians of such options. The legal shackling of Missouri would be discriminatory and deny it the "Privileges and Immunities" enjoyed by other states. Stripped of its rights, Missouri would be transformed into a pale, feeble imitation of a state. Congress's failure to respect the will of the people of Missouri would furthermore send the nation down the slippery slope of tyranny. If Congress took away Missouri's right to decide on slavery, what other rights might Congress deprive it of? If Congress regulated slavery in Missouri, might it seek to prevent slavery elsewhere in the trans-Mississippi West? Or attempt to abolish slavery in states where the institution was long established?

Smyth, Philip P. Barbour, Scott, and Van Dyke all believed that the unequal treatment of Missouri violated the very principles of republican government. The Constitution limited Congress's power over Missouri. Although anti-restrictionists conceded Congress's right to legislate for the territories, they observed that, if implemented, the Tallmadge amendments would apply to Missouri once it entered the Union as a state. Congress, however, lacked authority over states other than to guarantee them "a Republican Form of Government," as stated in Article IV, Section 4. Forcing a state to prohibit additional slaves hardly seemed republican. States must maintain sovereignty over their own affairs, for, according to the Tenth Amendment, "The powers not delegated to the United States by the Constitution, nor prohibited by it to the States, are reserved to the States respectively, or to the people." Anti-restrictionists therefore reasoned that the power to rule on the slave question resided with the states.

The Tallmadge amendments violated not only Missouri's sovereignty, but also, according to Smyth, masters' property rights. Article IV, Section 3, of the Constitution vested Congress with the power to "make all needful Rules and Regulations respecting the . . . Property belonging to the United States." Slaves, however, belonged not to the U.S. government but to individual masters, and the Fifth Amendment prohibits the government from depriving anyone of "property, without due process of law." For Smyth, the Tallmadge amendments represented an assault on masters' private property in slaves. First, they threatened the property rights of those slaveholders who had already carried their slaves into Missouri, unaware that their ownership of them might be endangered. Second, restricting slavery in Missouri would effectively preclude settlement by residents from the southern half of the country. James Barbour noted that the Louisiana Territory, of which Missouri was a part, was purchased with $15 million paid out of the common treasury. It would therefore be unjust to exclude slaveholders from the area. Southerners and northerners should be equally eligible to settle in the state.

But according to the anti-restrictionists, masters would never consider relocating to Missouri without their slaves. James Barbour and others explained that paternalistic ties between master and slave made bond people extensions of the white family to whom they belonged. Enslaved women helped raise white children, black and white youngsters played together in friendship, and masters felt affection for their slaves. Slaves might have been a socially degraded form of property, but masters could not conceivably sever the paternalistic bond with their slaves. Nor could they stand losing their favorite, devoted, faithful bond people. Resettling in Missouri without them was unthinkable. For masters to relocate, they would have to sell off their slaves in violation of the paternalistic obligation to care for them. Hence, the Tallmadge amendments would prevent settlement by slaveholding southerners.

Many anti-restrictionists—James Barbour, Philip P. Barbour, Scott, Smyth, and Van Dyke among them—asserted that Congress was obligated by treaty to admit Missouri without restriction. The third article of the treaty that the United States had signed with France to purchase the Louisiana Territory stipulated that "the inhabitants of the ceded territory shall be incorporated in the union of the United States, and admitted, as soon as possible, according to the principles of the Federal Constitution." As Scott, Philip P. Barbour, and other anti-restrictionists argued, that clause left no room for congressional discretion. States such as Missouri, formed out of the Louisiana Purchase, *shall be incorporated*—free of conditions—and granted all the rights of the existing states. Restricting slavery would mark a breach of a solemn contract with France and potentially invite French diplomatic or military retribution.

Peering into the past, anti-restrictionists found no precedents for prohibitions of slavery in Missouri. James Barbour indicated that Kentucky, Tennessee, and other states were admitted without any restrictions. Louisiana, by contrast, did face restrictions. It was required to guarantee republican government and the freedoms already common elsewhere throughout the Union. But Louisiana was an exceptional case. Its history as the former colony of both Spain and France merited special regulation. According to Philip P. Barbour, Van Dyke, and Smyth, the Northwest Ordinance's prohibition against slavery in 1787 was irrelevant, for several reasons. Barbour argued that because the Confederation Congress passed the Northwest Ordinance, it had no bearing on U.S. policy now that the Constitution was in effect. Others noted that in relinquishing claims on the Northwest to Congress, Virginia agreed with the restriction in advance. Van Dyke pointed to the timing of the ordinance, which took effect before many whites had settled in the region. Migrants to the Northwest understood prior to settlement that slavery was restricted there, whereas in Missouri, the Tallmadge amendments were attempting to change the rules unfairly after settlement had already begun in earnest. In addition, Smyth and other anti-restrictionists insisted that the states in the Northwest—Ohio, Indiana, and Illinois—had been illegitimately denied a choice about slavery and retained the legal right to amend their state constitutions to institute slavery at their discretion. If northern congressmen were truly interested in legislating against slavery, anti-restrictionists observed, they should begin in the District of Columbia, where Congress maintained undisputed sovereignty, as outlined in Article I, Section 8, of the Constitution.

Representative Robert W. Reid of Georgia argued that the diffusion of slaves into new states served the interests of both humanity and safety. (See "Speech of Representative Robert W. Reid, 1820," on page 188 in the Primary Sources section.) James Barbour, Tyler, and Smyth all shared this view. Most southerners in 1819 still spoke of slavery as a necessary evil. By freely extending slavery into Missouri, the slave population would be less concentrated in the slaveholding states, increasing the standard of living for all bond people. Anti-restrictionists furthermore claimed, in stark contrast to their Tallmadge amendment foes, that the smaller numbers of slaves in a state's population encouraged emancipation, as the experience of the northern states in the Revolutionary era bore out. Lower concentrations of slaves had the added benefit of reducing the danger of slave insurrections, ensuring "domestic Tranquility" and providing greater security for the southern white population.

The possible sealing off of Missouri to slavery alarmed southern politicians. Slaveholding state congressmen unleashed an arsenal of arguments to portray the prohibition of slavery as an illegal usurpation of power by Congress. Should Congress adopt the Tallmadge amendments, the ramifications would be profound. The Ohio River already partitioned the United States into slaveholding and nonslaveholding regions. Declaring the Mississippi River a similar boundary would perpetuate sectional division and jeopardize national unity.

OUTCOME AND IMPACT

Missouri's odyssey to statehood spanned two and one-half years. The House of Representatives first engaged the Missouri question in early 1819. On February 15, the House Committee of the Whole voted 79 to 67 in favor of the Tallmadge amendment. The next day, the House divided the amendment into two distinct parts and voted separately on each. It passed the provision prohibiting additional slaves from entering Missouri by a vote of 87 to 76. The provision providing for the "post-nati" emancipation of slaves born after statehood upon reaching age 25 was approved by the narrower margin of 82 to 78. With the Tallmadge amendments successfully appended, the House passed the bill to admit Missouri to statehood and on February 17 sent it to the Senate for approval. Ten days later, after heated debate, the Senate struck out the antislavery amendments, voting against the restriction on the further introduction of slaves 22 to 16 and against the post-nati emancipation of slaves 31 to 7. The increased power of slaveholding states in the Senate, where all states were represented equally, was evident in these votes. In the House, northern states' greater populations gave nonslaveholding states the edge, despite the additional representation slaveholding states gained from the three-fifths compromise. Stripped of the Tallmadge amendments, the bill returned to the House. Representatives opposed the Senate alterations to the bill by a vote of 78 to 66, and the measure failed. When the 15th Congress adjourned on March 4, Missouri remained a territory.

The growth of the United States nevertheless continued unabated. Alabama joined the Union as a slave state in December 1819, again giving slave states and (nominally) free states parity, at 11 apiece. That same month, Maine, at the time a northern portion of Massachusetts despite being geographically separated by the state of New Hampshire, applied for statehood. In January 1820, the House approved Maine's statehood, but in a calculated move, proslavery forces in the Senate, led by Virginia's James Barbour, made the admission of Maine—undoubtedly intending to be a free state—contingent upon the admission of Missouri as a slave state. This amounted to nothing less than political blackmail. Senators from slaveholding states held Maine hostage, using it as a bargaining chip in exchange for the admission of a Missouri with slavery. On February 16, the Senate passed a bill admitting Maine to statehood by a vote of 23 to 21, with the stipulation that slavery face no restrictions in Missouri.

That same day, Senator Jesse B. Thomas, a Maryland native representing the state of Illinois, proposed that slavery be prohibited in the Louisiana Purchase north of the 36°30' line of latitude (Missouri's southern boundary), except in Missouri itself. (See "Thomas Amendment, 1820," on page 189 in the Primary Sources section.) Thomas was not the first congressman to suggest a dividing line between slave and free territory. Almost exactly one year earlier, on February 17, 1819, while debating the organization of the Arkansas Territory, Representative Louis McLane of Delaware recommended that a line be established in the territories, north of which slavery would be outlawed. New York representative John W. Taylor proposed an amendment to the Arkansas Territory bill prohibiting the further introduction of slaves into any territory north of 36°30', which would have excluded Arkansas but included Missouri. Some representatives mocked the idea that an artificial line could possibly divide slave from free. Stiff opposition forced Taylor to withdraw the amendment, and Congress organized Arkansas as a slave territory in 1819. Senator Thomas's suggestion in February 1820, then, merely revived Taylor's year-old idea of restricting slavery north of 36°30', with the noteworthy difference that, under Thomas's proposal, masters could continue to take slaves into Missouri. With the admissions of both Maine and Missouri already linked in congressmen's minds, Thomas's compromise measure surrendered Missouri to slavery but excluded the peculiar institution from other lands of the Louisiana Purchase. The deal passed the Senate on February 17, 1820, 34 to 10.

The Senate version of the Missouri statehood bill faced challenges when it went to the House, which initially defeated it 97 to 76 on February 28. When the Senate refused to budge on the construction of the bill, House leaders broke it up into its constituent parts and voted on them separately. The Thomas amendment, which established the 36°30' Missouri Compromise line, passed the House 134 to 42. Northern representatives approved it 95 to 5; delegates from the South were almost equally divided: 39 in favor, 37 opposed. That measure achieved, the House of Representatives then voted 90 to 87 in favor of admitting Missouri without restrictions on slavery. The Tallmadge amendments were defeated.

Although Maine entered the Union soon thereafter, Missouri statehood met another hurdle. The proposed Missouri state constitution excluded free blacks and mulattoes. Northern congressmen objected to Missouri's restriction preventing free people of color from entering the state, considering it a violation of Article IV, Section 2, of the Constitution, which guarantees that citizens' rights are protected equally in all of the states. Missouri's entry into the Union again appeared in jeopardy, until Representative Henry Clay of Kentucky concocted an agreement sometimes called the Second Missouri Compromise. The obscure language of the compromise measure resolved nothing in reality but had the advantage of letting each side read into it what it wanted. For the North, it seemed to say that Missouri would not act on the controversial provision of its constitution. For the South, the provision remained, suggesting that black Americans were not citizens of the United States. Congress adopted the second compromise, and Missouri entered the Union, belatedly, in August 1821, after a two-and-one-half-year ordeal. No new states would join the Union for another 15 years.

Following the example of the founding generation, congressmen during the Missouri crisis compromised with slavery. The Tallmadge amendments put at the fore a serious constitutional question: Should slavery be allowed to expand into the territories? The question laid bare, once again, the paradox of slavery in a land of freedom by exposing the cracks in the constitutional compromises of 1787. The Missouri controversy unlocked the latent passions surrounding the slavery issue and exacerbated sectional division between North and South. Some contemporary observers shuddered as they watched the country's geographic chasm widen. The Missouri Compromise was designed to reunify a nation under strain. Just as each side of the contest could claim it sacrificed more than the other, it offered features appealing to both. Implicitly conceding the principle that Congress had the right to legislate against slavery in the territories, the South received assurances that slavery would be protected in Missouri and south of 36°30'. Slaveholders could accept the prohibition of slavery west of Missouri because that region of the Great Plains was widely—albeit mistakenly—believed to be the Great American Desert anyway. The North suffered the expansion of slavery but banned it in vast Louisiana Purchase lands west and north of Missouri. The region cordoned off from slavery by the Missouri Compromise was much larger geographically than the

Known as the Great Compromiser, Henry Clay helped negotiate the settlement that made Missouri a slave state in 1821. (© Classic Image/Alamy)

area where slavery was protected, some of it even south of the existing slaveholding states of Kentucky and Maryland. The compromise also admitted the new free state of Maine.

If the Missouri Compromise alleviated sectional tensions for the time being, it was also a precursor, as former president Thomas Jefferson warned, of future controversy. (See "Letter, Thomas Jefferson to John Holmes, 1820," on page 190 in the Primary Sources section.) It led some to redouble efforts to colonize black Americans in Africa and elsewhere. But the 36°30' Missouri Compromise line lasted only until 1854, when it was overturned by the Kansas-Nebraska Act. Three years later, the Supreme Court declared the Missouri Compromise unconstitutional in its infamous *Dred Scott* decision. The Missouri Compromise thus had ramifications for political debates for decades.

WHAT IF?

What if slavery had been restricted in Missouri?

The crisis might have turned out much differently than it did. In the final 90–87 House vote that approved the Missouri statehood bill without restrictions on slavery, representatives from slaveholding states cast their ballots unanimously with the majority. The 87 votes against Missouri's unrestricted admission were all from the North. The North, however, did not demonstrate the same political unity as did the South. Fourteen northern representatives voted with the majority, while four—a sufficient number to change the outcome of the vote—abstained. If only four northern votes had gone the other way (or been cast at all), Missouri would have retained only territorial status. The defeat of the Tallmadge amendments can also be attributed to the three-fifths compromise in the Constitution. Subtract the additional representatives bestowed on the southern states for their slaves, and any Missouri statehood bill permitting slavery would have met with failure.

Odds were against a Missouri statehood bill that included the Tallmadge amendments' passing both houses of Congress. Vote tallies suggest that enough pro-southern sentiment in the Senate precluded that possibility. Had senatorial objections somehow been overcome, Missouri might have accepted statehood with Congress's restrictions on slavery, but it seems unlikely. During the debates in Congress, some suggested that if Missouri accepted statehood under the provisions of the Tallmadge amendments, it could, once admitted to the Union, amend its state constitution to delete the antislavery restrictions in defiance of Congress's limitation. Congressional speeches suggested other, even more ominous, prospects for the future. With masters of 10,000 slaves already residing there, Missouri appeared willing to challenge any prohibitions against slavery. A few voices raised the possibility of Missouri's withdrawing its application for statehood and becoming an independent republic. Others suggested that Missouri settlers might take up their muskets and march to Congress to compel their admission to the Union. At least some slaveholding states, such as South Carolina, might have shown solidarity with Missouri, as threats of disunion flew freely in the halls of Congress. Threats like that issued by Senator James Barbour, that the Missouri crisis might force slaveholding states to secede from the Union, might have been nothing more than political bluster, used for rhetorical effect to impress upon northern congressmen their passionate feelings on the subject of slavery. (See "Speech of Senator James Barbour, 1820," on page 192 in the Primary Sources section.) But, given the subsequent events of 1860 and 1861, they might not have been bluffing. Certainly, the Missouri controversy contained the potential for disastrous consequences, whether or not secession was a realistic possibility. In the unexpectedly poisonous political atmosphere of the early 1820s, most observers agreed that the Missouri Compromise averted a legitimate crisis of union. In the process, however, Congress established a line that perpetuated the sectional division already delineated by the Ohio River.

CHRONOLOGY

1787 The Confederation Congress prohibits slavery in the Northwest Territory.

1803 The United States acquires the Louisiana Purchase through treaty with France.

1819 *Feb. 13:* Rep. James Tallmadge, Jr., of New York proposes restrictions on slavery in Missouri

Dec. 14: Alabama enters the Union as the 22nd state.

1820 *Feb. 16:* Sen. Jesse B. Thomas of Illinois proposes outlawing slavery in the Louisiana Purchase north of the 36°30' line.

Mar. 2: Congress passes the Missouri Compromise.

Mar. 3: President James Monroe signs a bill admitting Maine to the Union.

Mar. 6: President James Monroe signs a bill admitting Missouri to the Union.

Mar. 15: Maine enters the Union as the 23rd state.

1821 Missouri enters the Union as the 24th state.

DISCUSSION QUESTIONS

1. How relevant to the Missouri question was the prohibition in 1787 of slavery in the Northwest Territory?

2. How significant was the timing of Tallmadge's proposal? Should the distinction between a territory and a state have made a difference in determining congressional power over slavery? Why or why not?

3. In the debates over Missouri's admission to statehood, who had the stronger *constitutional* arguments: the proslavery forces or antislavery forces? Why?

4. The North or the South: who gained more from the Missouri Compromise? Why?

5. In what ways was the Missouri Compromise a success? A failure? How did Thomas Jefferson regard it?

WEB SITES

Library of Congress. "A Century of Lawmaking for a New Nation: U.S. Congressional Documents and Debates, 1774–1875," American Memory. Available online. URL: http://memory.loc.gov/ammem/amlaw/lawhome.html. Accessed September 11, 2009.

Library of Congress. "Missouri Compromise," Primary Documents in American History. Available online. URL: http://www.loc.gov/rr/program/bib/ourdocs/Missouri.html. Accessed September 11, 2009.

Library of Congress. "The Thomas Jefferson Papers," American Memory. Available online. URL: http://memory.loc.gov/ammem/collections/jefferson_papers/. Accessed September 11, 2009.

National Archives and Records Administration. "Missouri Compromise," Our Documents: A National Initiative on American History, Civics, and Service. Available online. URL: http://www.ourdocuments.gov/. Accessed September 11, 2009.

BIBLIOGRAPHY

Fehrenbacher, Don Edward. *The South and Three Sectional Crises*. Baton Rouge: Louisiana State University Press, 1980. A compact volume that examines the Missouri controversy, the Wilmot Proviso, and Bleeding Kansas. From the Walter Lynwood Fleming lectures in southern history at Louisiana State University.

Forbes, Robert Pierce. *The Missouri Compromise and Its Aftermath: Slavery and the Meaning of America*. Chapel Hill: University of North

Carolina Press, 2007. Argues that the Missouri crisis moved slavery to the forefront of political debate in the 1820s and reshaped American politics itself by the 1830s. Chapters 2 and 3 focus specifically on the Missouri controversy.

Freehling, William W. *The Road to Disunion*. Vol. 1, *Secessionists at Bay 1776–1854*. New York: Oxford University Press, 1990. A monumental work that devotes only one chapter to the Missouri crisis but examines the episode as one in a series of events that culminated in the Civil War.

Hammond, John Craig. *Slavery, Freedom, and Expansion in the Early American West*. Charlottesville: University of Virginia Press, 2007. Examines the westward expansion of slavery from the 1780s to 1820. Chapters 4 and 8 focus on Missouri. Mississippi, Louisiana, Ohio, Indiana, and Illinois are also covered.

Mason, Matthew. *Slavery and Politics in the Early American Republic*. Chapel Hill: University of North Carolina Press, 2006. Chapter 8 examines the constellation of concerns and arguments the North and South carried into the Missouri controversy and the ways in which they changed as a result of the crisis.

Moore, Glover. *The Missouri Controversy, 1819–1821*. Lexington: University of Kentucky Press, 1953. The classic account of the Missouri crisis, now somewhat dated.

PRIMARY SOURCES

1. Tallmadge Amendments, 1819

On Saturday, February 13, 1819, New York Democratic-Republican representative James Tallmadge, Jr., introduced amendments to a bill authorizing the people of Missouri to write a constitution, create a state government, and enter the Union. His proposals ignited a firestorm of controversy. Debate began in earnest the following Monday.

In the course of the consideration, Mr. TALLMADGE moved an amendment, substantially to limit the existence of slavery in the new State, by declaring all free who should be born in the Territory after its admission into the Union, and providing for the gradual emancipation of those now held in bondage. This motion gave rise to an interesting and pretty wide debate.

The question being on the proposition of Mr. TALLMADGE to amend the bill by adding to it the following proviso: "*And provided,* That the further introduction of slavery or involuntary servitude be prohibited, except for the punishment of crimes, whereof the party shall have been fully convicted; and that all children born within the said State, after the admission thereof into the Union, shall be free at the age of twenty-five years:" The debate which commenced on Saturday was to-day resumed on this proposition.

Source: Annals of the Congress of the United States. Fifteenth Congress.—Second Session (Washington, D.C.: Gales & Seaton, 1855), 1166, 1170.

―⚭―

2. Excerpts from the U.S. Constitution, 1787

The following excerpts from the U.S. Constitution of 1787 were the passages with the most direct bearing on the Missouri question.

Preamble: "We the People of the United States, in order to form a more perfect Union, establish Justice, insure domestic Tranquility, provide for the common defence, promote the general Welfare, and secure the Blessings of Liberty to ourselves and our Posterity, do ordain and establish this Constitution for the United States of America."

Article I, Section 8: "The Congress shall have power . . . To exercise exclusive Legislation in all Cases whatsoever, over such District (not exceeding ten Miles square) as may, by Cession of Particular States, and the Acceptance of Congress, become the Seat of the Government of the United States."

Article I, Section 9: "The Migration or Importation of such Persons as any of the States now existing shall think proper to admit, shall not be prohibited by the Congress prior to the Year one thousand eight hundred and eight."

Article IV, Section 2: "The Citizens of each State shall be entitled to all Privileges and Immunities of Citizens in the several States."

Article IV, Section 3: "New States may be admitted by the Congress into this Union. . . . The Congress shall have Power to dispose of and make all needful Rules and Regulations respecting the Territory or other Property belonging to the United States."

Article IV, Section 4: "The United States shall guarantee to every State in this Union a Republican Form of Government, and shall protect each of them against Invasion; and . . . domestic Violence."

Amendment V: "No person shall . . . be deprived of life, liberty, or property, without due process of law."

Amendment X: "The powers not delegated to the United States by the Constitution, nor prohibited by it to the States, are reserved to the States respectively, or to the people."

—⁂—

3. Speech of Representative John W. Taylor, 1819

Hailing from the same state as James Tallmadge, Jr., Representative John W. Taylor of New York delivered an extensive speech in support of the Tallmadge amendments on Monday, February 15, 1819, just two days after his colleague introduced the proposed restriction on slavery. Taylor's speech laid the groundwork for restrictionists' arguments throughout the Missouri controversy.

First.—Has congress power to require of Missouri a constitutional prohibition against the further introduction of slavery, as a condition of her admission into the Union? Second.—If the power exists, is it wise to exercise it? The third section of the fourth article [of the Constitution] declares that "the congress shall have power to dispose of, and make all needful rules and regulations respecting the territory, or other property, belonging to the United States." . . . Congress . . . has . . . the power of prescribing such conditions of admission as may be judged reasonable. The exercise of this power, until now, has never been questioned. The act of 1802, under which Ohio was admitted into the union, prescribed the condition that its constitution should not be repugnant to the ordinance of 1787. The sixth article of that ordinance declares "there shall be neither slavery nor involuntary servitude in the said territory, otherwise than in the punishment of crimes, whereof the party shall have been duly convicted." The same condition was imposed by congress on the people of Indiana and Illinois. These states have all complied with it and framed constitutions excluding slavery. . . . The same principles of government should be ap[p]lied to it [Missouri]. . . . The sovereignty of congress in relation to the states is limited by specific grants; but in regard to the territories is unlimited. Missouri was purchased with our money; and, until incorporated into the family of states, it may be sold for money. Can it then be maintained that, although we have the power to dispose of the whole territory, we have no right to provide against the further increase of slavery within its limits? . . . No, sir, it cannot. . . . Having proved . . . our right to legislate in the manner proposed, I proceed to illustrate the propriety of exercising it. And here I might rest satisfied with reminding my opponents of their own declarations on the subject of slavery. How often, and how eloquently, have they deplored its existence among them! What willingness, nay, what solicitude have they not manifested to be relieved from this burden! How have they wept over the unfortunate policy that first introduced slaves into this country! How have they disclaimed the guilt and shame of that original sin, and thrown it back upon their ancestors! I have with pleasure heard these avowals of regret and confided in their sincerity; I have hoped to see its effects in the advancement of the cause of humanity. Gentlemen have now an opportunity of putting their principles into practice: if they have tried slavery and found it a curse; if they desire to dissipate the gloom with which it covers their land; I call upon them to exclude it from the territory in question: plant not its seeds in this uncorrupt soil; let not our children, looking back to the proceeding of this day, say of them, as they have been constrained to speak of their fathers, "we wish their decision had been different; we regret the existence of this unfortunate population among us; but we found them here; we know not what to do with them; it is our misfortune, we must bear it with patience." . . . It is . . . objected, that the amendment is calculated to disfranchise our brethren of the south, by discouraging their emigration to the country west of the Mississippi . . . but when we place all on an equal footing, denying to all what we deny to one, I am unable to discover the injustice or inequality of which honourable gentlemen have thought proper to complain. . . . If slavery shall be tolerated, the country will be settled by rich planters, with their slaves; if it shall be rejected, the emigrants will chiefly consist of the poorer and more laborious classes of society. If it be true that the prosperity and happiness of a country ought to constitute the grand object of its legislators, I cannot hesitate for a moment which species of population deserves most to be encouraged by the laws we may pass. . . . If the rejection of slavery will tend to discourage emigration from the south, will not its admission have the same effect in relation to the north and east? . . . Do you believe . . . that these people will settle in a country where they must take rank with negro slaves? Having neither the ability nor will to hold slaves themselves, they labour cheerfully while labour is honorable; make it disgraceful, they will despise it. You cannot degrade it more effectually than by establishing a system whereby it shall be performed principally by slaves. . . . It is considered low, and unfit for freemen.

Source: Papers Relative to the Restriction of Slavery: Speeches of Mr. King, in the Senate, and of Messrs. Taylor & Talmadge in the House of Representatives, of the United States, on the Bill for Authorising the People of the Territory of Missouri to Form a Constitution and State Government, and for the Admission of the Same into the Union: In the Session of 1818–19, with a Report of a Committee of the Abolition Society of Delaware (Philadelphia: Hall & Atkinson, 1819), 14–20.

—☸—

4. Speech of Senator Rufus King, 1819

New York senator Rufus King was among the most outspoken advocates of the Tallmadge amendments in the Senate. In this excerpt from a speech delivered in 1819, he reviewed many of the arguments in favor of the restriction of slavery in Missouri.

The constitution declares "that congress shall have power to dispose of, and make all needful rules and regulations respecting the territory and other property of the United States." . . . The power to make all needful regulations, includes the power to determine what regulations are needful; and if a regulation prohibiting slavery within any territory of the United States be . . . deemed needful, congress possess the power to make the same, and moreover to pass all laws necessary to carry this power into execution. . . . The constitution further provides, that "new states may be admitted by congress into the union."—As this power is conferred without limitation, the time, terms, and circumstances of the admission of new states are referred to the discretion of congress, which may admit new states, but are not obliged to do so. . . . When admitted by congress into the union, whether by compact or otherwise, the new state becomes entitled to the enjoyment of the same rights, and bound to perform the like duties as the other states—and its citizens will be entitled to all privileges and immunities of citizens in the several states.

The citizens of each state possess rights, and owe duties that are peculiar to, and arise out of the constitution and laws of the several states. These rights and duties differ from each other in the different states; and among these differences none is so remarkable or important as that which proceeds from the constitution and laws of the several states respecting slavery;—the same being permitted in some states, and forbidden in others.

The question respecting slavery in the old thirteen states had been decided and settled before the adoption of the constitution, which grants no power to congress to interfere with, or to change what had been so previously settled; the slave states therefore, are free to continue or to abolish slavery. Since the year 1808, congress have possessed power to prohibit and have prohibited the further migration or importation of slaves into any of the old thirteen states; and at all times under the constitution have had power to prohibit such migration or importation into any of the new states, or territories of the United States. The constitution contains no express provisions respecting slavery in a new state that may be admitted into the union; every regulation upon this subject belongs to the power whose consent is necessary to the formation and admission of such state. Congress may, therefore, make it a condition of the admission of a new state, that slavery shall be forever prohibited within the same. We may with the more confidence pronounce this to be the true construction of the constitution. . . .

If congress possesses the power to exclude slavery from Missouri, it still remains to be shewn that they ought to do so. . . . Slavery unhappily exists within the United States. Enlightened men in the states where it is permitted, and every where out of them, regret its existence among us, and seek for the means of limiting and of mitigating it. . . . The reasons which shall be offered in favor of the interposition of the power of congress to exclude slavery from Missouri, shall be only such as respect the common defence, the general welfare, and that wise administration of the government which as far as possible may produce the impartial distribution of benefits and burdens throughout the nation. . . .

There is nothing new or peculiar in a provision for the exclusion of slavery: it has been established in the states north west of the river Ohio, and has existed from the beginning in the old states where slavery is forbidden. The citizens of states where slavery is allowed, may become inhabitants of Missouri, but cannot hold slaves there, nor in any other state where slavery is prohibited.

Source: Papers Relative to the Restriction of Slavery: Speeches of Mr. King, in the Senate, and of Messrs. Taylor & Talmadge in the House of Representatives, of the

United States, on the Bill for Authorising the People of the Territory of Missouri to Form a Constitution and State Government, and for the Admission of the Same into the Union: In the Session of 1818–19, with a Report of a Committee of the Abolition Society of Delaware (Philadelphia: Hall & Atkinson, 1819), 3–4, 8, 12.

—⚹—

5. Speech of Representative Timothy Fuller, 1819

On Monday, February 15, 1819, Massachusetts representative Timothy Fuller was counted among the first to speak in favor of the Tallmadge proposal to restrict slavery in Missouri. Unlike many of his colleagues, he emphasized the immorality and the injustice of slavery.

The Constitution expressly makes a republican form of government in the several States a fundamental principle, to be preserved under the sacred guarantee of the National Legislature. [Art. IV, Sec. 4.] It clearly, therefore, is the duty of Congress, before admitting a new sister into the Union, to ascertain that her constitution or form of government is republican. Now, sir, the amendment proposed by the gentleman from New York, Mr. TALLMADGE, merely requires that slavery shall be prohibited in Missouri. Does this imply anything more than that its constitution shall be republican? The existence of slavery in any State is so far a departure from republican principles. The Declaration of Independence, penned by the illustrious statesman then and at this time a citizen of a State which admits slavery, defines the principle on which our National and State Constitutions are all professedly founded. The second paragraph of that instrument begins thus: "We hold these truths to be self-evident—that all men are created equal—that they are endowed by their Creator with certain inalienable rights—that among these are life, liberty, and the pursuit of happiness." Since, then, it cannot be denied that slaves are men, it follows that they are in a purely republican government born free, and are entitled to liberty and the pursuit of happiness. . . . Now it becomes the right and duty of Congress to guard against the further extension of the intolerable evil and the crying enormity of slavery.

Source: Annals of the Congress of the United States. Fifteenth Congress.—Second Session (Washington, D.C.: Gales & Seaton, 1855), 1180, 1184.

—⚹—

6. Speech of Representative Alexander Smyth, 1820

An Irish immigrant to colonial Virginia, Alexander Smyth was a lawyer active in Virginia state politics and a member of the U.S. House of Representatives. On January 28, 1820, Smyth delivered one of the more powerful attacks upon the Tallmadge amendments. Among his many points in the following speech, he referred to the Fifth and Tenth Amendments to the Constitution, raised the specter of war with France, and bandied about the possibility of secession and civil war.

If, then, a new state is admitted into "this Union," must it not be on terms of equality? Can the old states, the first parties to this Union, bind other states farther than they themselves are bound? Can they bind the new states not to admit slavery, and preserve to themselves the right to admit slavery? Shall the old states preserve rights of which the new states shall be deprived? . . . Has the power to legislate over slavery been delegated to the United States? It has not. Has it been prohibited to the states? It has not. Then it is reserved to the states respectively, or to the people. Consequently, it is reserved to the state of Missouri, or to the people of that state. And any attempt, by Congress, to deprive them of this reserved power, will be unjust, tyrannical, unconstitutional, and void. . . . The right to own slaves being acknowledged and secured by the constitution, can you proscribe what the constitution guarantees? Can you touch a right reserved to the states or the people? You cannot. . . . If you possessed power to legislate concerning slavery, the adoption of the proposition on your table, which goes to emancipate all children of slaves hereafter born in Missouri, would be a direct violation of the Constitution, which provides that "no person shall be deprived of property without due process of law; nor shall private property be taken for public use without just compensation." If you cannot take property even for public use, without just compensation, you certainly have not power to take it away for the purpose of annihilation, without compensation. . . . If you cannot take the slaves, you cannot take their issue, who, by the laws of slavery, will be also slaves. You cannot force the people to give up their property. You cannot force a portion of the people to emancipate their slaves. By adopting this proposition, you will have proved that the clauses of the Constitution deemed most sacred by the people, are not sacred with you. . . . Treaties are in part the supreme law of the land, and paramount to the constitution of any state: yet you propose to violate the treaty with France. . . . The former sovereign of the country has made a stipulation on behalf of the people, and to that stipulation we have agreed in the most solemn manner. If we do not perform our engagements, we shall be deemed a perfidious, faithless nation. . . . Beware! You have no right to Missouri but what the treaty gives you. The treaty gives you Missouri on condition that you secure the property of the inhabitants, and incorporate them into the Union of the United States with all the rights of citizens, according to the principles of the Federal Constitution. . . . Perhaps they are mistaken who suppose that the present Government of France is deficient in spirit and honor, and will not insist on the observance of existing treaties made with France. . . . If fifteen millions of dollars of the money raised by taxes paid by the whole people, are appropriated to purchase a territory, is it just to exclude therefrom the inhabitants of a part of the states? The inhabitants of the slave-holding states, being slave-holders, you exclude them if you exclude their slaves. . . . Shall the slave-holders be declared incapable of holding any share of the territory purchased with the money of the whole people? Have they not contributed their full proportion of the money paid for the territory? By such a measure you will deprive the southern people of an equal privilege—that of taking with them their families. Will you compel the citizen of Kentucky, the wants of whose children require more lands, when he is about to remove to Missouri, to sell the nurse who has fed his children from her breast, the faithful man who has long attended on his person, the maids of his wife & daughters, and the little children born in his family, before he can remove to the country of his choice? Yes; this you propose to do; yet talk of your humanity! . . . The plan of our opponents seems to be, to confine the slave population to the southern states . . . and this under pretence of humanity to the blacks. But do you not perceive . . . that by confining the slaves to a part of the country where the crops are raised for exportation, and bread and meat are purchased, that you doom them to scarcity and hunger? Is it not obvious that the way to render the situation of those people more comfortable is to allow them to be taken to those parts of the country where bread and meat are produced in profusion, with little labor, and where, consequently, there is not the same motive to force the slaves to incessant toil, that there is in the countries where cotton, sugar, and tobacco are raised for exportation. . . . The proposed measure, recommended under the mask of humanity, would be extreme cruelty to the blacks. . . .

If you are truly desirous that the slaves shall be treated with humanity, let them be as much as possible dispersed. The smaller their number in any district, the better will be their situation. It is well known that those farmers who have only two or three slaves, feed, clothe, and govern them as they do their children; while those of the great proprietors are not so well fed or clothed, more restrained, and more constantly engaged in labor. . . . Equal dispersion would produce not only an increase of comfort to the slaves, but also perfect security to the whites. . . . You are about to prove to the Southern and Western people that their property and their lives are unsafe under your government; that you mean to violate their claim of a right to make laws for themselves. It will not be good policy to convince the Southern and Western people of this. Are you certain that injustice cannot have the effect of breaking the bands of the Union? Doubtless they are strong; but the attachment to life, property, and the rights of freemen, is stronger. The states who hold slaves cannot consent that any state shall surrender to this government power over that description of property. Its value amounts to five hundred millions of dollars. . . . Shall the Union be destroyed, and the future fame, power, and happiness of the nation lost? . . . Are there none here who would wish to have it recorded that they are the men who saved the Union[?]

Source: Speech of Mr. Smyth, on the Restriction of Slavery in Missouri. Delivered in the House of Representatives of the United States, January 28, 1820 (N.p.: n.p., 1820).

---

7. Speech of Representative Robert W. Reid, 1820

In debates over the Tallmadge amendments, Representative Robert W. Reid of Georgia offered one of the more straightforward explanations of the anti-restrictionists' diffusion argument. He delivered the following speech on February 1, 1820.

Can we incorporate them [the blacks] with us, and make them and us one people? The prejudices of the North and of the South rise up in equal strength against such a measure; and even those who clamor most loudly for the sublime doctrines of your Declaration of Independence, who shout in your ears, "all men are by nature equal!" would turn with abhorrence and disgust from a parti-colored progeny! . . . I would hail that day as the most glorious in its dawning which should behold, with safety to themselves and our citizens, the black population of the United States placed upon the high eminence of equal rights, and clothed in the privileges and immunities of American citizens! But this is a dream of philanthropy which can never be fulfilled; and whoever shall act in this country upon such wild theories shall cease to be a benefactor and become a destroyer of the human family. . . . Slaves, divided among many masters, will enjoy greater privileges and comforts than those who, cooped within a narrow sphere and under few owners, will be doomed to drag a long, heavy, and clanking chain through the space of their existence. Danger from insurrection will diminish. Confidence will grow between the master and his servant. The one will no longer be considered as a mere beast of burden, the other as a remorseless despot void of feeling and commiseration. In proportion as few slaves are possessed by the same individual will he look with less reluctance to the prospect of their ultimate liberation. Emancipations will become common, and who knows but that the Great Being, to whose mercies all men have an equal claim, may, in the fulness of his time, work a miracle in behalf of the trampled rights of human nature?

Source: Marion Mills Miller, ed., *Great Debates in American History: From the Debates in the British Parliament on the Colonial Stamp Act (1764–1765) to the Debates in Congress at the Close of the Taft Administration (1912–1913).* Vol. 4, *Slavery from 1790 to 1857.* New York: Current Literature Publishing Company, 1913, 80–81.

—⁊⁊—

8. Thomas Amendment, 1820

On February 17, 1820, Illinois senator Jesse B. Thomas introduced a significant amendment banning slavery in the Louisiana Purchase north of Missouri's southern border, Missouri itself notwithstanding. He revised his own proposal to guarantee protections for masters whose slaves absconded into Missouri. The Senate adopted the amendment by a vote of 34 to 10.

The following amendment, offered by Mr. THOMAS, and pending when the Senate adjourned yesterday, being still under consideration: *"And be it further enacted,* That the sixth article of compact of the ordinance of Congress, passed on the thirteenth day of July, one thousand seven hundred eighty-seven, for the government of the territory of the United

States northwest of the river Ohio, shall, to all intents and purposes be, and hereby is, deemed and held applicable to, and shall have full force and effect in and over, all that tract of country ceded by France to the United States, under the name of Louisiana, which lies north of thirty-six degrees and thirty minutes north latitude, excepting only such part thereof as is included within the limits of the State contemplated by this act." Mr. THOMAS withdrew this amendment, and offered the following as a new section: "*And be it further enacted*, That, in all that territory ceded by France to the United States, under the name of Louisiana, which lies north of thirty-six degrees and thirty minutes north latitude, excepting only such part thereof as is included within the limits of the State contemplated by this act, slavery and involuntary servitude, otherwise than in the punishment of crimes whereof the party shall have been duly convicted, shall be and is hereby forever prohibited: *Provided, always*, That any person escaping into the same, from whom labor or service is lawfully claimed in any State or Territory of the United States, such fugitive may be lawfully reclaimed and conveyed to the person claiming his or her labor or service as aforesaid."

Source: Annals of the Congress of the United States. Sixteenth Congress—First Session (Washington, D.C.: Gales & Seaton, 1855), 426–427.

—⁓—

9. Letter, Thomas Jefferson to John Holmes, 1820

Former president Thomas Jefferson authored the most famous response to the Missouri Compromise. He wrote the following letter on April 22, 1820, to his friend John Holmes, a Jeffersonian Republican and Massachusetts representative in the House. Although a Yankee, Holmes consistently voted with southern anti-restrictionists against the Tallmadge amendments, earning him the derisive label of "doughface" from his northern restrictionist counterparts.

I thank you, Dear Sir, for the copy you have been so kind as to send me of the letter to your constituents on the Missouri question. It is a perfect justification to them. I had for a long time ceased to read newspapers or pay any attention to public affairs, confident they were in good hands, and content to be a passenger in our bark to the shore from which I am not distant. but this momentous question, like a fire bell in the night, awakened and filled me with terror. I considered it at once as the knell of the Union. it is hushed indeed for the moment, but that is a reprieve only, not a final sentence. a geographical line, coinciding with a marked principle, moral and political, once conceived and held up to the angry passions of men, will never be obliterated; and every new irritation will mark it deeper and deeper. I can say with conscious truth that there is not a man on earth who would sacrifice more than I would to relieve us from this heavy reproach, in any *practicable* way. the cession of that kind of property, for so it is misnamed, is a bagatelle which would not cost me a second thought, if, in that way a general emancipation and *expatriation* could be effected: and, gradually, and with due sacrifices, I think it might be. but, as it is we have the wolf by the ear, and we can neither hold him, nor safely let him go. justice is in one scale, and self-preservation in the other. of one thing I am certain, that as the passage of slaves from one state to another would not make a slave of a single human being who would not be so without it, so their diffusion over a greater surface would make them individually happier and proportionally facilitate the accomplishment of their emancipation, by dividing the burthen on a greater number of co-adjutors. an abstinence too from this act of power would remove the jealousy excited by the undertaking of Congress, to regulate the condition of the different descriptions of men composing a state. this certainly is the exclusive right of every state, which nothing in the constitution has taken from them and given to the general government. could congress, for example say that the Non-freemen of Connecticut, shall be freemen, or that they shall not emigrate into any other state?

I regret that I am now to die in the belief that the useless sacrifice of themselves, by the generation of '76, to acquire self government and happiness to their country, is to be thrown away by the unwise and unworthy passions of their sons, and that my only consolation is to be that I live not to weep over it. if they would but dispassionately weigh the blessings they will throw away against an abstract principle more likely to be effected by union than by scission, they would pause before they would perpetrate this act of suicide on themselves and of treason against the hopes of the world. to yourself as the faithful advocate of union I tender the offering of my high esteem and respect. Th. Jefferson

Source: http://www.loc.gov/exhibits/jefferson/159.html.

—⚭—

10. Speech of Senator James Barbour, 1820

James Barbour served as governor of Virginia, U.S. senator, and secretary of war over the course of his long political career. In the Senate, Barbour earned a reputation for his oratorical skills. The following brief excerpt from a powerful speech on January 31, 1820, opposing the Tallmadge amendments illustrates the rhetoric threatening to the Union that entered the Missouri controversy.

Sir, there is a point where submission becomes a crime, and resistance a virtue. . . . Beware how you touch it, in regard to the South! Our people are as brave as they are loyal. They can endure any thing but insult. The moment to pass the Rubicon, they will redeem their much-abused character; they will throw back upon you your insolence and your aggression. . . . To what end do you encounter this great risk? To exclude slavery from Missouri? That cannot be your object. You have slaves there already. These, you say, you do not mean to touch. The principle, then, is given up; the stock they have already there will multiply and fill the land.

Source: Annals of the Congress of the United States. Sixteenth Congress—First Session (Washington, D.C.: Gales & Seaton, 1855), 328–329.

6

SLAVE RESISTANCE:
Should Virginia Abolish Slavery in Light of the Nat Turner Revolt?

—⁂—

THE CONTROVERSY

The Issue

After the slave Nat Turner led a bloody insurrection in Virginia in 1831, the state legislature reconsidered the future of human bondage in the Old Dominion. Should Virginia abolish slavery after the Turner revolt?

♦ *Arguments in favor of Virginia's abolishing slavery in light of Nat Turner's revolt:* After the slave Nat Turner led the bloody Southampton insurrection in 1831, the Virginia House of Delegates reconsidered the future of slavery in the state. Some legislators, primarily from the nonslaveholding region west of the Blue Ridge Mountains, favored delegate Thomas Jefferson Randolph's plan for the gradual emancipation of Virginia's slaves. The safety of white Virginians depended upon it, they believed. The growth of Virginia's black population outpaced that of whites and threatened to overwhelm the West's white majority. An influx of slaves westward, they predicted, would repel the state's whites and damage the economy. No less vested in slavery than Virginians who owned enslaved property, westerners were willing to sacrifice masters' property rights in the interests of security by appropriating slaves without any costly program of compensation.

♦ *Arguments against Virginia's abolishing slavery in light of Nat Turner's revolt:* Primarily from the slaveholding eastern portion of Virginia, opponents of gradual abolition reviled the Randolph plan for confiscating private property without compensation. Randolph's proposal, they argued, did little to ensure white Virginians' safety in the short term. To the contrary, publicly discussing emancipation endangered Virginia's citizenry by raising hopes among blacks that must be dashed. According to the anti-emancipationists, the Randolph plan invited

193

economic crisis. By decreasing the value of Virginia land and slaves, it would drive whites away from the state to locations where their property was more secure. The immediate crisis of the Turner revolt had passed. Anti-emancipationists preferred not to agitate the slavery issue just when peace and tranquility had been restored. If the abolition of slavery must be discussed at all, the decision was best left to slaveholders themselves without interference from antislavery demagogues in the legislature.

—⁓—

INTRODUCTION

Nat Turner launched a slave insurrection in Southampton County, Virginia, in 1831 that killed almost 60 whites before it dissolved. The massacre horrified white Virginians and prompted the most intense debate over the future of slavery ever witnessed in Virginia's history or in any southern legislature. The reconsideration of slavery in Virginia's House of Delegates, the lower chamber of the General Assembly, revealed a variety of opinions on the subject: Virginians were not all of one mind. Geography served as a good indicator of legislators' positions on the slavery issue. Those representing the predominantly nonslaveholding western part of the state supported Thomas Jefferson Randolph's plan for gradual emancipation, while their colleagues in the slaveholding East— where the Turner revolt took place—opposed it. For two weeks in early 1832, the competing political cultures of the aristocratic East and the democratic West carried on a debate—unthinkable before the Turner revolt—over the abolition of slavery in the Old Dominion. The discussion in the Virginia House of Delegates proved a pivotal moment in the history of American slavery. Never again would Virginia or any other southern state question its commitment to the institution. The debate furthermore previewed proslavery arguments that would be developed in the years ahead.

Delegates in favor of gradual emancipation shared several concerns. They feared repetition of the Turner revolt if they failed to act. Virginia's growing black population, already a majority east of the Blue Ridge Mountains, threatened to overspread the West and drive off hardworking, enterprising white Virginians. The safety and security of Virginia whites demanded a gradual emancipation program even at the expense of masters' right to enslaved property. According to the emancipationists, property rights were not absolute when weighed against the public welfare. They also argued that masters did not merit compensation for slaves manumitted under the terms of a gradual abolition plan because the liberation of slaves marked a public benefit to the state, and reimbursement would burden state coffers. In addition, they challenged masters' claims to slaves yet unborn. The western portion of Virginia did not contain the numbers of slaves found in the East, but the West still recognized its interest in the slavery question.

Legislators from eastern Virginia objected to plans for gradual abolition. They viewed the Southampton tragedy through rose-colored lenses, arguing that it was an isolated incident unlikely to be repeated. The real danger, anti-emancipationists charged, lay in discussing abolition publicly in the House of Delegates, thereby heightening black expectations for change. Anti-emancipationists believed the Randolph plan for gradual abolition inappropriate to meet its stated goals. Worse still, it permitted the confiscation of private property without compensation. While maintaining the inviolability of property, the legislators critical of emancipation feared that abolition would invite economic catastrophe, lowering the value of Virginia's land and slaves and pushing whites out of the state. In their minds, slaveholders alone were best equipped to determine the fate of their property.

BACKGROUND

In the early morning hours of Monday, August 22, 1831, the most famous slave uprising in U.S. history erupted in remote, sparsely inhabited Southampton County in Southside Virginia, near the forebodingly named Dismal Swamp. Nat Turner, an influential slave in the neighborhood, and a handful of enslaved followers launched what they considered a spiritual mission by murdering Turner's master and his family. They then marched to nearby farmhouses, gathering new slave recruits to continue their works of death. Local whites put down the revolt within two days, but not before rebellious slaves had murdered upward of 60 whites, the vast majority of whom were women, children, and infants. Reprisal was swift and harsh. Almost all of the rebels were either killed outright or captured, tried, and then executed. More than 100 blacks

The slave Nat Turner and his followers killed approximately 60 whites in Southampton County, Virginia, in August 1831. (Fotosearch/Getty Images)

rightly or wrongly suspected of participating in the revolt were indiscriminately killed in extralegal, vigilante activity. Turner escaped and took refuge in the Dismal Swamp. He remained at large for two months before he was apprehended, placed on trial, convicted, and hanged. (See the sidebar "*The Confessions of Nat Turner*" on page 198.)

The Southampton massacre stands as a rare event in the slaveholding South. Although anxious whites routinely detected slave conspiracies in their midst, these schemes were frustrated prior to any bloodshed. In Virginia, the enslaved blacksmith Gabriel plotted, in 1800, to seize the capital of Richmond but was betrayed by fellow slaves before he could implement his plan. Whereas Gabriel undoubtedly planned to revolt, sometimes white fears manifested themselves in claims of purported slave plots where none existed. Compared to the ubiquitous reports of slave conspiracies, whether real or imagined, actual slave rebellions that spilled white blood proved exceptional in the American South. In fact, in addition to the Turner revolt, there were only two. The colonial era witnessed the eruption of the Stono Rebellion in South Carolina in 1739, and a revolt broke out in Louisiana in 1811. The rarity of slave rebellions in the slaveholding South led some to treat the first reports of the Southampton insurrection with incredulity. It also made the event that much more momentous in the history of Virginia and the United States. (See "Articles, *Richmond Enquirer*, 1831," on page 222 in the Primary Sources section.)

Several concerns and anxieties of white Virginians coalesced around the Turner rebellion. The 1830 census showed that Virginia had more slaves than any other state, including South Carolina and Louisiana, the two states with a majority black population. Almost 50 percent more slaves lived in the Old Dominion than in South Carolina, which ranked second in total slave population. Virginia had more than double Georgia's 218,000 slaves and more than Louisiana, Mississippi, Alabama, and Tennessee combined. Virginia's demographic realities made the state's whites particularly sensitive to the machinations of outside agitators. In 1829, David Walker, a North Carolina–born free black man involved in the abolitionist movement in Boston, published his *Appeal to the Coloured Citizens of the World*. Directed to the slaves, Walker's militant pamphlet urged bond people to resist slavery and approved the use of violence against their masters. Walker ran a used clothing store on the Boston waterfront that catered to mariners. To reach his target

THE CONFESSIONS OF NAT TURNER

A major source of knowledge about the Southampton insurrection, *The Confessions of Nat Turner* was the product of a struggling, financially strapped 31-year-old slaveholder and lawyer named Thomas R. Gray. Benjamin Phipps, a white man armed with a shotgun, discovered the secreted Nat Turner on October 30, 1831, and the revolt leader surrendered without a fight. Gray gained access to the captive and interviewed him during the first three days of November. These meetings culminated in the publication of *The Confessions of Nat Turner* by the end of the month, just weeks after his subject's execution.

The Confessions of Nat Turner is no straightforward, verbatim transcript of Turner's recollections. Gray's presence is evident in parenthetical editorial remarks, questions inserted into the text, and telltale wordings that suggest his influence. As a local man, Gray was surely acquainted with many of Turner's victims and not predisposed to sympathize with the revolt leader. He described Turner as a fiendish fanatic and noted that the sight of him, manacled and still covered in the blood of his victims, filled him with horror. His interview with Turner impressed him in other, more positive ways as well, however. Gray could not avoid, for example, commending Turner's intellect and composure.

Although filtered through the lens of Thomas R. Gray, *The Confessions of Nat Turner* still offers insight into the leader of the Southampton insurrection.

audience, he smuggled his *Appeal* into the South by sewing copies into the linings of clothing he sold to black sailors and others sympathetic to the abolitionist cause. Unlike Walker, abolitionist William Lloyd Garrison opposed the violent uprising of slaves. He seemed no less threatening to the slaveholding South, however, in his role as editor of the abolitionist newspaper the *Liberator*. Despite Garrison's pacifist views, it appeared no coincidence to Virginia whites that the first issue of the paper appeared in January 1831, a little more than eight months before the Southampton insurrection. Virginia governor John Floyd was not alone in his suspicion that an insidious Yankee influence lurked behind the Turner revolt. (See "Letter, Virginia Governor John Floyd to South

Gray became the conduit through which Turner shared his personal story. Even if Turner was not entirely forthcoming, consciously withholding some information, he nevertheless intimated details of his childhood, his religious experiences, and the events of the massacre. Nat was born in 1800, the slave of Benjamin Turner of Southampton County, but by the time of the rebellion belonged to Joseph Travis. From a young age, Turner believed himself destined for a special purpose. Precocious and literate, he developed into a respected figure among his fellow slaves, serving as an exhorter, or preacher. Turner communicated with the biblical Holy Spirit and grew to think of himself as a prophet, a Christlike figure, and an instrument of divine will. He experienced frequent visions, the most significant of which was a battle between white and black spirits under a darkened sun. Turner interpreted a solar eclipse in February 1831 as a sign to commence a race war and slaughter of whites. Delayed until August, he and a half dozen followers launched their rebellion, vowing to spare none. The rebels first attacked the household of Turner's master, Joseph Travis, and then traversed the countryside on a murderous spree, gathering supporters as they went. At its height, Turner's force numbered perhaps 60 blacks wielding hatchets, axes, swords, and guns. White military forces quickly mobilized, and when the rebellion collapsed, Turner went into hiding. He evaded detection for more than two months before his capture. Though somewhat problematic as a source, *The Confessions of Nat Turner* nevertheless gives voice to the most famous of American slave revolt leaders.

Carolina Governor James Hamilton, Jr., 1831," on page 223 in the Primary Sources section.)

Turner's rebellion panicked many Virginia whites. Turner had played out planters' worst nightmares by attacking their families as they slept. The race war he undertook had resulted in dozens of white fatalities. White Virginians might try to dismiss Turner as an aberration, a one-of-a-kind religious lunatic on a fanatical crusade, but how could they be certain? They remained on edge, fearful that another Turner skulked about, poised to strike. In the wake of the Southampton insurrection, sensitized whites perceived conspiracies in various parts of the state. They also petitioned the Virginia General Assembly for legislative

William Lloyd Garrison published the first issue of his abolitionist newspaper, the *Liberator*, on January 1, 1831. (Library of Congress)

relief. Perhaps 40 petitions, from all corners of Virginia, made their way to the House of Delegates in the 1831–32 session. Most of them appealed for the elimination of the state's free people of color, a curious solution for easing their anxiety, given free blacks' almost complete absence from the Southampton revolt (but understandable in light of the pervasive racial sentiments of the time). A few notable exceptions petitioned for the abolition of slavery from Virginia. A Loudoun County memorial asked for deliverance from the evil of slavery. Another petition from King William County called for the gradual and peaceful removal of Virginia's slaves out of the United States. Most significant, however, was a petition from Charles City County Quakers, introduced on December 14, 1831, by William Roane of Hanover County. Quakers opposed slavery for moral and religious reasons and in their petition requested its abolition and the emancipation of Virginia's slaves. (See "Petition from the 'Females of the County of Augusta,' 1832," on page 225 in the Primary Sources section.)

Virginia legislators were uniquely primed to undertake a debate over abolition. Nat Turner's Southampton insurrection had alarmed their constituents, and the situation demanded some sort of legislative response. It would have been unimaginable to conceive of a discussion of emancipation without the impetus of the Turner revolt, but the momentary fear that gripped Virginia whites suddenly laid bare new possibilities for the future of slavery in the state. (See "Speech of Samuel Moore, 1832," on page 227 in the Primary Sources section.) Emancipation schemes that would have been derided in the past as delusional might now, under dramatically altered circumstances, earn a fair hearing. As one delegate explained in a speech in the House of Delegates, slavery was "a subject heretofore hermetically sealed, our opinions upon which, we have been accustomed to breathe in the lowest whispers. I have almost felt as though I were in a dream, and have been tempted to ask myself can it be real—am I actually in the Legislative Hall of Virginia, listening to such a discussion?"[1]

It was a discussion not all Virginians in the legislature wanted to have. A deep political fissure divided Virginia into eastern and western portions. Slaveholding in Virginia was unequally distributed, concentrated overwhelmingly in the Tidewater and Piedmont regions of the East. The preponderance of political power within Virginia likewise resided in the East because the state constitution, reflecting the elitist political sensibilities of the late 18th century, counted both white *and* slave populations in determining representation in the General Assembly. Planters in the East openly argued that the inflated representation they gained from the mixed principle Virginia followed was necessary to guarantee the security of slave property. In the decade before the Southampton insurrection, westerners challenged the East's conservative, aristocratic ethos. By the 1820s, Virginia's white population had grown and expanded in the West as it remained stagnant in the East, but the distribution of delegates remained unchanged. Westerners clamored for greater, more equitable representation on an exclusively white basis. They favored, in short, a more egalitarian government than the undemocratic East. Without intending to make any concessions to their western brethren, the East bowed to mounting pressure to remedy legislative malapportionment by agreeing to hold the Virginia Constitutional Convention of 1829. Essentially, the convention pitted a slaveholding East against a nonslaveholding West. At the convention, the politically powerful East fought the West's calls for reapportionment based on the state's white population from the 1830 census. Ultimately, the two halves of the state struck a compromise that strongly favored the East. The slave population still mattered in determining representation, and representation based on the white population was based on the decade-old 1820 census, which showed fewer Virginia whites living in the western part of the state. The West therefore gained a greater number of representatives, but the region was still shortchanged because the arrangement did not take into account

---

[1] *Richmond Enquirer,* 31 January 1832.

whites who had moved there after 1820. In addition, the terms of the convention effectively prevented further legislative reapportionment. The constitutional convention thus took only a meager half-step toward repairing the problem of disproportional representation and virtually guaranteed that malapportionment would be exacerbated in the future. The compromise resulted in a legislature that was only somewhat less malapportioned than before the convention. The West still felt cheated. Some historians have argued that Virginia's debate over emancipation after the Southampton insurrection stemmed less from fear of future slave rebellions than from western resentment of the slaveholding East and the West's drive for increased political power.

Anticipating the "gag rule" in the U.S. House of Representatives by four years, William O. Goode, a conservative delegate representing slave-heavy Mecklenburg County in the Virginia Southside, made a motion to reject the Quaker abolitionist petition of December 1831. Goode's attempt to stymie discussion of the memorial struck many of his colleagues as shockingly undemocratic. By a vote of 93 to 27, the House defeated Goode's motion and, out of respect for the petitioners, referred the memorial to a committee, as per custom. The East owned a clear majority in the House and had the numbers to arrest any discussion of the Quaker petition. That Goode's motion garnered only 27 votes illustrated that not only western representatives but also a fraction of delegates from the slaveholding East favored debating slavery's future in Virginia. "All this they looked at with indifference," grumbled one disgruntled correspondent to the *Richmond Enquirer*, "supposing no man in the State could be found mad enough seriously to consider of the propositions." A "mistaken courtesy to the Quakers" sent the petition to the House Select Committee on Slaves, Free Negroes, and Mulattoes.[2]

Goode made another effort to suppress debate on the petition the following month. By January 11, 1832, Goode believed the select committee tardy in reporting back to the House. To dispense quickly with the question of emancipation and allay the anxieties of his constituents, he made a resolution to discharge all petitions in favor of abolition from the committee preemptively, before it had the opportunity to report. Goode's resolution inflamed the very debate he hoped to avoid. Thomas

---

[2] *Richmond Enquirer*, 26 January 1832.

Benjamin Phipps, a resident of Southampton County, Virginia, captured the slave rebel Nat Turner on October 30, 1831. (MPI/Getty Images)

Jefferson Randolph, namesake of his famous grandfather and delegate from Albemarle County, unexpectedly introduced an amendment to Goode's resolution that asked the committee to explore the possibility of submitting a plan of gradual abolition to the qualified voters of Virginia. Randolph was not offering a bill for the General Assembly to vote upon but merely a resolution in support of a plan for gradual emancipation. (See "Resolution and Amendment of William O. Goode, 1832," on page 228 in the Primary Sources section.)

The Committee on Slavery and Free Negroes issued its report on January 16. After spending much of the previous month discussing the complicated, time-consuming issue of removing Virginia's free people of color, the committee drafted a resolution declaring "that it is inexpedient for the present Legislature to make any legislative enactment for the abolition of slavery." William Ballard Preston, a delegate from Montgomery County and nephew of Virginia governor John Floyd, moved to strike the word *inexpedient* and replace it with *expedient,* reversing the meaning of the resolution. Delegates conflated the debate on the committee report with the debate over the Goode and Randolph resolutions into a single protracted struggle over the status of bondage in Virginia. Should Virginia abolish slavery?

THE DEBATE

The Case for Abolishing Slavery after Nat Turner's Revolt

Many representatives in the House of Delegates welcomed the opportunity afforded by the Turner revolt to discuss the possibility of abolishing slavery in Virginia. Typically hailing from the western portions of the state, they included Henry Berry of Jefferson County; Philip A. Bolling of Buckingham; Charles James Faulkner of Berkeley; James McDowell, Jr., and Samuel Moore, both of Rockbridge; William Ballard Preston of Montgomery; and George Summers of Kanawha. They eagerly seized the chance to broach a subject that from their perspective had become taboo in the General Assembly. As one delegate explained, "a mystic sort of right, and a superstitious sort of veneration" for slavery had taken hold in the legislature, but "thank God, . . . the spell is broken, and the scales have fallen from our eyes."[3] Representatives in favor of the gradual elimination of slavery dreaded the demographic changes already under way in Virginia, decried slavery's negative effects on the state, emphasized the theme of white safety and security, and asserted the right of the state's westerners to pursue the question of abolition. Their analysis pointed to the conclusion that the gradual emancipation of Virginia's slaves was both "expedient" and "practicable."

Many proponents of gradual abolition in Virginia cited alarming census data in support of emancipation. In 1790, almost 293,000 slaves lived in Virginia. By 1830, that figure had increased to nearly 470,000. With a white population of a little more than 694,000 in 1830, white Virginians still outnumbered slaves, but their percentage of the overall

---

[3] *Richmond Enquirer,* 9 February 1832.

population was on the decline. East of the Blue Ridge Mountains, blacks composed a majority of the population in each census from 1800 to 1830, and black population growth was accelerating compared to that of whites. From a majority of only 3,000 in 1800, blacks outnumbered whites by more than 81,000 east of the Blue Ridge in 1830. The precipitous rise in the numbers of blacks relative to whites endangered white Virginians' safety. A program of gradual emancipation could arrest the dangerously widening gap between black and white populations in the eastern part of the state.

Antislavery delegates asserted that the dramatic rise of the black population relative to that of whites produced deleterious effects on the state. Rising numbers of slaves, they claimed, drove off valuable white citizens. The honest, hardworking laboring man was exiled from Virginia, demoralized, as skilled slave carpenters, masons, and coopers robbed him of employment in his native land. The presence of slaves degraded free labor and made work disreputable. In consequence, argued James McDowell, Jr., of Rockbridge in the House of Delegates, slavery generated economic distress, producing a "delinquent prosperity." Moreover, slaves lacked any genuine incentive to work industriously. The results were "desolated fields" and "torpid enterprise" in the slaveholding region of Virginia.[4] Thomas Jefferson Randolph's plan held forth a remedy. As slaves born on or after July 4, 1840, were emancipated, they would create a labor shortage, rejuvenating economic opportunity for free whites. Gradual abolition, in short, would promote free white labor in Virginia.

The greatest benefits of gradual emancipation, however, would be the safety and security of white Virginians. Hysteria gripped the slaveholding states in the wake of the Turner revolt, and in Virginia as in other slave states, alarmed whites detected conspiracies in many quarters. As McDowell explained, "it was the suspicion . . . that a Nat Turner might be in every family, that the same bloody deed could be acted over at any time and in any place." To prevent a repetition of the Southampton insurrection, prompt and decisive action was imperative. The presence of slaves compromised white Virginians' safety in

---

[4] *Speech of James M'Dowell, Jr. (of Rockbridge,) in the House of Delegates of Virginia, on the Slave Question: Delivered Saturday, January 21, 1832*, 2nd ed. (Richmond, Va.: Thomas W. White, 1832), 9.

other ways as well. Describing slaves as "the enemy within," George Summers of Kanawha County feared that foreign invaders could tempt willing bond people to commit horrific acts of "domestic butchery." Rockbridge County representative Samuel Moore concurred that slaves, "restrained by no moral or patriotic considerations, will ever be ready to act as guides to an invading foe, and to flock to his standard." Militarily, the country would need to divert a significant portion of its armed forces from fighting the enemy to suppressing domestic slave insurrections. "The time will come, and at no distant day," Moore gravely predicted, "when we shall be involved in all the horrors of a servile war, which will not end until . . . the slaves or the whites are totally exterminated." In the interests of self-preservation, Virginia needed to emancipate its slaves. The state had much more to fear by doing nothing than by doing something.[5] (See "Letter, James Goodwyn to Virginia Governor John Floyd, 1832," on page 229 in the Primary Sources section.)

Advocates of gradual emancipation prioritized the safety of white Virginians over masters' property interests in slaves. Thomas Jefferson Randolph expressed surprise that his resolution was "received with deep and damning reprobation, as a scheme of robbery and plunder." While still upholding the sanctity of private property, several delegates observed that property rights were not limitless when they conflicted with the security and welfare of the community and the state. McDowell and others argued that when the public safety was at stake, government maintained the authority to interfere with private property. Jefferson County representative Henry Berry thought Randolph's gradual emancipation plan quite similar to those successfully implemented in Pennsylvania, New York, and other states shortly after the American Revolution. He expressed indignation that anyone would dare jeopardize public safety for the sake of property. "The right of property in the colored class generally, has been brought into this debate, and I am sorry for it," Berry said. "But I think our eastern brethren are to blame for it; they rather arrogantly advanced their right of property, as an insuperable barrier to our doing any thing for the removal of the evil

---

[5] *Speech of James M'Dowell*, 29; *Richmond Enquirer*, 14 February 1832; *Richmond Enquirer*, 19 January 1832.

of slavery, and rather challenged an investigation of their title. . . . I am sick with the clamor in this debate, about this property, this wealth. I consider it all as mere trash, when weighed against the public safety."[6] (See "Speech of James McDowell, Jr., 1832," on page 230 in the Primary Sources section.)

Those in favor of gradual emancipation contended that masters need not be compensated for the slaves appropriated by the state after July 4, 1840. After asserting the primacy of public safety over private rights, Berkeley County's Charles James Faulkner argued that there was no legal precedent for providing full compensation for a form of property that "is a nuisance and found injurious" to society. The danger posed by the presence of slaves abrogated Virginia's responsibility to pay, and, on a practical level, the state lacked the financial resources to implement a program to reimburse masters the full value of their emancipated slaves. Faulkner, Berry, and other like-minded colleagues also challenged masters' property claims to unborn slaves. Slaveholders had a vested right only in slaves now living, they contended, not in those yet to be born. By this reasoning, Randolph's gradual emancipation plan did not violate masters' rights to slave property because it deprived them of no slaves currently living. Put another way, slaveholders *lost* nothing; they would simply be prevented from profiting from the "increase" of slaves in the future. As an added bonus for slaveholders, the value of bond people born before July 4, 1840, would increase as slaves became more scarce over time.[7]

Despite western Virginia's relative lack of slaves compared to the East, that portion of the state considered itself no less invested in the gradual abolition of slavery. More than 416,000 slaves lived east of the Blue Ridge in Virginia, compared to some 53,000 from the Blue Ridge to the Ohio River. The West was indeed home to fewer slaves than the East, but western representatives such as George Summers of Kanawha

---

[6] *The Speech of Thomas J. Randolph, (of Albemarle,) in the House of Delegates of Virginia, on the Abolition of Slavery: Delivered Saturday, Jan. 21, 1832,* 2nd ed. (Richmond, Va.: Thomas W. White, 1832), 10; *The Speech of Henry Berry, (of Jefferson,) in the House of Delegates of Virginia, on the Abolition of Slavery* (1832), 4.

[7] *The Speech of Charles Jas. Faulkner, (of Berkeley) in the House of Delegates of Virginia, on the Policy of the State with Respect to Her Slave Population. Delivered January 20, 1832* (Richmond, Va.: Thomas W. White, 1832), 15, 21.

expressed fears that surplus slaves from the East would infiltrate and overrun the West, which seemed the natural dumping ground for eastern Virginia's excess bond people. And what if other slaveholding states banned the importation of bond people through the domestic slave trade? Should that occur, Virginia slaves would be confined within the state's borders. Their rapidly growing population must then inevitably spill out of the East, advance westward, and overwhelm the entirety of Virginia's landscape. "We cannot desire to see our mountains blackened with the slave," Summers declared, "or that the fresh grass of our vallies should wither beneath his tread."[8] Now is the time, insisted western representatives, for the West to cooperate with the East to effect a program of gradual emancipation before growing numbers of slaves made the task impossible. The safety of Virginia's white population—a common concern in both sections of the state—required prompt action, and all whites—slaveholders as well as nonslaveholders—should rightfully participate in the discussion.

Thomas Jefferson Randolph confidently asserted that most representatives in the Virginia House of Delegates were "in favor of abolition in the abstract."[9] Most considered slavery an evil and dangerous "curse" upon society. For a number of those interested in the gradual liberation of Virginia slaves, Randolph's proposal seemed a moderate and perfectly reasonable plan. It applied to future generations, freeing no slave currently living or any who would be born prior to July 4, 1840. For those born on or after that date, female slaves would be turned over to the state at the age of 18, male slaves at 21. Masters thus retained enslaved women until at least 1858, enslaved men until at least 1861, during which time they benefited from the slaves' labor and were at liberty to relocate them to another state or to sell them for profit. Under the Randolph plan, no emancipated slave was permitted to remain in Virginia, yet no new taxes were imposed on the people of Virginia to support the colonization of freed slaves. Instead, the state hired out surrendered slaves as long as necessary to procure sufficient funds to finance their removal. Randolph predicted that, under his proposal, over a protracted period of perhaps 80 years, slavery would become extinct in the state of Virginia.

---

[8] *Richmond Enquirer,* 14 February 1832.
[9] *Speech of Thomas J. Randolph,* 13.

The Case Against Abolishing Slavery after Nat Turner's Revolt

The Virginia House of Delegates did not rally unanimously behind Randolph's program of gradual emancipation. Its most vocal foes consisted of representatives from the region east of the Blue Ridge Mountains. William H. Brodnax of Dinwiddie County, John Thompson Brown of the town of Petersburg, James Bruce of Halifax County, James Gholson of Brunswick, and William O. Goode and Alexander Knox, both of Mecklenburg, all represented areas with large slave populations engaged in the production of tobacco. Some opponents had no interest in tampering with slavery at all, while others were sympathetic to the goal of emancipation but objected to the manner in which abolition would be achieved under the Randolph plan. They decried Randolph's measures as "wild and revolutionary," "unjust, partial, tyrannical and monstrous."[10] During debates in the legislature, eastern delegates downplayed the severity of the Southampton insurrection and insisted that even discussing Randolph's plan publicly endangered white Virginians. The proposal, they argued, actually made black Virginians more restless. The plan itself struck them as ineffective in meeting the immediate need for safety. Above all, it authorized the confiscation of private property without compensation. Implementing it would have the undesirable effects of depressing slave prices and lowering the value of Virginia land, thereby banishing much of the state's white slaveholding population. Eastern slaveholders, not non-slaveholding westerners or the masses of Virginia voters, were best suited to determine questions of slavery in the state. The radical Randolph plan, its opponents argued, was utterly "impracticable."

In the House of Delegates, foes of gradual emancipation dismissed the dangers of Nat Turner's uprising. Without wishing to dishonor those who lost their lives in the rebellion or to diminish its horrors, they believed that the panic and hysteria left in the wake of the Turner revolt were disproportionate to the actual threat. From their perspective, several months comfortably removed from the quelled insurrection, the rebellion was limited in scope. No general uprising, it affected only one particular neighborhood in Southampton. One "fanatic" and a small band of followers stood no realistic chance for success in the face

---

[10] *Richmond Enquirer,* 11 February 1832; *Richmond Enquirer,* 24 January 1832.

of white military mobilization. To be sure, the tragic events of August 1831 generated excitement and terror, but white fears were exaggerated. As John Thompson Brown explained, the "atrocity" of servile revolt "has happened only once, in the course of near sixty years, which have elapsed since we became an independent people. And is this solitary calamity—so brief and rare—to change the whole tenor of our lives and uplift the very foundations of society?" Gradually to emancipate Virginia's slaves after one, isolated tragedy, he concluded, was "absurd." There was no present cause for alarm; any threat white Virginians now felt was imaginary. Representative James Gholson testified that "the people of our country again sleep quietly on their pillows," confident in "the most steadfast fidelity and devoted loyalty" of their "happy," "harmless" slaves. His colleague William H. Brodnax agreed.[11] (See "Speech of William H. Broadnax, 1832," on page 231 in the Primary Sources section and the sidebar "William H. Broadnax" on page 212.)

Gholson and other anti-emancipationists alleged that merely raising the possibility of abolition in the House of Delegates threatened Virginia's security and invited danger where none existed. The Southampton insurrection had been suppressed months ago, and Nat Turner had been captured and executed. The turmoil had finally begun to subside, tranquility restored, when the assembly began injudiciously to ponder emancipation. What delegates debated the Virginia press reported and the people discussed. "And all this is done," Gholson said, "as if the slaves around us had neither eyes nor ears—or that having ears, they heard not, and having eyes, they saw not." William O. Goode concurred. "The slaves themselves were not unconscious of what was going forward here," he explained. "They are not an ignorant herd of Africans. On the contrary, they are an active and intelligent class, watching and weighing every movement of the Legislature."[12] Discussion of emancipation in the House of Delegates thus artificially raised the expectations of Virginia's slaves. It excited their hopes and inspired dreams of freedom that must prove fleeting and illusory. Destined for disappointment, they might channel their frustration and resentment into another

---

[11] *The Speech of John Thompson Brown, in the House of Delegates of Virginia, on the Abolition of Slavery. Delivered Wednesday, January 18, 1832* (Richmond, Va.: Thomas W. White, 1832), 30; *Richmond Enquirer,* 21 January 1832.

[12] *Richmond Enquirer,* 21 January 1832; *Richmond Enquirer,* 19 January 1832.

insurrection. Debating unnecessary legislative action against slavery therefore served only to prolong the sense of unrest among Virginia's citizenry. If emancipation must be discussed at all, it should be behind closed doors and kept out of the press to prevent inciting trouble.

Anti-emancipationists in the House of Delegates predicted that the Randolph proposal might actually cause Virginia slaves to rebel. While an older generation of bond people remained permanently enslaved, those born on or after July 4, 1840, could expect eventual freedom. The same plan that freed enslaved children, brothers, and sisters asked enslaved parents and older siblings to reconcile themselves to perpetual bondage, all on the basis of a symbolic but nonetheless arbitrary date. The structure of the Randolph plan thus created a large restless and disaffected bloc of slaves. Enslaved parents overjoyed at the impending freedom of at least some of their children would desire liberty for themselves and other family members. Meanwhile, explained James Gholson, emancipated slaves would sympathize with loved ones still in captivity. The result, he predicted, would be a servile revolt on an unprecedented scale.

If the Randolph plan was calculated to ensure the safety of white Virginians, it simply did not make sense. To Gholson, it was ill suited to the widely perceived circumstances existing in Virginia in early 1832. Gholson observed that the emancipationists imagined the state in immediate peril. If the danger was so imminent, the need to allay white fears of revolt so pressing, Gholson asked, why did the Randolph proposal apply only to future generations of slaves? It did not promptly reduce the number of Virginia slaves, turning over to the state no enslaved men (considered far more physically threatening than enslaved women) for 29 years. The plan, in short, did nothing to restore and guarantee security *now*. Gholson discounted the prospect of another massacre, but even if dire warnings of violent slaves on a second murderous rampage came to pass, the Randolph plan afforded no protection for almost three decades.

Most significantly, critics of the Randolph plan saw it as a gross violation of masters' property rights in slaves. The Fifth Amendment to the U.S. Constitution, they indicated, guaranteed that no one shall "be deprived of . . . property, without due process of law." Slaveholders regarded slaves as property, as valuable economic assets. By forcing masters to surrender to the state any slaves born on or after July 4, 1840,

WILLIAM H. BRODNAX

William Henry Brodnax was counted among the most visible figures in Virginia's debate over emancipation. Born around 1786 in Brunswick County, Virginia, Brodnax attended his home state's Hampden-Sydney College. He rose to prominence as a lawyer in Petersburg and surrounding areas and acquired a 1,600-acre plantation in Dinwiddie County he called Kingston. He also owned more than 100 slaves, placing him in the top 1 percent of all southern slaveholders. Brodnax was a prosperous man.

Brodnax held a number of important posts throughout his life. He represented Greensville County in the House of Delegates from 1818 to 1819 and attended the Constitutional Convention of 1829 as one of the four representatives of Brunswick, Dinwiddie, Lunenburg, and Mecklenburg counties. At the convention, his voting record reflected the attitudes of the conservative, slaveholding East, unsurprising considering the substantial slave population in his district as well as his own investments in enslaved property.

In 1824, Brodnax was elected a brigadier general in the state militia. Seven years later, he commanded militia units dispatched to suppress Nat Turner and his rebels in Southampton County, but the insurrection had collapsed prior to the arrival of his thousands of troops. Nevertheless, Brodnax witnessed the resulting carnage. He was deeply affected by the sight of the untended bodies of infants and children exposed to ravenous dogs and

when they reached the age of 18 or 21, the Randolph plan authorized the "monstrous and unconstitutional" confiscation of private property. Running roughshod over the sanctity of private property represented an attack not only upon republican government but also upon masters' economic interests. James Bruce of Halifax County complained that the Randolph plan charged masters "with the expense of feeding and clothing a slave, until he is of an age to be useful, and at that moment he is to be taken from his possession, and become the property of the State." Anti-emancipationists argued that masters were rightfully entitled to the labor of their slaves' unborn children as well. According to James Gholson, "steady and old-fashioned people" believed "that the owner of land had a reasonable right to its annual profits; the owner of orchards, vultures. His firsthand encounter with the aftermath of a slave insurrection gave shape to his views on gradual abolition in Virginia.

Beginning in 1830, Brodnax served as a delegate from Dinwiddie County in the House. Inundated by petitions from concerned citizens after the Turner revolt, the House named Brodnax chairman of the Select Committee on Slaves, Free Negroes, and Mulattoes to sift through the memorials. Most of the petitions pleaded for the removal of Virginia's free black population, but a distinct minority implored the legislature to rid the state of its slaves. Unlike most of his eastern colleagues, Brodnax welcomed a debate on emancipation. A self-proclaimed moderate, he believed slavery endangered the safety and economic well-being of the commonwealth but vehemently opposed Thomas Jefferson Randolph's proposal for gradual abolition. Brodnax developed his own plan for the relocation of Virginia's black population. A member of the American Colonization Society, he recommended deporting 6,000 free blacks per year, then, after demonstrating the success of his proposal, launching a program of compensated emancipation for slaves. Without a plan for the removal of Virginia blacks, Brodnax predicted another Turner-style rebellion that would result in the indiscriminate slaughter of the state's black population. The House rejected Brodnax's proposal, and despite his dire warnings for the future, the select committee he chaired determined that it was "inexpedient" to discuss emancipation in 1832. Just two years after the abolition debate in the House of Delegates, he died of cholera on his Kingston plantation.

to their annual fruits; the owner of brood mares, to their product; and the owner of female slaves, to their *increase.*"[13] In Virginia and throughout the antebellum South, the legal principle of *partus sequitur ventrem* held that the status of offspring followed the condition of the mother. Enslaved mothers bore enslaved children, and no compelling reason could justify depriving owners of their next generation of slaves. Financial ruin and bankruptcy would result. Slave property, the antiemancipationists concluded, could only be taken with the consent of the master. (See "Speech of William H. Broadnax, 1832" and "Speech of

---

[13] *Richmond Enquirer,* 21 January 1832; *Richmond Enquirer,* 26 January 1832; *Richmond Enquirer,* 21 January 1832.

Alexander Knox, 1832," on pages 232 and 233 in the Primary Sources section.)

Almost all of the representatives opposed to gradual abolition insisted that any viable emancipation program must provide masters full compensation for slaves appropriated by the state. The Fifth Amendment to the U.S. Constitution, as well as the state constitution of Virginia, declared that "private property" shall not "be taken for public use, without just compensation." Reimbursing masters for their slaves— a feature absent from the Randolph plan—would not be cheap. Delegates Alexander Knox and John Thompson Brown did the math. The average slave in 1832 was worth about $200, and Virginia was home to roughly half a million slaves. Compensating masters for their slaves would therefore cost an estimated $100 million, excluding the costs of freed slaves' transportation out of the country, which virtually all white Virginians presumed was a requisite component to any emancipation program. From where was this money to come? The state lacked the fiscal resources to finance compensation and removal. Knox assumed new taxes would be imposed to secure the necessary funding. Slaveholders would therefore end up paying money out of their own pockets to reimburse themselves for the loss of their slaves. Such a scenario seemed nonsensical to the anti-emancipation contingent.

To make matters worse, any scheme of emancipation would depress the value of both slaves and land. According to John Thompson Brown, emancipating Virginia's $100 million worth of slaves would legislate away about one-third of the entire state's wealth. Prices for female slaves in particular would suffer, noted Brown and William H. Brodnax, because an essential component of their value was attached to their fecundity and their ability to provide the next generation of plantation laborer. The loss of slave labor would exert a ripple effect on the Virginia economy. With no slaves to work the soil, land values would plummet. The combination of depreciated slaves and land, said James Gholson, "would be productive of much pecuniary embarrassment and distress to a large portion of Eastern Virginia."[14] Deprived of their most valuable slave laborers and burdened with the responsibilities of raising relatively unproductive young slaves and maintaining elderly slaves past their prime, Virginia masters mindful of their own

---

[14] *Richmond Enquirer,* 24 January 1832.

economic interests would abandon their native land and migrate to other slaveholding states where their property rights were more secure. Thus, whereas supporters of the Randolph plan predicted that Virginia whites would flee the state if the General Assembly failed to adopt a program of gradual abolition, opponents argued that the Randolph plan of gradual abolition would have the effect of driving whites away.

The anti-emancipationists Brodnax, Gholson, and Knox saw gradual abolition as a thinly veiled scheme to undermine the political power of eastern Virginia planters. Only a minority of all white households in Virginia owned slaves, and interests in enslaved property were not equally distributed throughout the state. Although it made up about half of Virginia's territory and contained roughly half of the state's whites, western Virginia was home to only a little more than 50,000 slaves, or one-eighth of the state's entire slave population. With well more than 400,000 slaves, it was argued, the East had a comparatively greater stake in slavery. Eastern delegates claimed that because slavery was predominantly the sectional concern of the East, it was more appropriate to let those most directly interested in slavery—slaveholders—determine the fate of the institution. The East strenuously objected to Thomas Jefferson Randolph's suggestion that eligible voters across Virginia be permitted to vote directly on his plan at the polls. Under that scenario, eastern masters feared, the nonslaveholding majority in Virginia could unfairly strip them of their enslaved property and force its surrender. Moreover, it appeared to the East that a West unreconciled to recent political compromises at the Constitutional Convention of 1829 was attempting to use the emancipation issue to rehash the divisive political battles of the past few years. The convention of 1829 had explicitly rejected an equal distribution of political power among Virginia whites and bestowed greater representation upon the East on the basis of the region's slave population. Submitting emancipation to a direct popular vote would therefore undermine the spirit of the convention. Eastern slaveholders considered it the legislature's express responsibility to protect their interest in slave property. Their concerns required them to make the rather undemocratic argument that a popular vote on emancipation was subversive of state government.

For those opposed to the gradual abolition of slavery, the Randolph plan had no shortage of weaknesses. Ultimately, its fundamental flaw was that it targeted the wrong segment of the black population altogether. Slaveholders urged their representatives to leave slavery untouched and instead redirect their energies to expelling Virginia's free blacks. Although few free persons of color participated in the Turner rebellion, James Gholson argued that "removal of the *free* colored population . . . should claim the first consideration and regard of this Legislature." According to the 1830 census, Virginia's 47,000 free blacks made up less than 4 percent of the total population in a state with more than 1.2 million people, and just one-tenth of the overall black population. Nevertheless, for many white Virginians, free blacks posed a greater threat than slaves. Gholson described Virginia's free blacks as "the most depraved, dissolute, miserable and dangerous portion" of the population: "With no regular occupations to restrain them from mischief, they act as the procurers of news, and the carriers of intelligence; and by their presence and association, are continually reminding the slave, of the difference in *their* condition, and the bondage in which *he* lives." The overwhelming majority of white Virginians did not believe they could cohabit the same society as free or freed blacks. But especially for eastern Virginia whites, a well-regulated slave population fulfilled an important economic role. An editorial from slave-rich Mecklenburg County neatly summarized the anti-emancipationist position, arguing that tampering with slavery "is endangering to our safety, destructive of our property, and an invasion of our rights."[15]

OUTCOME AND IMPACT

Virginia's future pivoted on the outcome of the emancipation debate in the House of Delegates. One representative likened the state to a house teetering on the edge of a volcanic crater. Would Virginia metaphorically plummet to its death in a bubbling cauldron of lava? Delegates understood that their decision held ramifications for not only Virginia but the entire South. Some feared that the assembly was behaving rashly and irresponsibly. Questions of such magnitude demanded the utmost discretion. Considering the importance of the question, they recommended consulting fellow slaveholding states to preclude acting prematurely.

---

[15] *Richmond Enquirer*, 24 January 1832; *Richmond Enquirer*, 26 January 1832.

After two weeks of debate, on January 25, 1832, William Ballard Preston's amended resolution calling it "expedient" to consider legislation abolishing slavery in Virginia came up for a vote. It failed to pass, 73 to 58. A majority of legislators found it "inexpedient" to discuss any scheme of emancipation, preferring instead to leave the issue alone. The zenith of antislavery political agitation in a southern legislature had been reached without producing a gradual abolition law. The subject never again resurfaced in Virginia or any other slaveholding state. Even without implementing an emancipation program, Virginia avoided a repeat of the Turner revolt. In 1859, however, the radical white abolitionist John Brown led an interracial group in a raid on the federal arsenal at Harpers Ferry, Virginia, as part of an ill-conceived plan to arm slaves and incite an insurrection. The Virginia militia commanded by Robert E. Lee quickly mobilized and crushed the insurgents before any genuine slave revolt could erupt.

Unable to reach a consensus on gradual abolition, the Virginia assembly passed a stricter black code than had been on the books. Laws prohibited a range of independent slave activities, such as unsupervised black religious gatherings. Slave preaching was forbidden, and new restrictions were imposed on slave movement. Legislation outlawed free blacks from possessing firearms. They could also not own slaves, immediate family members excepted, and any charged with felonies were now to be tried in slave courts. Virginia lawmakers also agreed that the relocation of the state's free blacks was a desirable goal, briefly lending renewed impetus to colonization efforts. The legislature in 1833 appropriated $18,000 annually for the next five years for the voluntary removal of free black Virginians to Africa. The General Assembly never authorized the compulsory deportation of either free blacks or slaves.

In the wake of the Nat Turner revolt and the debate over gradual emancipation in Virginia, southern slaveholders more vociferously defended the peculiar institution. Virginia delegates in 1832 did not describe bondage as a "positive good," however. At this transitory moment, they continued to speak of slavery as an "evil" and a "curse" rather than as a blessing. Nevertheless, the legislative debate in Virginia presaged many arguments that became staples in the proslavery repertoire. Proslavery delegates, for instance, conjured images of happy slaves with affectionate ties to their masters, and they insisted that Virginia slaves were better off than working-class whites in the North or in Europe. Shortly after the debate over emancipation concluded in the House of Delegates, Thomas Roderick Dew, a Virginia Tidewater native and young professor at the College of William & Mary, composed an essay, first published in the *American Quarterly Review* as "Abolition of Negro Slavery," that became a classic in the emerging proslavery argument. Soon expanded into a substantial pamphlet entitled *Review of the Debate in the Virginia Legislature of 1831 and 1832,* Dew's work circulated widely in the South. Though confused and even contradictory at points, a reflection of changing attitudes toward slavery, it dismissed emancipation and colonization as unrealistic and provided a foundation for more elaborate and internally consistent defenses of slavery in future decades.

WHAT IF?

What if Virginia had abolished slavery after the Nat Turner revolt?

By a margin of 15 votes, 73 to 58, the House of Delegates ruled against consideration of a gradual emancipation program. An analysis of the votes reveals a clear sectional division within Virginia. From the Shenandoah Valley west to the Ohio River, delegates declared a discussion of abolition expedient by a vote of 49 to 6. William Ballard Preston's amended resolution suffered defeat thanks to the East, where only 9 delegates voted to discuss emancipation, compared to 67 who preferred silence on the subject. Without a legislative apportionment that favored the East, the vote on the Preston amendment might have been much closer than it was. If seats in the Virginia legislature in 1832 were determined strictly on the basis of the state's white population, the East would have had to surrender seven of its votes to the West, producing a theoretically possible result of 66 to 65, in which a scant one vote prevented setting slavery on the road to extinction in Virginia. Some who voted for the Preston amendment in 1832 might have done so symbolically, knowing the resolution was doomed to failure. Had their votes truly mattered, they might have switched sides. Nevertheless, apportioning the vote exclusively according to the white population would probably have narrowed the gap in the final tally.

Alternatives existed to the Randolph plan, upon which most legislators based their vote. Henry Berry of Jefferson County offered tweaks to the Randolph proposal. Unlike Randolph's, his plan declared the children of slaves free from birth but mandated that they work as servants long enough for their masters to recoup the costs of raising them. The Berry plan also prohibited the sale of slaves' children.

William H. Brodnax advanced his own distinct scheme for ridding Virginia of its black population. He proposed the removal of 6,000 blacks per year, roughly their annual natural increase, to their ancestral home of Africa. Brodnax recommended first deporting free blacks, starting with young adults yet to begin their families. Their absence, he predicted, would increase the value of slave labor and the slaves themselves. After the successful colonization of free blacks, the state could turn its attention to the slaves. Brodnax, Thomas Marshall of Fauquier County, and others entertained the idea of using monies from the sale of public lands in the West for federally funding the removal of Virginia's slave population.

Sectionalism and the apportionment of delegates in Virginia make it difficult to imagine a scenario in which any scheme of emancipation would pass. If western nonslaveholders somehow miraculously united with like-minded easterners, overcame the West's legislative handicaps, and managed to institute gradual abolition, would slaveholding eastern Virginians even have accepted it? In 1832, the East detected in the Randolph proposal a western ambush. One delegate observed that "sectional jealousy" in Virginia had "awakened" to the point that, according to some contemporaries, "the State must be divided."[16] Western Virginia eventually did split from Virginia in 1861 as loyal westerners refused to secede from the Union along with the remainder of the state. Western Virginia joined the Union as the separate state of West Virginia in 1863.

After Nat Turner's rebellion, Virginia—the cradle of U.S. slavery—briefly questioned its commitment to the peculiar institution. Had the House of Delegates found it expedient to embark upon gradual abolition, Alexander Knox feared that the "baneful contagion" of emancipation might spread across the South. Perhaps other slaveholding states in the Upper South could have mustered the courage to imitate Virginia's example, but Deep South states such as South Carolina, more devoted to slavery than more northerly slaveholding states, would never have consented to a program of gradual emancipation. Knox was right to doubt that southern states "will be so blind to their interest, or so callous of their rights," as to undertake abolitionist schemes.[17] At the national level, southern states that succumbed to gradual emancipation would have sacrificed the political benefits of the three-fifths clause. Ultimately, Virginia fell 15 votes short of toppling the pillar of slavery in the Old Dominion as delegates showed greater interest in removing free blacks than in freeing slaves. Thanks to the political uproar he prompted, however, in a roundabout way, Nat Turner nearly succeeded in liberating Virginia's slaves.

---

[16] *Richmond Enquirer,* 27 April 1832.
[17] *Richmond Enquirer,* 11 February 1832.

CHRONOLOGY

1712   A slave rebellion breaks out in New York City.

1739   The Stono Rebellion erupts in South Carolina.

1800   The Gabriel conspiracy is unearthed in Richmond, Virginia.
Nat Turner is born.

1811   A large slave uprising takes place in Louisiana.

1822   Denmark Vesey reportedly plots a slave revolt in Charleston,
South Carolina.

1831   *Jan. 1:* William Lloyd Garrison publishes the first issue of the
Liberator.

Feb. 12: Nat Turner witnesses and attaches significance to a solar
eclipse.

Aug. 22: The Turner revolt begins.

Oct. 30: Turner is captured.

Nov. 5: Turner is put on trial.

Nov. 11: Turner is executed.

1832   The Virginia House of Delegates debates gradual emancipation
of the state's slaves.

1859   John Brown's raid at Harpers Ferry, Virginia, fails to incite a
slave insurrection.

1863   After breaking away from Virginia, West Virginia enters the
Union during the Civil War.

1865   The Thirteenth Amendment abolishes slavery in the United States.

DISCUSSION QUESTIONS

1. How successful was the Turner uprising? By what criteria do you
   gauge success?
2. How appropriate is it to label Nat Turner a "hero" or his actions
   "heroic"?
3. How valid were legislators' reasons for wanting to abolish slavery
   gradually in Virginia?
4. How valid were other legislators' reasons for rejecting the gradual emancipation of slavery in Virginia?
5. What did the debate in the House of Delegates indicate about
   the state of slavery in Virginia? How typical was Virginia of other
   slaveholding states?

WEB SITES

Public Broadcasting Service. "Nat Turner's Rebellion," Africans in America, Resource Bank. URL: http://www.pbs.org/wgbh/aia/part3/3p1518.html. Accessed October 24, 2009.

University of North Carolina at Chapel Hill. Documenting the American South. *The Confessions of Nat Turner, the Leader of the Late Insurrection in Southampton, Va.* Baltimore: T. R. Gray, 1831. URL: http://docsouth.unc.edu/neh/turner/menu.html. Accessed October 24, 2009.

BIBLIOGRAPHY

Freehling, Alison Goodyear. *Drift Toward Dissolution: The Virginia Slavery Debate of 1831–1832.* Baton Rouge: Louisiana State University Press, 1982. The fullest, most complete account of the Virginia debate over slavery. It stresses the continuity of antislavery sentiment within the state and the divisions among Virginia whites. Chapter 3 examines the Constitutional Convention of 1829, chapter 5 the debate in the House of Delegates.

French, Scot. *The Rebellious Slave: Nat Turner in American Memory.* Boston: Houghton Mifflin, 2004. A cultural examination of the figure of the rebellious slave and later generations' memory of Nat Turner.

Greenberg, Kenneth S., ed. *The Confessions of Nat Turner and Related Documents.* Boston: Bedford/St. Martin's, 1996. A classroom-friendly volume containing an insightful introductory essay, a reprint of Thomas R. Gray's *Confessions of Nat Turner,* and several primary sources related to the uprising.

———. *Nat Turner: A Slave Rebellion in History and Memory.* New York: Oxford University Press, 2003. A collection of essays by prominent scholars that examines the Turner revolt from many different perspectives.

Oates, Stephen B. *The Fires of Jubilee: Nat Turner's Fierce Rebellion.* New York: Harper & Row, 1975. The standard narrative account of the Southampton insurrection.

Rucker, Walter C. *The River Flows On: Black Resistance, Culture, and Identity Formation in Early America.* Baton Rouge: Louisiana State University Press, 2006. Chapter 6 examines the Turner revolt through the lens of spiritualism, conjure, and Christianity.

Tragle, Henry Irving. *The Southampton Slave Revolt of 1831: A Compilation of Source Material.* Amherst: University of Massachusetts Press, 1971. An impressive collection of primary sources related to the Turner rebellion.

Wolf, Eva Sheppard. *Race and Liberty in the New Nation: Emancipation in Virginia from the Revolution to Nat Turner's Rebellion.* Baton Rouge: Louisiana State University Press, 2006. Traces white Virginians' changing attitudes toward emancipation and their growing commitment to slavery. The sixth chapter examines the legislative debate of early 1832.

PRIMARY SOURCES

1. Articles, *Richmond Enquirer*, 1831

Reports of slave plots and slave conspiracies abounded in the American South. Many of them had no basis in fact and merely reflected active white imaginations. Accustomed to hearing unsubstantiated rumors, Thomas Ritchie and John L. Cook, the editors of the Richmond Enquirer, *downplayed the first reports of the events in Southampton County in August 1831. But while they urged readers to remain calm, they also assured them that if the reports were true, white Virginians would be avenged.*

A letter was received on Tuesday morning . . . that an "insurrection" had broken out among the blacks—that several white families had been destroyed; that arms and ammunition were wanting in Southampton, and that a considerable military force might be required to subdue the disturbers. . . .

No *authentic* accounts have been received of the character of this unexpected transaction—of the number of blacks collected, of their designs, of the mischief they have done; whether they are the mere runaways who have broken out from the Swamps, or how many slaves of the neighboring plantations have joined—whether they have got together for mere rapine and robbery, or for what.—But that these wretches will rue the day on which they broke loose upon the neighboring population, is most certain. A terrible retribution will fall upon their heads.—Dearly will they pay for their madness and their misdeeds.

Rumors are, of course, as "plenty as blackberries."—There is, of course, much exaggeration in all our verbal and written accounts. The short letters which have been received are themselves the mere statements of rumors—none of them having been written by actual observers of the scene. We give such as have been received—the reader will know how to make allowance for the exaggerations in all such matters.

Source: Richmond Enquirer, 26 August 1831.

Once more reliable information filtered into the Enquirer *offices, the editors struck a different, more resolute tone.*

What strikes us as the most remarkable thing in this matter, is the horrible ferocity of these monsters. They remind one of a parcel of blood thirsty wolves rushing down from the Alps; or, rather like a former incursion of the Indians upon the white settlements. Nothing is spared; neither age nor sex respected—the helplessness of women and children pleads in vain for mercy. The danger is thought to be over—but prudence still demands precaution. The lower county should be on the alert.— The case of Nat. Turner warns us. No black man ought to be permitted to turn a Preacher through the country. The law must be enforced—or the tragedy of Southampton appeals to us in vain. . . . The alacrity with which our troops turned out, and the number which so quickly collected on the scene, will have its effect hereafter. It will show how utterly hopeless is every attempt to do any thing against the whites—and how surely such misguided wretches bring down ruin upon their own heads.

Source: Richmond Enquirer, 30 August 1831.

—∽∽—

2. Letter, Virginia Governor John Floyd to South Carolina Governor James Hamilton, Jr., 1831

Governor John Floyd of Virginia wrote to his fellow governor James Hamilton, Jr., of South Carolina on November 19, 1831. Like many Virginia whites, Floyd blamed northern troublemakers for inciting the Turner uprising. A western Virginian, he anticipated in his letter the implementation of restrictive legislation against Virginia's black population and suggested his support for a scheme of gradual emancipation. He later retreated from his earlier, controversial abolitionist stance.

Richmond
November 19, 1831

Sir:

I received your letter yesterday and with great pleasure will give you my impressions freely—

I will notice this affair in my annual message, but here only give a very careless history of it, as it appeared to the public—

I am fully persuaded, the spirit of insubordination which has, and still manifests itself in Virginia, had its origin among, and eminated [sic] from, the Yankee population, upon their *first* arrival amongst us, but mostly especially the Yankee pedlers and traders.

The course has been by no means a direct one—they began first, by making them religious—their conversations were of that character—telling the blacks, God was no respecter of persons—the black man was as good as the white—that all men were born free and equal—that they cannot serve two masters—that the white people rebelled against England to obtain freedom, so have the blacks a right to do.

In the mean time, I am sure without any purpose of this kind, the preachers, principally Northern—were very assiduous in operating upon our population, day and night, they were at work—and religion became, and is, the fashion of the times—finally our females and of the most respectable were persuaded that it was piety to teach negroes to read and write, to the end that they might read the *Scriptures*—many of them became tutoresses in Sunday schools and, pious distributors of tracts, from the New York Tract Society.

At this point, more active operations commenced—our magistrates and laws became more inactive—large assemblages of negroes were suffered to take place for religious purposes—Then commenced the efforts of the black preachers, often from the pulpits these pamphlets and papers were read—followed by the incendiary publications of Walker, Garrison and Knapp of Boston, these too with songs and hymns of a similar character were circulated, read and commented upon—We resting in apathetic security until the Southampton affair.

From all that has come to my knowledge during and since this affair—I am fully convinced that every black preacher in the whole country east of the Blue Ridge was in the secret, that the plans as published by those Northern presses were adopted and acted upon by them—that their congregations, as they were called knew nothing of this intended rebellion, except a few leading and intelligent men, who may have been head men in the Church—*the mass* were prepared by making them aspire to an equal station by such conversations as I have related as the first step.

I am informed that they had settled the form of government to be that of white people, whom they intended to cut off to a man—with the difference that the preachers were to be their Governors, Generals and Judges. I feel fully justified to myself, in believing the Northern incendiaries, tracts, Sunday schools, religion and reading and writing has accomplished this end.

I shall in my annual message recommend that laws be passed—To confine the Slaves to the estates of their masters—prohibit negroes from preaching—absolutely to drive from this State all free negroes—and to substitute the surplus revenues in our Treasury annually for slaves, to work for a time upon our Rail Roads etc etc and these sent out of the country, preparatory, or rather as the first step to emancipation—This last point will of course be tenderly and cautiously managed and will be urged or delayed as your State and Georgia may be disposed to co-operate. . . .

I am Sir,
with consideration and respect
Your obt Sevnt
John Floyd

Source: Kenneth S. Greenberg, ed., *The Confessions of Nat Turner and Related Documents* (Boston: Bedford/St. Martin's, 1996), 110–111.

—⁓—

3. Petition from the "Females of the County of Augusta," 1832

The Turner rebellion sparked numerous petitions for relief to the Virginia legislature. In an era of small government, men in antebellum America frequently petitioned their state assemblies. The following memorial was unusual in that it was signed not by men, but by more than 200 women from Augusta County in western Virginia in 1832. Reflecting contemporary gender conventions, the female petitioners shared their fears for themselves and their families and humbly implored male legislators to perform their masculine duty to protect them.

To . . . the General Assembly of the State of Virginia, the memorial of the subscribing females of the county of Augusta humbly represents that although it be unexampled, in our beloved State, that females should interfere in its political concerns, and although we feel all the timidity incident to our sex in taking this step, yet we hold our right to do so to be unquestionable, and feel ourselves irresistably *[sic]* impelled to the exercise of that right by the most potent considerations and the perilous circumstances which surround us. We pretend not to conceal from you, our fathers and brothers, our protectors by your investment with the political power of the land, the fears which agitate our bosoms, and the dangers which await us, as revealed by recent tragical deeds. Our fears, we admit, are great; but we do not concede that they are the effects of blind & unreflecting cowardice; we do not concede that they spring from the superstitious timidity of our sex. Alas! we are indeed timid; but we appeal to your manly reason, to your more matured wisdom to attest the justice & propriety of our fears, when we call to your recollection the late slaughter of our sisters & their little ones, in certain parts of our land, & the strong probability that that slaughter was but a partial execution of a widely projected scheme of carnage. We know not, we cannot know the night, nor the unguarded moments by day or by night, which is pregnant with our destruction, & that of our husbands, & brothers, & sisters, & children; but we do know that we are, at every moment, exposed to the means of our own excision, & of all that is dear to us in life. The bloody monster which threatens us is warmed & cherished on our own hearths. O hear our prayer, & remove it, ye protectors of our persons, ye guardians of our peace!

Tell us not of the labors & hardships which we shall endure when our bond-servants shall be removed from us. They have no terrors for us. Those labors & hardships cannot be greater, or so great as those we now endure in providing for & ruling the faithless beings who are subjected to us. Or were they greater, still they are, in our esteem, less than the small dust in the balance, compared with the burden of our fears and our dangers. . . . However we may be flattered, we will not be argued out of our senses, & persuaded into a belief which is contradicted by experience, & the testimony of sober facts. Many, very many of our sisters & brothers have fled to other lands, from the evils which we experience. . . . Do not slight our importunities. Do not disregard our fears. Our destiny is identified with your's. If we perish, alas! What will become of you & your offspring?

We are no political economists; but our domestic employments, our engagements in rearing up the children of our husbands & brothers, our intimate concern with the interest & prosperity of society, we presume, cannot but inform us of the great & elementary principles of that important science. . . . What is a nation but a family on a large scale? Our fears teach us to reflect & reason and our reflections & reasonings have taught us that the peace of our homes, the welfare of society, the prosperity of future generations call aloud & imperiously for some decisive & efficient measure—and that measure cannot, we believe, be efficient, or of much benefit, if it have not, for its ultimate object, the extinction of slavery, from amongst us. Without, therefore, entering upon a detail of facts & arguments, we implore you by the urgency of our fears, by the love we bear you as our fathers & brothers, by our anxieties for the little ones around us, by our estimate of domestic & public weal, by present danger, by the prospects of the future, by our female virtues, by the patriotism which glows in & animates our bosoms, by our prayers to Almighty God, not to let the power with which you are invested be dormant, but that you exert it for the deliverance of yourselves, of us, of the children of the land, of future ages, from the direct curse which can befal[l] a people. Signalize your legislation by this might deed. This we pray: and in duty bound will ever pray.

Source: Virginia, General Assembly, Legislative Petitions, Augusta County, January 19, 1832, Reel 13, Box 17, Folder 28, Library of Virginia, Richmond.

—⚹—

4. Speech of Samuel Moore, 1832

In the following excerpt, delegate Samuel Moore of Rockbridge County explained the direct relationship between the Turner revolt and the consideration of abolition in the Virginia legislature. Sympathetic to emancipation, Moore considered it manly to grapple with the slavery issue.

The evils and the dangers arising from the continued existence of slavery among us, had escaped the observation of all. . . ; yet recent events had opened the eyes of the whole people to the magnitude of these evils, and to the imminence of the danger which is impending over them. And in my estimation, to have attempted under these circumstances, to shrink from the investigation of this important subject, would have been to disregard the dictates of wisdom, and of prudence. It is utterly impossible, Sir, for us to avoid the consideration of this subject, which forces itself upon our view, in such a manner that we cannot avoid it. . . . The monstrous consequences which arise from the existence of slavery, have become exposed to open day; the dangers arising from it, stare us in the face, and it becomes us as men, as freemen, and the representatives of freemen, to meet and overcome rather than attempt to escape by evading them.

Source: *Richmond Enquirer,* 19 January 1832.

—⁓—

5. Resolution and Amendment of William O. Goode, 1832

Mecklenburg County representative William O. Goode offered the following resolution in January 1832 to discharge a committee in the House of Delegates from considering abolitionist petitions. Albemarle County's Thomas Jefferson Randolph proposed an amendment that in substance reversed Goode's intent.

WEDNESDAY, JANUARY 11, 1832.

MR. GOODE of Mecklenburg, rose to move the following resolution: *Resolved,* That the select committee raised on the subject of slaves, free negroes, and the melancholy occurrences growing out of the tragical massacre in Southampton, be discharged from the consideration of all petitions, memorials and resolutions, which have for their object, the manumission of persons held in servitude under the existing laws of this commonwealth, and that it is not expedient to legislate on the subject.

MR. RANDOLPH moved the following substitute to be inserted after the word "Southampton:"—"be instructed to inquire into the expediency of submitting to the vote of the qualified voters in the several towns, cities, boroughs, and counties of this commonwealth, the propriety of providing by law, that the children of all female slaves, who may be born in this state, on or after the 4th day of July 1840, shall become the property of the commonwealth, the males at the age of twenty-one years, and females at the age of eighteen, if detained by their owners within the limits of Virginia, until they shall respectively arrive at the ages aforesaid, to be hired out until the nett sum arising therefrom, shall be sufficient to defray the expense of their removal, beyond the limits of the United States, and that said committee have leave to report by bill or otherwise."

Source: *The Speech of Thomas J. Randolph, (of Albemarle,) in the House of Delegates of Virginia, on the Abolition of Slavery: Delivered Saturday, Jan. 21, 1832,* 2nd ed. (Richmond, Va.: Thomas W. White, 1832), 3.

—m—

6. Letter, James Goodwyn to Virginia Governor John Floyd, 1832

For several months after the Southampton insurrection, Virginia whites detected other purported conspiracies in many parts of the state. In the following letter of January 9, 1832, to Governor John Floyd, one correspondent related some suspicious events that had occurred recently in Dinwiddie County.

Sir, As the subject of this letter may be of some importance to the publick, I have thought it adviseable to detail to you the occurrences in this county on yesterday, when their *[sic]* were seven slaves brought before me, charged with plot[t]ing and conspiring to Murder the white people of this commonwealth. The Witness was a boy (slave) about fourteen or fifteen years old and appears to be a simple unoffending lad; His evidence was that for the last two or three weeks he had been in company where the prisoners were, and had heard each of them say they were ready to rise, and would do so as soon as their *[sic]* was an opertunity *[sic]*; and that they talked much of murdering the white people stating they should begin at home first; that they should have began sooner, but was delaid *[sic]* by the defeat of Nat (Turner) one he heard say that he should go, or send to the rail road to get men, all this the witness says he heard in a low tone of voice, and could only understand parts of their conversations which he related as above; I asked the boy what induced him to give this information; he readily answered he was afraid they would kill his Mistress. The prisoners were committed to the Jail of the county and will be tried on Monday next. Now if the boy has really told the truth, their *[sic]* are numbers of others concerned with them, as we have a large number of Slaves in this neighbourhood and they very much indulged for we have departed from the ancient discipline of slaves, and have adopted that Lenient course which will surely end in insurrection; We have out our little patrols, and the people, ready to meet any event with out fear

I am Sir very respectfully
Your ob^t Servt
Ja^s Goodwyn

Source: Executive Papers, John Floyd, Nov. 1, 1831–Jan. 31, 1832, Box 5, Folder 10, Library of Virginia, Richmond.

—٭—

7. Speech of James McDowell, Jr., 1832

James McDowell, Jr., represented western Virginia's Rockbridge County in the House of Delegates before he became governor and a U.S. congressman. He emerged as one of the leading voices in favor of gradual emancipation. In the following selection of a speech delivered in the House of Delegates on January 21, 1832, he discussed the relationship between private property and public safety.

The power . . . of correcting the evil tendencies of an authorized property, is inherent in all governments, and the exercise of that power in effecting the correction, when such tendencies arise, is no infringement of private rights—no infringement, because, as these exist within the limitation that they do not conflict with the general weal. . . . An individual cannot hold a property when its general qualities are dangerous or baneful. . . .

On the one side the sanctity and inviolability of private property is plead for the preservation of the total number of our slaves, present and to come: on the other side, there is plead, the increasing danger of this slave population to the public security, and the consequent necessity of arresting it by a gradual reduction of its numbers. Allow the private claim of property to prevail, and you authorize a progressive and indefinite increase of the slave:—Allow the public claim to security to prevail, and you authorize an immediate restriction of that increase. How, sir, are these opposite claims, both of them of acknowledged legitimacy . . . to be reconciled with each other in their practical effects? If a limitation is imposed on the right to this property or its increase, an abridgment of private rights is complained of: if no limitation is imposed, an abridgment of personal and public security is complained of. Upon this opposition how are we to decide? How can we decide but against the inferior right?

The rights of private property and of personal security exist under every government, but they are not *equal*. Security is the primary purpose for which men enter into government; property, beyond a sufficiency for natural wants, is only a secondary purpose. . . . When it loses its utility—when it no longer contributes to the personal benefits and wants of its holder in any equal degree with the expense or the risk or the danger of keeping it—much more—when it jeopards the security of the public—when this is the case, then the original purpose for which it is authorized is lost; its character of prosperity, in the just and beneficial sense of it, is gone, and it may be regulated, without private injustice, in any manner which the general good of the community, by whose laws it was licensed, may require. . . .

The claim to property cannot balance, much less, cancel the claim to security; and when the two come into collision, . . . then the property must yield and the claim to security must be satisfied.

Source: Speech of James M'Dowell, Jr. (of Rockbridge,) in the House of Delegates of Virginia, on the Slave Question: Delivered Saturday, January 21, 1832, 2nd ed. (Richmond, Va.: Thomas W. White, 1832), 11, 15–16.

—⚏—

8. Speech of William H. Brodnax, 1832

William H. Brodnax represented Dinwiddie County in the Virginia House of Delegates. In the following excerpt of his speech of January 19, 1832, he minimized the danger of the Turner revolt.

The real extent of the danger—and God knows that is bad enough!—is, that in insulated neighborhoods, a few misguided fanatics, like Nat Turner—or reckless infatuated desperadoes, like his followers, in total ignorance of the extent of such an enterprise, or of the means necessary to accomplish it, may, in moments of sudden excitement, make desperate attempts, and commence partial excesses of pillage and massacre. Much mischief—(yes, sir, as important to the wretched individuals assailed, as if all the world was involved,)—much injury might be inflicted, before the insurgents could be met with and arrested. But, so far from their overwhelming the whites, conquering the country, overturning our political dynasty, and usurping the seats of legislation, *the very act of their imbodying, would be the immediate signal for their annihilation.* Sir, I assure you, that whatever little of military information I may possess, confirms and corroborates this obvious view of the subject. The only difficulty consists in *finding them*—The danger to be apprehended is entirely of a temporary character, and while they advance unseen and unopposed. The idea of a military force invading and conquering any country, without uniting in a mass, or by avoiding the opposing force of the invaded, would be ridiculous. In truth, there was never a single moment, from the commencement, to the termination, of this celebrated Southampton insurrection, in which ten resolute, well armed men, could not easily have put the whole down. With the relative moral, intellectual and scientific advantages which we possess, the numerical superiority of our slaves would have to become at least twenty to one, before any probable prospect could exist, of a successful general rebellion. . . . Another attempt soon after the recent one, would, in my judgment, lead the way to an indiscriminate slaughter of all the blacks, whether concerned in it or not.

Source: The Speech of William H. Brodnax, (of Dinwiddie) in the House of Delegates of Virginia, on the Policy of the State with Respect to Its Colored Population. Delivered January 19, 1832 (Richmond, Va.: Thomas W. White, 1832), 25.

—⚹—

9. Speech of William H. Brodnax, 1832

William H. Brodnax opposed the Randolph plan for gradual abolition but in the following excerpt from a speech he delivered on January 19, 1832, he set the parameters under which he would support the emancipation of Virginia's slaves.

Yes, sir, your table almost literally groans with petitions, from all quarters of the state, looking to us for some remedy, and crying out in language so strong, and so loud, as not to be disregarded, for *something* to be done—and, sir, *something* must be done. But they have not petitioned you to decree the abolition of slavery—or the confiscation of their property. They have not applied to you to avert an evil portentous, it is true, in its appearance, by bringing sudden and obvious ruin on them. They have not called on you to tear all their property away from them, or manumit their slaves without indemnity or compensation. No, sir, far from it. With a very few exceptions, this is a vision which had not crossed their imaginations. They have prescribed no system, and indicated no plan. This they have submitted to the judgment and intelligence of their delegates in this assembly. They expected, and wish *us* to do *something. What is that something to be?* That is the question. Sir, let us not prescribe a remedy, like that which come to us from Albemarle, nauseous to the palate, and far more pernicious in its effects, than the disease which it would remove. . . .

I have always regarded the following as axioms, which should never be disregarded, and from which, for one, I will never consent to depart:

1st. That no emancipation of slaves should ever be tolerated, unaccompanied by their immediate removal from among us.

2d.   That no system should be introduced, which is calculated to interfere with, or weaken the *security* of private property, or affect its *value.*—And

3d.   That not a single slave, or any other property he possesses, should be taken from its owner, *without his own consent,* or an ample compensation for its value.

Unless some plan can be struck out, in our united councils, entirely consistent with these essential principles, dreadful as would be the alternative, I will sit down in silent despair, and fold my arms with the desperate resolution, of letting the evil roll on to its horrid consummation. . . . I do believe that measures of incalculable benefit may be adopted, entirely consistent with those great principles which I have assumed.

Source: The Speech of William H. Brodnax, (of Dinwiddie) in the House of Delegates of Virginia, on the Policy of the State with Respect to Its Colored Population. Delivered January 19, 1832 (Richmond, Va.: Thomas W. White, 1832), 11–12.

—∞—

10. Speech of Alexander Knox, 1832

Alexander Knox represented Mecklenburg County in the Virginia House of Delegates. He called the Randolph plan a "flagrant . . . violation of our rights" in the 1832 speech excerpted here.

Can any one seriously believe, that the people of this Commonwealth are so destitute of common sense, as to consent to submit to the care and expense of rearing slaves, when they are to be wrested from their possession so soon as they shall arrive at an age capable of rendering efficient service, under the operation of this scheme? The time, Sir, would soon arrive, when the slave-holder would have in his possession none but the old and infirm, or those of a tender age, which, so far from being a source of emolument, would be that of trouble and expence; and a principle of common sense, would induce an immediate surrender of the property. What does it signify, then, Sir, for gentlemen to tell us, that this measure only proposes to operate upon the after-born . . . when its effects will be to destroy the value of the property, and force its surrender at the hands of every individual in the Commonwealth? If, Sir, you have the right to legislate the people out of the increase of this property, you have the power to attack that which is now in their possession. . . . Sir, you may disguise this proposition in any form in which the ingenuity of man can clothe it, but its ostensible object is to deprive the people of this Commonwealth of their inherited and vested rights. . . . To proceed in the manner proposed, would be an act of legislative usurpation, because the Constitution of the State expressly prohibits the Legislature from passing any law, whereby private property shall be taken for public uses without just compensation. . . . We cannot surrender our property to the demands of deluded fanaticism; we cannot yield to the exactions of a power that must strip us of all that is worth preservation in our political association: and if gentlemen are determined to force this measure upon us, a principle of self-preservation will drive us to the maintenance of our rights—for, submission to this arbitrary exaction is more than freemen will bear. The bonds of this Confederacy must be dissolved, or the inhabitants of the East driven to other States, in which they may find that protection for their property which this measure seeks to destroy. The fertile field that heretofore waived with rich foliage, will yield its verdure to the thistle.

Source: Richmond Enquirer, 11 February 1832.

7

SLAVERY AND RELIGION:
Was the Bible Proslavery?

—ᴍ—

THE CONTROVERSY

The Issue

As the debate over slavery intensified in the mid-19th century, both supporters and opponents of the institution invoked religion to defend their positions. Was the Bible proslavery or antislavery?

♦ *Arguments that the Bible was proslavery:* Many theologians in the South as well as in the North believed that the Bible provided divine sanction for the institution of American slavery. In their view, the curse of Ham (or Canaan) condemned Africans and their descendants to slavery. The biblical patriarchs of the Old Testament owned slaves and nevertheless held favor with God, and the law of Moses offered clear instructions governing the keeping of slaves. In the New Testament, Jesus remained silent on the issue of slavery, never explicitly condemning the institution. Instead, the New Testament is filled with passages imploring slaves to obey their masters. One letter of the apostle Paul also ordered the runaway slave Onesimus to return to his owner. Looking at these passages collectively suggested to many clergymen and southern slaveholders that the Bible justified slavery.

♦ *Arguments that the Bible was antislavery:* Abolitionist ministers in the North found ample condemnations of slavery in the Bible. They pointed out that the forms of bondage practiced in biblical times differed markedly from the institution of southern slavery. Slavery was permitted in the Old Testament, but that did not make holding slaves morally right. Like slavery, polygamy and divorce occurred in the Bible, and theologians now denounced them. Slavery, too, had become morally repugnant over time and should be outlawed. Indeed, when God's chosen people were held in slavery in Egypt, God appointed Moses to deliver them to freedom. In the New Testament, Jesus never attacked the institution

235

of slavery directly, but neither did he identify many sins by name. They were nonetheless wrong. Jesus's teachings—to love one another, to treat others as you would want to be treated—condemned slavery implicitly. Slavery, in short, violated the entire spirit of the Bible, with its emphasis on freedom from oppression, equality, and love.

—⁓—

INTRODUCTION

In the late 1820s and 1830s, a radical abolitionist movement took shape in the North. In 1829, the free black David Walker published in Boston his *Appeal to the Coloured Citizens of the World,* a pamphlet that endorsed violence as means to end slavery. The blossoming of radical abolitionism continued in 1831 with the publication of William Lloyd Garrison's weekly newspaper, the *Liberator.* Although small in numbers and confined mainly to the New England states and the Northeast, abolitionists proved exceptionally vocal in their denunciations of slavery as sinful, a great moral evil to be eradicated. In a departure from previous antislavery efforts, they called not for the gradual abolition of slavery but rather for the slaves' immediate emancipation. To achieve their goal, they organized antislavery societies, launched a mass mailing of abolitionist materials into the South, and deluged Congress with abolitionist petitions. (See the sidebar "Abolitionists' Petitions to Congress and the Gag Rule" on page 252.) Their efforts consistently emphasized the immorality of bondage in the American South and provided biblical evidence of the sinfulness of slavery.

Surprised by the new vehemence of antislavery forces, proslavery theologians gathered biblical evidence of their own in justification of slavery. By the early 1840s, Thornton Stringfellow and other proslavery ministers both South and North unfurled a list of proslavery arguments culled from the Bible. They attributed slavery to the curse Noah placed on Canaan, which condemned his descendants to bondage. They pointed out that even though Abraham and other great patriarchs and prophets of the Old Testament owned slaves, God did not smite them but bestowed his grace upon them. Moreover, Mosaic law codified the rules governing slaveholding in ancient times. Turning to the New Testament, proslavery forces observed Jesus' failure to condemn slavery as evil. To the contrary, the New Testament repeatedly entreats slaves to comply with their masters' wishes. The Bible furthermore beseeches fugitive slaves to return to their masters. Proslavery forces made the Bible central to the intellectual defense of slavery.

Abolitionists had drawn upon the Good Book even earlier than their proslavery foes and arrived at the opposite conclusion. For them, the Bible offered no rationale for the continuation of slavery in the American South. A vast gulf separated American slavery from the more benevolent varieties of bondage of the Old Testament. Old Testament slavery existed side by side with polygamy and divorce, two practices widely condemned in mainstream 19th-century Christian churches. If polygamy and divorce had begun to be recognized as wrong over time, slavery merited a similar moral judgment. In the Old Testament itself, Moses had redeemed the Israelites from bondage in Egypt. Surely, the abolitionists figured, God wanted the same for enslaved black Americans. That Jesus in the New Testament failed to censure slavery by name did not make the practice of slaveholding any less sinful. His instructions to love one another and to follow the Golden Rule betrayed the broad antislavery spirit contained within the pages of the Bible.

BACKGROUND

Eighteen thirty-one proved a pivotal year in the development of the abolitionist movement as well as of proslavery thought. William Lloyd Garrison published the first issue of his abolitionist newspaper, the *Liberator*, in Boston on January 1. In it, he rejected gradual emancipation schemes in favor of the immediate liberation of American slaves. Many southerners believed it no coincidence that Nat Turner launched the bloody Southampton insurrection late in the summer of the same year. Although contemporaries in the South linked Garrison to the massacre, Turner had probably never heard of the northern abolitionist. Furthermore, Garrison, despite his antislavery invective, was a pacifist opposed to the utilization of violence. Nevertheless, the Turner rebellion sparked debate in the Virginia legislature over the future of slavery in the Old Dominion and whether or not to abolish the institution. Proslavery forces emerged from the contest victorious, inspiring Thomas Roderick Dew's seminal proslavery essay "Abolition of Negro Slavery," a work that dismissed plans to colonize blacks abroad and enumerated the horrific consequences of emancipation.

On the whole, however, the rise of radical abolitionism caught slavery's supporters off guard. Abolitionists, a small but very vocal minority concentrated most heavily in the northeastern states, busied themselves in pursuit of immediate emancipation, laboring under the conviction that slavery was morally wrong. Garrison was involved in the formation of the New England Anti-Slavery Society in 1832 and the following year joined brothers and New York merchants Arthur and Lewis Tappan to establish the American Anti-Slavery Society (AASS), a national organization dedicated to the abolitionist cause. The AASS was founded shortly after a notable abolitionist success overseas, as Parliament in 1833 freed slaves in the British West Indies through a program of compensated emancipation. At the instigation of Lewis Tappan, abolitionists in 1835 launched a mass mailing campaign that inundated the South with antislavery pamphlets. In Charleston, South Carolina, and other locations, crowds of angry southerners seized from the post office bags of undelivered abolitionist literature and set them ablaze. Although historians estimate that fewer than 10 percent of all slaves could read, the arrival in the U.S. mail of abolitionist propaganda posed a real threat to southern slaveholding interests.

The abolitionists' postal campaign roused slavery's defenders to action. Despite the rise of Garrison and radical abolitionism in 1831, proslavery voices remained remarkably silent for the next few years, seemingly stunned by the sudden assault upon the "peculiar institution." Although South Carolina politician John C. Calhoun proclaimed slavery a "positive good" by 1837, the southern white masses after the Turner revolt did not instantly spurn past characterizations of slavery as a "necessary evil." Like George Washington, Thomas Jefferson, and other members of the founding generation, they continued to look forward to slavery's eventual demise. Most southern whites between 1831 and 1835 continued to lament the presence of slavery, describing it as a burden and regrettable inheritance from their ancestors, and willingly discussed plans of gradual abolition and black colonization abroad. Only in 1835 did the antislavery mailings mobilize a more concerted effort to defend slavery. That year, the number of proslavery works began to mount. With time, their initially inchoate arguments coalesced into a distinctive proslavery ideology.

Religion featured prominently in the developing proslavery and antislavery arguments of the 1830s, 1840s, and 1850s. Biblical justifications and refutations of American slavery were nothing new, having

Angry southern mobs destroyed abolitionist propaganda mailed to the South in 1835. (Library of Congress)

appeared early in the 1700s. More recently, pro- and antislavery biblical references surfaced occasionally during both the congressional debates over Missouri's admission into the Union and the Virginia legislature's deliberations over the abolition of slavery. The antebellum decades therefore witnessed an elaboration of existing arguments that demonstrated continuity with the past rather than a sharp break from it. But while antebellum Americans did not invent biblical pro- and antislavery arguments, the debate did enter a new phase after 1831. The rise of the radical abolitionist movement placed a new emphasis on the morality—or, rather, the immorality—of slavery. Garrison and his colleagues condemned slaveholding as sinful, a moral evil to be eradicated. "If Slavery is ever abolished from the world," wrote Methodist minister LaRoy Sunderland, "it will be done by the influence of the Christian Religion. Men never will abandon slave-holding, till they feel it to be a sin against God."[1] Abolitionist critiques of slavery's immorality forced slaveholders to articulate more thorough and sophisticated proslavery defenses, and debate over slavery's morality therefore grew more pronounced. An

---

[1] LaRoy Sunderland, *The Testimony of God Against Slavery, or a Collection of Passages from the Bible, Which Show the Sin of Holding Property in Man; with Notes* (Boston: Webster & Southard, 1835; reprint, St. Clair Shores, Mich.: Scholarly Press, 1970), v.

examination of scripture became central to the project of determining the justice or injustice of American slavery. The respective theological allies of slaveholders and abolitionists reached contradictory answers to the question, Was the Bible proslavery?

THE DEBATE

The Case that the Bible Was Proslavery

By 1841, proslavery forces were prepared to skillfully use the Bible to defend the peculiar institution from abolitionist attacks. More than any other individual, Thornton Stringfellow, a Baptist minister in Culpeper County, Virginia, made the Bible a centerpiece in the defense of slavery, scouring the good book for scriptural evidence in support of bondage. Other southern clergymen, including South Carolina Baptist Richard Fuller, Kentucky-born Episcopalian Albert Taylor Bledsoe, and Presbyterian Fred A. Ross in Alabama, lent their voices to the chorus of religious proslavery arguments. Southerners were not alone, however, in insisting that slavery was divinely ordained. Many northern-born ministers such as Charles Hodge, the moderate head of Princeton Theological Seminary, and Samuel Blanchard How, pastor of the First Reformed Dutch Church of New Brunswick, New Jersey, also agreed that the Bible sanctioned slavery. They were joined by northern Congregational ministers Nathan Lord and Moses Stuart and the Irish-born Episcopal bishop John Henry Hopkins. Together, the writings of clerics South and North informed the more secular proslavery tracts of southern intellectuals James Henry Hammond and George Fitzhugh. Despite their denominational differences, Stringfellow and other pastors located frequent references amenable to slavery in scripture. They argued that they maintained complete fidelity to the Bible, unlike their antislavery opponents, who deviated from the Bible's plain language creatively but erroneously to pervert the true meaning of God's word.

Much of the religious proslavery argument was rooted in the Old Testament, especially in the books of Genesis and Exodus. Some proslavery clerics viewed enslavement as the by-product of the curse of Cain. After Cain murdered his brother Abel in the fourth chapter of Genesis, God angrily cursed Cain, but, to prevent others from killing him, placed a mark upon Cain, which some assumed to be black skin.

Many other clergymen traced the origins of slavery to the so-called curse of Ham, or, more accurately, the curse of Canaan, explained in Genesis 9:18–27. The story centered on Noah and his three sons, Shem, Ham, and Japheth. After the great flood, Noah planted a vineyard. On one occasion, he drank too much of his wine, became intoxicated, and passed out naked inside his tent. Ham stared at his father's immodesty and reported it to his two brothers. To avoid seeing Noah nude, Shem and Japheth walked backward into their father's tent and covered his body with a robe. When Noah awakened and learned what Ham had done, he cursed Ham's son Canaan and made him a slave to Shem and Japheth. According to many supporters of slavery, Shem's progeny migrated to Asia and Japheth's to Europe; Africans were the descendants of Ham and Canaan. For Thornton Stringfellow and others, then, blacks were condemned to perpetual bondage as punishment for their ancestor's biblical wrongdoing. The subordination of one race to another was divinely ordained. As Stringfellow put it, "God *decreed slavery.*"[2] (See "Thornton Stringfellow, *Slavery: Its Origin, Nature, and History,* 1861," on page 261 in the Primary Sources section and the sidebar "Ethnology and Polygenesis" on page 256.)

God not only sanctioned slavery but showed favor to those who held others in bondage. Many of the Old Testament patriarchs and prophets, Stringfellow noted, were slave owners. Slavery "did exist in the *patriarchal age,* and . . . the persons most extensively involved . . . are the very persons who have been singled out by the Almighty, as the objects of his special regard—whose character and conduct he has caused to be held up as *models* for future generations." Central to this argument was the figure of Abraham. According to Albert Taylor Bledsoe's 1857 *Essay on Liberty and Slavery,* "Abraham himself . . . was the owner and holder of more than a thousand slaves," and the Lord never expressed disapproval of him. The book of Genesis reported that Abraham purchased servants with money and promptly had them circumcised, bringing them into covenant with God and demonstrating the authority he exercised over them. Abraham bequeathed his slaves to his son Isaac, who in turn passed them on to his son Jacob. "How, then," Bledsoe asked, "could . . . professing Christians proceed to condemn and excommunicate a poor

---

[2] Thornton Stringfellow, *Scriptural and Statistical Views in Favor of Slavery,* 4th ed. (Richmond, Va.: J. W. Randolph, 1856), 9.

brother for having merely approved what Abraham had practiced?" Job, too, was a wealthy slaveholder when God tested his faith. Concluded Stringfellow, "from the fact that he has singled out the greatest slaveholders of that age, as the objects of his special favor, it would seem that the institution was one furnishing great opportunities to exercise grace and glorify God, as it still does, where its duties are faithfully discharged."[3]

Proslavery ministers insisted that God would never sanction an institution that was an unmitigated moral evil or countenance a practice he deemed sinful. Slavery, then, was not innately immoral, as the abolitionists supposed. Bledsoe argued that "slavery among the Hebrews . . . was not wrong, because there it received the sanction of the Almighty. . . . We affirm that since slavery has been ordained by him, it cannot be always and everywhere wrong." In *Slavery Ordained of God* (1857), the Reverend Fred A. Ross added that since "Abraham lived in the midst of a system of slave-holding exactly the same in nature with that in the South," then it was also appropriate for "the Southern master in the present day."[4] Baptist minister Richard Fuller made an appeal to moral consistency over time. If God looked favorably upon slavery in the Old Testament, it could not have somehow devolved into a great wrong by the 19th century. To argue otherwise suggested that God had once withheld a spiritual truth from his people. (See "Letter, Richard Fuller to Francis Wayland, 1840s," on page 262 in the Primary Sources section.)

Many proslavery clergymen observed that Mosaic law permitted slaves to be held as property. That Moses made laws governing slavery and slave treatment implied God's approbation of bondage. "Our argument from this acknowledged fact," remarked Charles Hodge, "is, that if God allowed slavery to exist, if he directed how slaves might be lawfully acquired, and how they were to be treated, it is in vain to contend that slaveholding is a sin, and yet profess reverence for the Scriptures."

---

[3] Thornton Stringfellow, *A Brief Examination of Scripture Testimony on the Institution of Slavery, in an Essay, First Published in the Religious Herald, and Republished by Request: With Remarks on a Letter of Elder Galusha, of New York, to Dr. R. Fuller, of South Carolina* (Washington, D.C.: Congressional Globe Office, 1850), 2, 6–7; Albert Taylor Bledsoe, "Liberty and Slavery: or, Slavery in the Light of Moral and Political Philosophy," in *Cotton Is King, and Pro-Slavery Arguments Comprising the Writings of Hammond, Harper, Christy, Stringfellow, Hodge, Bledsoe, and Cartwright, on This Important Subject*, ed. E. N. Elliott (1860; reprint, New York: Negro Universities Press, 1969), 339.

[4] Bledsoe, "Liberty and Slavery," 337–338; Fred A. Ross, *Slavery Ordained of God* (1857; reprint, Miami: Mnemosyne, 1969), 153.

One biblical passage recurring in proslavery ministers' defense of bondage was Leviticus 25:44–46: "Thy bond-men and thy bond-maids which thou shalt have, shall be of the heathen that are round about you; of them shall ye buy bond-men and bond-maids. Moreover, of the children of the strangers that do sojourn among you, of them shall ye buy, and of their families that are with you, which they begat in your land. And they shall be your possession. And ye shall take them as an inheritance for your children after you, to inherit them for a possession; they shall be your bond-men forever." As Ross explained, "I do not see how God could tell us more plainly that he did command his people to buy slaves. . . . The passage has no other meaning." Mosaic law permitted God's chosen people to hold foreigners as slaves who could be bought, owned, sold, or bequeathed to the next generation in perpetual bondage. The 21st chapter of Exodus completed the objectification and commodification of the slave, describing servants and maids as "money." According to the law of Moses, a master who struck his slave faced certain punishment if the bond person died immediately. If, however, the servant lingered a day or two before succumbing to death, the master escaped penalty because he intended only to correct, not to kill, the slave. The slaveholder, explained Samuel Blanchard How, avoided prosecution "because the servant or maid was his property, and he had the right suitably and not cruelly to chastise them when they, by their improper conduct, merited it."[5]

Proslavery writers found evidence in the New Testament as compelling as that in the Old. Even though he lived in a slaveholding region and would have been familiar with the practice, Jesus never took the opportunity to refute the law of Moses and explicitly condemn the institution of slavery. No New Testament figure either denounced or abolished it. Albert Taylor Bledsoe marveled that "the most profound silence reigns through the whole word of God with respect to the sinfulness of slavery," and he was not alone in making the point.[6] (See "Charles Hodge, 'The Bible Argument on Slavery,' 1860," on page 263 in the Primary Sources section.) In contrast, Jesus did single out for rebuke polygamy and divorce, both practices formerly permitted under

---

[5] Charles Hodge, "The Bible Argument on Slavery," in *Cotton Is King*, 860; Leviticus quoted in Stringfellow, *Scriptural and Statistical Views*, 29; Ross, *Slavery Ordained of God*, 63; Samuel Blanchard How, *Slaveholding Not Sinful: Slavery, the Punishment of Man's Sin, Its Remedy, the Gospel of Christ* (1855; reprint, Freeport, N.Y.: Books for Libraries Press, 1971), 114.

[6] Bledsoe, "Liberty and Slavery," 347.

Old Testament law. His failure likewise to censure slavery in the new covenant underscored his acceptance of the institution. (See "Thornton Stringfellow, The New Testament on Polygamy, Divorce, and Slavery, 1860," on page 263 in the Primary Sources section.)

Rather than assail bondage, the New Testament repeatedly implored slaves to obey their masters. Paul's letters to the Ephesians 6:5 and the Colossians 3:22, 1 Timothy 6:1, the letter to Titus 2:9, and 1 Peter 2:18 all instructed bond people to respect and serve their owners. In Paul's brief letter to the slaveholder Philemon, Paul explained that he had converted Onesimus, a fugitive slave belonging to Philemon, to Christianity but then ordered him to return to his master. The apostle's instructions mirrored those of the Old Testament's Book of Genesis, in which an angel told the runaway bondwoman Hagar to return and submit to her mistress Sarah, Abraham's wife. Both the Old and New Testaments demanded that slaves fulfill their duties to their masters.

Proslavery churchmen also countered the abolitionists' claim that Jesus ushered in a new moral principle antithetical to slavery, the Golden Rule: "Do to others as you would they should do to you." Thornton Stringfellow contended that the Golden Rule introduced nothing unique to the New Testament. He viewed it, rather, as merely a rewording of the Old Testament command in Leviticus 19:18 to love your neighbor as yourself. If the underlying principle was identical, as Stringfellow supposed, and slavery was sanctioned by God in the Old Testament, Jesus' teaching of the Golden Rule in the New provided no impetus for the prohibition of slavery. For proslavery clergymen, the Golden Rule implied only that masters should treat slaves as they would wish to be treated if they, too, were enslaved.

Many southern theologians upheld the model of the Christian slaveholder. They considered slaveholders in the South divinely chosen masters who mitigated the possible ill effects of slavery through their own Christian character. In conformity with the golden rule, they insisted, masters treated slaves well, as members of an extended family, civilizing and Christianizing heathen slaves and guiding their moral improvement. When benevolent masters fulfilled their obligations to their slaves, they made slavery acceptable as an institution. Nothing about slavery was inherently immoral; it was quite possible for good Christians to own slaves, assuming they executed their duty to serve as guardians of their bond people.

Proslavery clergymen and their secular allies viewed antislavery northerners as stunningly ignorant of God's word. The South adhered loyally to the letter of the Bible, whereas the North betrayed it. (See "James Henry Hammond, 'Slavery in the Light of Political Science,' 1860," on page 264 in the Primary Sources section.) "With men from the North," Thornton Stringfellow scoffed, "I have observed for many years a palpable ignorance of the Divine will, in reference to the institution of slavery. . . . How can any man, who believes the Bible, admit for a moment that God intended to teach mankind by the Bible, that all are born free and equal?" Some proslavery theologians acknowledged that God may someday choose to eradicate slavery, but in seeking to dismantle the institution prematurely, abolitionists were interfering with God's divine plan, which embraced the master-slave relationship no less than that between husband and wife or parent and child. Any potential disappearance of slavery must occur in its own time, consistent with God's will. In the meantime, Stringfellow concluded, "The moral precepts of the Old or New Testament cannot make that wrong which God ordained to be his will, as he has slavery."[7]

The Case that the Bible Was Antislavery

Although proslavery forces laid claim to a biblical argument, abolitionists had no intention of surrendering the Good Book to their rivals. For them, slaveholding was unquestionably a sin, "a heinous crime in the sight of God," and only a tortured reading of the Bible could conclude otherwise. Presbyterian minister and abolitionist Albert Barnes declared the biblical proslavery argument "among the most remarkable instances of mistaken interpretation and unfounded reasoning furnished by the perversities of the human mind." Northern and foreign-born abolitionist preachers such as Barnes and his fellow Presbyterian George Bourne; Baptists Nathaniel Colver and Elon Galusha; Methodists Charles Elliott, William Hosmer, and LaRoy Sunderland; Congregationalist Charles Beecher; and William Ellery Channing, a Unitarian, joined unordained allies, including Francis Wayland and Theodore Dwight Weld, among others, to marshal biblical evidence in condemnation of slavery. As one contemporary observed, "The Abolitionists

---

[7] Stringfellow, *Scriptural and Statistical Views*, 6, 75, 70.

have quoted Scripture quite as much as their opponents, but . . . on the side of right and justice."[8]

Antislavery theologians distinguished between biblical slavery and the form practiced in the Old South. Their arguments took different tacks. According to Albert Barnes, Theodore Dwight Weld, and others, the complicated task of translating the Bible had obscured the original meaning of several passages purported to endorse slavery. The linguistic confusion between Greek and Hebrew and English had resulted in the mistaken belief that 19th-century southern masters and the patriarchs of the Old Testament understood slavery in the same way. What modern readers thought was slavery in the Bible, however, actually referred to various other forms of servitude or apprenticeship less oppressive than American slavery. Other antislavery ministers such as LaRoy Sunderland acknowledged slavery in the Bible but agreed that "it differed radically from the system of slave-holding, which prevails now in these United States." Bondage in the Old Testament, concurred the Methodist William Hosmer, "has scarcely any resemblance to American Slavery."[9]

Clergymen such as Barnes, Sunderland, and Charles Beecher highlighted the brutality of the American brand of slavery compared to the various labor regimes employed in biblical times. For instance, unlike in the American South, slaves in the Old Testament enjoyed legal recourse if maltreated. And whereas southern slavery was perpetual and hereditary, the Mosaic law outlined in the book of Exodus clearly stated that Hebrew servants would serve six years and be freed on the seventh, a point repeated in the 15th chapter of Deuteronomy. Non-Hebrews could be held in servitude only until Jubilee, every 50 years. (See "Albert Barnes, *An Inquiry into the Scriptural Views of Slavery*, 1846," on page 265 in the Primary Sources section.) Such regulations appeared in the Old Testament not because God sanctioned slavery but because the institution antedated Mosaic law. The major point that antislavery churchmen

---

[8] The American Anti-Slavery Society described slavery as "a heinous crime," quoted in Charles K. Whipple, *Relations of Anti-Slavery to Religion* (New York: American Anti-Slavery Society, 1856), 1; Albert Barnes, *An Inquiry into the Scriptural Views of Slavery* (1846; Philadelphia: Parry and McMillan, 1857), 381; Whipple, *Relations of Anti-Slavery to Religion*, 2.

[9] Sunderland, *Testimony of God against Slavery*, 10; William Hosmer, *Slavery and the Church* (Auburn: William J. Moses, 1853; reprint, Freeport, N.Y.: Books for Libraries Press, 1970), 51.

stressed was that the nature of bondage practiced in the Old Testament was unique to its time, without parallel in the 19th-century South.

Francis Wayland contended that although God had indeed allowed slavery in the Old Testament, he restricted the institution to a people at a particular moment in history. Through a process of progressive revelation, Christianity had evolved over time to shun bondage. (See "Letter, Francis Wayland to Richard Fuller, 1845," on page 266 in the Primary Sources section.) Many antislavery voices—those of Wayland, William Ellery Channing, LaRoy Sunderland, and Albert Barnes, for example— dismissed the proslavery argument that God must have approved of bondage since it existed in biblical times. "It should be understood in the outset," William Hosmer indicated, "that the Old Testament is not, in all respects, a standard of morals for the present day. The New Testament has revised the ethical code of the Old, and several things, once allowed, are now prohibited," such as polygamy. Like slavery, polygamy occurred in the Old Testament. Sunderland observed that "Abraham has two wives, David had two, and. . . . Solomon had seven hundred wives, and three hundred concubines."[10] That did not imply, however, that God either commanded or sanctioned the practice. Moreover, as Barnes observed, modern-day Christians had since rejected polygamy, despite its presence in the Bible. The same could be said of divorce. Therefore, how could slavery's advocates, with any consistency, invoke the existence of biblical slavery in support of the enslavement of blacks in the American South? Proslavery forces were conveniently cherry-picking biblical evidence in favor of bondage while ignoring facts that contradicted their logic. (See "Albert Barnes on Slavery and Polygamy, 1846," on page 267 in the Primary Sources section.)

Scanning the Old Testament itself, some clergymen detected an obvious antislavery message in the book of Exodus. With his demand to pharaoh to "let my people go," Moses delivered the Israelites from bondage in Egypt. God, then, must have advocated freedom from the oppression of slavery. "God regarded their groanings," Sunderland wrote of the Hebrew slaves, "and when they cried unto him, he saved them from the power of their oppressors." (See "LaRoy Sunderland, *The Testimony of God Against Slavery*, 1835," on page 269 in the Primary Sources section.) English-born Presbyterian George Bourne agreed that scripture

---

[10] Hosmer, *Slavery and the Church*, 44; Sunderland, *Testimony of God Against Slavery*, 10–11.

resoundingly condemned "the great sin of human oppression, including of course [slavery] the most oppressive practice in the world." It followed that God would support the liberation of bond people from the yoke of their southern masters.[11]

Nor could Jesus' silence on the subject of slavery in the New Testament be contorted into support for the institution. Sunderland and Channing again applied the polygamy example. According to Sunderland, "if any kind of slavery may be tolerated now, under the gospel dispensation, because a certain species of it existed among the Jews anciently, or because Christ and his Apostles did not say in just so many words, that 'slave-holding under all circumstances of the case, is a sin against God,' then it follows by the same rules of interpretation . . . that polygamy is justifiable now, by the Bible, for some of the patriarchs were polygamists, and they carried out their views by their practice." Jesus may have remained mum on the slavery issue, Sunderland conceded, but "by this same silence, we may justify the making[,] selling and drinking of ardent spirits; if Christ never condemned slavery, then neither did he condemn . . . polygamy, nor lotteries, nor theatres, nor offensive wars, nor tyranny of any kind, nor gladiatorial exhibitions," all of which 19th-century Christians recognized as moral offenses against God. Jesus neglected to enumerate a whole host of activities now regarded as sinful, but the lack of explicit denunciation made them no more acceptable.[12]

Despite Jesus' failure to target slavery by name as evil, his teachings fundamentally attacked slaveholding. By the Golden Rule, Jesus implored people to treat others as they would like to be treated themselves. "It is impossible for any person to practise human slavery an hour without violating the law of Love, the Golden Rule," wrote George Bourne. "The common pro-slavery pretence, therefore, that Christ and his apostles did not condemn human slavery, is a naked and obvious untruth. They did in various other ways indirectly condemn such slavery, as by their denunciations of oppression." Barnes, Channing, and others agreed. Jesus also repeated the imperative from the Old Testament's book of Leviticus to "love thy neighbor as thyself." In John 15:12,

---

[11] Sunderland, *Testimony of God Against Slavery,* 32; George Bourne, *A Condensed Anti-Slavery Bible Argument; By a Citizen of Virginia* (New York: S. W. Benedict, 1845), 54.

[12] Sunderland, *Testimony of God Against Slavery,* 10, 11.

Jesus offered a similar piece of advice, to "love one another, as I have loved you." These instructions, wrote LaRoy Sunderland, implicitly condemned slavery. In holding slaves, no master could obey the greatest commandments in the moral law of Christ.[13]

For antislavery preachers, the New Testament espoused a message of equality inimical to slavery. Albert Barnes urged his audience to "look more closely at the very precepts which the apostles gave to 'masters,' and on which reliance is placed to justify them in holding their fellow-men in bondage." The apostle Paul's letter to the Ephesians 6:9, Barnes explained, "enjoins it on masters to 'do the same things unto them, forbearing threatening, knowing that they had a master in heaven, and that *there is no respect of persons with him.*'" (See "Albert Barnes on Equality, 1846," on page 269 in the Primary Sources section.) God, in short, drew no distinction between master and slave. Likewise, in his letter to the Colossians 4:1, Paul wrote, "Masters, render unto your servants *that which is just and equal;* knowing that ye also have a master in heaven." Moreover, when Paul sent Onesimus back to his master, Philemon, he returned him "not as a servant, but as a brother beloved." Onesimus "was not now to be received as a slave," LaRoy Sunderland emphasized, "but *above a slave.*" As Irish-born Methodist Charles Elliott put it, "Onesimus is now the *brother* of his master."[14]

Taken in its totality, the Bible embraced a fundamentally antislavery stance. As Presbyterian abolitionist John Rankin explained, "The whole Bible is opposed to slavery. The sacred volume is one grand scheme of benevolence. Beams of love and mercy emanate from every page, while the voice of justice denounces the oppressor, and speaks to his awful doom." Great theological principles superseded specific words and passages that seemingly sanctioned bondage. In one of the Bible's recurring themes, for instance, the Lord championed the cause of the lowly and heard the cries of the poor. Biblical denunciations of oppression,

---

[13] Bourne, *Condensed Anti-Slavery Bible Argument,* 64–65, 67; Sunderland, *Testimony of God Against Slavery,* 71, 72, 74, 75.

[14] Barnes, *Inquiry into the Scriptural Views of Slavery,* 316; Sunderland, *Testimony of God Against Slavery,* 92; Charles Elliott, *The Bible and Slavery: In Which the Abrahamic and Mosaic Discipline Is Considered in Connection with the Most Ancient Forms of Slavery; and the Pauline Code on Slavery as Related to Roman Slavery and the Discipline of the Apostolic Churches* (Cincinnati: L. Swormstedt & A. Poe, 1857), 328.

the advocacy of the meek and humble, and injunctions to provide aid and relief for those suffering and in distress all conveyed a broad message of fairness, justice, and righteousness. In the New Testament especially, God condemned those features that together composed the reality of slavery. Even "if the New Testament has left no precept justifying, and no prohibition forbidding slavery," wrote Francis Wayland, "the Saviour and his apostles . . . promulgat[ed] such truths concerning the nature and destiny of man, his relations and obligations both to man and to his Maker, as should render the slavery of a human being a manifest moral absurdity." Slavery, in short, violated the entire spirit of the New Testament. "It is a solemn fact," affirmed abolitionist minister LaRoy Sunderland, "that there is scarcely any one *sin* described in the inspired writings, in all its parts, features and consequences, so clearly and explicitly, as is *the sin of holding property in man;* and scarcely any other sin has been so frequently denounced in the Bible."[15]

OUTCOME AND IMPACT

The impasse between proslavery and antislavery theologians defied resolution. Neither side intended to compromise its moral position. Many clergymen in the South as well as in the North found abundant and incontrovertible evidence in the Bible of the divine sanction of slavery. In contrast, abolitionists, certain of the sinfulness of bondage, continued to denounce slavery as an immoral institution and persisted in their goal of effecting immediate emancipation. Abolitionists in the 1830s hoped to transform the nation's churches into instruments of the antislavery cause. In the North, ministers could persuade congregants of abolitionism's righteousness, while southern ministers could coerce slaveholding members to liberate their slaves or risk church disciplinary action or expulsion. The exclusion of slaveholding congregants seemed to abolitionists a small sacrifice for the maintenance of moral principle.

---

[15] John Rankin quoted in John R. McKivigan, *The War Against Proslavery Religion: Abolitionism and the Northern Churches, 1830–1865* (Ithaca, N.Y.: Cornell University Press, 1984), 31; Richard Fuller and Francis Wayland, *Domestic Slavery Considered as a Scriptural Institution: In a Correspondence Between the Rev. Richard Fuller, of Beaufort, S.C., and the Rev. Francis Wayland, of Providence, R.I.,* rev. ed. (1845; reprint, New York: Sheldon & Co., 1860), 89–90; Sunderland, *Testimony of God Against Slavery,* v.

To the frustration of such abolitionists as Boston's Charles K. Whipple, however, their appeals to the churches were largely unheeded. The abolitionists gained little ecclesiastical or popular support for their program of immediate emancipation. Scoffed Whipple, "the clergy should have taken the lead in preaching and enforcing it. They have not done this; they have constantly maligned and obstructed the Abolitionists, who *did* do it."[16]

Churches' failure to meet abolitionists' expectations conformed to historical precedent. Of the nation's major denominations, only the Quakers and Mennonites had distinguished themselves as genuine and consistent opponents of slavery. Some evangelical churches such as the Baptists and Methodists initially opposed the peculiar institution but, in a drive for respectability in southern slaveholding circles, tamed their early antislavery impulses to make evangelical religion more palatable to the southern gentry. The vast majority of all denominations avoided entering the highly charged debate and neglected to offer a clear, forceful statement of slavery's immorality. By 1830, almost all churches tolerated bondage. According to Whipple, "The great majority of ministers, of every denomination, remained utterly indifferent . . . concerning slavery."[17]

Garrisonians grew disillusioned with the nation's religious institutions and the clergy's failure in their duty to convert the masses of American churchgoers to abolitionism. Although some ordained Garrisonian ministers still labored to reform their own denominations through moral suasion, others lost faith in the power of churches to effect change. By contrast, a developing and more moderate non-Garrisonian wing of the abolitionist movement emphasized reform from within the church and continued to appeal to churches for moral leadership on the slavery issue. This so-called "Christian abolitionist" faction included Lewis Tappan, Joshua Leavitt, and former slaveholder James G. Birney. Garrisonians and non-Garrisonians also disagreed over the proper scope of social reform. Garrisonians argued that decay permeated American society. Their commitment to social perfection led them to embrace reform in all its guises, including not only the

(continues on page 254)

---

[16] Whipple, *Relations of Anti-Slavery to Religion,* 19.
[17] Whipple, *Relations of Anti-Slavery to Religion,* 1.

ABOLITIONISTS' PETITIONS TO CONGRESS AND THE GAG RULE

After northern abolitionists concluded their mass mailing campaign to the South, they struck upon a new tactic: They determined to flood Congress with petitions pleading for the abolition of slavery in Washington, D.C. Constitutionally, Congress exercised authority over the District of Columbia; liberating slaves there might serve as an inroad to the immediate abolition of slavery nationwide. The planned deluge of petitions was still just a trickle when freshman representative James Henry Hammond of South Carolina took a stand in the House. Hammond, an ambitious young man still in his 20s, had wed a homely but wealthy woman to gain access to her fortune. The marriage had helped catapult him from his humble origins to the House of Representatives. In late 1835, Hammond unexpectedly made a motion not to receive petitions dealing with slavery in the House. Customarily, the House had received antislavery petitions and then either tabled them or cast them into the vortex of a congressional committee. In either case, the petitions were at least read before being dismissed. Hammond's proposal, by contrast, disposed of antislavery petitions without a hearing. The first-term congressman believed that gagging the antislavery petitions was necessary for the safety of slavery from increasingly emboldened fanatical abolitionists.

In January 1836, South Carolina's John C. Calhoun introduced Hammond's measure in the Senate. James Buchanan of Pennsylvania recommended instead that the Senate receive but then immediately reject antislavery petitions. He believed that petitions must be received in a democratic society, yet his proposal kept the petitions out of committee. Kentucky's Henry Clay went further than Buchanan. He preferred receiving the antislavery petitions, sending them to committee, and then refusing them for the sake of expediency. The Senate voted down the proposals of Calhoun and Clay but passed Buchanan's in March 1836.

The House of Representatives rejected Hammond's suggestion not to receive antislavery petitions. (Hammond soon resigned his House seat, ostensibly for health reasons.) Instead, the House voted in May 1836 to receive but automatically table such memorials. It voted annually to continue this so-called gag rule and passed it in roughly the same form until 1840. That year, Waddy Thompson of South Carolina introduced, and William Cost Johnson of Maryland promoted, a stricter gag rule in which the House would refuse to accept antislavery petitions. The measure passed narrowly.

Former president John Quincy Adams, then serving as a representative from Massachusetts, emerged as the greatest foe of the gag rule in the House. From the moment abolitionist petitions began pouring into Congress in 1836, Adams—although not an avowed abolitionist himself—defended the right of white Americans to petition their government. When the more stringent gag rule of 1840 passed, Adams redoubled his efforts to overturn it. Craftily, he called the gag rule to the House's attention almost daily

Former president and Massachusetts congressman John Quincy Adams led the fight against the gag rule in the U.S. House of Representatives in the late 1830s and early 1840s. (The Art Archive/ Culver Pictures)

by asking whether certain petitions qualified for gagging, thereby forcing the South to debate the issue. Repeatedly, Adams presented petitions that he knew would be rejected, but each year, House votes to prolong the gag rule passed by increasingly narrower margins. Momentum shifted in Adams's favor, and the House finally repealed the gag rule in December 1844. The gag rule that James Henry Hammond had initiated to silence the abolitionists had the ironic effect of turning more northerners than ever toward the antislavery cause.

(continued from page 251)
abolitionist but also the temperance and women's rights movements. Non-Garrisonians preferred an exclusively antislavery focus, fearing that the simultaneous pursuit of a variety of social reforms—especially the unpopular feminist agenda—would dilute or even derail the abolitionist cause. Finally, Garrisonians demonstrated outright hostility toward the U.S. government, the allegedly proslavery U.S. Constitution, and voting or participating in American politics. Non-Garrisonians ventured into the American political system and supported the creation of a third party built around an abolitionist platform. In both 1840 and 1844, they nominated James G. Birney, a onetime southern slaveholder converted to the abolitionist cause, as the presidential candidate of the abolitionist Liberty Party. The Liberty Party met with little success, but Birney garnered far more votes in 1844 than in 1840.

Never a monolithic group, abolitionists succumbed to their internal differences. Disputes over attitudes toward churches, women's rights, and the propriety of participation in politics created unbearable pressures. The pervasive strife and factionalism under the abolitionist umbrella ultimately splintered the abolitionist movement in 1840. Led by the Tappan brothers, non-Garrisonians founded the American and Foreign Anti-Slavery Society (AFASS), an organization distinct from its parent, the American Anti-Slavery Society (AASS). AFASS members tended to be churchgoers, more religiously orthodox than their counterparts in the Garrisonian-controlled AASS. After the 1840 schism, the AASS grew increasingly radicalized. Longtime critics of church complicity in buttressing slavery, more and more Garrisonians began to view churches as hopelessly corrupt institutions. Deeming them beyond possibility of reform, they severed their ties to them. That Garrisonians publicly questioned the authority of the Bible at various religious conventions in the 1840s and 1850s because scripture could be used to insulate slaveholders from criticism further contributed to the Garrisonians' reputation for outright hostility toward organized religion.

If the abolitionist movement fractured, so did a number of evangelical churches. Divergent views toward slavery in the North and South prompted sectional schisms of the Methodist Church in 1844 and the Baptist Church the following year, resulting in the creation, respectively, of the Methodist Episcopal Church, South, and the Southern Baptist

Convention. The Methodists' dispute originated in a debate over the permissibility of allowing Bishop James Andrew to remain in his post after he became a slaveholder through marriage. The rift among the Baptists primarily concerned the employment of slaveholding missionaries. The Presbyterians divided in 1837 into Old and New Schools, but the separation did not occur neatly along sectional lines. New School Presbyterians subsequently split into northern and southern factions in 1857, Old School Presbyterians in 1861. More than northern antislavery agitation, southern commitment to slavery forced the denominational schisms of the antebellum period. The regional schisms freed southern clergymen to pursue proslavery policies and to preach proslavery sermons unapologetically to slaveholding audiences. The separations exerted less influence in the North. Even after the splintering of the evangelical churches and the defection of their southern halves, most northern churches refused to embrace the abolitionist cause, disappointing the non-Garrisonians, who hoped to use the churches to advance their antislavery agenda. Northern Methodists and Baptists did not condemn slaveholding outright as sinful or initiate disciplinary actions against proslavery churchgoers. Their antislavery credentials derived instead from the northern Methodists' repudiation of slaveholding bishops, the northern Baptists' rejection of slaveholding missionaries, and both denominations' calls for gradual, but not immediate abolition. The moderate antislavery sentiments of many northerners dismayed the radical abolitionists, who bemoaned what they considered the North's lackadaisical toleration of slavery. Northern churches adopted a stronger antislavery stance only when the sectional politics of the 1850s swelled popular antislavery sentiment and galvanized the North against the institution. Nevertheless, historian John R. McKivigan observed, "before the Civil War no major denomination endorsed immediate emancipation." For its part, the South marched to war in 1861 confident in the righteousness of its cause. As John Patrick Daly explained, "Moral and biblical justifications of slaveholding constituted the first, and remained the most widely disseminated, foundation of southern proslavery."[18]

---

[18] McKivigan, *War Against Proslavery Religion*, 15; John Patrick Daly, *When Slavery Was Called Freedom: Evangelicalism, Proslavery, and the Causes of the Civil War* (Lexington: University Press of Kentucky, 2002), 31.

ETHNOLOGY AND POLYGENESIS

In the 1840s and 1850s, proslavery writers employed not only the scriptures but also science in defense of the peculiar institution. Physicians Josiah C. Nott, Samuel A. Cartwright, and others pioneered the study of racial difference, or ethnology. Nott, a native South Carolinian who practiced medicine in Mobile, Alabama, and Cartwright, a medical doctor in Alabama, Mississippi, and Louisiana, spent much of their careers studying anatomical and physiological differences between blacks and whites. Their efforts offered an early glimpse of the widespread scientific racism of the late 19th and early 20th-century United States.

Ethnologists found blacks inferior to whites physically and mentally. They discerned striking physical similarities between Africans and apes, such as long, simian arms. They frequently observed that blacks emitted a strong, pungent odor unlike that of whites. By taking cranial measurements of skulls, ethnologists also found that "negro" heads were 10 percent smaller than those of Caucasians. In contrast to the African jaw, which protruded from the face, the forehead receded markedly, creating a smaller cavity to house the brain. The reduced cranial capacity of Africans and their descendants, the ethnologists believed, made them intellectually deficient to whites. Unlike thoughtful, reflective Caucasians, blacks were emotional, passionate, and imitative. Their lack of linguistic skills, evidenced by poor grammar, testified to their mental defects. Ethnologists, in short, employed pseudoscience to justify whites' enslavement of "uncivilized" blacks.

According to some ethnologists, blacks were so different from whites that they constituted an altogether different species. Dr. Nott argued in the 1840s that blacks and whites were discrete products of distinct origins. For Nott, Africans and Caucasians did not descend from a common ancestral couple—Adam and Eve—but from separate, multiple creations. The theory of polygenesis, however, contradicted the biblical account of creation. Southern clergymen took offense and did not welcome ethnologists' attempts to rally science in defense of slavery. Nott's ethnology clashed with religious proslavery arguments and did not gain much traction in the South. Ironically, his ideas took greater hold in the North, where they were utilized by Stephen Douglas and northern Democrats in their politicking of the 1850s.

WHAT IF?

What if the Bible had unequivocally condemned or endorsed slavery?

Beginning in the 1830s, abolitionists injected morality into debates over slavery to an unprecedented extent, and biblical proslavery counterarguments followed within a few years. Abolitionist and proslavery clergymen each mined the Bible to uncover relevant truths buried in scripture. Rather than supplying clear answers, however, their efforts merely heightened resolve on both sides. Vying for public opinion, they published tracts and sermons continuously through the end of the Civil War, although with the passage of the Fugitive Slave Act in 1850, they focused their attention increasingly on the Bible's instructions for dealing with runaways.

Had the Bible unequivocally condemned slavery, radical abolitionists would have been validated in their moral stand. Slaveholders would have had to justify enslavement in other ways. The Bible undergirded the proslavery defense of the antebellum decades, but southern whites did not rely solely on the Good Book to rationalize the perpetuation of slavery. Proslavery thinkers such as Virginia's George Fitzhugh were prepared to offer secular defenses of the institution. Author of *Sociology for the South; or, The Failure of Free Society* (1854) and *Cannibals All! or, Slaves Without Masters* (1857), Fitzhugh touted the benefits of slavery. For slaves, bondage offered protection. Masters cared for their chattel, even during old age and infirmity, Fitzhugh argued. Bondage thus provided a social welfare network for the slaves that no northern white wage worker similarly enjoyed. Lacking the same protections as southern slaves, white laborers in the North toiled long hours, horribly exploited during their most productive years by the factory system and a callous market economy, only to be cast into the streets and left to their own devices when their productivity decreased. A harsher, more brutal system Fitzhugh could hardly imagine. Moreover, slavery was valuable economically. Slaves produced southern cotton, the United States' leading export. Even divested of their biblical cudgels, proslavery writers could still argue that slavery benefited the slave, the South as a region, and the nation as a whole.

If the Bible indisputably endorsed slavery, theology would have continued to figure prominently in the defense of slavery, but the radical abolitionist movement might have been eviscerated. William Lloyd Garrison and other radical abolitionists predicated their antislavery views upon the moral certainty that slavery was wrong and an abomination in the eyes of God. If the Bible denied them support, they would have had to unite against and debate slavery on other terms. Although abolitionists were certainly capable intellectually of contesting the notions that slavery was profitable both socially and economically, it is not clear whether debates organized along those lines could have generated the same passion that motivated abolitionists infused with religious zeal. Stripped of its moral imperative, abolitionism might have had greater difficulty attracting support and attacking slavery.

CHRONOLOGY

1829 David Walker publishes his *Appeal to the Coloured Citizens of the World.*

1831 *Jan. 1:* William Lloyd Garrison publishes the first issue of the *Liberator.*

Aug. 22: Nat Turner launches his revolt in Southampton County, Virginia.

1832 The Virginia House of Delegates decides against gradual emancipation of the state's slaves.

The nullification crisis erupts in South Carolina.

1833 Parliament abolishes slavery in the British Empire through a program of compensated emancipation.

The American Anti-Slavery Society (AASS) is founded in Philadelphia.

1835 Abolitionists launch a mass antislavery mailing in the South.

1837 The Presbyterian Church divides into Old School and New School wings.

Antislavery newspaper editor Elijah Lovejoy is murdered.

1840 Abolitionist schism into Garrisonian and non-Garrisonian wings. Non-Garrisonians found the American and Foreign Anti-Slavery Society (AFASS).

The Liberty Party nominates former slaveholder James G. Birney for president.

1844 The Methodist Church divides over slavery into northern and southern conferences.

1845 The Baptist Church divides over slavery into northern and southern conventions.

1857 New School Presbyterians split into northern and southern factions.

1861   The Confederate States of America form.

The Civil War begins.

Old School Presbyterians split into northern and southern factions.

1865   The Civil War ends.

The Thirteenth Amendment abolishes slavery in the United States. Some biracial congregations begin expelling their African-American members.

DISCUSSION QUESTIONS

1. How applicable were justifications of biblical slavery to the institution of racial slavery in the American South?
2. How persuasive were the biblical proslavery and antislavery arguments?
3. How was it possible for antebellum Americans to use the Bible both to support and to oppose slavery?
4. What role should religion play in politics?

WEB SITES

Maffly-Kipp, Laurie. "African American Religion, Pt. I: To the Civil War," National Humanities Center, Teacher Serve, Divining America, the 19th Century. Available online. URL: http://nationalhumanities center.org/tserve/nineteen/nkeyinfo/aareligion.htm. Accessed February 5, 2010.

University of Michigan. Making of America. *The Bible Gives No Sanction to Slavery: By a Tennessean.* Available online. URL: http://quod.lib. umich.edu/cgi/t/text/text-idx?c=moa;idno=AEU2037. Accessed February 5, 2010.

University of Michigan. Making of America. Isaac Allen. *Is Slavery Sanctioned by the Bible? A Premium Tract.* Available online. URL: http:// quod.lib.umich.edu/cgi/t/text/text-idx?c=moa;idno=AEV3891. Accessed February 5, 2010.

University of North Carolina at Chapel Hill. Documenting the American South. George Bourne. *A Condensed Anti-Slavery Bible Argument; By a Citizen of Virginia.* Available online. URL: http://docsouth.unc.edu/ church/bourne/bourne.html. Accessed February 5, 2010.

BIBLIOGRAPHY

Boles, John B., ed. *Masters and Slaves in the House of the Lord: Race and Religion in the American South.* Lexington: University Press of Kentucky, 1988. A collection of essays that document black and white religious life in the American South.

Daly, John Patrick. *When Slavery Was Called Freedom: Evangelicalism, Proslavery, and the Causes of the Civil War.* Lexington: University Press of Kentucky, 2002. Argues that evangelicals in the North and the South shared common beliefs and values. Chapters 2 and 3 chart the emergence of religious proslavery arguments.

Faust, Drew Gilpin, ed. *The Ideology of Slavery: Proslavery Thought in the Antebellum South.* Baton Rouge: Louisiana State University Press, 1981. An anthology whose selections sample the many strains of proslavery thought.

Genovese, Eugene D. *A Consuming Fire: The Fall of the Confederacy in the Mind of the White Christian South.* Athens: University of Georgia Press, 1998. Explores theological defenses of slavery as well as proslavery reformers' efforts to respond to northern critics and ameliorate the ugliest realities of slaveholding.

Haynes, Stephen R. *Noah's Curse: The Biblical Justification of American Slavery.* New York: Oxford University Press, 2002. Focuses on one biblical proslavery argument, the curse that Noah placed on Ham's son, Canaan. Also mentions Ham's grandson, Nimrod.

Irons, Charles F. *The Origins of Proslavery Christianity: White and Black Evangelicals in Colonial and Antebellum Virginia.* Chapel Hill: University of North Carolina Press, 2008. Contends that white evangelicals' interactions with black churchgoers shaped white views about slavery and helped construct their proslavery arguments.

McKivigan, John R. *The War Against Proslavery Religion: Abolitionism and the Northern Churches, 1830–1865.* Ithaca, N.Y.: Cornell University Press, 1984. Studies abolitionists' attempts to enlist the aid of northern churches in the antislavery cause.

Snay, Mitchell. *Gospel of Disunion: Religion and Separatism in the Antebellum South.* New York: Cambridge University Press, 1993. Explores the role of religion in the approach of the Civil War. Includes a discussion of the biblical justification of slavery.

Tise, Larry E. *Proslavery: A History of the Defense of Slavery in America, 1701–1840.* Athens: University of Georgia Press, 1987. A thorough examination of the history of proslavery thought. It explodes many myths surrounding the subject.

PRIMARY SOURCES

1. Thornton Stringfellow, *Slavery: Its Origin, Nature, and History,* 1861

Over the course of two decades, Reverend Thornton Stringfellow elaborated upon the racial implications of the curse of Ham (or Canaan). In the following excerpt from a tract he published in 1861, Stringfellow explained how the descendants of Ham and Canaan—blacks—were unsuited to rule and fitting objects of subordination.

The descendants of Ham, in Gen. ix. 25, 26, 27, are devoted to slavery, and Shem and Japheth are made their masters. In the days of Jacob, Ham's descendants in Egypt were free, and were about to perish for the want of proper qualifications to use freedom. God sent Shem, in the person of Joseph, to subject them to a more efficient government than they were capable of inaugurating or disposed to exercise. One hundred and fifty years after this the descendants of Ham, by the power of numbers and the worst of motives, subjected in the same kingdom the descendants of Shem to their control. They soon demonstrated, by imbecility and merciless cruelty, that the inferior ought not to rule over the superior race. Hence the Almighty made a most signal display of his displeasure against such unnatural subordination, and the savage cruelty to which it led. By Moses he released the Israelites, the superior race, from this bondage to the inferior, and visited his wrath upon the usurpers of his power for their unnatural and savage cruelty. He had delegated his power to Shem and Japheth to control Ham. But he never delegated his power to Ham to rule over Shem or Japheth. The divine subordination of these races is written in the Scriptures for our learning. It is only necessary to look upon the domestic and national fields of experiment up to the present period of the world's history, to satisfy us that God's plan of subordinating individuals and races is wise, humane and good, and that the infidel theory of "freedom and equality" is only evil.

Source: Thornton Stringfellow. *Slavery: Its Origin, Nature, and History, Considered in the Light of Bible Teachings, Moral Justice, and Political Wisdom* (New York: John F. Trow, 1861), 55–56.

—⁓—

2. Letter, Richard Fuller to Francis Wayland, 1840s

In the 1840s, the slaveholding South Carolina minister Richard Fuller debated slavery's place in the Bible with his fellow Baptist, the northerner Francis Wayland. In the following excerpts from their collected letters, Fuller insisted that slavery had divine sanction from biblical times to the present, attacking in the process Wayland's notion of progressive revelation.

But it is affirmed that the moral character of actions is immutable; that sin is always "the abominable thing which God hates;" that if slavery be essentially and necessarily a sin, it was a sin among the Hebrews; and that it is impiety to say that God, at any time, or in any place, gave his express sanction to sin. . . .

It is to assert that Jehovah first, by his conduct and express enactment, confirmed his chosen people in a sin of appalling magnitude, because he saw fit to keep back the truth as to some things, and then completed the only revelation he will ever give, and assured the world it was complete, and still suppressed the truth as to this sin, unless they had the strange penetration to discover . . . that the Author of the Bible said one thing and meant another—and the singular sanctity to detect, behind the plain language and law of God, a subtle spirit and lurking principle which contradict that language, and condemn that law as a license to commit crime! If any man can believe this, and thus charge God with mocking his poor creatures, and sporting with their guilt and consequent wretchedness, and trying on their blindness and weakness and corruption an experiment which he knew would prove fatal even to those most sincerely desirous to do his will—then that man can surmount the first New Testament objection to your broad statement that slavery is in itself and always a heinous sin.

Source: Richard Fuller and Francis Wayland, *Domestic Slavery Considered as a Scriptural Institution: In a Correspondence Between the Rev. Richard Fuller, of Beaufort, S.C., and the Rev. Francis Wayland, of Providence, R.I.,* rev. ed. (1845; reprint, New York: Sheldon & Co., 1860), 180–181, 187–188.

—⁓—

3. Charles Hodge, "The Bible Argument on Slavery," 1860

A native of Pennsylvania, Charles Hodge counted among the many northern ministers willing to defend slavery. In the following excerpt published in 1860, he indicated that Christ failed to condemn slavery, thereby authorizing the holding of slaves in the American South.

The subject is hardly alluded to by Christ in any of his personal instructions. The apostles refer to it, not to pronounce upon it as a question of morals, but to prescribe the relative duties of masters and slaves. They caution those slaves who have believing or Christian masters, not to despise them because they were on a perfect religious equality with them, but to consider the fact that their masters were their brethren, as an additional reason for obedience. It is remarkable that there is not even an exhortation to masters to liberate their slaves, much less is it urged as an imperative and immediate duty. . . .

When Southern Christians are told that they are guilty of a heinous crime, worse than piracy, robbery, or murder, because they hold slaves, when they know that Christ and his apostles never denounced slaveholding as a crime, never called upon men to renounce it as a condition of admission into the church, they are shocked and offended, without being convinced. They are sure that their accusers can not be wiser or better than their divine Master, and their consciences are untouched by denunciations.

Source: Charles Hodge, "The Bible Argument on Slavery," in *Cotton Is King, and Pro-Slavery Arguments Comprising the Writings of Hammond, Harper, Christy, Stringfellow, Hodge, Bledsoe, and Cartwright, on This Important Subject*, ed. E. N. Elliott (1860; reprint, New York: Negro Universities Press, 1969), 848, 851.

—∞—

4. Thornton Stringfellow, The New Testament on Polygamy, Divorce, and Slavery, 1860

The leading proslavery minister Thornton Stringfellow observed in 1860 that the New Testament specifically attacked polygamy and divorce but not slavery. All three practices had been accepted in the Old Testament. The failure to identify slavery by name as sinful lent sanction to bondage.

If slavery under the gospel is sinful, then its sinfulness would have been made known by the gospel, as has been done with respect to polygamy and divorce. All three, polygamy, divorce and slavery, were *sanctioned* by the law of Moses. But under the gospel, slavery has been *sanctioned* in the church, while polygamy and divorce have been *excluded* from the church. It is manifest, therefore, that under the gospel, polygamy and divorce have been made sins, *by prohibition*, while slavery remains lawful because *sanctioned* and *continued*. The *lawfulness* of slavery under the gospel, rests upon the sovereign pleasure of Christ, in *permitting it*; and the *sinfulness* of polygamy and divorce, upon his sovereign pleasure in *prohibiting* their continuance. The law of Christ gives to the relation of slavery its full sanction. *That law* is to be found, first, in the *admission, by the apostles*, of slaveholders and their slaves into the gospel church; second, in the *positive injunction* by the Holy Ghost, of obedience on the part of Christian slaves in this relation, to their believing masters; third, in the *absence* of any injunction upon the believing master, under any circumstances, to dissolve this relation; fourth, in the *absence* of any instruction from Christ or the apostles, that the relation is sinful; and lastly, in the *injunction* of the Holy Ghost, delivered by Paul, to *withdraw* from all such as teach that this relation is sinful.

Source: Thornton Stringfellow, "An Examination of Elder Galusha's Reply to Dr. Richard Fuller of South Carolina," in *Cotton Is King, and Pro-Slavery Arguments Comprising the Writings of Hammond, Harper, Christy, Stringfellow, Hodge, Bledsoe, and Cartwright, on This Important Subject*, ed. E. N. Elliott (1860; reprint, New York: Negro Universities Press, 1969), 515.

—m—

5. James Henry Hammond, "Slavery in the Light of Political Science," 1860

No minister, South Carolina planter and politician James Henry Hammond claimed the mantle of the misunderstood southern intellectual. His typically secular defenses of slavery were complemented by occasional references to religion. In the following excerpt from 1860, Hammond criticized northern antislavery forces for attempting to establish an authority surpassing the Bible.

It is . . . absurd to say that American slavery differs in form or principle from that of the chosen people. . . .

I fear there has grown up in our time a transcendental religion, . . . a religion too pure and elevated for the Bible; which seeks to erect among men a higher standard of morals than the Almighty has revealed, or our Saviour preached; and which is probably destined to do more to impede the extension of God's kingdom on earth than all the infidels who have ever lived. Error is error. It is as dangerous to deviate to the right hand as to the left. And when men, professing to be holy men, . . . declare those things to be sinful which our Creator has expressly authorized and instituted, they do more to destroy his authority among mankind than the most wicked can effect, by proclaiming that to be innocent which he has forbidden. To this self-righteous and self-exalted class belong all the abolitionists whose writings I have read. With them it is no end of the argument to prove your propositions by the text of the Bible, interpreted according to its plain and palpable meaning, and as understood by all mankind for three thousand years before their time. They are . . . ingenious at construing and interpolating to accommodate it to their new-fangled and ethereal code of morals. . . . *They deny the Bible, and set up in its place a law of their own making.*

Source: J. H. Hammond, "Slavery in the Light of Political Science," in *Cotton Is King, and Pro-Slavery Arguments Comprising the Writings of Hammond, Harper, Christy, Stringfellow, Hodge, Bledsoe, and Cartwright, on This Important Subject,* ed. E. N. Elliott (1860; reprint, New York: Negro Universities Press, 1969), 636–637.

—⚏—

6. Albert Barnes, *An Inquiry into the Scriptural Views of Slavery,* 1846

Born in New York, Albert Barnes was one of the most eloquent antislavery ministers of the 1840s and 1850s. In the following selection, Barnes contrasted biblical and southern slavery.

We have seen that under the Mosaic institutions, the rights of the slave were carefully guarded . . . , and that if he were subjected to such usage he had a redress by claiming his freedom. We have seen that there were express statutes requiring that slaves should be treated with humanity and kindness; that if they were maimed by their masters they had a right to liberty; and that there were many solemn injunctions to treat the *stranger* with kindness, no matter what relation he might sustain.

The question now is, whether there are any such provisions in the laws in this land, or whether there is any security that the slave will be preserved from hard and oppressive usage? The question is not, whether there may not be masters who treat their slaves with kindness, but whether the *laws* furnish any security for the slave on this point? It is not whether a master may not *abuse* his power, but it is whether the law does not give him such power that the slave has no redress, as he had under the Hebrew commonwealth? If it be so, certainly the Mosaic enactments cannot, so far as this point is concerned, be adduced in defence of slavery in the United States. . . .

There is no provision made in this land for general emancipation. We found, in the examination of the Jewish law, that it was a fundamental provision there that every Hebrew servant was to be set at liberty at the close of the sixth year, and that there was to be a general proclamation of freedom throughout the land in the year of jubilee. The practical operation of this, it was shown, would be to abolish slavery altogether, for it was seen that the system could not be perpetuated under such an arrangement.

It is not necessary to attempt to show that there is no such general arrangement in this country for freedom. It has never been contemplated, for it must be seen at once that it would be the destruction of the system. Let the Mosaic laws be applied to slavery in this land, just as they are found in the Pentateuch, and in half a century slavery in the United States would be at an end.

Source: Albert Barnes, *An Inquiry into the Scriptural Views of Slavery* (1846; reprint, Philadelphia: Parry and McMillan, 1857), 171, 192–193.

—⚬—

7. Letter, Francis Wayland to Richard Fuller, 1845

A prominent professor trained at a theological seminary, Francis Wayland carried on a correspondence with South Carolina's Richard Fuller that debated the message of the Bible toward slavery. Although both Baptists, the two men reached starkly different conclusions. Wayland argued that through a process of ethical development since the days of the Old Testament, God had made slavery wrong over time, a point Fuller disputed. In the following letter, Wayland addressed Fuller directly.

Your view, I think, may be briefly expressed as follows: Slavery was sanctioned in the Old Testament; and, since the Old Testament is a revelation from God, and since He would not sanction any thing morally evil, therefore slavery is not a moral evil. . . .

I grant, at once, that the Hebrews held slaves from the time of the conquest of Canaan, and that Abraham and the patriarchs had held them many centuries before. I grant also that Moses enacted laws with special reference to that relation. . . .

Granting all this, I do not see that it contradicts aught that I have said. I believe slavery then, as now, to have been wrong, a violation of our obligations to man, and at variance with the moral laws of God. But I believe that God did not see fit to reveal his will on this subject, nor indeed on many others, to the ancient Hebrews. He made known to them just as much of his moral law as he chose, and the law on this subject belonged to the part which he did not choose to make known. Hence, although they did what was in itself *wrong*, yet, God not having made known to them his will, they were not *guilty*. . . .

But this grant [to hold slaves] was made to one people, and to one people only, *the Hebrews*. It *had respect to one people only*, the Canaanites. It can be of force at no other time, and to no other people.

Source: Richard Fuller and Francis Wayland, *Domestic Slavery Considered as a Scriptural Institution: in a Correspondence Between the Rev. Richard Fuller, of Beaufort, S.C., and the Rev. Francis Wayland, of Providence, R.I.*, rev. ed. (1845; reprint, New York: Sheldon & Co., 1860), 49–50.

—⁂—

8. Albert Barnes on Slavery and Polygamy, 1846

In this selection from 1846, Presbyterian minister Albert Barnes denied that actions of the Old Testament patriarchs automatically met with divine approval.

How far would it go to demonstrate that *God* regards it as a good system, and one that is to be perpetuated, in order that society may reach its highest possible elevation? Who would undertake to vindicate all the conduct of the patriarchs, or to maintain that all which they practised was in accordance with the will of God? They practised concubinage and polygamy. Is it therefore certain that this was the highest and purest state of society, and that it was a state which God designed should be perpetuated? Abraham and Isaac were guilty of falsehood and deception . . . and Noah was drunk with wine . . . and these things are recorded merely *as facts*, without any decided expression of disapprobation; but is it therefore to be inferred that they had the approbation of God, and that they are to be practised still, in order to secure the highest condition of society?

Take the single case of polygamy. Admitting that the patriarchs held slaves, the argument in favour of polygamy, from their conduct, would be, in all its main features, the same as that which I suggested . . . as employed in favour of slavery. The argument would be this:—that they were good men, the "friends of God," and that what such men practised freely cannot be wrong; that God permitted this; that he nowhere forbade it; that he did not record his disapprobation of the practice; and that whatever God permitted in such circumstances, without expressing his disapprobation, must be regarded as in itself a good thing, and as desirable to be perpetuated, in order that society may reach the highest point of elevation. It is perfectly clear that, so far as the conduct of the patriarchs goes, it would be just as easy to construct an argument in favour of polygamy as in favour of slavery—even on the supposition that slavery existed then essentially as it does now. But it is not probable that polygamy would be defended now, as a good institution, and as one that has the approbation of God, even by those who defend the "domestic institutions of the South." The truth is, that the patriarchs were good men in their generation, and, considering their circumstances, were men eminent for piety. But they were imperfect men; they lived in the infancy of the world; they had comparatively little light on the subjects of morals and religion; and it is a very feeble argument which maintains that a thing is *right, because any one or all of the patriarchs practised it.*

But after all, what *real* sanction did God ever give either to polygamy or to servitude, as it was practised in the time of the patriarchs? Did he command either? Did he ever express approbation of either? Is there an instance in which either is mentioned with a sentiment of approval? The mere *record* of actual occurrences, even if there is no declared disapprobation of them, proves nothing as to the divine estimate of what is recorded.

Source: Albert Barnes, *An Inquiry into the Scriptural Views of Slavery* (1846; reprint, Philadelphia: Parry and McMillan, 1857), 78–79.

9. LaRoy Sunderland, *The Testimony of God Against Slavery,* 1835

Although not one of the most widely known abolitionist preachers, Methodist minister LaRoy Sunderland offered one of the earliest, sustained indictments of slavery on biblical grounds. Sunderland argued in the following selection from 1835 that God's pity on the Hebrew slaves in Egypt suggested his identical sympathy with slaves in the American South.

The people of God, at this time were held in slavery by the Egyptians; and though the bondage which they were compelled to endure, was certainly not so cruel and severe as that which nearly three millions of American citizens are now doomed to suffer; yet the Infinite Being manifested the most feeling pity for their sorrows. And how can a believer in the truth of the Bible suppose, for one moment, that this same unchangeable God is now an indifferent spectator merely, to the accumulated wrongs which thousands of the poor slaves are forced to endure in this Christian land,—thousands who are his people, who love him, but who are not permitted to read his word, nor to worship him according to the dictates of their own consciences?

Source: LaRoy Sunderland, *The Testimony of God Against Slavery, or a Collection of Passages from the Bible, Which Show the Sin of Holding Property in Man; with Notes* (Boston: Webster & Southard, 1835; reprint, St. Clair Shores, Mich.: Scholarly Press, 1970), 14.

—⚏—

10. Albert Barnes on Equality, 1846

In Ephesians 6:9, Albert Barnes located evidence that God did not draw distinctions between masters and slaves. Such a verse struck at the inherent inequalities of the master-slave relationship.

Would the effect of *this* precept be to lead him to infer that slavery was a good thing, and was to be perpetuated? The manifest object of the apostle in this passage is, to secure for servants a proper treatment; to require the master to evince towards them the same spirit which he had enjoined on servants; and to teach them to remember that they had a master in heaven who would require a strict account; for *"there was no respect of persons with him."* But this great and central truth of the Christian religion, that "there is no respect of persons with God," is one which is by no means favourable to the perpetuity of slavery. A man who should have this constantly before his mind, and allow it to have its full influence on his heart, would not be long the owner of a slave. The direct tendency of it is to show him that his slave, in the sight of God, is equal to himself.

Source: Albert Barnes, *An Inquiry into the Scriptural Views of Slavery* (1846; reprint, Philadelphia: Parry and McMillan, 1857), 316.

8

FUGITIVE SLAVES:
Should Congress Pass the Fugitive Slave Bill of 1850?

—⚉—

THE CONTROVERSY

The Issue

In 1850, Congress worked out a series of compromise measures to ease tensions between North and South over the issue of slavery. One point of contention was the southern demand for a more effective law for the return of escaped slaves. Should Congress pass the Fugitive Slave Bill?

♦ *Arguments that Congress should pass the Fugitive Slave Bill:* Southern masters considered a new fugitive slave law essential to the preservation of the South's slave regime. The existing Fugitive Slave Act of 1793 was proving ineffective. Too many in the North, it seemed, were shirking their constitutional duty to help apprehend runaway slaves and, in defiance of the law, even aiding and encouraging them to the detriment of their masters. Economic losses in enslaved property mounted most significantly for masters in the slaveholding states bordering the North. In 1850, slaveholders turned to Congress to devise a legislative remedy for the shortcomings of the current law.

♦ *Arguments that Congress should not pass the Fugitive Slave Bill:* Many northern congressmen opposed the Fugitive Slave Bill. The proposal appropriated public funds—in part, northern tax monies—for the apprehension and return of runaways. It denied accused fugitives a jury trial and instead established a system of special commissioners whose compensation for their work varied with the decision they rendered. The very structure of the bill jeopardized the safety of northern free blacks by promoting their kidnapping and sale into slavery. Moreover, federal agents maintained the authority to draft northern citizens to aid them in their duties. Some in the North resolved to follow their individual conscience, a "higher law" than the Constitution itself. The Fugitive Slave Bill threatened their rights in many ways.

—⚉—

INTRODUCTION

Tensions between slaveholding and nonslaveholding states had escalated by 1850. With the conclusion of the Mexican-American War in 1848, the United States added a vast quantity of land in the Southwest. Americans' success in expanding westward raised a divisive question about the status of slavery in the territories. Northerners and southerners maintained contrasting visions for the future of slavery in the West. Their disagreements proved so profound that they began to reevaluate their relationship to one another and the broader American community. The strains on the American family led some contemporaries to fear a civil war. The Compromise of 1850—a collection of laws passed separately by Congress in 1850—was designed to defuse sectional antagonisms and maintain the integrity of the Union.

While the Compromise of 1850 staved off civil war, it encompassed a controversial Fugitive Slave Bill that generated its own set of contradictions. Although the South generally upheld a belief in states' rights principles, slaveholders demanded an effective fugitive slave law through which the federal government aided in tracking down runaway slaves. Hostile to the existing Fugitive Slave Act of 1793, many northern state legislatures had passed personal liberty laws with the intent of undermining federal legislation. Such a maneuver was reminiscent of the nullification controversy of the 1830s, in which South Carolina's John C. Calhoun took states' rights doctrine to its logical though unsuccessful conclusion. Designed to help reconcile North and South, the Fugitive Slave Bill also exposed divisions within the South itself. Border-state congressmen took far greater interest in securing a new fugitive slave law than did their counterparts in the Deep South, who typically spearheaded proslavery causes.

Suffering the brunt of the economic losses from runaways, masters in the Upper South demanded a new fugitive slave act as a substitute for the inadequate law of 1793. They argued that the North had a constitutional duty to "deliver up" runaway slaves captured on northern soil. Contrary to law, many in the North exerted no effort and openly defied constitutional imperatives. Congressmen from the border states led the legislative effort to pass a new fugitive slave law.

Many in the North objected to the proposed Fugitive Slave Bill. Under its provisions, funds collected partially from northern taxes financed the apprehension and return of runaway slaves. Alleged fugitives were denied a jury trial but instead appeared before special commissioners, who received more pay for sending purported fugitives to the South than for liberating them. Critics of the Fugitive Slave Bill feared that it encouraged the kidnapping of free black northerners for sale in the South as slaves. The bill also authorized federal marshals to conscript northerners in the pursuit or delivery of fugitives. Some northerners appealed to a "higher law" of individual conscience to justify disobedience to the Fugitive Slave Act.

BACKGROUND

In 1846, the Mexican-American War erupted between the United States and its neighbor to the south. President James Knox Polk, a southerner, was largely responsible for engineering the conflict to fulfill a campaign promise to stretch American boundaries from the Atlantic coast to the Pacific. Polk's critics condemned what they deemed an aggressive war to extend slavery. Soon after hostilities began, Congress needed to appropriate money for the war effort. During the debate over funding, Representative David Wilmot of Pennsylvania unexpectedly added a controversial amendment to the appropriations bill, dubbed the Wilmot Proviso. The congressman proposed prohibiting slavery in any territory taken from Mexico as a result of the ongoing war. No abolitionist, Wilmot presented no threat to slavery in regions where it already existed; however, he did oppose the extension of slavery into new territories.

Although never enacted, the Wilmot Proviso haunted the Capitol for the next four years. The Mexican-American War unfolded favorably for American expansionists. By the Treaty of Guadalupe Hidalgo, which formally ended the conflict in 1848, Mexico turned over to the United States basically half of its territory, 500,000 square miles of land known as the Mexican Cession. Mexico surrendered what would become the southwestern United States, including all of modern-day California, Nevada, and Utah, as well as parts of Arizona, New Mexico, Colorado, and Wyoming. Ironically, American success in accumulating new lands bred political controversy and jeopardized national harmony as the nation struggled to determine what policy to adopt respecting slavery in the territories.

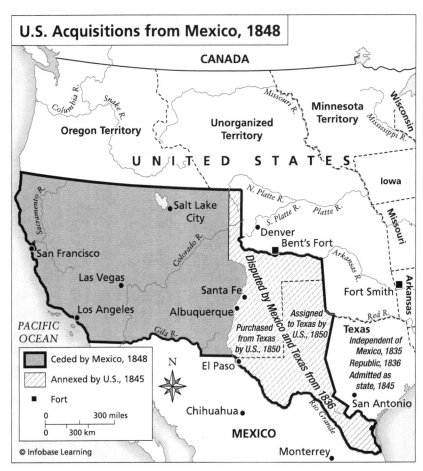

U.S. Acquisitions from Mexico, 1848

The treaty that ended the Mexican-American War in 1848 transferred nearly half of Mexico's territory to the United States. The acquisition of that land forced Americans to debate the fate of slavery in the territories.

Several options were available. The Wilmot Proviso proposed a ban on slavery in territories acquired from Mexico. At the opposite extreme, southerners such as John C. Calhoun of South Carolina argued that the Constitution protected masters' right to carry slaves wherever they wished. Any restriction, they said, would violate Fifth Amendment guarantees that no citizen could be "deprived of life, liberty, or property"—including property in slaves—"without due process of law." Two more moderate proposals lay between these extremes. Senator Lewis Cass of Michigan advanced a plan known as popular sovereignty, by which the people living in a given territory would vote to decide the fate of slavery in that territory. Still others, including Senator Jefferson Davis of Mississippi, recommended the extension of the 36°30' Missouri Compromise line of 1820 all the way to the Pacific, perpetuating the division between a free North and a slave South.

Debate in 1850 concentrated on the admission of California into the Union. Acquired in the Mexican Cession, California saw its population skyrocket after the discovery of gold in 1849. Very soon, California had a sufficient number of residents to apply for statehood. Any new state, however, would upset the sectional balance of power between slaveholding and nonslaveholding states, which at the time stood at 15 apiece. Mexican-American War hero and U.S. president Zachary Taylor, although a large slaveholder with a sprawling plantation in Louisiana, preferred a free California. His sudden death in office in July 1850, probably from food poisoning, complicated an already complex situation.

Thus, a cluster of perplexing issues shared the political stage in 1850. The country had reached an impasse on the California question, and there was uncertainty over the organization of the remaining Mexican Cession lands. The precise status of slavery in the territories hung in doubt. In addition, there were disputes over Texas's western boundary claims and the presence of slave auctions in the District of Columbia, the latter of which many northerners found embarrassing and a source of national disgrace.

Moreover, many southerners, predominantly from the Upper South, agitated for a strengthened Fugitive Slave Law. The Constitution of 1787 included a fugitive slave clause that authorized the return of runaways apprehended in other states. Article IV, Section 2, held that "No Person held to Service or Labour in one State, under the Laws thereof, escaping into another, shall, in Consequence of any Law or Regulation therein, be discharged from such Service of Labour, but shall be delivered up on Claim of the Party to whom such Service or Labour may be due." The Constitution neglected, however, to include any enforcement mechanisms. This oversight became clear after three white men abducted a free black man in Pennsylvania in 1788 and conveyed him to Virginia. The whites were charged with kidnapping, but Virginia's governor refused to extradite them to Pennsylvania since no law mandated their rendition. As a result, Congress passed the first Fugitive Slave Act in 1793 to lend teeth to the constitutional provision.

(See "Fugitive Slave Act of 1793," on page 300 in the Primary Sources section.) The act provided for the arrest of fugitives and their appearance before a judge vested with the authority to order runaways' return. Anyone who interfered with the process of recovery faced a hefty $500 fine. Most Southerners were unimpressed with the Fugitive Slave Act of 1793, however, and criticized it as inadequate. They believed that it demanded too much time and expense of masters and subjected them to the dangers posed by hostile Northern crowds. Attempts to revise the law as early as 1818 all proved unsuccessful.

The next step in the evolution of the legal understanding of the Fugitive Slave Act of 1793 occurred with the Supreme Court decision of *Prigg v. Pennsylvania* in 1842. In 1837, Edward Prigg, acting as a slaveholder's agent, arrested as a fugitive Margaret Morgan, who had fled slavery in Maryland several years before. Prigg sent Morgan, as well as her Pennsylvania-born children, back to Maryland but was charged with violating an 1826 Pennsylvania law designed to deter the kidnapping of the state's free blacks and to protect fugitives who sought safe haven in the Keystone State. Prigg's case progressed to the Supreme Court, which ruled the Pennsylvania state law unconstitutional. The *Prigg* decision upheld the right of a master or master's representative lawfully to pursue a fugitive slave into any state or territory, including in the North.

But in the most momentous component of the verdict, the Court went on to argue that the national government alone had the authority to legislate and enforce laws regarding fugitive slaves. Individual states had no obligation to help apprehend runaways. (See "Excerpts from *Prigg v. Pennsylvania*, 1842," on page 301 in the Primary Sources section.) The federal government, however, had long relied upon state and local authorities to implement the Fugitive Slave Act of 1793, aiding in the apprehension of fugitives and the adjudication of their cases. Although the *Prigg* decision affirmed the constitutionality of the Fugitive Slave Act, it excused state and local officials from enforcing it. The capture and recovery of fugitives were suddenly exclusively federal responsibilities. Within six years of *Prigg v. Pennsylvania*, several northern states took the legal opportunity to pass personal liberty laws or strengthen existing ones. In conformity with the *Prigg* verdict, personal liberty laws absolved state officials from aiding in the recovery of fugitives. Combined with a shortage of U.S. government manpower, the reclamation of fugitives grew more burdensome than ever for southern masters.

Southern calls for a stronger, more effective fugitive slave law thus intensified after the *Prigg* case. In 1850, U.S. government figures showed that more than 1,000 slaves—roughly one in every 3,200 bond people—fled to the North. Although this amounted to a little more than 3/100 of 1 percent of all slaves, fugitives were not distributed equally across the South. Masters in border states suffered the preponderance of these losses. The dollar value of absconded slaves reportedly tallied in the tens of thousands of dollars in several states and, according to some estimates, reached $200,000 annually for the South as a whole. Consequently, many slaveholders welcomed the proposed Fugitive Slave Bill of 1850, designed to remedy the perceived shortcomings of the 1793 law. But should Congress pass it?

THE DEBATE

The Argument that Congress Should Pass the Fugitive Slave Bill

Although normally the states of the Deep South led the agitation on slavery issues, an improved fugitive slave law was of greatest interest to masters in the Upper South border states of Maryland, Virginia, and Kentucky. In the Lower South, slaves had relatively little realistic chance of launching a successful flight to freedom. The distance to the North, the dangers of traveling without a pass, and uncertain supplies of food and other essentials for survival all militated against endeavoring to escape permanently from bondage. Desiring a break from their routine labors or perhaps wanting to visit a spouse on a neighboring plantation, slaves usually ran off for only a few days or weeks at a time before returning to their master of their own volition and suffering punishment for their truancy. Because runaway slaves did not present as pressing a problem for their constituents, members of Congress from the Lower South, such as Mississippi's Jefferson Davis or South Carolina's Andrew P. Butler, offered only tepid support for a new fugitive slave law. By contrast, border-state congressmen such as Senator Joseph R. Underwood of Kentucky recognized a more urgent need to pass effective fugitive slave legislation. The proximity of slaves in the border states to the free North made flight a risk worth taking. An inadequate fugitive slave law therefore called into question the safety of slave property in regions adjacent to the free states. By no accident, then, the primary author of the Fugitive Slave Bill of 1850 was border-state senator James Mason of Virginia, and congressmen from the Upper South gave his proposal its most enthusiastic support.

The Fugitive Slave Act of 1793 already on the books failed to overcome the difficulties of reclaiming slaves who absconded to the North. According to Senator Mason, "you may as well go down into the sea, and endeavor to recover from his native element a fish which had escaped from you, as expect to recover such fugitive—I mean under existing laws." Many southern members of Congress charged northerners with obstructing or evading the implementation of the 1793 law. Imagining themselves benevolent paternalists, southern masters frequently scapegoated northern residents for enticing away slaves who otherwise purportedly had no legitimate reason for seeking freedom. It was unscrupulous northerners who lured and seduced slaves away and welcomed them with hospitality. Moreover, antislavery mobs sometimes rescued apprehended fugitives. That northerners occasionally abducted bond people from their owners and escorted them to freedom made it unsafe for slaveholders even to journey in the North with their enslaved property. "I think it is a mark of no good brotherhood, of no kindness, of no courtesy, that a man from a slave State cannot now, in any degree of safety, travel in a free State with his servant," lamented Kentucky senator and slaveholder Henry Clay on the floor of the Senate. "It is unkind, unneighborly, . . . [and] not in the spirit of that fraternal connection existing between all parts of this Confederacy." Many masters also found it prohibitively costly to pursue a fugitive very far north, for the expense to apprehend the slave exceeded his or her monetary value. The costs, time, and inconvenience—with no guarantee of success—all presented impediments to the implementation of the existing fugitive slave law.[1]

Senator George Badger of North Carolina counted among the many southern congressmen who argued that the North had nothing less than a constitutional obligation to aid the South in recovering runaways. "This is a claim of right," Badger declared; "this is a demand founded upon the Constitution; this is not a matter of question or

---

[1] *Appendix to the Congressional Globe, for the First Session, Thirty-first Congress: Containing Speeches and Important State Papers*, vol. 22, pt. 2 (Washington, D.C.: John C. Rives, 1850), 1583; *Appendix*, vol. 22, pt. 1, 123.

debate. If there is anything in the Constitution free from doubt, difficulty, or dispute, it is that that instrument gives us a right to have our fugitives surrendered to us." Article IV, Section 2, of the Constitution stated, without equivocation, that a fugitive from labor "shall be delivered up" to the party claiming the slave. The word *shall* left no doubt as to the framers' intent: The Constitution mandated the return of fugitive slaves. The Supreme Court decision of *Prigg v. Pennsylvania* reinforced the point, authorizing masters to retrieve their runaway slaves from any state or territory where they might have fled. Logically, then, northerners who failed to return fugitives or impeded recovery in any way shirked their constitutional responsibility, showed blatant irreverence toward that sacrosanct document, and exhibited their own fanaticism on the subject of slavery. At the very least, insisted Senator Badger, the North should respect the Fugitive Slave Act of 1793 because it was passed early in the nation's history, by the great and wise men of the founding generation, and signed into law by the venerable George Washington. Notably, he added, at the time of its passage, the measure elicited little dispute in either house of Congress.[2]

Congressmen in favor of the new Fugitive Slave Bill challenged the audacity of a few northern antislavery colleagues who candidly asserted that personal conscience represented a "higher law" than the U.S. Constitution and permitted the brazen disregard of fugitive slave laws. Kentucky senator Joseph R. Underwood argued that individual citizens could not elevate themselves above the laws and arbitrarily decide for themselves which statutes to obey. According to Underwood, laws were not only ordained by God but also crucial to the prevention of social disorder and chaos. All citizens, he concluded, had an ethical duty to obey fugitive slave laws regardless of any scruples they personally felt toward slavery. (See "Speech of Senator Joseph R. Underwood, 1850," on page 302 in the Primary Sources section.)

Convinced that the North was not "sound" on the slavery issue, southerners in Congress lobbied strenuously during debates over the Fugitive Slave Bill of 1850 to prevent any jury trials for fugitive slaves from taking place on northern soil. Some objected to jury trials altogether; Clay, Badger, and others entertained the prospect, but only in the South. Northern hostility to the institution of slavery made jury

---

[2] *Appendix,* vol. 22, pt. 1, 385.

trials in the nonslaveholding states unacceptable. In the North, Clay explained, "the feelings and the sympathy of the neighborhood are naturally and necessarily excited in favor of the colored person." Badger informed his northern colleagues that "none but fools or madmen" would think the master of a fugitive slave granted a trial in the North could obtain a favorable verdict. If, as southern lawmakers suggested, no bond people would be returned to the South, jury trials in the North would be tantamount to the virtually automatic, wholesale liberation of runaway slaves. In the unlikely event of an outcome sympathetic to the master, an extralegal mob might obstruct the execution of justice. The "protracted litigation" common in northern jury trials, Badger further observed, would only add to masters' expense and delay or prevent the return of their property. As the Constitution stated, fugitives must be delivered up on claim—not proof—of the master.[3]

If a fugitive insisted on a jury trial, it must take place in the state from which the slave fled. There, it would be easier to prove the slave's identity with certainty and establish all of the facts surrounding the case because people who knew the bond person would be present, unlike in a theoretical northern jury trial. Badger considered northern intimations that fugitives taken south for trial would not receive justice an affront to the entire region. "Are we to be told that our judicatures are not to be trusted? that we will not administer justice? that we are in the habit of suffering persons who are free to be converted into slaves? that freemen may be kidnapped, introduced among us, held among us as slaves, and refused redress by our courts and our laws?" Badger asked with indignation. "It is direct, wanton, inexcusable insult upon the character and the judicature of every southern State."[4]

The ineffectiveness of the Fugitive Slave Act of 1793 and the resulting lack of security for their enslaved property convinced border-state and other southern masters of the need for a new law to apprehend fugitive slaves. They claimed a constitutional right to recover runaway chattel. For the North to interfere in any way with that process marked an unjust violation of their property rights. Passage of the Fugitive Slave Bill of 1850 would both reaffirm a constitutional pledge to slaveholders and maintain brotherly harmony between North and South.

---

[3] *Appendix*, vol. 22, pt. 1, 571, 387.
[4] *Appendix*, vol. 22, pt. 1, 386.

The Argument that Congress Should Not Pass the Fugitive Slave Bill

Supporters of the Fugitive Slave Bill derisively labeled its opponents fanatical abolitionists on the political fringe. In reality, northern congressmen who spoke against the bill held a range of opinions on slavery. Congressional enemies of the Fugitive Slave Bill included abolitionists such as Senator Salmon P. Chase and Representative Joshua R. Giddings of Ohio, but other more moderately antislavery politicians also lobbied against its passage. Still other northern congressmen, including New Jersey's William L. Dayton, expressed a willingness to vote for a reasonably constructed fugitive slave bill but could not endorse the 1850 proposal as written. Members of Congress need not don the abolitionist mantle to oppose the Fugitive Slave Bill.

Many northern congressmen were alarmed at the Fugitive Slave Bill's lack of a jury trial for alleged fugitives. Instead of a jury trial, purported runaways were to appear before special commissioners who would determine whether or not they would be sent south. The commissioners heard evidence from the master but no testimony from the purported slave. Thus, under the bill, a slaveholder could venture into the North, lay claim to an individual as enslaved property, and, subject only to the whims of the commissioner, convey the alleged slave to bondage in the South. As Senator Chase explained, "I do not believe that a slave claimant can go into any State of the Union and take a person . . . and, upon his mere assertion that the person seized is a fugitive from labor, carry him off, without process, by private force."[5] Exacerbating matters, commissioners received $10 in compensation for returning a purported runaway to the South but only five dollars for releasing a captive, a disparity attributed to the additional paperwork required in extradition cases. Northern congressmen decried the injustice that, by law, the unsalaried commissioners had a financial incentive to return those who had reportedly fled their masters. Any bill that denied alleged fugitives the benefit of a jury or the ability to prove their freedom and instituted a compensation scheme that rewarded commissioners monetarily for sending supposed fugitives to the South doomed the accused to slavery.

---

[5] *Appendix,* vol. 22, pt. 2, 1587.

Dayton, Giddings, and other northern critics of the Fugitive Slave Bill immediately grasped that the system it established promoted the kidnapping of northern free blacks. Dayton imagined the scenario: "Upon some calm day a stranger unknown to the community" arrives and, "without process or evidence, simply says, that man, or that woman is my slave!" Over the denials and protests of the targeted person of color, the slaveholder "lays violent hands upon that slave, and carries him or her off by force." Once taken to the South, individuals abducted as runaways would have virtually no opportunity to establish their freedom and escape permanent enslavement. Through such a process, unscrupulous, predatory masters might claim northern free blacks as slaves and add them to their holdings. Meanwhile, stunned communities in the North would be divested of their black residents. "That community," Dayton continued, "know nothing of the man who presents himself, nor of his right. They only know that the black has been there, perhaps for years, and supposed to be free." Southern politicians scoffed at the prospect of kidnapping, admitting only a remote possibility of anyone's falsely claiming a free black at the risk of perjury. Nevertheless, Dayton recognized, the law was stacked in slaveholders' favor. "Can it be [a] matter of surprise," he asked, "that, under such circumstances, there should be mobs, and riots, and outrages? The case is calculated to create excitement, and the feelings of all free communities revolt against it."[6]

Many in the North believed they had good reason to fear for free blacks' safety. Opponents of the Fugitive Slave Bill—George W. Julian of Indiana, Roger Baldwin of Connecticut, and John Davis and Robert Charles Winthrop of Massachusetts among them—charged that already the South was engaged in the practice of kidnapping northern free blacks. They most frequently pointed to a South Carolina law—not entirely unique in the South—that affected free black mariners from the North when they entered southern ports such as Charleston. Fearing that free black outsiders would incite rebellion among the state's slaves, South Carolina permitted their seizure, arrest, and confinement in jail until their ship departed. If the captain of the ship neglected to retrieve the free black sailors and pay the costs of their detainment before pulling out of port, the unfortunate crewmen could legally be sold into slavery. Northern free blacks commonly manned ships in the antebellum

---

[6] *Appendix*, vol. 22, pt. 1, 438–439.

era, often as stewards or cooks. According to northern observers, South Carolina's law not only attacked the freedoms of northern free blacks, but also impinged on the right of northern shippers to employ whomever they wished. The controversial piece of legislation contributed to a feud between South Carolina and Massachusetts, a commonwealth heavily involved in the maritime trades as well as one that recognized free blacks as citizens, even granting free black men the right to vote. When Massachusetts dispatched an agent to South Carolina to investigate the matter of northern free blacks sold into slavery, he was quickly intimidated into leaving the state.

Several Northern congressmen believed the best antidote to a potential plague of free black kidnappings was to adopt a provision for jury trials for alleged runaways. Those jury trials must be held in the North. Unlike his Northern colleagues with abolitionist leanings, Dayton conceded that slaveholders had a constitutional right to have a slave delivered up *"on claim made,"* but he interpreted that to mean in the North, "where the claim is made." Before a purported fugitive could possibly be surrendered, Baldwin agreed, "it must be satisfactorily proved that he is a fugitive from another State, and that he owes involuntary service under its laws to the claimant." Whereas southern whites presumed black persons to be enslaved, African Americans in the North were presumed free. Even if the northern states did not grant free blacks all the same rights as whites, they recognized them as citizens who needed protection. As a presumptively free citizen, Baldwin concluded, a person of color in the North maintained the right "to assert his freedom in the State where he happens to be, until his right is disproved by evidence."[7]

Baldwin explained the reasons a fugitive by right deserved a jury trial in the North. Justice demanded that ownership be proven prior to removal. Anything less gave extraterritoriality to the laws of the state from which the alleged fugitive reportedly fled and necessarily validated the master's claim. To deprive a purported runaway of the benefit of law in the state of capture extracted him from the community where people knew him and where friends could testify on his behalf. (See "Speech of Senator Roger Baldwin, 1850," on page 303 in the Primary Sources section.) If the North merely surrendered fugitives on the claim of the master, those taken up as runaways would have no hope of a fair trial, or

---

[7] *Appendix,* vol. 22, pt. 1, 439; *Appendix,* vol. 22, pt. 2, 420, 421.

any trial whatsoever, in the South. Northern congressmen were aware of southern distrust of northern courts' ability to administer fugitive slave laws but believed it wholly misplaced. They offered examples of their states' having returned runaways in the past as evidence of their good faith. They simultaneously dismissed the ubiquitous southern charge that jury trials in the North posed an undue inconvenience for masters in terms of both the time and expense involved in travel and the adjudication of the case.

Critics of the Fugitive Slave Bill objected to its infringement on northern rights. They questioned why federal revenues should finance the return of fugitive slaves from the North to the South. Many in the North doubted the propriety of using funds taken out of the public treasury—northern tax dollars—to underwrite the expenses associated with the recovery of southern slaveholders' property. According to Representative Julian, the bill also placed undue burdens on northerners by forcing free people, possibly against their will and in violation of conscience, to act as the agents of slavery. Federal marshals were authorized to draft northern citizens into service capturing or returning fugitives, regardless of their personal opinions of slavery as an institution. (See "Speech of Representative George W. Julian, 1850," on page 304 in the Primary Sources section.) Abolitionist congressman Giddings asked rhetorically, "did those framers of the Constitution intend that northern freemen should leave their shops, their plows, their merchandise to give chase to fugitive slaves?" Giddings stood firm against the bill: "No! The freemen of Ohio will never turn out to chase the panting fugitive; they will never be metamorphosed into bloodhounds, to track him to his hiding place, and seize and drag him out, and deliver him to his tormentors. . . . Let no man tell me there is no higher law than this fugitive bill."[8]

Northern resolve to resist the Fugitive Slave Law found moral and philosophical underpinning in the "higher law" doctrine enunciated by antislavery New York senator William H. Seward. Countering southern claims that it was the North's constitutional duty to obey the Fugitive Slave Act, Seward claimed a higher law than the Constitution forbade

---

[8] *Congressional Globe, New Series: Containing Sketches of the Debates and Proceedings of the Second Session of the Thirty-first Congress*, vol. 23 (Washington, D.C.: John C. Rives, 1851), 14–15.

violating human rights or taking immoral, unchristian actions. (See "Speech of Senator William H. Seward, 1850," on page 304 in the Primary Sources section.) Foes of the Fugitive Slave Bill did not rally unanimously behind Seward's argument, however. Senator Dayton, for one, voiced his reservations: "As soon . . . as we begin to speculate, not upon what the Constitution is, but upon what it ought to be—to try it by the laws of God, and the powers of conscience, as we understand them— I fear that our anchorage is gone, that we are adrift in the night."[9] The "higher law" doctrine sparked controversy not only in the halls of Congress but also in church pulpits across the North. Antislavery ministers in the North waged theological battle with other northern pastors, who, though often opposed to slavery, nevertheless stressed the need for people to obey laws as divinely ordained. Sermons on both sides were printed and widely distributed in pamphlet form. (See "Northern Ministers Expound upon the Fugitive Slave Act, 1851," on page 305 in the Primary Sources section.)

Some who opposed the Fugitive Slave Bill reviled the institution of slavery on principle; others did not agree with various specific features of the bill. Regardless of their differences, the bill's enemies saw the South as attempting to extend its reach northward. They could not vote for a law that automatically presumed alleged fugitives were indeed enslaved, stripped supposed runaways of any realistic opportunity to prove their status as free, encouraged the kidnapping of free black northerners, or legally mandated the violation of conscience.

OUTCOME AND IMPACT

Introduced in January 1850, the Fugitive Slave Bill was debated early in the year and taken up again in August. Despite the addition of various amendments, the bill remained true to Senator James Mason's proposal. The Senate completed its work on the Fugitive Slave Bill in August, approving it by a margin of 27 to 12, with more than 20 abstentions. The following month, the House of Representatives passed the bill 109 to 76, with unanimous support from southern congressmen. Only 30 percent of all northern representatives approved the bill. Twenty-seven

---

[9] *Appendix*, vol. 22, pt. 1, 438.

northern Democrats voted for it, compared to 16 opposed, but only three of 74 northern Whigs sided with the majority. Northern Democrats united with southern politicians to push the bill through. "I do not believe that ten of those northern gentlemen who supported it

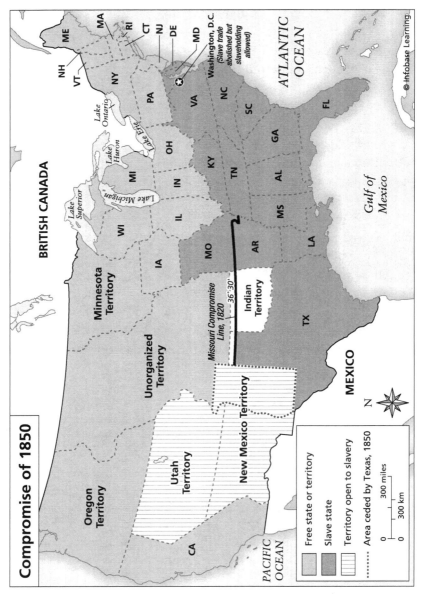

The Compromise of 1850 admitted California to the Union as a free state, created the territories of Utah and New Mexico, and included a new Fugitive Slave Act.

had looked into its provisions with any care," grumbled Representative Julian, "or knew what the bill contained."[10] Nevertheless, President Millard Fillmore signed the Fugitive Slave Act into law on September 18.

The final provisions of the Fugitive Slave Act of 1850 clearly favored the South. They established a stronger federal government role for the return of fugitives. Special commissioners determined the fates of alleged runaways after hearings in which masters gave evidence, but purported fugitives were unable to testify and denied a jury trial. The compensation scheme encouraged judgments in favor of bondage rather than freedom. The Fugitive Slave Act also authorized federal officials to call upon "all good citizens" and "bystanders" to form a "posse comitatus" to aid them in the completion of their duties. Those who refused faced fines of up to $1,000 and a prison sentence as long as six months. The same penalties applied to anyone who actively obstructed the apprehension of a fugitive or who harbored, concealed, or rescued a slave. All northerners, in short, were burdened with the obligation to serve as de facto slave catchers. Furthermore, the U.S. Treasury underwrote these revised slave-catching provisions. Arrested in New York, James Hamlet, a runaway from Baltimore, became the first fugitive remanded to slavery under the Fugitive Slave Act of 1850.

The inclusion of the Fugitive Slave Act was designed to make the Compromise of 1850 more palatable to the South. That agreement, engineered by Senator Clay in the interest of national unity, appeared to southern critics too generous to the North. It theoretically tilted the balance between slaveholding and nonslaveholding states in favor of the North by admitting California as a free state. The Compromise of 1850 also bowed to northern demands by abolishing the slave trade in the District of Columbia. Moreover, while it did not exclude slavery from the newly organized Utah and New Mexico Territories, neither did it guarantee slavery there. Exacerbating matters, Texas accepted a $10 million payment as part of the compromise in exchange for surrendering land claims that extended westward to the upper Rio Grande. A sizable portion of the New Mexico Territory, where slavery was now possible but not certain, was carved out of this land ceded by Texas, where slavery was an established institution. Southern politicians in 1850 saw themselves on the losing end of the compromise. The Fugitive Slave Act made it somewhat easier to swallow, especially for legislators from the border states, where

---

[10] *Appendix*, vol. 22, pt. 2, 1302.

escaped slaves presented a more pressing problem than they did farther south. President Fillmore declared the Compromise of 1850 a "final settlement," but while it staved off the immediate political crisis, it resolved few of the underlying issues that lay at its source.

Many southerners proved skeptical that the new Fugitive Slave Act was enforceable. Senator Robert Barnwell Rhett of South Carolina and others from the Deep South expressed their reservations publicly more frequently than their more optimistic border-state colleagues. (See "Speech of Senator Robert Barnwell Rhett, 1851," on page 308 in the Primary Sources section.) Initially, the North greeted the Fugitive Slave Act with indignation. The northern outcry expressed itself in different ways. Some opponents, including Indiana Quakers, petitioned for its repeal. (See "Petition Against the Fugitive Slave Act, 1850," on page 308 in the Primary Sources section.) The citizens of Danvers, Massachusetts, appealed for the passage of "a law exempting them, and all others having tender consciences upon this subject from all participation in carrying into effect the fugitive slave law, and from the pains and penalties enacted in said law for the non-performance of its provisions. They . . . feel pained . . . to be set like bloodhounds upon the track of the panting fugitive."[11] Representative Giddings of Ohio and others vowed resistance, and a minority of all northerners fulfilled the pledge not to enforce the law. In 1851, African Americans burst into a Boston courtroom, hustled away a Virginia fugitive named Shadrack, and delivered him to Montreal, Canada, where he married an Irish woman and ran a restaurant. The eight men—four whites and four blacks—indicted in Shadrack's liberation all avoided conviction. Three cases ended in hung juries; the others were dropped. The same year, an escaped slave from Missouri named Jerry was arrested in Syracuse, New York. Abolitionists abducted Jerry from the police station and conveyed him safely to Ontario, Canada. A year earlier, and only a month after the Fugitive Slave Act became law, federal troops in Detroit, Michigan, had to form a protective cocoon around a fugitive as he was led from the jail to the courthouse in order to prevent his rescue by an angry mob.

The Fugitive Slave Act and the resistance that immediately followed its passage informed the writing of Harriet Beecher Stowe's antislavery novel *Uncle Tom's Cabin*, published in 1852. When the fugitive slave Eliza

---

[11] *Congressional Globe*, vol. 23, 425.

Harriet Beecher Stowe's novel *Uncle Tom's Cabin* depicted the horrors of slavery for a wide audience. (Library of Congress)

escaped with her child by hopscotching from one ice chunk to another across a partially frozen Ohio River, she encountered on the northern bank a Mr. Symmes from Kentucky. Symmes did not help Eliza directly but advised her where to go for assistance. Critical of the Fugitive Slave Act, Stowe explained that if the fictional Symmes had understood his legal responsibility, he would not have offered any aid at all. (See "Harriet Beecher Stowe, *Uncle Tom's Cabin*, 1852," on page 310 in the Primary Sources section.) In the short term, the Fugitive Slave Act and the publication of *Uncle Tom's Cabin* galvanized antislavery forces.

Northern abolitionists, dedicated to the complete overthrow of slavery, were bitterly, vehemently opposed to the Fugitive Slave Act. They represented only a small number of all northerners, however. Most in the North felt little sympathy for southern masters whose slaves had run off but did not actively oppose enforcement of the law. The initial period of resistance notwithstanding, the North generally acquiesced and did its constitutional duty to support the Fugitive Slave Act. Many fugitives were returned with little fanfare, especially in southern Illinois and other parts of the North where significant numbers of native-born Southerners had settled. Commissioners remanded to slavery the vast majority of all fugitives claimed by southern masters. In the first six years of the Fugitive Slave Act, almost 200 slaves were returned. During the same period, only three fugitives were forcibly liberated. The publicity surrounding the dramatic rescues lent them notoriety, however, and fed a perception among southerners that the law was ineffective. In reality, the administrations of presidents Millard Fillmore, Franklin Pierce, and James Buchanan all strictly enforced the Fugitive Slave Law. Between 1850 and 1860, more than 300 slaves were remanded to the South, while only 11 were released.

Northern hostility to the law revived in 1854. That year, antislavery sentiment spiked as the Kansas-Nebraska Act repealed the Missouri Compromise line of 1820. If the South could violate the Missouri Compromise agreement, the North believed that it was justified in resisting the Fugitive Slave Act. In addition, other highly publicized cases, including that of Anthony Burns, heightened northern resolve. (See the sidebar "Anthony Burns" on page 292.) In one notable case, an abolitionist editor in Milwaukee, Wisconsin, named Sherman M. Booth roused a mob to rescue Joshua Glover, a fugitive slave. Glover had fled bondage in Missouri but was taken up as a runaway in Racine, Wisconsin, and detained in Milwaukee. The next day an antislavery mob broke Glover out of jail and carried him to safety in Canada. Booth was arrested for his role in the escape and convicted of violating the Fugitive Slave Act. On appeal, the Wisconsin state supreme court freed Booth because, it argued, the Fugitive Slave Act was unconstitutional. The case eventually made its way to the U.S. Supreme Court, where in 1859 Chief Justice Roger B. Taney rendered a verdict overturning the Wisconsin ruling. In *Ableman v. Booth,* the Supreme Court unanimously affirmed the constitutionality of the Fugitive Slave Act.

In the latter half of the 1850s, several northern state legislatures passed new rounds of personal liberty laws. Laws varied from one state to the next. Consistent with the *Prigg* decision of 1842, many statutes forbade state officials to aid federal agents and prohibited the use of state jails for the incarceration of fugitives. Some states passed anti-kidnapping laws, imposing fines and prison sentences as a deterrent to the abduction and sale of northern free blacks by unscrupulous individuals. Some provided legal counsel for alleged fugitives. Four states authorized jury trials for accused runaways. Although the vast majority of personal liberty laws were not technically unconstitutional, their intent was nevertheless to undermine or obstruct the implementation of the Fugitive Slave Act. Any measure that increased the time or expense required of a slaveholder to recover a fugitive might accomplish that end. Southern masters recognized the personal liberty laws as hostile in their design and saw them as evidence of northern intransigence. It was already potentially dangerous to venture northward in search of a slave. Personal liberty laws that, from a slaveholder's perspective, seemed to shirk constitutionally prescribed duties made recovery that much more difficult. According to historian Stanley W. Campbell, however, such measures "did not prevent even one slave from being returned to the South where the claim was legitimate."[12]

The secession of southern states beginning in December 1860 raised a significant new question about the enforcement of the Fugitive Slave Act. If a state now belonged to the Confederacy and no longer considered itself a member of the Union, was there a constitutional obligation to return an apprehended fugitive? If northerners had accepted the Compromise of 1850 as a means of reducing sectional conflict and complied with the Fugitive Slave Act primarily to maintain national unity, the incentive to abide by the act evaporated. Nevertheless, from 1861 to mid-1863, amid some of the bloodiest fighting of the Civil War, U.S. marshals continued to restore fugitives to states that had seceded. President

---

[12] Stanley W. Campbell, *The Slave Catchers: Enforcement of the Fugitive Slave Law, 1850–1860* (Chapel Hill: University of North Carolina Press, 1968), viii.

ANTHONY BURNS

In May 1854, a black man named Anthony Burns was arrested in Boston, Massachusetts, as a fugitive slave belonging to Charles F. Suttle of Virginia. Apparently Burns was, in fact, Suttle's bondman. He had been working in the Virginia capital of Richmond when he absconded aboard a vessel bound for Boston. Once in port, Burns sneaked off the boat unnoticed, blended into the anonymity of the city, and secured a job at a clothing store.

When Burns's luck ran out in 1854, he became the first fugitive slave in three years apprehended in Boston. The last had been Thomas Sims of Chatham County, Georgia. In 1851, Sims was remanded to slavery, placed onboard a ship, and delivered to Savannah. Sims had nearly evaded this fate; however, a plan to liberate him by having Sims leap from his jail cell onto a pile of mattresses on the street three stories below was frustrated when masons cemented iron bars into his window. Sims's attempt to gain freedom was foiled.

The city of Boston was well known as a hotbed of abolitionism. That public opinion was so hostile to slavery dissuaded many masters from even attempting to recover any runaways discovered there. Anthony Burns's arrest met with stiff public opposition as Bostonians hoped to avoid repetition of the Sims case of three years before. Aware of the threat of riots and the possible abduction of Burns by antislavery forces, the U.S. marshal called in federal troops to keep the tense situation under control. Indeed, Burns' antislavery allies hatched a plot to create a diversion by rushing into the courtroom and yelling that a mob of African Americans was attacking

Abraham Lincoln continued to enforce the Fugitive Slave Act as a means of placating the slaveholding border states of Maryland, Kentucky, and Missouri, maintaining their loyalty to the Union and preventing their defection to the Confederacy. Enforcement grew increasingly difficult during the war, however, when fugitive slaves began flocking to Union armies by the thousands in search of safe haven. It would have been virtually impossible, not to mention morally objectionable, to return runaways seeking liberty to their masters. In December 1863, Representative Thaddeus Stevens, a Pennsylvania Republican and leading voice the courthouse. Burns could then slip out during the mayhem when no one was looking. A throng numbering perhaps 20,000 massed outside the courthouse, but the presence of U.S. soldiers prevented Burns's rescue. The court ordered his rendition.

At the conclusion of the courtroom proceedings, the troops escorted Burns to the wharf, where a ship was waiting for his return trip to Virginia. Burns witnessed an overwhelming scene en route to the vessel. Bostonians lined the streets and verbally assaulted the soldiers with shouts of "Kidnappers!" Buildings were draped in black sheets of mourning. From one corner building hung a coffin. Despite the menace of the crowd, the soldiers succeeded in ushering Burns to the docks, and he was placed aboard a revenue cutter President Franklin Pierce had made available to convey the fugitive to Norfolk, Virginia. Altogether, returning Burns to slavery cost the U.S. government more than $14,000 (almost $360,000 in current dollars).

Burns's case illustrated that the Fugitive Slave Act could be enforced even in Massachusetts, but it contributed to an increase in northern hostility toward the law in 1854. Burns became the last fugitive remanded to slavery from the city of Boston, the commonwealth of Massachusetts, and all the New England states. Burns himself was detained in Norfolk for a time, then sent to Richmond. He was confined in a slave pen for four months before sale to a speculator. At that point, his fortunes improved. The African-American community of Boston pooled its resources and purchased Burns's freedom in February 1855. Burns went on to study theology in Cincinnati, Ohio, and became a Baptist minister in Ontario, Canada. He died in 1862 at the age of 28.

in the House, renewed an effort begun two years earlier, in late 1861, to repeal the Fugitive Slave Act. In February 1864, Charles Sumner of Massachusetts introduced the bill to repeal in the Senate, which passed the measure by a vote of 27 to 12. President Lincoln signed the repeal of the Fugitive Slave Act on June 28, 1864.

During its 14 years on the books, the Fugitive Slave Act generated resentment in the North and suspicion in the South that it was not being enforced. A few publicized rescues and the passage of personal liberty laws obscured the effectiveness of the law in returning fugitives.

JANE JOHNSON

In July 1855, North Carolina planter Col. John Hill Wheeler was traveling in company with his bondwoman, Jane Johnson, and her enslaved sons, Daniel and Isaiah, in Philadelphia. A former superintendent of the U.S. Branch Mint at Charlotte, North Carolina, state legislator, and personal assistant to President Franklin Pierce, Colonel Wheeler was en route to take his latest political post as U.S. minister to the Central American nation of Nicaragua. Johnson was his wife's personal servant and would offer his spouse some of the conveniences of home in their new tropical residence.

While Wheeler and his slaves were still in port awaiting departure, Passmore Williamson, a Quaker abolitionist and secretary of the Pennsylvania Antislavery Society, interrupted Wheeler's itinerary. He strode onto the boat and boldly entered into a conversation with Johnson. Ignoring Wheeler's presence, Williamson informed the slave woman that since she was in the free state of Pennsylvania, she was therefore also free. Wheeler protested, but Williamson shoved him away as some black men who had accompanied Williamson escorted Johnson and her children off the boat and whisked them away in a carriage. Williamson divested Wheeler of his slaves under Pennsylvania's Liberty Law of 1847, one provision of which freed any slave taken onto Pennsylvania soil. He knew neither the name nor the stature of the aggrieved master.

(See the sidebar "Jane Johnson" above.) The North generally complied because tolerating the Fugitive Slave Law meant the preservation of the Union. Northern whites' freedoms were compromised for the sake of enforcement, but their sacrifices paled beside those of black Americans. The Fugitive Slave Act prioritized sectional reconciliation over fugitive slaves' desire for freedom, as well as the rights of southern masters over those of northern free blacks. No longer confident that their liberty was assured, some free blacks began an exodus to Canada to avoid kidnapping and sale into bondage. Others contributed money to purchase fugitives' freedom legally or participated in extralegal actions to liberate enslaved captives. The Fugitive Slave Act had far-reaching consequences for black and white, North and South.

Wheeler petitioned the U.S. District Court to compel Williamson to reveal his slaves' whereabouts. The abolitionist had taken no direct part in the physical abduction of the slaves, however. When he truthfully stated that the slaves were not in his possession, Judge John Kintzing Kane imprisoned him on a contempt charge. Williamson lingered in jail for more than three months, quite consciously an abolitionist martyr.

During subsequent court proceedings, Johnson made a dramatic reappearance. She had been taken to Massachusetts but, in a daring move that risked her own freedom, returned to Pennsylvania in company with abolitionist Lucretia Mott and other members of the Female Anti-Slavery Society to help rescue the man who had rescued her. As federal marshals ready to seize her and policemen prepared to protect her lined opposite walls of the courtroom, Johnson gave testimony refuting her master's story and corroborating Williamson's account of her liberation. Never, she said, were she and her children in Williamson's custody. Upon concluding her testimony, Johnson was hurried away out a back door. With abolitionists' assistance, she evaded arrest and returned to Boston, where she and her children lived in freedom. Johnson occasionally aided other runaway slaves before her death in August 1872. Some scholars postulate that Jane Johnson is the real identity of the pseudonymous Hannah Crafts, whose *Bondwoman's Narrative* is the only known novel authored by an African-American slave woman.

WHAT IF?

What if Congress had not passed the Fugitive Slave Act?

Despite the cohesion implied by its name, the Compromise of 1850 did not ultimately pass Congress as a package. To promote passage of its respective measures, Senator Stephen A. Douglas of Illinois unbundled Henry Clay's compromise into its constituent parts and secured a majority vote on each individual component in September. That, it seemed, was the only way to secure passage of the whole and prevent the collapse of the compromise. Douglas's action might very well have saved the compromise and made the Fugitive Slave Act law.

The Fugitive Slave Act marked the one part of the Compromise of 1850 that was unequivocally pro-southern. Textbooks often take the position that the fate of slavery in the Utah and New Mexico Territories, left an open question by the compromise, counted as a Southern victory, but contemporary Southerners did not necessarily view it that way. In June 1850, as debates over California state-hood and the status of slavery in the territories still raged, disgruntled southerners convened a meeting in Nashville, Tennessee. The Nashville Convention, called to discuss the many pressing political issues facing the South, attracted secession-ists such as James Henry Hammond of South Carolina, who saw the meeting as a platform to promote their disunionist agenda. Hammond's hopes were dashed, however, as the slaveholding border states, Louisiana, and North Carolina sent no delegates to the meeting, and Texas, Arkansas, Virginia, and Florida all sent a few at most. Only South Carolina arrived in full force. Clearly more extremist in their views than their fellow southerners, the South Carolina delegation retreated from the spotlight. Rather than pursue secession, the Nashville Convention offered dec-larations that all territories should be open to slavery but that the extension of the Missouri Compromise line to the Pacific Ocean, permitting slavery south of 36°30', was an acceptable alternative. Still, many Americans believed the Union in grave danger. From their perspective, the Compromise of 1850, of which the Fugitive Slave Act was a crucial part, defused mounting sectional tensions and averted a possible civil war between North and South. As Indiana representative George W. Julian cautioned at the time, however, "let not the slaveholder nor the slaveholder's friend be deceived by the delusive hope that harmony is now to be restored between the two sections of the Union."[13]

Worth considering are the alternatives to the passage of the Fugitive Slave Act of 1850 as written. Senator Thomas Hart Benton of Missouri, for example, wrote that he and others preferred merely amending and strengthening the existing act of 1793. Instead, Congress "made a new law—long and complex—and[,] striking the public mind as a novelty," unnecessarily provoked an uproar.[14] Several propos-als not ultimately included in the final form of the Fugitive Slave Act, such as a provision for jury trials for fugitive slaves, might have reduced northern opposition to the resulting law but antagonized the South. Senator Thomas Pratt of Maryland

---

[13] *Appendix*, vol. 22, pt. 2, 1302.

[14] Thomas Hart Benton, *Thirty Years' View; or, a History of the Working of the American Government for Thirty Years, from 1820 to 1850. Chiefly Taken from the Congress Debates, the Private Papers of General Jackson, and the Speeches of Ex-Senator Benton, with His Actual View of Men and Affairs: With Historical Notes and Illustrations, and Some Notices of Eminent Deceased Contemporaries. By a Senator of Thirty Years. In Two Volumes*, vol. 2 (New York: D. Appleton and Company, 1856), 778.

offered the most intriguing amendment of the entire debate. Pratt reasoned that if the federal government had the responsibility to return fugitive slaves, it should compensate masters the value of their slaves when their agents failed to apprehend or safely deliver them. The Pratt amendment had notable advantages for North and South. First, it promised to eliminate the need to capture fugitives in hostile communities vehemently opposed to slavery, thereby reducing the physical danger to federal agents. Second, an indemnification program meant that fugitive slaves might remain free without damaging the master's economic interests.

What Senator Pratt envisioned as a statesmanlike means to reconcile North and South, however, revealed divisions internal to the South. Border-South commitment to slavery paled compared to that of the Deep South. Senator Andrew P. Butler of South Carolina alleged that the Pratt amendment was but a thinly veiled scheme of federally funded, gradual emancipation for the benefit of border-state slaveholders seeking to free their bond people. He feared that if compensated for the loss of fugitives, masters might make only halfhearted attempts at recovery or fail to pursue them at all. Dishonest owners might even strike a bargain with slaves to run away so that masters could fraudulently collect an inflated value from the government. Such swindling would tax the U.S. Treasury as it undermined slavery as an institution. With no interest in supporting a program of compensated emancipation or weakening slavery, the Deep South voted with the North to defeat the Pratt amendment by a large majority. Had it been included in the bill, the aborted measure might have reduced the ill will generated by the Fugitive Slave Act. It also offered a small, peaceful step toward the liberation of American slaves.

CHRONOLOGY

1787   The founders sign the Constitution, which includes a fugitive slave clause.

1793   Congress passes the nation's first Fugitive Slave Law.

1842   The Supreme Court hands down its verdict in *Prigg v. Pennsylvania.*

1846   The Wilmot Proviso proposes restrictions on slavery in any territory acquired through war with Mexico.

1848   The Treaty of Guadalupe Hidalgo grants the Mexican Cession to the United States.

1850   Congress passes the Compromise of 1850, which includes the Fugitive Slave Act of 1850.

1852   Harriet Beecher Stowe publishes the novel *Uncle Tom's Cabin.*

1859   The Supreme Court affirms the constitutionality of the Fugitive Slave Act in the unanimous decision of *Ableman v. Booth.*

1864   Congress repeals the Fugitive Slave Act.

DISCUSSION QUESTIONS

1. Did the Fugitive Slave Law of 1850 treat northerners unfairly? Why or why not?
2. Whose responsibility should it have been to apprehend runaway slaves? Why?
3. If you had lived in the North in the 1850s and a fugitive slave appeared at your door late at night, what do you think you would have done?
4. How do you assess the "higher law" doctrine? Should you always obey the law, or are there times when disobeying the law is justified?

WEB SITES

Library of Congress. "African American Odyssey: Abolition, Anti-Slavery Movements, and the Rise of the Sectional Controversy," American Memory. Available online. URL: http://memory.loc.gov/ammem/aaohtml/exhibit/aopart3b.html. Accessed September 28, 2009.

National Archives and Records Administration. "Compromise of 1850," Our Documents: A National Initiative on American History, Civics, and Service. Available online. URL: http://www.ourdocuments.gov/. Accessed September 28, 2009.

Public Broadcasting Service. "Eric Foner on the Fugitive Slave Act," Africans in America, Resource Bank. Available online. URL: http://www.pbs.org/wgbh/aia/part4/4i3094.html. Accessed September 28, 2009.

U.S. Constitution Online. "The Fugitive Slave Act." Available online. URL: http://www.usconstitution.net/fslave.html. Accessed September 28, 2009.

BIBLIOGRAPHY

Baker, H. Robert. *The Rescue of Joshua Glover: A Fugitive Slave, the Constitution, and the Coming of the Civil War.* Athens: Ohio University Press, 2006. Explores an 1854 case in which citizens of Wisconsin prevented the return of a fugitive slave to his master.

Brandt, Nat, and Yanna Kroyt Brandt. *In the Shadow of the Civil War: Passmore Williamson and the Rescue of Jane Johnson.* Columbia: University of South Carolina Press, 2007. An account of Jane Johnson and her two children, slaves belonging to Col. John Hill Wheeler of North Carolina, who were liberated by abolitionists when Wheeler journeyed to the North in 1855. An extensive legal battle ensued.

Campbell, Stanley W. *The Slave Catchers: Enforcement of the Fugitive Slave Law, 1850–1860.* Chapel Hill: University of North Carolina Press, 1968. Despite its age, still the best place to begin any investigation of the Fugitive Slave Act.

Cover, Robert M. *Justice Accused: Antislavery and the Judicial Process.* New Haven, Conn.: Yale University Press, 1975. Skillfully examines the conundrum faced by antislavery judges in having to enforce proslavery laws.

Finkelman, Paul. *An Imperfect Union: Slavery, Federalism, and Comity.* Chapel Hill: University of North Carolina Press, 1981. Studies the "comity clause" of the Constitution, documenting a gradual decrease in cooperation between slave and free states in the decades before the Civil War.

Gara, Larry. *The Liberty Line: The Legend of the Underground Railroad.* Lexington: University of Kentucky Press, 1961. Challenges the popular belief in a smooth, efficient, and coordinated system for whisking slaves to freedom in the North or Canada.

Mitchell, Laura L. "'Matters of Justice Between Man and Man': Northern Divines, the Bible, and the Fugitive Slave Act of 1850." In *Religion and the Antebellum Debate over Slavery,* edited by John R. McKivigan and Mitchell Snay, 134–165. Athens: University of Georgia Press, 1998. Examines sermons on the Fugitive Slave Act in light of white Americans' conceptions of neighborhood and community.

Northup, Solomon. *Twelve Years a Slave.* Edited by Sue Eakin and Joseph Logsdon. Baton Rouge: Louisiana State University Press, 1996. An autobiography of a free black Northerner kidnapped and sold into slavery in 1841.

Slaughter, Thomas P. *Bloody Dawn: The Christiana Riot and Racial Violence in the Antebellum North.* New York: Oxford University Press, 1991. Explores in superb detail an 1851 riot over the recapture of four fugitive slaves in southeastern Pennsylvania.

PRIMARY SOURCES

1. Fugitive Slave Act of 1793

President George Washington signed the Fugitive Slave Act of 1793 into law on February 12. The first two sections of the law dealt with fugitives from justice, or escaped criminals. Sections 3 and 4, excerpted here, addressed fugitives from labor, including runaway slaves. They established U.S. government policy and procedures for the return of slaveholders' escaped property.

Sec. 3. *And it be also enacted,* That when a person held to labor in any of the United States, or in either of the Territories on the Northwest or South of the river Ohio, under the laws thereof, shall escape into any other part of the said States or Territory, the person to whom such labor or service may be due, his agent or attorney, is hereby empowered to seize or arrest such fugitive from labor, and to take him or her before any Judge of the Circuit or District Courts of the United States, residing or being within the State, or before any magistrate of a county, city, or town corporate, wherein such seizure or arrest shall be made, and upon proof to the satisfaction of such Judge or magistrate, either by oral testimony or affidavit taken before and certified by a magistrate or any such State or Territory, that the person so seized or arrested, doth, under the laws of the State or Territory from which he or she fled, owe service or labor to the person claiming him or her, it shall be the duty of such Judge or magistrate to give a certificate thereof to such claimant, his agent, or attorney, which shall be sufficient warrant for removing the said fugitive from labor to the State or Territory from which he or she fled.

Sec. 4. *And be it further enacted,* That any person who shall knowingly and willingly obstruct or hinder such claimant, his agent, or attorney, in so seizing or arresting such fugitive from labor, or shall rescue such fugitive from such claimant, his agent or attorney, when so arrested pursuant to the authority herein given and declared; or shall harbor or conceal such person after notice that he or she was a fugitive from labor, as aforesaid, shall, for either of the said offences, forfeit and pay the sum of five hundred dollars. Which penalty may be recovered by and for the benefit of such claimant, by action of debt, in any Court proper to try the same, saving moreover to the person claiming such labor or service his right of action for or on account of the said injuries, or either of them.

Source: http://www.ushistory.org/presidentshouse/history/slaveact1793.htm.

—⚬⚬—

2. Excerpts from *Prigg v. Pennsylvania,* 1842

Justice Joseph Story delivered the majority opinion in the Supreme Court's Prigg v. Pennsylvania *decision in 1842.*

The [Fugitive Slave] clause manifestly contemplates the existence of a positive, unqualified right on the part of the owner of the slave, which no state law or regulation can in any way qualify, regulate, control, or restrain. The slave is not to be discharged from service or labour, in consequence of any state law or regulation. . . . If this be so, then all the incidents to that right attach also; the owner must, therefore, have the right to seize and repossess the slave, which the local laws of his own state confer upon him as property; and we all know that this right of seizure and reception is universally acknowledged in all the slaveholding states. . . . Upon this ground we have not the slightest hesitation in holding, that, under and in virtue of the Constitution, the owner of a slave is clothed with entire authority, in every state in the Union, to seize and recapture his slave, whenever he can do it without any breach of the peace, or any illegal violence. . . .

The slave is to be delivered up on the claim. By whom to be delivered up? In what mode to be delivered up? How, if a refusal takes place, is the right of delivery to be enforced? Upon what proofs? What shall be the evidence of a rightful reception or delivery? When and under what circumstances shall the possession of the owner, after it is obtained, be conclusive of his right, so as to preclude any further inquiry or examination into it by local tribunals or otherwise, while the slave, in possession of the owner, is in transit to the state from which he fled?

These, and many other questions, will readily occur upon the slightest attention to the clause; and it is obvious that they can receive but one satisfactory answer. They require the aid of legislation to protect the right, to enforce the delivery, and to secure the subsequent possession of the slave. If, indeed, the Constitution guarantees the right, and if it requires the delivery upon the claim of the owner, (as cannot well be doubted,) the natural inference certainly is, that the national government is clothed with the appropriate authority and functions to enforce it. . . . The clause is found in the national Constitution, and not in that of any state. It does not point out any state functionaries, or any state action to carry its provisions into effect. The states cannot, therefore, be compelled to enforce them; and it might well be deemed an unconstitutional exercise of the power of interpretation, to insist that the states are bound to provide means to carry into effect the duties of the national government, nowhere delegated or intrusted to them by the Constitution. . . .

The remaining question is, whether the power of legislation upon this subject is exclusive in the national government, or concurrent in the states, until it is exercised by Congress. In our opinion it is exclusive.

Source: 41 U.S. 539 (1842); 10 L. Ed. 1060; 1842 U.S. LEXIS 387.

—m—

3. Speech of Senator Joseph R. Underwood, 1850

Senator Joseph R. Underwood of Kentucky was actively involved in the creation of the Fugitive Slave Bill, offering amendments to Senator James Mason's proposal. He delivered the following critique of the "higher law" doctrine in the Senate on April 3, 1850.

It is upon the ground that the laws we may pass for the reclamation of fugitive slaves are violations of the Divine law, and that no citizen is bound to execute human law when it comes in conflict with the law of God. In other words, it is the opinion of those who intend to disobey any act of Congress for the reclamation of fugitive slaves that the laws of God are paramount and superior to the laws of man, and every citizen is bound to resist the laws of men, when they conflict with his duties to his Maker. . . . I . . . [oppose] this thing of assuming the responsibility and just executing the law as we understand it—enforcing or not enforcing it, according to our will and pleasure, and setting up individual conscience and conviction to override the laws of the country. This idea permits the private citizen to say to the law makers, elected to make regulations for the government of society, "You have violated your duty; you have not understood what you were elected for; you have trampled upon the principles of the Divine law; you don't understand the laws of God, but I do, and therefore I will set all your legislation at defiance." It is the very essence of nullification, the quintessence of revolution and despotism. It is a doctrine which subverts everything like order, stability, and good government on earth. . . .

Sir, these people, who profess to live up to the laws of God with such strictness, forget the doctrine which is taught in the holiest of all books, that government is ordained of God; that it is a duty to submit to the powers that be, and to render unto Cæsar the things which are Cæsar's. . . . If these laws are morally wrong, it is the citizen's privilege to attempt to change them, through the ballot box and right of suffrage. But submission to them, while they are in force, is a duty. . . . There is a proper and constitutional mode by which bad laws may be assailed and repealed; but until repealed, they must be obeyed, or there is an end of government.

Source: Appendix to the Congressional Globe, for the First Session, Thirty-first Congress: Containing Speeches and Important State Papers, vol. 22, pt. 1 (Washington, D.C.: John C. Rives, 1850), 533.

—⁂—

4. Speech of Senator Roger Baldwin, 1850

Probably best known for his legal work in the Amistad *case, Roger Baldwin served as a Connecticut senator during the debates over the Fugitive Slave Bill. In this speech of March 18, 1850, Baldwin defended the right of alleged fugitives to have a jury trial in the North.*

Has not the man who is seized in a free State as a slave, but who claims to be a freeman, a right, before he shall be withdrawn from his own jurisdiction, from a region where he is surrounded by his friends, who can prove his title to freedom, to have a full trial before a competent tribunal, which shall ascertain the facts in controversy by unquestionable evidence? . . . The alleged fugitive stands there as a freeman, and with the rights of a freeman, until he is proved to have been a slave. How, then, can the court discriminate between the claimant and him whom he has seized, and say that anything short of full and entire proof shall be enough to authorize his transportation beyond the limits of the State to which he claims to belong?

Source: Appendix to the Congressional Globe, for the First Session, Thirty-first Congress: Containing Speeches and Important State Papers, vol. 22, pt. 2 (Washington, D.C.: John C. Rives, 1850), 420.

—⁂—

5. Speech of Representative George W. Julian, 1850

An antislavery member of the House of Representatives, George W. Julian of Indiana offered one of the most powerful indictments of the Fugitive Slave Bill in a speech he delivered on September 25, 1850.

I must say that a tissue of more heartless and cold-blooded enactments never disgraced the legislation of a civilized people. On the one hand, every possible guard is thrown around the rights of the slaveholder, as if his institution had the stamp of divinity upon it, and as if it was to be cherished and fostered as the nation's life; whilst on the other hand, the way of the poor fugitive, whose only crime is a desire to be free, is not only so hedged about with nets and snares as to leave him utterly without hope, but at the same time to expose the free colored man of the North to any southern land-pirate who may seize him as his prey. . . . It commends the *citizens* of the free States to join in the hellish employment of capturing runaway slaves; and sending them back to hopeless bondage and despair. . . . I would resist the execution of this latter provision, if need be, at the peril of my life. I am sure that my constituents will resist it. . . . There is no earthly power that can induce us thus to take sides with the oppressor. If I believed the people I represent were base enough to become the miserable flunkies of a God-forsaken southern slave hunter by joining him or his constables in the blood-hound chase of a panting slave, I would scorn to hold a seat on this floor by their suffrages, and I would denounce them as fit subjects themselves for the lash of the slave-driver. Sir, they will do no such thing, and I give notice now to our southern brethren that their newly-vamped fugitive bill cannot be executed in that portion of Indiana which I have the honor to represent. The moral sense of our people will revolt at its provisions and set them at defiance, while the man who shall attempt to enforce them will cover himself with the infamy which belongs to the trade of a pirate. This is my judgment.

Source: Appendix to the Congressional Globe, for the First Session, Thirty-first Congress: Containing Speeches and Important State Papers, vol. 22, pt. 2 (Washington, D.C.: John C. Rives, 1850), 1301.

—∞—

6. Speech of Senator William H. Seward, 1850

William H. Seward of New York was one of the most vocal opponents of slavery in the U.S. Senate. His famous "higher law" speech of 1850 was not broadly representative of northern opinion, however. Some northern senators specifically disavowed his remarks and expressed a willingness to enforce the Fugitive Slave Bill.

We deem the principle of the law, for the recapture of fugitive slaves, unjust, unconstitutional, and immoral; and thus, while patriotism withholds its approbation, the conscience of our people condemn it. You will say that these convictions of ours are disloyal. Grant it, for the sake of argument. They are nevertheless honest; and the law is to be executed among us, not among you; not by us, but by the Federal authority. Has any Government ever succeeded in changing the moral convictions of its subjects by force? But these convictions imply no disloyalty. We reverence the Constitution, although we perceive this defect, just as we acknowledge the splendor and the power of the sun, although its surface is tarnished with here and there an opaque spot.

We cannot, in our judgment, be either true Christians, or real freemen, if we impose on another a chain that we defy all human power to fasten on ourselves. You believe and think otherwise, and doubtlessly with equal sincerity. We judge you not, and He alone, who ordained the conscience of man and its laws of action, can judge us. Do we then, in this conflict, demand of you an unreasonable thing, in asking that, since you will have property that can and will exercise human powers to effect its escape, you shall be your own police, and in acting among us as such, you shall conform to principles indispensable to the security of admitted rights of freemen? If you will have this law executed, you must alleviate, not increase, its rigors.

The Constitution regulates our stewardship; the Constitution devotes the domain to union, to justice, to defence, to welfare, and to liberty.

But there is a higher law than the Constitution, which regulates our authority over the domain, and devotes it to the same noble purposes.

Source: Appendix to the Congressional Globe, for the First Session, Thirty-first Congress: Containing Speeches and Important State Papers, vol. 22, pt. 1 (Washington, D.C.: John C. Rives, 1850), 387

—⚬⚬⚬—

7. Northern Ministers Expound upon the Fugitive Slave Act, 1851

What was the proper Christian response to the Fugitive Slave Act? Northern ministers addressed the law's spiritual imperatives from the pulpit, publishing approximately 70 sermons on the Fugitive Slave Act in 1850 and 1851. Regardless of denomination, most sermons stressed the Christian duty to obey the law, however morally repulsive it may have been. Without necessarily supporting slavery or endorsing the Fugitive Slave Act, many northern preachers explained to their flocks that they need not agree with the law but must nevertheless submit to it until the law was peacefully amended or repealed. In the following excerpt from a sermon delivered in 1851, Reverend John C. Lord implored his audience to abide by the Fugitive Slave Act, justifying his position with biblical references to Romans 13:1–7 and Matthew 22:15–22. Lord delivered this sermon in Buffalo, New York, hometown of President Millard Fillmore, who thanked him for encouraging obedience to the controversial law.

In the discussions which the recent agitations of the country have originated, grave questions have arisen in regard to the obligation of the citizen to obey laws which he may disapprove; appeals have been made to a HIGHER LAW, as a justification, not merely of a neglect to aid in enforcing a particular statute, but of an open and forcible resistance by arms. . . . *We take the ground, that the action of civil governments within their appropriate jurisdiction is final and conclusive upon the citizen;* and that, to plead a higher law to justify disobedience to a human law . . . is to reject the authority of God himself; who has committed to governments the power and authority which they exercise in civil affairs. This is expressly declared by the Apostle [Paul] in the Epistle to the Romans: "Let every soul be subject to the higher powers, for there is no power but of God; the powers that be are ordained of God; whosoever, therefore, resisteth the power, resisteth the ordinance of God." . . . The language here cannot be misunderstood. Obedience to governments, in the exercise of their legitimate powers, is a religious duty, positively enjoined by God himself. The same authority which commands us to render to God the things which are God's, enjoins us, by the same high sanctions, to render to Cæsar the things which are Cæsar's.

Source: John C. Lord, *"The Higher Law," in Its Application to the Fugitive Slave Bill. A Sermon on the Duties Men Owe to God and to Governments. Delivered at the Central Presbyterian Church, Buffalo, on Thanksgiving-Day* (New York: Union Safety Committee, 1851), 4–6.

Other northern ministers proved equally adept at finding biblical sanc-tion for support of the "higher law" doctrine and resistance to the Fugitive Slave Act. Acts 5:29, for example, states, "We ought to obey God rather than men." In the following sermon from 1851, Congregationalist minis-ter Charles Beecher, a member of the same extended New England fam-ily of abolitionists that included his older sister, Harriet Beecher Stowe, drew upon the biblical injunction of Deuteronomy 23:15–16 forbidding the return of runaway servants. His conclusion suggested a reference to Matthew 25:33–46, in which Jesus explains that the way to inherit the kingdom of heaven is to feed the hungry, give drink to the thirsty, wel-come the stranger, clothe the naked, and visit the imprisoned.

Has a man, made in God's image, a right to himself greater than another man has to him? Has a man in the interior of Africa a right to himself greater than the right of the slave-trader? . . . If it is a right by law to recapture him in a free State, and reconsign him to slavery, it would be right by law to capture him in Africa in the first place. Therefore this clause of the Constitution is wrong. It legalizes kidnapping. The legis-lature pronounces lawful here precisely what it condemns as piracy in Africa. . . . The slave is a man. He has a right to be free. It is wrong to deliver him up when he has made himself free. And that clause of the Constitution which says, Deliver him up, is wrong. It is unrighteous, and God will so declare it and treat it in the day of judgment. . . . But what common sense teaches, the Bible explicitly confirms:—"THOU SHALT NOT deliver unto his master the servant which is escaped from his mas-ter unto thee: he shall dwell with thee, even among you, in that place which he shall choose, in one of thy gates where it liketh him best; thou shalt not oppress him." . . .

In conclusion, therefore, my application of the subject is—Disobey this law . . . If a fugitive claim your help on his journey, break the law and give it him. . . . Feed him, clothe him, harbor him, by day and by night, and conceal him from his pursuers and from the officers of the law. If you are summoned to aid in his capture, refuse to obey. If you are commanded by the officer to lay hands on the fugitive, decline to com-ply; rather, if possible, detain the officer, if you conveniently can, without injury to his person, until the victim is clean gone. If for these things you are accused and brought to trial, appear and defend yourself . . . tell the court that you obey Christ.

Source: Charles Beecher, *The Duty of Disobedience to Wicked Laws: A Sermon on the Fugitive Slave Law* (New York: John A. Gray, 1851), 7–8, 21–22.

—∿—

8. Speech of Senator Robert Barnwell Rhett, 1851

In February 1851, Robert Barnwell Rhett, the South Carolinian who filled the Senate seat left vacant by the death of John C. Calhoun, delivered a speech doubting that the Fugitive Slave Act would be effective because it lacked popular support in the North. On this point, Rhett, known as a "fire-eater" for his radical secessionist views, was in rare agreement with northern antislavery forces.

> A law, to have its practical effect, must move in harmony with the opinions and feelings of the community where it is to operate. In this case no one can doubt that the feeling of the whole and entire North . . . is opposed to the institution of slavery and opposed to this law. Now, you may multiply officers as much as you please; you may make every ship a prison; you may make every custom house a guard-room; you may, in all your great central points, make every effort you can for the purpose honestly of enforcing the law; nay, you may have a large majority in all the free States in favor of its enforcement; and yet, if there be a formidable minority that determine upon the defeat of the operation of the law, they can defeat it, and they will defeat it. . . . Although the Government may be perfectly honest in its determination to enforce the law, although you may legislate with the utmost rigor, yet, after all, the statutes may be nothing more than so much waste paper, of no use but to deceive those who are willing to be deceived. . . . [T]his law cannot and will not be so enforced as practically to secure the rights of the South.

Source: Marion Mills Miller, ed., *Great Debates in American History: From the Debates in the British Parliament on the Colonial Stamp Act (1764–1765) to the Debates in Congress at the Close of the Taft Administration (1912–1913)*. Vol. 4, *Slavery from 1790 to 1857* (New York: Current Literature Publishing Company, 1913), 245–246.

—∿—

9. Petition Against the Fugitive Slave Act, 1850

In January 1851, Representative George W. Julian of Indiana submitted the following petition from his home state's Yearly Meeting of the

Society of Friends, signed in Newport, Wayne County, the previous October. Quakers had been active in the abolitionist movement since before the American Revolution. Congress received many such petitions from northern citizens opposed to the Fugitive Slave Act.

Whenever the powers of any Government are so wielded as to conflict with the Divine law as laid down in the Scriptures—whenever they support any institution subversive of justice, it is evident that that government is perverted from its true object; and from such an administration we believe it our duty to withhold all active support. That the system of chattel slavery, as tolerated and legalized in the southern portion of this Union . . . is an institution of injustice, is too plain a proposition to require argument for its support. . . .

We feel called upon at the present time, particularly, to denounce a bill recently passed for the reclamation of fugitives, the whole of which seems to be based on the assumption that the legal slaveholder has a right of property in the person of the unfortunate man whom he claims as his slave. Were it possible for you to divest yourselves of the prejudice of education, and come out of the mists in which the habit of considering slaves as property has enveloped you, and look upon man in his true light—as the noblest creature of Infinite Wisdom, an object of Divine grace, and heir of immortality—the proposition that he could become property, would certainly appear preposterous in the extreme.

We are aware that it is argued by some that the people of the free States are bound by a certain compromise in the Federal Constitution, to refuse assistance to the stranger, fleeing from Republican oppression to monarchical liberty; yet, while we must ever contend that there is a binding law higher than any human enactments, we must view the above-named bill as a law far more unjust and wicked than is required even by that unholy compromise.

In paying the salaries of the commissioners provided for by this act, we see nothing but a useless, worse than useless, and prodigal expenditure of the national treasure.

According to the provisions of this bill, the testimony of the claimant, or agent, is to be *prima facie* evidence against the alleged fugitive, and so he is prevented from giving his own evidence, which makes every colored person liable to be taken, though legally free; and renders the law unfair and odious in the sight even of those who believe that that is property which the law makes property.

By another provision, it is made a criminal offence, punishable by a heavy fine, to assist a fugitive peaceably and laudably striving to regain his lost liberty—his natural and inherent rights. How plainly is this contrary to the equitable and merciful precepts of the Gospel!

To feed the hungry, clothe the naked, defend the fatherless, and plead for the widow—in short, to perform deeds of charity and mercy, is made the duty of the followers of Christ, and will be taken as evidence of their love of and faith in him; but by this law it is made a crime! Thus has Congress at its last session, in the passage of this bill, set good for evil, and evil for good. . . .

Immediately repeal this cruel, wicked, and infamous law.

Source: Congressional Globe, New Series: Containing Sketches of the Debates and Proceedings of the Second Session of the Thirty-first Congress. Vol. 23 (Washington, D.C.: John C. Rives, 1851), 177.

—ᴍ—

10. Harriet Beecher Stowe, *Uncle Tom's Cabin*, 1852

Harriet Beecher Stowe's abolitionist novel Uncle Tom's Cabin *sold 300,000 copies in its first year of publication. In the 19th century, it was second in sales only to the Bible. The following scene excerpted from the book condemned the Fugitive Slave Act of 1850.*

A thousand lives seemed to be concentrated in that one moment to Eliza. Her room opened by a side door to the river. She caught her child, and sprang down the steps towards it. The trader caught a full glimpse of her just as she was disappearing down the bank; and throwing himself from his horse, . . . he was after her like a hound after a deer. In that dizzy moment her feet to her scarce seemed to touch the ground, and a moment brought her to the water's edge. Right on behind they came; and, nerved with strength such as God gives only to the desperate, with one wild cry and flying leap, she vaulted sheer over the turbid current by the shore, on to the raft of ice beyond. It was a desperate leap—impossible to anything but madness and despair. . . .

The huge green fragment of ice on which she alighted pitched and creaked as her weight came on it, but she staid there not a moment. With wild cries and desperate energy she leaped to another and still another cake; stumbling—leaping—slipping—springing upwards again! Her shoes are gone—her stockings cut from her feet—while blood marked every step; but she saw nothing, felt nothing, till dimly, as in a dream, she saw the Ohio side, and a man helping her up the bank.

"Yer a brave gal, now, whoever ye ar!" said the man, with an oath.

Eliza recognized the voice and face for a man who owned a farm not far from her old home.

"O, Mr. Symmes!—save me—do save me—do hide me!" said Eli[z]a.

"Why, what's this?" said the man. "Why, if 'tan't Shelby's gal!"

"My child!—this boy!—he'd sold him! There is his Mas'r," said she, pointing to the Kentucky shore. "O, Mr. Symmes, you've got a little boy!"

"So I have," said the man, as he roughly, but kindly, drew her up the steep bank. "Besides, you're a right brave gal. I like grit, wherever I see it."

When they had gained the top of the bank, the man paused.

"I'd be glad to do something for ye," said he; "but then there's nowhar I could take ye. The best I can do is to tell ye to go *thar*," said he, pointing to a large white house which stood by itself, off the main street of the village. "Go thar; they're kind folks. Thar's no kind o' danger but they'll help you,—they're up to all that sort o' thing."

"The Lord bless you!" said Eliza, earnestly.

"No 'casion, no 'casion in the world," said the man. "What I've done's of no 'count."

"And, oh, surely, sir, you won't tell any one!"

"Go to thunder, gal! What do you take a feller for? In course not," said the man. "Come, now, go along like a likely, sensible gal, as you are. You've arnt your liberty, and you shall have it, for all me."

The woman folded her child to her bosom, and walked firmly and swiftly away. The man stood and looked after her.

"Shelby, now, mebbe won't think this yer the most neighborly thing in the world; but what's a feller to do? If he catches one of my gals in the same fix, he's welcome to pay back. Somehow I never could see no kind o' critter a strivin' and pantin', and trying to clar theirselves, with the dogs arter 'em and go agin 'em. Besides, I don't see no kind of 'casion for me to be hunter and catcher for other folks, neither."

So spoke this poor, heathenish Kentuckian, who had not been instructed in his constitutional relations, and consequently was betrayed into acting in a sort of Christianized manner, which, if he had been better situated and more enlightened, he would not have been left to do.

Source: Harriet Beecher Stowe, *Uncle Tom's Cabin; Or, Life Among the Lowly,* ed. Ann Douglas (New York: Penguin, 1986), 117–119.

THE KANSAS-NEBRASKA BILL:
Should the Missouri Compromise Line of 1820 Be Repealed?

—⁂—

THE CONTROVERSY

The Issue

In 1854, Senator Stephen A. Douglas of Illinois engineered a bill to organize the Kansas and Nebraska territories according to the principle of popular sovereignty. This bill, however, would overturn decades-old restrictions against slavery in the region. Should the Missouri Compromise line of 1820, which imposed the prohibition against slavery, be repealed?

♦ *Arguments that the Missouri Compromise line of 1820 should be repealed:* In the Kansas-Nebraska bill of 1854, Democratic senator Stephen A. Douglas of Illinois and his allies in Congress, a majority of whom represented the South, sought to overturn the Missouri Compromise line of 1820. They considered the principle of a dividing line between slavery and freedom both unfair to the South and unconstitutional in depriving slaveholders access to public lands with their slaves. The South patriotically submitted to the arrangement in 1820 despite its misgivings and accepted the principle of the 36°30′ parallel. In contrast, the North repudiated the Missouri Compromise line on multiple occasions. Douglas and his supporters argued that the Compromise of 1850, which applied the principle of popular sovereignty to the Utah and New Mexico Territories, replaced the Missouri Compromise line with a doctrine of nonintervention. This new principle forbade congressional interference with slavery in the territories. Because the Missouri Compromise line symbolized that interference, consistency demanded the Missouri Compromise line be declared "inoperative and void."

♦ *Arguments that the Missouri Compromise line of 1820 should not be repealed:* The critics of the Kansas-Nebraska bill, overwhelmingly from the North, wanted to preserve the Missouri Compromise line.

They believed the compromise of 1820 constitutional. The country had acknowledged its force for more than 30 years, with southern support. Repeal was unnecessary: Since Kansas and Nebraska lands were thought hostile to slavery, few whites occupied the region, and plenty of organized territories were already available for settlement. Nothing about the abrogation of the Missouri Compromise line had been mentioned during debates over the Compromise of 1850. As a sacred and perpetually binding compact between North and South, the Missouri Compromise could not be repealed. The South was seeking to skirt its obligation to honor the restriction placed on slavery in the Louisiana Purchase north of the compromise line. Voiding the line would also jeopardize treaties made with the Indians in the unorganized territory. Moreover, the South's proposed substitute, popular sovereignty, was fraught with danger. Opponents of the Kansas-Nebraska bill saw it as a means for Senator Douglas to pursue his personal political ambitions and for the slavepower conspiracy to claim for slavery territory previously deemed free.

—␣␣—

INTRODUCTION

Tensions between North and South over slavery had subsided after the passage of the Compromise of 1850. Although the publication of Harriet Beecher Stowe's *Uncle Tom's Cabin* in 1852 prevented slavery from fading into the background, sectional hostility seemed to be on the wane. In 1854, however, Illinois senator Stephen A. Douglas's proposed Kansas-Nebraska bill shattered the veneer of tranquility and reignited the sectional dispute over slavery. Douglas hoped to establish government in the remaining unorganized territory of the 1803 Louisiana Purchase, lands that spanned the area from the present-day state of Kansas northward to the Canadian border. To attract southern support for his Nebraska bill, as contemporaries called Douglas's measure, the senator recommended that popular sovereignty decide the slavery question in the region. This meant the invalidation of the eighth section of the Missouri Compromise of 1820, which prohibited slavery in lands of the Louisiana Purchase north of the 36°30' line of latitude, Missouri excepted. The Nebraska bill thus proposed to declare "inoperative and void" a Missouri Compromise line that had been in place for more than three decades. The controversy over the proposed legislation reset the nation on the path to civil war.

Douglas and other proponents of the Nebraska bill urged the repeal of the Missouri Compromise line. They argued that the restriction against slavery north of the line unconstitutionally deprived masters of the right to share in the common lands of the United States. The identical argument had been made in 1820, but northern votes in Congress had overwhelmed a divided South and carried the measure. With time, the South became reconciled to the principle of a line separating slavery from freedom and repeatedly campaigned for its extension beyond its original confines of the Louisiana Purchase. The South understood the North's refusal as a rejection of the line. Then, the Compromise of 1850 employed the principle of popular sovereignty to determine the future of slavery in the Utah and New Mexico Territories, a vast region recently won by war with Mexico. In 1854, Douglas and his predominantly Southern supporters argued that the Compromise of 1850's embrace of the principle of self-government established a new doctrine of congressional nonintervention in the territories. The people living in the territory, rather than Congress, should decide the fate of slavery there. The Missouri Compromise line conflicted with the great principle of popular sovereignty and therefore must be repealed.

Almost all from the North, enemies of the Kansas-Nebraska bill worked to maintain the Missouri Compromise line. Denying its alleged unconstitutionality, they observed that it had been in effect for 34 years and had even gained southern backing. There was no reason to abrogate the line, because virtually everyone agreed the soil and climate in the unorganized territory discouraged plantation agriculture. Few whites inhabited the region, and white settlers had many other states and organized territories available to them. In addition, the Missouri Compromise line applied only to the Louisiana Purchase, and the North was under no obligation to extend it. Foes of the Kansas-Nebraska bill upheld the Missouri Compromise as a sacred and inviolable agreement between North and South. More than just a regular piece of legislation, it was, they argued, not subject to revision. No one during debates over the Compromise of 1850 had suggested that the measures had introduced a principle of nonintervention that invalidated the Missouri Compromise line. Tampering with the restriction on slavery north of the line would moreover generate chaos with treaties negotiated with the Indians living in the unorganized territory. The entire effort to repeal the Missouri Compromise line struck many in the North as a plot through which Douglas could gain political fame and the South could eschew its political obligations with the North and extend slavery's influence.

BACKGROUND

The Compromise of 1850, extolled as a "final settlement" to the slavery question, failed to meet its lofty expectations. The agreement that admitted California as a free state, organized the Utah and New Mexico Territories, abolished the slave trade in Washington, D.C., and created a new fugitive slave law subdued tensions between North and South for a time, but after only four years, sectional strains resurfaced. Senator Stephen A. Douglas played the most prominent role in the drama that unfolded.

Several factors conspired to renew the conflict over slavery in 1854. Pressure was mounting from whites eager to settle the vast unorganized lands of the Louisiana Purchase west of Missouri, Iowa, and the Minnesota Territory. At the same time, California's admission to the Union in 1850 generated calls for a transcontinental railroad to link the new state to the rest of the country, half a continent away. A railroad line traversing the West would greatly facilitate the movement of people and goods across the country and improve communication between the coasts. The advantages of a transcontinental railroad seemed obvious enough, but members of Congress disagreed over the precise route a prospective rail line should take. Southerners, naturally, favored a southern path that sent tracks westward from New Orleans or Memphis to the Pacific. To bolster the odds of a southern route for the railroad, Secretary of War Jefferson Davis of Mississippi spearheaded the acquisition of the Gadsden Purchase from Mexico in 1853. The United States paid its southern neighbor $10 million for roughly 30,000 square miles of land south of the Gila River in modern-day Arizona and New Mexico. The additional territory boasted terrain more conducive to railroad construction than other paths across the Rocky Mountains that separated California from the East.

Senator Douglas of Illinois championed a northerly route for the transcontinental railroad with an eastern terminus in Chicago. Such a rail line would benefit his home state as well as his own political fortunes. Besides the topographic obstacle of the Rocky Mountains, however, any plan for a railroad line heading west from Chicago faced an

Democrat Stephen A. Douglas represented Illinois in the U.S. Senate. He championed popular sovereignty as the best solution for dealing with slavery in the territories. (The Art Archive)

additional impediment. Between Iowa's western boundary and the Rockies, and from Texas to the Canadian border, lay an unorganized expanse of land occupied by Native Americans, some indigenous to the Great Plains and others relocated there from points east after the passage of the Indian Removal Act in 1830. White presence in the region was limited, and no official U.S. governmental institutions were established. Douglas understood the need to organize the sprawling territory in the West to enhance the chance for a northern route for the railroad. Prior to 1854, he had attempted—unsuccessfully—to create a Nebraska Territory, thwarted by southern opposition. Southern lawmakers recognized that Section 8 of the Missouri Compromise of 1820 had declared the territory in question, nestled within the Louisiana Purchase and entirely north of the 36°30' line, free. They had little interest in paving the way for the creation of new states in a region where slavery had been "forever prohibited." In particular, Missourians such as Senator David Rice Atchison had no desire to be surrounded on three sides by nonslaveholding states. Making the region due west of Missouri a slave state would help keep the Show Me State safe for slavery. Maneuvering to secure a transcontinental railroad route out of Chicago and in the process define his Democratic Party as the party of progress and western development, Douglas realized an accommodation with slavery was politically necessary.

Douglas chaired the Senate's Committee on Territories. When Democratic senator Augustus C. Dodge of Iowa introduced a bill in December 1853 to create a territorial government for Nebraska, it headed to Douglas's committee. To attract southern support, Douglas proposed a bill to organize a vast Nebraska Territory that incorporated the principle of popular sovereignty. The brainchild of Michigan's Democratic senator Lewis Cass, popular sovereignty had emerged in the latter 1840s as a possible solution for dealing with the expansion of slavery into territories obtained from Mexico as a result of the Mexican-American War (1846–48). Popular sovereignty maintained that the people actually living in a territory would vote to decide whether slavery would be permitted there; Congress would not participate in that determination. As the Democratic nominee for president in 1848, Cass promoted popular sovereignty during his campaign. Although he lost his bid for the presidency, the Compromise of 1850 applied the principle of popular sovereignty to the newly established Utah and New Mexico territories. Douglas found popular sovereignty genuinely appealing. It seemed to him fundamentally democratic and American to allow voters— white male citizens—to decide the fate of slavery where they resided. Although Douglas himself personally opposed slavery, he did not consider it a moral issue. As architect of the Nebraska bill, he was therefore perfectly willing to accept the principle of popular sovereignty in the new territory. If Douglas's political calculations were correct, he could gain Southern allies for the Nebraska bill because it potentially opened to slavery a region where it had been barred for more than 30 years.

Douglas's overtures to the South in the Nebraska bill were met with a critical eye. The initial bill Douglas reported out of committee on January 4, 1854, organized a single, vast Nebraska Territory but was worded so ambiguously that it was not entirely clear that the Missouri Compromise restriction upon slavery had been removed. To prevent the Democrats from taking all the political credit in the South should the prohibition on slavery north of 36°30' be lifted, Whig senator Archibald Dixon of Kentucky, serving out the unexpired term of the recently deceased Henry Clay, introduced an amendment to make the repeal of the Missouri Compromise line more explicit. Douglas responded with a bill on January 23 that divided the unorganized portion of the Louisiana Purchase into two territories. The smaller, Kansas, lay west of Missouri, while the much larger Nebraska Territory occupied lands west of Iowa and the Minnesota Territory, including all or part of present-day Nebraska, the Dakotas, Montana, Wyoming, and Colorado. It also stated that Section 8 of the Missouri Compromise of 1820 "was superseded by the principles of the legislation of 1850, commonly called the compromise measures, and is hereby declared inoperative." The bill was still not forceful enough to satisfy southern lawmakers, however. Douglas tinkered with its language again, to read that the Missouri Compromise line was "inconsistent with the principle of non-intervention by Congress with slaves in the States and Territories, as

HONOR IN THE KANSAS-NEBRASKA DEBATES

Although a concept typically associated with the South, honor infused the speech and informed the actions of both northern and southern politicians in antebellum debates over slavery. Obsessive concern with status and reputation was prevalent during the debates over the Kansas-Nebraska bill. Members of Congress customarily spoke in the language of honor and observed its rituals. They addressed one another as "honorable gentleman" and typically showed mutual respect in the chambers. As debate intensified over the Nebraska bill, however, cordiality was at times strained. Friends and foes of the legislation each charged the other with dishonorably breaking the Missouri Compromise, and disagreements sometimes turned personal.

In one instance, Senator Robert Toombs of Georgia insisted that his southern Whig colleagues in the Senate had held an impromptu meeting in which they united behind the Kansas-Nebraska bill. Renegade Whig John Bell of Tennessee, who ultimately voted against the measure, disputed Toombs' account of what transpired at the gathering. He took offense that Toombs presumed to speak for him, vehemently denied being present for the duration of the meeting, and declared "utterly false" any allegation that he had ever pledged his support for the bill—not that that made him an ally of the abolitionists, as Toombs alleged. Glancing in his colleague's direction, Bell observed that "the honorable Senator from Georgia looks at me sternly," apparently visibly perturbed that Bell's remarks impugned his character by insinuating he was a liar. Throughout the Kansas-Nebraska debate, senators and representatives, conscious of their colleagues' prickly sensitivities, repeatedly denied any intent to offend, clarified meanings that had been misconstrued, and apologized for misunderstandings. They perfected the strategy of speaking in the abstract ("It would be the height of folly to say . . .") to preclude directly insulting a congressional adversary.

recognized by the legislation of eighteen hundred and fifty, commonly called the Compromise Measures" and "is hereby declared inoperative and void." (See "Kansas-Nebraska Bill, 1854," on page 343 in the Primary Sources section.)

The Kansas-Nebraska bill aroused unexpectedly heated passions in the North and South and in the halls of Congress. (See the sidebar

Despite all precautions, tempers were bound to boil over the congressional cauldron of 1854. An exchange in the House led to a near-duel between Democratic representatives Francis B. Cutting of New York and John C. Breckinridge of Kentucky. The two men disagreed over which committee in the House should receive the bill. Cutting preferred the more legislatively cumbersome route, sending it to the Committee of the Whole to wait its turn behind 50 other bills already on the calendar, while Breckinridge favored the more expeditious path to passage via the Committee on Territories. Breckinridge questioned Cutting's motive for delay, and Cutting accused Breckinridge of ungratefully accepting political contributions from New York in his recent reelection campaign. Breckinridge denied the charge in "hot words" that Cutting called "one of the most violent, one of the most inflammatory, one of the most personal assaults that has ever been known upon this floor." As he elaborated, Cutting stated that Breckinridge "skulks behind the Senate bill," a comment the Kentucky representative demanded he retract. Cutting refused, saying, "It is not here that I will desecrate my lips by undertaking to retort on it in the manner which it deserves." Breckinridge interpreted the remark as a challenge to a duel, an antiquated means of settling disputes by the 1850s. No congressman had died in a duel since 1838, when Representative William J. Graves of Kentucky killed Maine's Jonathan Cilley. Nevertheless, Breckinridge and Cutting headed to Bladensburg, Maryland, to engage in the potentially lethal contest. Before any shots were fired, however, Representative Thomas Hart Benton of Missouri, who had himself killed a man in a duel decades earlier, brokered peace between the combatants. The duel averted, the pair cemented their truce by sharing a plug of tobacco when they next met in the House.[*]

---

[*] *Appendix*, 944 (Bell); *Congressional Globe*, 763, 764 (Cutting).

"Honor in the Kansas-Nebraska Debates" on page 318.) The response caught Douglas by surprise. Both supporters and opponents of the Nebraska bill, Democrats and Whigs, publicly doubted slavery would ever exist in either Kansas or Nebraska. "Does any man believe that you will have a slaveholding State in Kansas or Nebraska?" asked Virginia Democratic senator Robert M. T. Hunter, a proponent of the bill. Whig senator George Badger of North Carolina responded, "it is in the highest degree probable that with regard to these Territories of Nebraska and Kansas, there will never be any slaves in them." Douglas concurred, calling it "worse than folly" to imagine the region "permanently a slaveholding country." Senators Andrew P. Butler of South Carolina and William H. Seward of New York, the former a slaveholder and Democrat and the latter a leading antislavery advocate and Whig, agreed on little but found common ground in their belief "that slavery at most can get nothing more than Kansas; while Nebraska . . . will . . . escape, for the reason that its soil and climate are uncongenial with the staples of slave culture."[1] Although congressmen generally perceived the two territories as hostile to plantation agriculture, debate over the Kansas-Nebraska bill hinged on a far broader, more significant issue. At stake were the future of slavery's expansion and the possible substitution of popular sovereignty for a distinct line that for decades had been understood to separate slavery from freedom. Should Congress pass the Kansas-Nebraska bill and thereby repeal the Missouri Compromise line of 1820?

THE DEBATE

The Case that the Missouri Compromise Line Should Be Repealed

Senator Stephen Douglas led the fight to pass the Kansas-Nebraska bill. By 1854, he considered it essential to establish government in the unorganized territory of the West—then sparsely populated by

---

[1] *Appendix to the Congressional Globe, for the First Session, Thirty-third Congress: Containing Speeches, Important State Papers, Etc.,* vol. 31 (Washington, D.C.: John C. Rives, 1854), 224 (Hunter), 149 (Badger), 769 (Seward); *Congressional Globe: Containing the Debates, Proceedings, and Laws, of the First Session of the Thirty-third Congress,* vol. 28, pt. 1 (Washington, D.C.: John C. Rives, 1854), 279 (Douglas).

whites—to connect California to the rest of the United States and protect American citizens as they headed westward. (See "Speech of Senator Stephen Douglas on the Necessity of the Nebraska Bill, 1854," on page 343 in the Primary Sources section.) The Kansas-Nebraska bill Douglas crafted appealed to Senator Lewis Cass, a Michigan Democrat and the originator of popular sovereignty; Douglas's Illinois counterpart in the House, Democratic representative William A. Richardson; and many other northern congressmen. But Douglas's bill was primarily designed to attract southern votes, and it did gain strong, widespread support in the South. In the Senate, Andrew P. Butler of South Carolina, Robert M. T. Hunter of Virginia, and George Badger of North Carolina proved among the most outspoken and articulate backers of the bill, while Representatives Alexander H. Stephens of Georgia and Preston Brooks of South Carolina assumed influential roles in promoting it in the House. Central to the Kansas-Nebraska bill was the annulment of the 36°30' Missouri Compromise line. Southern congressmen in 1820 had grudgingly accepted the Missouri Compromise but over time gradually became its most ardent defenders. As the antebellum decades wore on, they grew to believe that the North had abandoned the agreement. In dealing with slavery in the Mexican Cession, the Compromise of 1850 had abandoned the 36°30' parallel and replaced it with the principle of popular sovereignty. By adopting popular sovereignty for the Kansas and Nebraska territories, Douglas's bill reaffirmed the Compromise of 1850's principle of congressional nonintervention. Because the Missouri Compromise line imposed by Congress in 1820 was inconsistent with territorial self-government, it required repeal.

Senator Butler best voiced the South's newfound contempt for the Missouri Compromise. Although intended to make peace, he argued, the Missouri Compromise alienated the North and the South by imposing an arbitrary, geographical line between slavery and freedom. This was a "fatal error." The North had dictated the terms of the agreement and passed it through superior northern numbers. In Butler's telling, Southerners chafed under the Missouri Compromise, an unconstitutional measure that denied slaveholding citizens equal access to the common territory of the United States. The persecuted South only acquiesced to the arrangement out of a sense of patriotic duty, but resentment lingered. As Butler observed, "repeal of the

Missouri compromise . . . would withdraw a festering thorn from the side of the South."[2]

As odious as it initially was to the South, the Missouri Compromise established a principle. It suggested that "a division of territory between the slaveholding and nonslaveholding States" must be maintained, explained Senator Hunter, because "justice required a partition of it amongst them, for purposes of use and occupation." As Douglas reasoned, the intent of the Missouri Compromise "was not simply to settle the question on that piece of country, but . . . to carry out a great principle, by extending that dividing line as far west as our territory went, and running it onward on each new acquisition of territory." Although admittedly section 8 of the compromise "only covered the territory acquired from France . . . the principles of the act, the objects of its adoption, the reasons in its support, required that it should be extended indefinitely westward, so far as our territory might go, whenever new purchases should be made." Badger concurred: "the principle of legislation embodied in the Missouri compromise was . . . that a line in the territories should be selected, and slavery excluded on the one side, and impliedly allowed on the other." Then, "as we acquired future territory, we should apply that line." Douglas, Badger, and others insisted that, because the Missouri Compromise line applied to *all* territory the United States possessed in 1820, the line should naturally be extended to all *new* territory in the West the nation should happen to acquire. Over the next three decades, the South reconciled itself to the Missouri Compromise line and recommended its continuation to the Pacific Ocean on several occasions. Its extension made sense, Badger explained, "because it gave a clear legal ground to stand upon; because it was associated with a patriotic settlement of a former difficulty; [and] because it had age on its side, and commanded, consequently, a large share of favor in the public mind." According to the North Carolina senator, "we asked nothing, we sought nothing, but the simple recognition of the Missouri compromise line, as carried still further out upon its original principle."[3]

As the South remained faithful to the principle of the Missouri Compromise, the North repeatedly repudiated it. Douglas argued that

---

[2] *Appendix*, 234, 937.

[3] *Appendix*, 221 (Hunter), 146, 147 (Badger); *Congressional Globe*, 276 (Douglas).

the North first disavowed the Missouri Compromise agreement within a year of its inception. A majority of northern congressmen had violated it by voting against Missouri's admission into the Union in 1821, under the pretext that the proposed state constitution forbade the entrance of free blacks. A separate bargain engineered by Henry Clay was required to gather the necessary northern support for statehood. Then, in 1836, the North opposed the admission of the slave state of Arkansas despite its location south of the 36°30' parallel. A dozen years later, the South proposed to extend the Missouri Compromise line to the Pacific during discussions to organize the Oregon Territory. Although Douglas and a majority in the Senate voted to adopt an amendment stating that the Oregon Territory would remain free precisely because it lay north of 36°30', Northern representatives in the House balked and struck it down. Oregon became a free territory in 1848 without mention of the Missouri Compromise line. Northern disregard of the line persisted during negotiations over the Compromise of 1850. If the Missouri Compromise retained any meaning, Douglas and the South argued, it would have been carried into the territory gained from Mexico in 1848. Northern congressmen, however, opposed the extension of the line into any part of the Mexican Cession. The North's repeated rejections of the 36°30' parallel demonstrated to the South that the Missouri Compromise marked no sacred compact impervious to revision. Thus, during debates over the Kansas-Nebraska bill, the South considered it disingenuous for the North to assail Douglas's proposal as a violation of the Missouri agreement because northern commitment to the compromise seemed so sudden. "I think it is a little unreasonable, and a little absurd," scoffed Senator Badger, "that gentlemen should call upon us to respect a compromise which they themselves have destroyed." The Missouri Compromise was, in Douglas's words, "an ordinary act of legislation" no more binding than any other law.[4]

According to Douglas and his allies, the Compromise of 1850 marked the final repudiation of the Missouri Compromise line. The Compromise of 1850, Douglas explained, implemented popular sovereignty in the region ceded by Texas to the New Mexico Territory, some of which lay north of 36°30' and hence had been subject to the

---

[4] *Appendix*, 148 (Badger); John Vance Cheney, ed., *Memorable American Speeches*, vol. 3 (Chicago: R. R. Donnelley & Sons Company, 1909), 170 (Douglas).

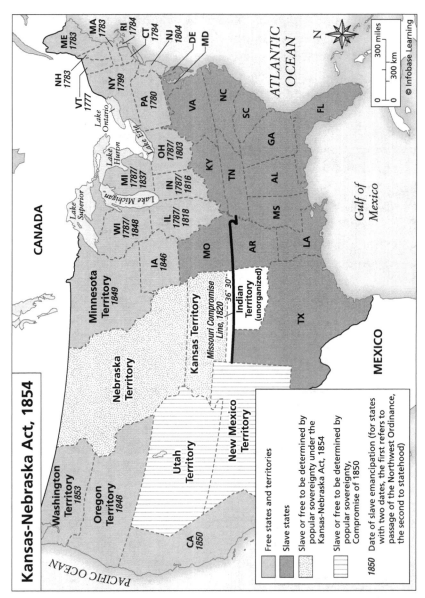

Kansas-Nebraska Act, 1854

CANADA

Lake Superior

Lake Michigan

Lake Huron

Lake Erie

Lake Ontario

ATLANTIC OCEAN

N

300 miles

300 km

© Infobase Learning

ME 1783
NH 1783
VT 1777
MA 1783
RI 1784
CT 1784
NY 1799
NJ 1804
DE
MD
PA 1780
VA
NC
SC
GA
FL

OH 1787/ 1803
MI 1787/ 1837
IN 1787/ 1816
IL 1787/ 1818
WI 1787/ 1848
KY
TN
AL
MS
AR
LA

IA 1846
MO
TX

MEXICO

Gulf of Mexico

Minnesota Territory 1849

Nebraska Territory

Kansas Territory

Missouri Compromise Line, 1820   36° 30'

Indian Territory (unorganized)

Washington Territory 1853

Oregon Territory 1848

Utah Territory

New Mexico Territory

CA 1850

PACIFIC OCEAN

Free states and territories

Slave states

Slave or free to be determined by popular sovereignty under the Kansas-Nebraska Act, 1854

Slave or free to be determined by popular sovereignty, Compromise of 1850

1850 Date of slave emancipation (for states with two dates, the first refers to passage of the Northwest Ordinance, the second to statehood)

In 1854, Senator Stephen A. Douglas of Illinois proposed the organization of the Kansas and Nebraska territories according to the principle of popular sovereignty.

Missouri Compromise restriction. Similarly, the measure incorporated a fragment of the Louisiana Purchase where slavery had been prohibited into the Utah Territory, where popular sovereignty was likewise imposed. Moreover, legislators in 1850 opted not to make the Missouri

Compromise line the boundary between the New Mexico and Utah territories. That the North succeeded in making California a free state, despite substantial lands south of 36°30', permanently defeated the principle of the Missouri Compromise line.

With the Missouri Compromise line effectively annulled and superseded, Douglas asserted that the Compromise of 1850 introduced in its place the doctrine of congressional nonintervention. The Missouri Compromise assumed that Congress had the constitutional authority to legislate upon slavery in the territories, excluding it on one side of a line and implicitly permitting it on the other. By contrast, in its embrace of popular sovereignty, the Compromise of 1850 stripped Congress of that power. As Douglas explained, "The Missouri Compromise was interference; the compromise of 1850 was non-interference, leaving the people to exercise their rights under the Constitution." Douglas and his allies understood the application of popular sovereignty to Utah and New Mexico in 1850 as a precedent for all future territories. In incorporating popular sovereignty in the Kansas-Nebraska bill of 1854, Douglas applied the identical principle of nonintervention from the compromise of 1850. He made his position on Kansas-Nebraska clear: "The principle which we propose to carry into effect by the bill is this: That *Congress shall neither legislate slavery into any territories or state, nor out of the same; but the people shall be left free to regulate their domestic concerns in their own way, subject only to the Constitution of the United States.*" Implementation of the vaunted principle of self-government required that the eighth section of the Missouri Compromise—legally incompatible with the new, enduring principle of 1850—be declared "inoperative and void."[5] (See "Speech of Senator Stephen Douglas on the Principle of the Kansas-Nebraska Bill, 1854," on page 345 in the Primary Sources section.)

Formerly an ardent proponent of the Missouri Compromise, Douglas threw his energies behind popular sovereignty after the principle of self-government supplanted it by the Compromise of 1850. Popular sovereignty seemed to him and many of his colleagues a perfectly reasonable solution for dealing with slavery in the territories. Asked North Carolina's Senator Badger, "if there is a strip of land belonging to the United States, upon which a southern planter can make cotton or

---

[5] Cheney, *Memorable American Speeches,* 217, 155–156.

sugar, why grudge it to him? He reduces no man from freedom to slavery in order to make it." A Yankee supporter of the Kansas-Nebraska bill likewise queried, "Why should northern men object to it? Will the institution be likely to prevail in those Territories? Climate, soil, the productions of the soil, forbid it. The laws of nature forbid it. . . . It is a grain country, a country of wheat and corn. . . . Is there any danger to the North?" Appeals to moderation and common sense proved rare, however, in a debate frequently clouded by passion.[6]

But what of the presence of Native Americans in Kansas and Nebraska? Douglas considered them no insurmountable obstacle to the implementation of his bill. Only an insignificant population of Indians lived in the territory to be organized, he claimed, and the bill did not infringe upon their rights to the lands they occupied. Shall a vast territory eligible for white settlement, Douglas asked rhetorically, "be consigned to perpetual barbarism merely on account of that small number of Indians, when the bill itself expressly provides that those Indians and their lands are not to be included within the limits of the proposed Territories, nor to be subject to their laws or jurisdiction?"[7] Douglas left it to the Committee on Indian Affairs to make regulations for the natives. The Kansas-Nebraska bill would not apply to them until the U.S. government negotiated treaties with the Indians placing them under the bill's provisions.

Proponents of the Kansas-Nebraska bill predicted that it was a legitimate legislative path to national peace and harmony. Although some support was garnered from those eager to see the South finally treated fairly, a sanguine Douglas cast the bill's anticipated effects more broadly. For him, its affirmation of the principle of nonintervention by Congress promised justice to settlers in the territories and the preemption of future controversy. Grounded in popular sovereignty, the Kansas-Nebraska bill "will have the effect to destroy all sectional parties and sectional agitations." "If we stand firm, and pass the bill," Representative Richardson prophesied, "my word for it, that the excitement which has been manufactured at the North will blow over before the elections next fall." Conversely, defeat of the Nebraska bill boded ill for the nation. "Before God," Representative Brooks forecast ominously, "I believe that

---

[6] *Appendix*, 149 (Badger), 318 (Toucey).
[7] *Appendix*, 325.

if this bill . . . fails to pass this House, we will be in greater danger of disunion than at any time since the formation of this Government."[8]

The Case that the Missouri Compromise Line Should Not Be Repealed

Section 8 of the Missouri Compromise in 1820 "forever prohibited" slavery north of the 36°30' line of latitude. By the agreement, the North and South divided the lands of the Louisiana Purchase between them. Preferring territory entirely free, northern antislavery forces opposed the creation of an arbitrary line separating freedom and slavery but conceded its political necessity. With time, the Missouri Compromise assumed a sacred status. The Kansas-Nebraska bill, crafted paradoxically by a man who had supported the Missouri Compromise line throughout his political career, attempted to change the terms of this historical bargain. Senator Stephen Douglas drastically underestimated the strength and intensity of antislavery sentiment in the North, however. Its opponents labeled the proposal a "fire-brand" that aimed to unravel a revered compromise crafted by esteemed statesmen. No stranger to hyperbole, Charles Sumner, the antislavery senator from Massachusetts, called it "the worst bill on which Congress ever acted," digging "the very grave of freedom in Kansas and Nebraska."[9] The doctrine of nonintervention and popular sovereignty (derisively dubbed "squatter sovereignty" in the North) were smokescreens of reputed principle to disguise the theft of free territory for slavery. Sumner and his northern senatorial colleagues William H. Seward of New York, Salmon P. Chase and Benjamin Wade of Ohio, Edward Everett of Massachusetts, and Truman Smith of Connecticut spoke forcefully against the bill, joined in the House by Massachusetts representatives Charles W. Upham and Tappan Wentworth, New York's Gerrit Smith, and others. A few isolated Southerners also opposed the Kansas-Nebraska bill, including Representative William Cullom and Senator John Bell of Tennessee and Texas senator Sam Houston. All argued against the repeal of the Missouri Compromise line.

Critics quickly discounted southern arguments that the Missouri Compromise line was unconstitutional. They reviewed the point from

---

[8] Cheney, *Memorable American Speeches*, 218; *Appendix*, 796 (Richardson), 375 (Brooks).
[9] *Appendix*, 785.

1820 that Article IV, Section 3, of the Constitution granted Congress the power "to make all needful Rules and Regulations" for U.S. territories. That constitutional provision fundamentally contradicted Douglas's doctrine of nonintervention. Nonintervention was a charade, Senator Wade observed. Congress had imposed legal limits on carrying gunpowder, firearms, or whiskey into the territories, yet slaveholders nevertheless felt entitled to a special exemption for enslaved property. More significant than that, however, southern lawmakers had long supported the Missouri Compromise that had been in effect for more than 30 years. Congress abided by it in the admissions to statehood of Missouri (1821), Arkansas (1836), and Iowa (1846), as well as in the organization of Minnesota Territory. It also incorporated the line into the Texas annexation resolutions of 1845, which authorized the possible creation of four additional states carved out of Texas's lands. In accordance with the Missouri Compromise, any states formed south of 36°30' could be either slave or free, according to the wishes of their voters; those north of the line were to become free. In all of these instances, Senator Chase and his northern colleagues saw validation of the Missouri Compromise line. Southern states approved the Texas annexation measure containing the slavery restriction. Douglas, then a member of the House of Representatives, also voted for it. Furthermore, Douglas and most southern members of Congress pressed for the continuation of the Missouri Compromise line to the Pacific in 1848 and 1850. How, with any consistency, wondered the Kansas-Nebraska bill's enemies, could the South seek to abrogate an agreement that had stood for 34 years *with* southern support? Had the South, asked Senator Wade, "deliberately voted for an act which they knew to be unconstitutional?" No, concluded northern congressmen; the South stumbled upon its newfound opposition for another reason. Wade averred that the South now attempted to invalidate the Missouri Compromise line out of spite that it was not extended. Representative Wentworth concurred. "After the South has peaceably enjoyed all the benefits of this settlement for thirty-four years, and so repeatedly and so solemnly recognized it by her votes in Congress," he insisted, "it is too late for her now to urge the unconstitutionality of the settlement."[10]

The bill's failure to honor the Missouri Compromise line unnecessarily disrupted national harmony, argued the measure's opponents.

---

[10] *Appendix*, 300 (Wade), 733 (Wentworth).

Given the widespread belief that the climate and soil discouraged slavery in Kansas and Nebraska, it made no sense to Seward and others to repeal the Missouri Compromise prohibition on slavery north of 36°30'. Senator Smith noted that the nation already had five existing territories in early 1854: Oregon, Minnesota, Utah, New Mexico, and Washington. Moreover, ample unsettled public lands were still available in Missouri, Arkansas, Michigan, Iowa, and Wisconsin. There seemed little need to organize the two additional territories. Smith echoed the concern of others when he observed that the unorganized territory was largely unpopulated by whites, except for a smattering of government officials, soldiers, missionaries, and traders. It appeared premature to establish territories with so few white inhabitants. A less expensive, more practical solution to protect settlers and travelers was to locate military posts strategically within the unorganized territory. Finally, Seward, Sumner, Houston, and others pointed out that no one to their knowledge had asked for the organization of Kansas and Nebraska. According to Representative Cullom, "No public meeting of the people, no primary assembly, no convention, no legislative body has called for this measure."[11] Rather, it sprang from the shrewd and active mind of Stephen Douglas for unabashedly political purposes. (See "Speech of Representative William Cullom, 1854," on page 346 in the Primary Sources section.)

Douglas had manufactured a bill that contained language too ambiguous for his opponents' comfort. His revised draft of the bill that for the first time divvied up the unorganized territory into two distinct political entities stated that the Missouri Compromise "was superseded by the principles of the legislation of 1850" and consequently "inoperative." The next version of the bill declared the compromise of 1820 "inconsistent with" that of 1850 and therefore "inoperative and void." The wording of the bill pressed the question of whether the Missouri Compromise line was still law. "If it is to be repealed," asked Senator Edward Everett, "why not say so? . . . Then we should know precisely." Smith wondered why Douglas felt compelled to install a uniform principle for all of the territories. "May you not have one set of provisions for one Territory, and a different set for another?" he asked. Perfectly content with an ad hoc system of territorial policy, Smith saw in the Kansas-Nebraska bill too many "excuses, or apologies." "The language

---

[11] *Appendix*, 538.

of the bill is so subtle, circumlocutory, and tautological," Cullom concurred, "that it seems to have been intended to bear a construction to
suit any meridian. If it is necessary to lay down a great principle, would
it not be becoming in Congress to strip it of all ambiguity, and to lay
down that naked principle so clearly that the country and future Congresses may be enabled to know what it is?"[12]

For opponents of the Kansas-Nebraska bill, the notion that the
Compromise of 1850 somehow invalidated the Missouri Compromise
surfaced unexpectedly. "This is a novel idea," Chase declared, "little
short of preposterous." During the debates in 1850, no one in Congress suggested or discussed the repeal of the Missouri Compromise.
Such a proposition would have upset the delicate balance of terms in
the agreement and handed an unequivocal victory to the South. No
thinking northern congressman would have voted for it. Indeed, it was
not until Douglas unveiled his revised bill on January 23, 1854, that
any word about the Missouri Compromise was uttered. According to
Smith, its alleged incompatibility with the Compromise of 1850 was
"all a pretense" and "an afterthought." The Compromise of 1850 established no new principle to supplant that of the Missouri Compromise,
as the South claimed. By the same flawed logic, Wade informed southern senators, one could deduce that the Compromise of 1850's abolition
of the slave trade in the District of Columbia established a principle to
destroy slave markets throughout the South. Nonintervention in the
territories was emphatically not settled U.S. policy when the Nebraska
bill was introduced.[13]

The sudden reversal of Douglas and his cronies against the Missouri Compromise line appeared to the bill's opponents a breach of
faith and betrayal of trust. Chase, Seward, and Sumner all stressed this
line of argument in their speeches against the bill. Since the language
of the Missouri Compromise prohibited slavery north of 36°30' "forever," the restriction was, in Chase's words, "absolute and perpetual."
Chase and many in the North understood the Missouri Compromise as
a binding compact between North and South. Early in the debate over
the bill, Chase served as the primary author of a noteworthy antislavery
pamphlet entitled "Appeal of the Independent Democrats in Congress

---

[12] *Appendix,* 160 (Everett), 173 (Smith), 541 (Cullom).
[13] *Appendix,* 134, 136 (Chase), 173 (Smith); *Congressional Globe,* 340 (Wade).

to the people of the United States." (See "'Appeal of the Independent Democrats in Congress to the People of the United States,' 1854," on page 347 in the Primary Sources section.) He argued that the South must preserve its "plighted faith" in the Missouri Compromise of 1820. In seeking aggressively to expand slavery into the territories, the South rescinded "a time-honored and sacred compact ... which has been universally regarded as inviolable, North and South ... and by which all have consented to abide." Seward concurred. The Missouri Compromise, he said, was "irrepealable in honor and conscience," "a covenant between the free States and the slave States, scarcely less sacred than the Constitution itself." At stake for southern legislators, Sumner contended, was "the preservation of that Public Faith to which they were pledged."[14]

Anti-Nebraska forces in Congress criticized its supporters for attempting to evade the Missouri Compromise. The North and the South mutually agreed to the compromise in 1820 for the sake of national peace, Senator Sumner explained, but now the South "repudiates the bargain" and "refuses to perform" its "outstanding obligations to freedom." Sumner, Chase, and Seward all observed that the South was attempting to annul the Missouri Compromise only after having derived all the advantages it could from the agreement. The South did not object to the 36°30' parallel until it came time to organize free territory north of the line. More than that, the South sought not to overturn the Missouri Compromise in its entirety but to cherry-pick just one section it adjudged onerous. Seward asked southern senators to empathize with the North by imagining how they would feel if they were suddenly told that slavery were no longer safe in Missouri or Arkansas as promised. He denied that "a mere ordinary law" such as the Kansas-Nebraska bill contained the legal force to negate a formal compromise like that of 1820. He also observed that if, as the South contended, the Compromise of 1850 superseded, impaired, or conflicted with the Missouri Compromise, then perhaps it was the Compromise of 1850 that should be abrogated.[15]

Many northern legislators upheld the Missouri Compromise line as still completely valid. They considered the Missouri Compromise a

---

[14] *Appendix*, 139–140 (Chase), 770 (Seward), 264 (Sumner).
[15] *Appendix*, 266, 264 (Sumner), 152 (Seward).

discrete agreement that applied only to the Louisiana Purchase. The North never promised explicitly or implicitly to extend it, so even though the line was applied to Texas, the refusal to carry it farther westward breached no obligation with the South. Seward, Chase, and other anti-Nebraska congressmen argued furthermore that the Missouri Compromise conformed to the founders' original intent to exclude slavery from the territories. The first generation of U.S. statesmen forbade slavery where it was possible—in the Northwest Territory—and anticipated the gradual elimination of slavery where it already existed. In a speech punctuated by applause, Representative Charles W. Upham of Massachusetts described the beleaguered Missouri Compromise as a renewal of a bargain struck by the founders. As in the Northwest Ordinance of 1787, slavery was forbidden in a carefully demarcated area, but, in both cases, masters could recover fugitive slaves from free territory. The real "principle," Upham explained, was one of compromise. In that spirit, the Missouri Compromise line stood as an extension of the Ohio River, the traditional boundary between slavery and freedom. The 36°30' parallel lay well south of the Ohio River because much of Missouri extended north of the latitude of the river. Similarly, the Compromise of 1850 admitted California as a free state, even though it fell partly south of 36°30', in exchange for allowing the possibility of slavery in lands north of the line in Utah as well as in a sliver of northern New Mexico. Representative Wentworth offered a different interpretation of the logic behind the Compromise of 1850. In his view, the fraction of California extending south of the 36°30' line compensated for the state of Missouri, which lay north of the line. Wentworth saw the compromises of 1820 and 1850 as ideologically consistent, mirror images of one another. In 1820, the slave state of Missouri joined the Union, with restrictions on slavery in the unorganized territory north of the compromise line. By contrast, in 1850, the free state of California was admitted, and New Mexico and Utah Territories were opened to the possibility of slavery. The anti-Nebraska contingent in Congress believed the North in perfect compliance with previous agreements.

According to its opponents, the proposed Kansas-Nebraska bill violated not only the Missouri Compromise but also compacts with Native Americans in the unorganized territory. The U.S. government had negotiated an array of treaties with Indian tribes in the region. The Indian Removal Act of 1830 had divested Native Americans of their lands east of the Mississippi River and deposited them on lands in the unorganized territory that the government guaranteed them perpetually. Territorial organization threatened these agreements. Preservation of native tribes, whether indigenous or already devastated by removal, demanded respect for their rights to the land. Mounting pressure from whites hoping to settle the surrounding region jeopardized the welfare of the native peoples. A few scattered voices in Congress defended the Indians. Maverick southern senators Sam Houston and John Bell, respectively a Democrat and a Whig, spoke at greatest length on the Indians' behalf. Of the two, Houston conveyed greater respect for native culture and civilization and, more so than Bell, believed Indians capable of further "advancement." Both, however, appealed to national honor in upholding treaties with the natives. (See "Speech of Senator Sam Houston, 1854," on page 349 in the Primary Sources section.) Are we, Bell asked, "at liberty to disregard our treaty stipulations with the Indian tribes, because they are a weak and feeble people—unable to resist our power—any more than we would our treaty obligations with the more powerful nations of the earth? Can we, as a Government or a people, act on such a principle—set aside, at our discretion, and trample under foot the most explicit and solemn guarantees?"[16] Others spoke more practically about the requisite costs to the government to extinguish Indian titles to the land and to fund military outposts in the area.

Only a few critics of the bill directly challenged the wisdom of popular sovereignty, the darling principle of Douglas and the South. Bell considered the doctrine of nonintervention "a wise and expedient principle, for general application"; however, its merits were not worth the disruption the repeal of the Missouri Compromise line would undoubtedly cause. Bell recognized the potential dangers of unlimited self-government freed of congressional oversight. The people's unchecked power to legislate for a territory might produce bad policies and indebtedness prior to statehood. Bell raised another practical point. If popular sovereignty left the slavery question to the territorial legislature, what would happen if elections replaced a proslavery legislature with an antislavery one, or vice versa? The result would be a "perpetual struggle" over slavery in the territory that could invite congressional intervention.[17] Although

---

[16] *Appendix*, 409.
[17] *Appendix*, 413, 939.

not a member of Congress in 1854, Springfield, Illinois, attorney Abraham Lincoln detected still other shortcomings with popular sovereignty. The possible introduction of slavery into territory previously immune from bondage discouraged the settlement of freemen—Northern farmers and working people—and deprived them of economic opportunities in the West. Popular sovereignty, Lincoln presciently predicted, would also set up a potentially bloody contest between slaveholders and non-slaveholders for control of the territory. (See "Speech of Abraham Lincoln, 1854," on page 349 in the Primary Sources section.)

Enemies of the Kansas-Nebraska bill puzzled over its commitment to "squatter sovereignty." What was the practical benefit of repealing the Missouri Compromise line in favor of popular sovereignty if it was generally understood that slavery could never take hold in the unorganized territory? Opponents discerned two possible motives lurking behind the legislation. One was the personal aggrandizement of Douglas himself. Douglas had known aspirations to the presidency and was cultivating southern ties by "out-southing" the South. Cheekily playing on the diminutive Douglas's nickname as the "Little Giant," Representative Cullom saw the bill as a way "to make great men out of small ones." But political ambition was just one explanation for the bill. Some in the North suspected a more sinister endgame. Chase and Wentworth believed the elimination of the Missouri Compromise line somehow central to a southern master plan for slavery's expansion. According to Chase, "the principle of the bill is to serve some great purpose . . . in respect to future territorial acquisitions." It was rumored in the Northern press that the South had designs on Cuba, Mexico, the Sandwich Islands (Hawaii), and Hispaniola. Although all south of 36°30', so was a portion of California now free. Substituting for the reputedly flawed principle of a line, popular sovereignty perhaps was intended "to achieve its greatest triumphs" in "theaters" not yet in American possession.[18]

Kansas-Nebraska foes imagined only dire consequences resulting from the bill's passage. Overturning the Missouri Compromise line would reopen sectional wounds and not tamp down but renew the slavery controversy. "Pass this bill," Sumner proclaimed, "and it will be in vain that you say, the Slavery question is settled." A profoundly moral issue was at stake, he continued, and *"nothing can be settled which is not*

---

[18] *Appendix,* 538 (Cullom), 782 (Chase).

right." Public reverence for the line in the free states was strong. Repealing the slavery restriction in the unorganized territory would awaken
and rally the North, united, against the South. Signing into law a polarizing measure that divided northern and southern Whigs would also
lead to their fatal, permanent fracture as a national party and prompt a
political realignment. According to Bell, the reorganized political landscape would include "a great northern and sectional party . . . founded
upon no common principle but hostility to the South." Finally, like their
congressional adversaries, Seward, Sumner, and other opponents of the
bill feared it would lead to disunion. "I do not believe this Union can
survive ten years the act of perfidy that will repudiate the great compromise of 1820," declared Benjamin Wade, but, he added resolutely, if
conflict did erupt, "it will not be liberty that will die in the nineteenth
century."[19] (See "Speech of Senator Benjamin Wade, 1854," on page 350
in the Primary Sources section.)

OUTCOME AND IMPACT

Citizens across the country contacted their congressmen to voice their
opinions on the Kansas-Nebraska bill. The majority of memorials were
from the North and urged Congress not to repeal the Missouri Compromise line. (See "Letter from the Chicago Clergymen, 1854," on page
351 in the Primary Sources section.) One petition from some 3,000
New England clergyman totaled 250 feet in length. Sumner alone introduced more than 125 remonstrances from such groups as the citizens
of New York, Michigan Quakers, and Baptist clergymen in Michigan
and Indiana. The appeals from the North to spare the Missouri Compromise line did not have their desired effect, however. The House of
Representatives passed the Kansas-Nebraska bill 113 to 100 on May 22,
1854, amid protracted applause and hisses. The Senate voted in favor
of the bill by a comfortable margin three days later. President Franklin
Pierce signed into law the "Act to Organize the Territories of Nebraska
and Kansas" on May 30.

Voting patterns in Congress divided along sectional and party
lines. In the House, northern Democrats split evenly over the bill,

---

[19] *Appendix*, 269 (Sumner), 415 (Bell); *Congressional Globe*, 340 (Wade).

while southern Democrats almost unanimously approved it. Northern Whigs in the House gave the measure no support whatsoever, while their southern counterparts voted two to one in favor. In the Senate, a majority of northern Democrats endorsed the Nebraska bill, and all southern Democrats except Sam Houston followed suit. Not a single northern Whig in the Senate voted for the bill, whereas almost every southern Whig approved it. Looking at Congress as a whole, northern Democrats divided over the Kansas-Nebraska bill, southern Democrats almost uniformly supported it, and the Whig vote split along sectional lines. Not a single northern Whig voted for the Nebraska bill in either house of Congress, but most southern Whigs were in favor.

Passage of the Kansas-Nebraska Act sparked outrage in the North as it surrendered territory once barred to slavery by the Missouri Compromise line. Douglas bore the brunt of northern criticism for appeasing the South and escalating sectional tensions dampened by the Compromise of 1850. Irate Northerners so vilified the Illinois senator for his central role in the Kansas-Nebraska drama that Douglas observed with only mild exaggeration that he could travel at night by the light of his own burning effigies. Even in Douglas's hometown of Chicago, a jeering, raucous audience shouted down his attempt to deliver a speech in defense of the Kansas-Nebraska Act. Reviled in the North, Douglas necessarily placed his presidential ambitions temporarily on hold. But Douglas was not the only politician to suffer as a result of the Kansas-Nebraska vote. In retribution for their cooperation with the South, 37 of the 44 northern Democrats in the House who voted for the bill lost their reelection bids in 1854. Democrats across the North were defeated in state elections as well. The party lost control of all but two northern states after having carried all but two in 1852.

Opponents of the Kansas-Nebraska Act detected in its passage a sinister slavepower conspiracy afoot. The repeal of the Missouri Compromise line seemed to many in the North evidence of an insidious scheme to expand slavery's reach. A small minority of southern slaveholders had somehow managed to dictate national policy and enhance southern political power at the expense of the North. The Kansas-Nebraska Act marked but one sign of an aggressively proslavery plot. Later in 1854, the Pierce administration set its sights on the slaveholding Spanish colony of Cuba. High-ranking U.S. officials intimated in an internal government document known as the Ostend Manifesto that the United States would be justified in "wresting" Cuba from Spain militarily if it refused to sell. When news of the Ostend Manifesto went public, northerners saw yet another example of slavepower machinations to extend the peculiar institution.

The polarizing Kansas-Nebraska controversy was crucial to a prolonged process of party realignment in U.S. politics in the 1850s. The Whig and Democratic parties did not survive the Kansas-Nebraska crisis unscathed. As several politicians predicted during the debates, the Whig Party succumbed to sectional divisions over slavery. Northern Whigs' unanimous opposition to the bill alienated them from their southern colleagues and destroyed the Whigs' viability as a national party. The Democrats escaped a similar demise as more than half of all northern Democratic congressmen joined their southern counterparts to vote for the bill; however, some in the unhappy minority of northern Democrats defected from their party. They joined northern politicians orphaned by the dissolution of the Whig Party to seek a political home in a number of anti-Nebraska fusion parties with various labels. Many former Whigs and smaller numbers of northern Democrats gravitated to the rising American, or Know-Nothing, Party, a fleetingly powerful anti-immigrant and anti-Catholic political organization. Others migrated to a nascent Republican Party, whose formation in 1854 was prompted by the Kansas-Nebraska controversy. With virtually identical constituencies, the Republicans and Know-Nothings vied for supremacy in the mid-1850s. The Republicans eventually overcame the Know-Nothings' challenge, absorbed them, and emerged as the primary political adversaries of the Democrats. Under a broad antislavery umbrella, the Republicans forged a coalition of disparate elements dedicated to the confinement of slavery to regions where it already existed. They were, in short, a sectional party of the North committed to opposing the extension of slavery into the territories.

The political showdown over slavery in the territories produced bloodshed in Kansas in 1856. "Bleeding Kansas" exposed a major flaw inherent in popular sovereignty. Because voters living in a territory decided the fate of slavery in that territory, popular sovereignty set up a contest to see who could most heavily populate the region. When Kansas was opened to settlement, both supporters and the defeated opponents of the Kansas-Nebraska Act poured in, each hoping to gain the political upper hand. Unwilling to surrender Kansas to slavery, the antislavery New England Emigrant Aid Society alone rushed more than 1,200 colonists to Kansas and inspired others to relocate there. It seemed that Kansas was destined to be free, but during the election for a territorial legislature in 1855, thousands of proslavery voters crossed into Kansas from neighboring Missouri and fraudulently cast ballots in the election, carrying the day for slavery. Within a year, antislavery forces unreconciled to the election results had chosen their

BLEEDING SUMNER

The controversy over slavery spilled blood not only in Kansas but also on the floor of the U.S. Senate. In May 1856, Senator Charles Sumner delivered a two-day diatribe against slavery and the South known as "The Crime against Kansas" speech. In it he heaped insults upon his fellow senator Andrew P. Butler of South Carolina, with whom over the years he had had a number of heated exchanges over slavery. Sumner drew an analogy between Butler and Don Quixote, a fictional literary character who found beauty in a prostitute named Dulcinea. Likewise, Butler loved a mistress "who, though ugly to others, is always lovely to him; though polluted in the sight of the world, is chaste in his sight;—I mean the harlot Slavery." (See "Senator Charles Sumner, 'The Crime Against Kansas' Speech, 1856," on page 352 in the Primary Sources section.) Sumner thus used overtly sexual language to insult another senator on the floor of Congress. Two days later, Sumner was sitting at his desk in the Senate chamber when Representative Preston Brooks of South Carolina, Butler's nephew, approached him and, in retribution for the assault on his uncle's honor, savagely beat Sumner about the head with his thick cane, ceasing only when it snapped. Brandishing a pistol, Brooks's South Carolina colleague Laurence M. Keitt warned away senators who rushed to intervene. Sumner lost consciousness during the attack and did not return to the Senate for three years as he recuperated from the assault. "Bleeding Sumner," as the caning was dubbed, transformed the Massachusetts senator into an antislavery martyr, his empty seat a reminder of the divisions wrought by slavery. Brooks was forced to resign his seat in the House, but the voters of his district hailed him as a hero and returned him to office, showering him with gifts of new canes. Shockingly, the events of "Bleeding Kansas" and "Bleeding Sumner" all occurred within the span of a single week.

SOUTHERN CHIVALRY_ ARGUMENTversus **CLUB'S.**

In May 1856, Representative Preston Brooks of South Carolina assaulted Senator Charles Sumner of Massachusetts with a cane after Sumner insulted Brooks's uncle, South Carolina senator Andrew P. Butler, in his "Crime Against Kansas" speech. (American Antiquarian Society, Worcester, Massachusetts, USA/The Bridgeman Art Library International)

own governor and territorial legislature for Kansas. Having competing territorial governments for Kansas invited bloodshed. On May 21, 1856, proslavery forces attacked the free town of Lawrence, destroying newspaper offices, burning the governor's home, and razing the Free State Hotel with cannon fire. Three days later, the "sack of Lawrence" was avenged by the radical abolitionist John Brown and a handful of followers who perpetrated the Pottawatomie Massacre. Venturing into a proslavery settlement at Pottawatomie Creek, they killed five men in retribution for an attack in which they had not participated. Guerrilla warfare for much of the remainder of 1856 resulted in the deaths of some 200 Kansans. (See the sidebar "Bleeding Sumner" on page 338.)

WHAT IF?

What if the Missouri Compromise line had not been repealed?
Because passage of the Kansas-Nebraska Act produced such profound political effects, American history might have looked much different had the bill been

defeated. Stephen Douglas's exertions on behalf of the bill secured sufficient votes to push it through Congress, but without the South's additional representatives courtesy of the three-fifths clause, it would not have passed safely through the House. In the absence of the Kansas-Nebraska Act, it is uncertain how long the relative calm between North and South after the Compromise of 1850 would have held. The "compromise measures" did not fully satisfy either section of the country, but they nevertheless might have at least postponed the national schism. The Kansas-Nebraska Act instead exacerbated sectional tension and accelerated the country down the road to war. The deadly debacle in Kansas might have been completely avoided had North and South continued to share a mutual understanding that the territory was free by the Missouri Compromise line. Moreover, party realignment might have proceeded differently without the Whigs' permanent division into northern and southern wings as a result of the Kansas-Nebraska vote. Although their decline began before 1854, the Whigs might have survived longer and perhaps even precluded the organization of the Republican Party. Another fateful consequence of the Kansas-Nebraska Act was the reemergence of Abraham Lincoln from political retirement. After serving one two-year term as a Whig representative in the U.S. House in the 1840s, Lincoln had returned to Springfield, Illinois, to practice law. The Kansas-Nebraska Act lured Lincoln back into the political arena. As a Republican, he debated Douglas over the issue of slavery in the territories in 1858 and captured the presidency in 1860, guiding the Union through the Civil War. The Kansas-Nebraska Act dramatically shaped the country's political landscape.

CHRONOLOGY

1803 The United States acquires the Louisiana Purchase through treaty with France.

1820 The Missouri Compromise is approved.

1830 President Andrew Jackson signs into law the Indian Removal Act.

1836 Arkansas enters the Union.

1845 The United States annexes the Republic of Texas.

1846 The Wilmot Proviso proposes restrictions on slavery in any territory acquired through war with Mexico.

1848 The Treaty of Guadalupe Hidalgo grants the Mexican Cession to the United States.

The Free-Soil Party platform endorses the Wilmot Proviso's restriction on slavery in the territories.

Congress organizes the Oregon Territory.

1850   The Compromise of 1850 is hailed as a "final settlement" of the slavery question.

1852   Franklin Pierce is elected president.

1853   The United States acquires the Gadsden Purchase from Mexico.

1854   The Kansas-Nebraska Act passes.

The Republican Party is founded.

The Ostend Manifesto is made public.

1855   Voter fraud takes place in elections for the Kansas territorial legislature.

1856   *May 19–20*: Charles Sumner delivers his "Crime Against Kansas" speech.

May 21: Proslavery forces launch the "sack of Lawrence."

May 22: Preston Brooks canes Charles Sumner in the Senate chamber.

May 24–25: John Brown leads the Pottawatomie Massacre.

1857   The U.S. Supreme Court declares the Missouri Compromise line unconstitutional in the case of *Dred Scott v. Sandford.*

DISCUSSION QUESTIONS

1. What were Senator Stephen A. Douglas's reasons for instigating the organization of the Nebraska and Kansas Territories? How wise was it for him to pursue organization in 1854? What is your opinion of Douglas?

2. Which side of the debate over the Kansas-Nebraska bill made better use of the nation's legislative history in crafting its argument? Why do you think so?

3. The North or the South: Who was more faithful to the Missouri Compromise? Defend your opinion.

4. Do you believe the Compromise of 1850 was "inconsistent with" the Missouri Compromise? Why or why not?

5. Why might popular sovereignty seem to be an attractive solution to settle the question of slavery's expansion into the territories? What advantages did it hold? How viable an option was it?

WEB SITES

Library of Congress. "Kansas-Nebraska Act," Primary Documents in American History. Available online. URL: http://www.loc.gov/rr/program/bib/ourdocs/kansas.html. Accessed December 28, 2009.

National Archives and Records Administration. "Kansas-Nebraska Act (1854)," Our Documents: A National Initiative on American History, Civics, and Service. Available online. URL: http://www.ourdocuments.gov/. Accessed December 28, 2009.

Northern Illinois University. "The Kansas-Nebraska Act and the Rise of the Republican Party, 1854–1856," Abraham Lincoln Historical Digitization Project. Available online. URL: http://lincoln.lib.niu.edu/biography6text.html. Accessed December 28, 2009.

University of Kansas and Kansas State Historical Society. "Territorial Kansas." Available online. URL: http://www.territorialkansasonline.org. Accessed December 28, 2009.

BIBLIOGRAPHY

Earle, Jonathan H. *Jacksonian Antislavery and the Politics of Free Soil, 1824–1854.* Chapel Hill: University of North Carolina Press, 2004. Studies the influence of the Free Soil movement on the political realignments of the 1850s.

Etcheson, Nicole. *Bleeding Kansas: Contested Liberty in the Civil War Era.* Lawrence: University Press of Kansas, 2004. Examines events in Kansas, the failure of popular sovereignty, and Kansas's role in national politics. Argues that in Kansas concerns over the liberty of white settlers superseded interest in freeing slaves.

Gienapp, William E. *The Origins of the Republican Party, 1852–1856.* New York: Oxford University Press, 1987. A prodigiously researched and formidable tome that argues that the process of Republican Party formation hinged more on ethnocultural issues than on antislavery sentiment.

Goodrich, Thomas. *War to the Knife: Bleeding Kansas, 1854–1861.* Lincoln: University of Nebraska Press, 2004. Chronicles the events of Bleeding Kansas as a prelude to the Civil War.

Holt, Michael F. *The Fate of Their Country: Politicians, Slavery Extension, and the Coming of the Civil War.* New York: Hill & Wang, 2004. Stresses the role of partisan politics in the sectional crisis that culminated in the Civil War.

Wunder, John R., and Joann M. Ross, eds. *The Nebraska-Kansas Act of 1854.* Lincoln: University of Nebraska Press, 2008. An edited collection of essays that, unlike most studies, emphasizes the place of Nebraska rather than Kansas in the controversy of 1854.

PRIMARY SOURCES

1. Kansas-Nebraska Bill, 1854

Senator Stephen Douglas, an Illinois Democrat, worked diligently to gain southern support for the Kansas-Nebraska bill. The following excerpt from Section 14 of the act as it eventually passed in 1854 rendered "inoperative and void" Section 8 of the Missouri Compromise of 1820.

The Constitution, and all Laws of the United States which are not locally inapplicable, shall have the same force and effect within the said Territory of Nebraska as elsewhere within the United States, except the eighth section of the act preparatory to the admission of Missouri into the Union approved March sixth, eighteen hundred and twenty, which, being inconsistent with the principle of non-intervention by Congress with slaves in the States and Territories, as recognized by the legislation of eighteen hundred and fifty, commonly called the Compromise Measures, is hereby declared inoperative and void; it being the true intent and meaning of this act not to legislate slavery into any Territory or State, nor to exclude it therefrom, but to leave the people thereof perfectly free to form and regulate their domestic institutions in their own way, subject only to the Constitution of the United States: *Provided,* That nothing herein contained shall be construed to revive or put in force any law or regulation which may have existed prior to the act of sixth March, eighteen hundred and twenty, either protecting, establishing, prohibiting, or abolishing slavery.

Source: http://www.loc.gov/rr/program/bib/ourdocs/kansas.html.

—∞—

2. Speech of Senator Stephen Douglas on the Necessity of the Nebraska Bill, 1854

In a speech delivered in the Senate on March 3, 1854, Democratic senator Stephen Douglas of Illinois dismissed objections that his bill to organize the Kansas and Nebraska territories was unnecessary.

It has been urged in debate that there is no necessity for these territorial organizations; and I have been called upon to point out any public and national considerations which require action at this time. Senators seem to forget that our immense and valuable possessions on the Pacific are separated from the states and organized territories on this side of the Rocky Mountains by a vast wilderness, filled by hostile savages; that nearly a hundred thousand emigrants pass through this barbarous wilderness every year, on their way to California and Oregon; that these emigrants are American citizens, our own constituents, who are entitled to the protection of law and government. . . .

I am told that there are not white inhabitants enough permanently settled in the country to require and sustain a government. True, there is not a very large population there, for the very good reason that your Indian code and intercourse laws exclude the settlers, and forbid their remaining there to cultivate the soil. You refuse to throw the country open to settlers, and then object to the organization of the territories, upon the ground that there is not a sufficient number of inhabitants. . . .

We have been told by nearly every senator who has spoken in opposition to this bill, that at the time of its introduction the people were in a state of profound quiet and repose; that the antislavery agitation had entirely ceased; and that the whole country was acquiescing cheerfully and cordially in the compromise measures of 1850 as a final adjustment of this vexed question. Sir, it is truly refreshing to hear senators who contested every inch of ground in opposition to those measures when they were under discussion, who predicted all manner of evils and calamities from their adoption, and who raised the cry of repeal and even resistance to their execution after they had become the laws of the land,—I say it is really refreshing to hear these same senators now bear their united testimony to the wisdom of those measures, and to the patriotic motives which induced us to pass them in defiance of their threats and resistance, and to their beneficial effects in restoring peace, harmony and fraternity to a distracted country. These are precious confessions from the lips of those who stand pledged never to assent to the propriety of those measures, and to make war upon them.

Source: John Vance Cheney, ed., *Memorable American Speeches,* vol. 3 (Chicago: R. R. Donnelley & Sons Company), 1909, 147, 148, 150.

—⚏—

3. Speech of Senator Stephen Douglas on the Principle of the Kansas-Nebraska Bill, 1854

On January 30, 1854, Illinois senator Stephen Douglas delivered a speech on the Kansas-Nebraska bill in which he explained how the Compromise of 1850 replaced the Missouri Compromise.

We took the principles established by the compromise act of 1850 as our guide. . . . Those measures established and rest upon the great principle of self-government—that the people should be allowed to decide the questions of their domestic institutions for themselves . . . instead of having them determined by an arbitrary or geographical line. . . .

The leading feature of the compromise of 1850 was congressional non-intervention as to slavery in the Territories; that the people of the Territories, and of all the States, were to be allowed to do as they pleased upon the subject of slavery, subject only to the provisions of the Constitution of the United States.

That, sir, was the leading feature of the compromise measures of 1850. Those measures therefore, abandoned the idea of a geographical line as the boundary between free States and slave States; abandoned it because compelled to do it from an inability to maintain it; and in lieu of that, substituted a great principle of self-government, which would allow the people to do as they thought proper. Now, the question is, when that new compromise, resting upon that great fundamental principle of freedom, was established, was it not an abandonment of the old one—the geographical line? Was it not a supersedure of the old one within the very language of the substitute for the bill which is now under consideration? I say it did supersede it, because it applied its provisions as well to the north as to the south of 36°30'. It established a principle which was equally applicable to the country north as well as south of the parallel of 36°30'—a principle of universal application. . . .

The object of the compromise measures of 1850 was to establish certain great principles, which would avoid the slavery agitation in all time to come. Was it our object simply to provide for a temporary evil? Was it our object just to heal over an old sore, and leave it to break out again? Was it our object to adopt a mere miserable expedient to apply to that territory, and that alone, and leave ourselves entirely at sea without compass when new territory was acquired, or new territorial organizations were to be made? . . .

I hold, then, that as to the territory covered by the Utah and New Mexico bills, there was an express annulment of the Missouri compromise; and as to all the other unorganized territories, it was superseded by the principles of that legislation, and we are bound to apply those principles in the organization of all new Territories, to all which we now own, or which we may hereafter acquire. If this construction be given, it makes that compromise a final settlement. . . . By any other construction you reopen the issue every time you make a new territorial government. But, sir, if you treat the compromise measures of 1850 in the light of great principles, sufficient to remedy temporary evils, at the same time that they prescribe rules of action applicable everywhere in all time to come, then you avoid the agitation forever, if you observe good faith to the provisions of these enactments, and the principles established by them. . . .

The legal effect of this bill, if it be passed as reported by the Committee on Territories, is neither to legislate slavery into these Territories nor out of them, but to leave the people do as they please, under the provisions and subject to the limitations of the Constitution of the United States. Why should not this principle prevail? Why should any man, North or South, object to it?

Source: Congressional Globe: Containing the Debates, Proceedings, and Laws, of the First Session of the Thirty-Third Congress, vol. 28, pt. 1 (Washington: John C. Rives, 1854), 275, 277–278.

—⁓—

4. Speech of Representative William Cullom, 1854

Representative William Cullom, a Tennessee Whig and rare southern opponent of the Kansas-Nebraska bill, gave the following speech in the House on April 11, 1854. In it, he regretted his generation's failure to abide by the Missouri Compromise.

I . . . denounce this scheme as a plot against the peace and quiet of the country, whether so designed or not. . . .

We are told . . . that now the eighth section of the act of 1820, called the Missouri compromise, must be repealed; a measure which was the work of our patriotic fathers, most of whom have now descended to the tomb; a measure which was passed in times of great public peril, and when the Union was in imminent danger, to quiet and assuage the angry feelings which sectional strife had engendered, and which did, happily, calm and subdue the sectional animosities of the day, and cement anew the bonds of our Union; a measure of such happy results that our fathers might well pledge their honor for its faithful observance, as they did by accepting and voting for it. The bill now before this House seeks to repudiate their plighted faith, and to pull down the work of their hands, which has stood as a monument of their wisdom and patriotism for thirty-four years; which has been cheerfully acquiesced in by all sections of the Confederacy, and for which the pure men of 1820 have been canonized in the hearts of the American people. This great measure of pacification is now, for mere party purposes, and party and personal advancement, to be trampled under foot. . . . I proclaim here to-day that this Nebraska bill presents the naked question of *repudiation* or *no repudiation* of the faith and honor of the South, plighted by the act of 1820. . . . I do not come forward, on this occasion, to defend the North. I am here to defend southern honor; and I would be the first to vindicate southern rights whenever and wherever violated or assailed. But I repeat, that the question now is, will we stand by the covenant of our fathers, by observing the compromise of 1820, and thereby maintain southern honor, the public tranquillity, and the integrity of the Union; or, shall we decide that the flood-gates of agitation shall be re-opened, with all the evil consequences which must flow from it, to say nothing of the danger to the stability of the Union itself?

Source: Appendix to the Congressional Globe, for the First Session, Thirty-Third Congress: Containing Speeches, Important State Papers, Etc., vol. 31 (Washington: John C. Rives, 1854), 538.

—ᵚ—

5. "Appeal of the Independent Democrats in Congress to the People of the United States," 1854

Authored primarily by Ohio senator Salmon P. Chase, the "Appeal of the Independent Democrats" was an antislavery pamphlet and masterful piece of propaganda designed to rouse public opinion against the Kansas-Nebraska bill. Its publication in January 1854 outlined the arguments that recurred during the four months of debate in Congress. Chase, Senator Charles Sumner of Massachusetts, Representatives

Joshua R. Giddings and Edward Wade of Ohio, Representative Gerrit Smith of New York, and Representative Alexander DeWitt of Massachusetts all affixed their names to the treatise.

We arraign this bill as a gross violation of a sacred pledge; as a criminal betrayal of precious rights; as part and parcel of an atrocious plot to exclude from a vast unoccupied region immigrants from the Old World, and free laborers from our own States, and convert it into a dreary region of despotism, inhabited by masters and slaves. . . .

Missouri could not have been admitted as a slave State had not certain members from the free States been reconciled to the measure by the incorporation of this prohibition into the act of admission. Nothing is more certain than that this prohibition has been regarded and accepted by the whole country as a solemn compact against the extension of slavery into any part of the territory acquired from France, lying north of 36°30', and not included in the new State of Missouri. . . . For more than thirty years—during more than half the period of our national existence under our present Constitution—this compact has been universally regarded and acted upon as inviolable American law. In conformity with it, Iowa was admitted as a free State, and Minnesota has been organized as a free Territory.

It is a strange and ominous fact, well calculated to awaken the worst apprehensions, and the most fearful forebodings of future calamities, that it is now deliberately purposed to repeal this prohibition, by implication or directly—the later certainly the manlier way—and thus to subvert this compact, and allow slavery in all the yet unorganized territory. . . .

The compromise measures of 1850, by one of which California was admitted as a free State; while two others, organizing the Territories of New Mexico and Utah, exposed all the residue of the recently acquired territory to the invasion of slavery.

These acts were never supposed to abrogate or touch the existing exclusion of slavery from what is now called Nebraska. They applied to the territory acquired from Mexico, and to that only. They were intended as a settlement of the controversy growing out of that acquisition, and of that controversy only. They must stand or fall by their own merits.

The statesmen whose powerful support carried the Utah and New Mexico acts never dreamed that their provisions would ever be applied to Nebraska. . . . This pretension had not then been set up. It is a palpable afterthought.

Source: Congressional Globe: Containing the Debates, Proceedings, and Laws, of the First Session of the Thirty-Third Congress, vol. 28, pt. 1 (Washington: John C. Rives, 1854), 281.

—᳁—

6. Speech of Senator Sam Houston, 1854

Almost unique in his concern for the Native Americans in the unorganized territory, Senator Sam Houston, a Texas Democrat, reminded his fellow senators in a speech on March 3, 1854, to honor the country's obligations to the Indians.

I am a friend of the Indian upon the principle that I am a friend to justice. We are not bound to make them promises, but if a promise be made to an Indian, it ought to be regarded as sacredly as if it were made to a white man. If we treat them as tribes, recognize them, send commissioners to form treaties and exchange ratifications with them, and the treaties are negotiated, accepted, ratified, and exchanged—having met with the approval of the Senate—I think they may be called compacts; and how are those compacts regarded? Just as we choose to construe them at the time, without any reference to the wishes of the Indians, or whether we do them kindness or justice in the operation or not. We are often prompted to their ratification by persons interested; and we lend ourselves unintentionally to an unjust act of oppression upon the Indians by men who go and get their signatures to a treaty. The Indian's mark is made; the employees of the Government certify or witness it; and the Indians do not understand it, for they do not know what is written. These are some of the circumstances connected with the Indians.

Source: Appendix to the Congressional Globe, for the First Session, Thirty-Third Congress: Containing Speeches, Important State Papers, Etc., vol. 31 (Washington: John C. Rives, 1854), 341.

—᳁—

7. Speech of Abraham Lincoln, 1854

Not a member of Congress during the Kansas-Nebraska affair, Abraham Lincoln reentered politics as a result of the controversy. In a speech delivered in Peoria, Illinois, on October 16, 1854, Lincoln criticized popular sovereignty for restricting opportunities for white people and creating a dangerous environment in the territories. He anticipated by one and one-half years the violence that erupted in Kansas in 1856.

Whether slavery shall go into Nebraska, or other new territories, is not a matter of exclusive concern to the people who may go there. The whole nation is interested that the best use shall be made of these territories. We want them for the homes of free white people. This they cannot be, to any considerable extent, if slavery shall be planted within them. Slave States are places for poor white people to remove FROM; not to remove TO. New free States are the places for poor people to go to and better their condition. For this use, the nation needs these territories. . . .

Some Yankees, in the east, are sending emigrants to Nebraska to exclude slavery from it. . . . But the Missourians are awake too. They are within a stone's throw of the contested ground. . . . They resolve that slavery already exists in the territory; that more shall go there; that they, remaining in Missouri will protect it; and that abolitionists shall be hung, or driven away. Through all this, bowie-knives and six-shooters are seen plainly enough; but never a glimpse of the ballot-box. And, really, what is to be the result of this? Each party WITHIN, having numerous and determined backers WITHOUT, is it not probable that the contest will come to blows, and bloodshed? Could there be a more apt invention to bring about collision and violence, on the slavery question, than this Nebraska project is? . . .

The Missouri Compromise ought to be restored. For the sake of the Union, it ought to be restored.

Source: Abraham Lincoln, Speeches and Writings 1832–1858: Speeches, Letters, and Miscellaneous Writings: The Lincoln-Douglas Debates (New York: Library of America, 1989), 330–331, 334–335.

—⚏—

8. Speech of Senator Benjamin Wade, 1854

Although less famous than Salmon P. Chase, his senatorial colleague from Ohio, Benjamin Wade delivered some of the most impassioned and eloquent speeches during the debate over the Kansas-Nebraska bill. In the following excerpt from his oration of May 25, 1854, the day of the Senate's final vote on the bill, Wade blamed the South for inflaming sectional tension.

This was a declaration of war on the institutions of the North; a deliberate sectional movement by the South for political power, without regard to either justice or consequences. . . .

Mr. President, radical as I am, and always have been, on this subject of slavery, if there is anything which I have labored to prevent, it has been to prevent one section of this country from coming in collision, face to face, with the other, without a possible mode of escape, on a direct sectional issue, North and South. But the South have deliberately made up that issue. They have sought this great sectional advantage. They have put the North at defiance, and declared a sectional war for the mastery; and I accept the issue thus tendered. Slavery must now become general, or it must cease to be at all. And, Mr. President, let it always be understood, that this sectional strife was commenced by the South alone. . . . They have forced it on the North without their knowledge, and against their will. Should evil result from this movement, the South, and not the North, are responsible for it.

Source: Appendix to the Congressional Globe, for the First Session, Thirty-Third Congress: Containing Speeches, Important State Papers, Etc., vol. 31 (Washington: John C. Rives, 1854), 764.

—⁊⁊⁊—

9. Letter from the Chicago Clergymen, 1854

On March 27, 1854, 25 clergymen in Chicago met to discuss the Kansas-Nebraska bill. They composed a letter of protest to both houses of Congress that appeared in the anti–Nebraska bill Chicago newspapers. They appended the names of more than 500 clergy who agreed with the sentiments contained in the protest.

To the honorable Senate and House of Representatives of the United States, in Congress assembled:

The undersigned clergymen of different religious denominations in the northwestern States, as citizens and as ministers of the Gospel of Jesus Christ, hereby, in the name of Almighty God, and in his presence, do solemnly protest against the passage of what is known as the "Nebraska bill," or any repeat or modification of existing legal prohibitions of slavery in that part of our national domain which it is proposed to organize into the Territories of Nebraska and Kansas.

We protest against it as a great moral wrong; as a breach of faith eminently injurious to the moral principles of the community, and subversive of all confidence in national engagements; as a measure full of danger to the peace and even existence of our beloved Union, and exposure of the righteous judgments of the Almighty.

Source: Appendix to the Congressional Globe, for the First Session, Thirty-Third Congress: Containing Speeches, Important State Papers, Etc., vol. 31 (Washington: John C. Rives, 1854), 654.

—⁓—

10. Senator Charles Sumner, "The Crime Against Kansas" Speech, 1856

"The Crime Against Kansas" speech delivered by Senator Charles Sumner of Massachusetts over two days in May 1856 stands as one of the most notorious orations in American history. Excerpted here are the personally offensive portions that spurred Representative Preston Brooks to reclaim the honor of his uncle and fellow South Carolina Democrat, Senator Andrew P. Butler, who was absent from the Senate chamber during the speech.

But, before entering upon the argument, I must say something of a general character, particularly in response to what has fallen from senators who have raised themselves to eminence on this floor in championship of human wrongs; I mean the senator from South Carolina [MR. BUTLER], and the senator from Illinois [MR. DOUGLAS], who, though unlike as Don Quixote and Sancho Panza, yet, like this couple, sally forth together in the same adventure. I regret much to miss the elder senator from his seat; but the cause against which he has run a tilt with such activity of animosity demands that the opportunity of exposing him should not be lost; and it is for the cause that I speak. The senator from South Carolina has read many books of chivalry, and believes himself a chivalrous knight, with sentiments of honor and courage. Of course he has chosen a mistress to whom he has made his vows, and who, though ugly to others, is always lovely to him; though polluted in the sight of the world, is chaste in his sight;—I mean the harlot Slavery. For her his tongue is always profuse with words. Let her be impeached in character, or any proposition made to shut her out from the extension of her wantonness, and no extravagance of manner or hardihood of assertion is then too great for this senator. The frenzy of Don Quixote in behalf of his wench Dulcinea del Toboso is all surpassed. The asserted rights of Slavery, which shock equality of all kinds, are cloaked by a fantastic claim of equality. If the slave States cannot enjoy what, in mockery of the great fathers of the Republic, he misnames equality under the constitution,—in other words, the full power in the National Territories to compel fellow-men to unpaid toil, to separate husband and wife, and to sell little children at the auction-block,—then, sir, the chivalric senator will conduct the State of South Carolina out of the Union! Heroic knight! Exalted senator! A second Moses come for a second exodus! . . .

Now, the Nebraska Bill, on its very face, openly cleared the way for Slavery, and it is not wrong to presume that its originators intended the natural consequences of such an act, and sought in this way to extend Slavery. Of course, they did. And this is the first stage in the crime against Kansas.

But this was speedily followed by other developments. . . . It was confidently anticipated, that . . . the interest of slaveholders everywhere, with the advantage derived from the neighborhood of Missouri, and the influence of the Territorial Government, Slavery might be introduced into Kansas, quietly but surely, without arousing a conflict; that the crocodile egg might be stealthily dropped in the sunburnt soil, there to be hatched unobserved until it sent forth its reptile monster. . . .

With regret, I come again upon the senator from South Carolina [MR. BUTLER], who, omnipresent in this debate, overflowed with rage at the simple suggestion that Kansas had applied for admission as a State; and, with incoherent phrases, discharged the loose expectoration of his speech, now upon her representative, and then upon her people. There was no extravagance of the ancient Parliamentary debate which he did not repeat; nor was there any possible deviation from truth which he did not make, with so much of passion, I am glad to add, as to save him from the suspicion of intentional aberration. But the senator touches nothing that he does not disfigure—with error, sometimes of principle, sometimes of fact. He shows an incapacity of accuracy, whether in stating the constitution or in stating the law, whether in the details of statistics or the diversions of scholarship. He cannot open his mouth but out there flies a blunder.

Source: Speech of Hon. Charles Sumner, in the Senate of the United States, 19th and 20th May, 1856 (Boston: John P. Jewett & Company, 1856), 9–10, 20, 21, 85–86.

Slavery and the Courts:
Was the Dred Scott *Decision of 1857 Legally Sound?*

—⚕—

THE COMPROMISE

The Issue

In 1857, the U.S. Supreme Court rendered one of its most controversial decisions of all time in the *Dred Scott* case. Slaveholders welcomed the verdict of *Dred Scott*, but was the decision legally sound?

♦ **Arguments that the Dred Scott *decision was legally sound:*** In the Supreme Court case of *Dred Scott v. Sandford*, the majority ruled against the Missouri slave Dred Scott in his bid for freedom. The Court judged that Scott was not a citizen qualified to bring his case to court and that blacks were not citizens of the United States. It also declared the Missouri Compromise unconstitutional. The majority on the Court interpreted Article IV, Section 3, of the Constitution narrowly, denying the power of Congress to legislate in territories acquired since the drafting of the Constitution. Limitations on slavery in the territories also violated masters' Fifth Amendment rights by depriving them of their enslaved property without due process. The laws of Missouri enslaving Dred Scott remained intact despite his travels in the free state of Illinois and free territory of Wisconsin.

♦ **Arguments that the Dred Scott *decision was not legally sound:*** To critics of the *Dred Scott* decision, much of the ruling seemed extrajudicial. The two dissenting justices on the Supreme Court believed Dred Scott a citizen and located ample historical evidence of black citizenship. Their reading of the Constitution held that it granted Congress broad legislative powers over American territories—powers Congress had exercised routinely in the past—so the Missouri Compromise could not be unconstitutional. If Congress chose to restrict slavery in a territory, it did not deprive masters of their rights without due process because the law was not designed to protect an individual's opportunity to settle there. The minority opinions in the *Dred Scott* case maintained that masters who took slaves to live in free states or territories forfeited their claim to

354

them, because the laws of a slave state did not have extraterritorial force outside that state.

—␣␣—

INTRODUCTION

In 1846, the slave Dred Scott sued for his freedom in the Missouri court system on the basis of having lived in the free state of Illinois and the free territory of Wisconsin. His case ultimately went to the Supreme Court, which ruled in 1857 that he would remain a slave. The magnitude of the *Dred Scott v. Sandford* decision far exceeded one man's individual pursuit of freedom, however. The Supreme Court's ruling engaged questions about slavery in the territories that had dogged the nation since debate in 1819 over Missouri's admission to the Union. The decision disrupted national politics, undermining the Republican Party's platform and eventually dividing the Democrats. It also unleashed sectional passions that further strained relations between North and South and culminated in the Civil War.

The Supreme Court decided that Dred Scott would remain enslaved. Since the majority of the Court determined that neither he nor blacks in general were citizens of the United States, he did not have a right to sue for his freedom. The Court also held that Congress did not have the constitutional authority to legislate against slavery in the territories. Therefore, the Missouri Compromise of 1820 that had imposed restrictions upon slavery in the Wisconsin Territory was unconstitutional. According to the Court, the Fifth Amendment's due process clause protected masters' right to take their slaves into the territories. Moreover, when masters traveled to free states and territories, the laws of the slaveholding state that they left remained in force.

Two dissenting justices on the Supreme Court as well as a number of Republican critics disagreed with the majority's decision in *Dred Scott.* They showed that people of color had been and still could be citizens of the United States. They therefore had the right to file suit in court. Moreover, the Constitution's "rules and regulations" clause bestowed upon Congress expansive powers to legislate in the territories, so the majority's grounds for voiding the Missouri Compromise were false. Masters, argued the minority on the Court, were not unlawfully deprived of their rights when slavery was prohibited in a territory.

If, in defiance of restrictions on slavery, slaveholders took their bond people to free states or territories, they surrendered ownership to them and could never again reduce them to slavery.

BACKGROUND

Born into bondage around 1799, Dred Scott belonged to a Virginia master, Peter Blow. Blow relocated to Alabama and was a planter there for a time before deciding in 1830 to migrate with his wife Elizabeth, seven children, and six slaves to St. Louis, Missouri, where he opened a boardinghouse. Elizabeth Blow died soon thereafter in 1831, her husband Peter the following year. By 1833, their slave Dred Scott was owned by Dr. John Emerson, a surgeon in the U.S. Army. In 1834, Dr. Emerson was transferred to Fort Armstrong, at Rock Island, Illinois. Scott accompanied his master to Fort Armstrong, where he met an enslaved woman named Harriet Robinson, the property of Indian agent Major Lawrence Taliaferro, also stationed there. The next year, the U.S. government ordered Major Taliaferro to Fort Snelling, an installation in unorganized territory on the west bank of the Mississippi River in modern-day Minnesota. Transferred the following year, Emerson made the identical journey to Fort Snelling, now encompassed within the newly organized Wisconsin Territory, reuniting the slaves Harriet and Dred. Emerson purchased Harriet from Taliaferro, and with their master's permission, Dred Scott and Harriet were wed in a ceremony performed by the major. Their union produced four children. Two sons died in infancy, but their two daughters survived. One of them was born aboard a stern-wheeled paddleboat on the Mississippi River, probably somewhere north of Missouri. Emerson had been dispatched to Louisiana in 1837; there, after a whirlwind courtship with Eliza Irene Sanford, he married in 1838 before retrieving his slaves Dred and Harriet from Fort Snelling. On their return trip to Fort Snelling, Harriet gave birth to baby Eliza, named for Mrs. Emerson. By the early 1840s, the Scott family was back in St. Louis with their mistress as Dr. Emerson followed his orders to go to Florida. Emerson was discharged in 1842, returned to St. Louis, and relocated with his wife to Davenport, Iowa, before dying in 1843. Dred and Harriet Scott stayed behind in St. Louis, working for relatives of the Emersons.

In 1846, Dred and Harriet Scott sued for their freedom on the basis of their far-flung travels. They alleged that their residence in the free state of Illinois and in the Territory of Wisconsin made them free.

The slave Dred Scott sued for his freedom on the basis of his travels outside the slaveholding states. (Library of Congress)

Consistent with the Northwest Ordinance of 1787, Illinois law prohibited slavery, and the region of the Wisconsin Territory in which the Scotts lived lay in a part of the Louisiana Purchase north of the 36°30′ line of latitude, where slavery had been forbidden by the Missouri Compromise of 1820. If the Scotts could make the case successfully that residence in either Illinois or the Wisconsin Territory (or both) liberated them from bondage and that they retained their free status once back in Missouri, they would permanently gain their liberty. The Scotts won their freedom suit in the State Circuit Court of St. Louis County in 1850, but on appeal the Missouri state supreme court in 1852 overturned that decision. They then took their case to the federal court system, where the U.S. Circuit Court upheld the state supreme court ruling. The case made its way to the U.S. Supreme Court in 1854 as *Dred Scott v. Sandford*. Mrs. Emerson had conveyed the title for Dred Scott to her brother, John F. A. Sanford of New York, sometime prior to the initiation of proceedings in federal court. His name, inadvertently misspelled in the case file, is attached to the Supreme Court decision.

The Supreme Court was prepared to deliver its verdict on the *Dred Scott* case in its 1855–56 session but opted to postpone its decision until after the upcoming presidential contest of 1856. Understanding the import of the case, a majority of the justices preferred to wait, fearing that the ruling could unduly sway the election results. In addition, Justice John McLean of Massachusetts, the lone justice with genuine antislavery credentials, was angling to become the 1856 Republican presidential candidate, and delaying judgment would deny him a platform for using his judicial opinion to audition for the nomination from the bench. The entire campaign season and the general election passed with no ruling on Scott. Democrat James Buchanan, candidate of the last remaining national party, won the election with 174 electoral votes to Republican John C. Frémont's 114. Third-party candidate Millard Fillmore garnered a paltry eight electoral votes by carrying the single state of Maryland.

President James Buchanan was sworn into office on March 4, 1857, just two days before the Supreme Court rendered the *Dred Scott* decision. In his inaugural address, Buchanan urged cheerful submission to the upcoming verdict, regardless of its content. (See "Inaugural Address of President James Buchanan, 1857," on page 382 in the Primary Sources section.) Through conversations with Chief Justice Roger B. Taney and other judges—whisperings, as suspicious Republicans described them—Buchanan apparently knew the outcome in advance. The Supreme Court formally issued its opinion on March 6. It supported the Missouri state supreme court in deciding that Dred Scott and his family would remain enslaved. The *Dred Scott* decision was unquestionably momentous, but was it legally sound?

THE DEBATE

The Case that the *Dred Scott* Decision Was Legally Sound

Chief Justice Roger B. Taney wrote the majority opinion for the Supreme Court against Dred Scott. Six of the eight other justices concurred with him: James Moore Wayne of Georgia, Samuel Nelson of New York, Robert Cooper Grier of Pennsylvania, Peter V. Daniel of Virginia, John A. Campbell of Alabama, and John Catron of Tennessee. The majority determined that (1) Scott was not a citizen and therefore had no right to sue in court; (2) he was not freed by his time spent in the Wisconsin Territory, because the Missouri Compromise that made the territory free was unconstitutional; and (3) his residence in Illinois did not liberate him because it was the laws of Missouri that applied to him. All of the concurring justices except Wayne filed an individual opinion in the case. Although the judges did not necessarily agree on all of the particulars, notwithstanding Justice Nelson's abstention on the Missouri Compromise question, they reached a general consensus on the broad conclusions of the case.

The majority decision first explored the question of Scott's citizenship and, by extension, his eligibility to take his case to court. Taney distinguished between state citizenship, on one hand, and federal citizenship, on the other. Whereas states could legally bestow state citizenship on whomever they wished, they exercised no authority over federal citizenship. Federal citizenship derived, in Taney's view, either from being a citizen when the Constitution was ratified or from the naturalization of foreigners, the latter the constitutional bailiwick of Congress. For Taney, it was immaterial whether Scott was a citizen of Missouri. The real question was whether he held federal citizenship and was therefore qualified to take his case to court. (See the sidebar "Roger B. Taney" on page 360.)

Taney located no historical evidence of black citizenship. He offered instead examples of colonial-era legislation that discriminated against blacks, including laws against interracial marriage. He then turned to the Declaration of Independence. "The general words . . . would seem to embrace the whole human family," Taney conceded. "But it is too clear for dispute, that the enslaved African race were not intended to be included, and formed no part of the people who framed and adopted this declaration." Had "the distinguished men who framed the Declaration of Independence" upheld black citizenship, "they would have deserved and received universal rebuke and reprobation. . . . They perfectly understood the meaning of the language they used, and . . . knew that it would not in any part of the civilized world be supposed to embrace the negro race, which, by common consent, had been excluded from civilized Governments and the family of nations, and doomed to slavery." The Constitution, Taney continued, further illustrated black degradation. That sacrosanct document, he said, included "two clauses . . . which point directly and specifically to the negro race as a separate class of persons, and show clearly that they were not regarded as a portion of the people or citizens of the Government then formed." First, it prevented restrictions on the transatlantic slave trade for 20 years, and, second, it mandated the return of fugitive slaves. Taney next reviewed a litany of discriminatory state laws and enactments in the North as

ROGER B. TANEY

Dred Scott v. Sandford defined the career of Chief Justice Roger B. Taney. A Marylander, Taney was born in Calvert County in 1777. He graduated from Dickinson College in Pennsylvania and, after reading law, was admitted to the bar in 1799. In 1806, Taney married Anne Key, whose brother, Francis Scott, would one day write the national anthem, "The Star-Spangled Banner." Taney served one term each in the Maryland House of Delegates and in the state senate before becoming state attorney general in 1827. He entered national politics as a Jacksonian Democrat, first serving Old Hickory as U.S. attorney general in 1831. Jackson next made Taney acting secretary of the treasury, in which capacity he did the president's bidding in his attack upon the "monster" Second Bank of the United States. In 1836, Taney succeeded the illustrious John Marshall to become the fifth chief justice of the Supreme Court.

Chronically ill and already 59 years old at the time of his appointment, Taney seemed an unlikely candidate to serve as chief justice for almost three decades. Historian Don E. Fehrenbacher described him as "six feet tall, flat-chested and stooped, with homely features and irregular, tobacco-stained teeth, . . . an unimpressive figure until he began to speak." Taney demonstrated a brilliant legal mind over his many years on the bench, a fact often overshadowed by the historical inaccuracies and suspect arguments contained in the *Dred Scott* decision. The young jurist and future Supreme Court justice Horace Gray remarked graciously that the "tone and manner of reasoning" in Taney's *Dred Scott* opinion were "unworthy of the reputation of that great magistrate." A onetime slaveholder, Taney freed his slaves in evidence of a persistent belief in black inferiority. Legislation prohibiting interracial unions, and black schooling, for instance, set blacks apart from whites. "Indeed," Taney summarized, "when we look to the condition of this race in the several States at the time, it is impossible to believe that these rights and privileges [of citizenship] were intended to be extended to them." Finally, Taney cited as precedents three federal laws passed by Congress that suggested blacks were not citizens. A naturalization law of 1790 defined "*aliens*" as "free white persons," a law of 1792 specified that only whites were eligible for militia service, and

---

1818, the same year he condemned the institution of slavery as he defended in court an abolitionist minister charged with inciting slaves. Throughout his judicial career, however, Taney proved himself reliably proslavery in his views.

As chief justice, a visibly uncomfortable Taney administered the oath of office to Republican president Abraham Lincoln in 1861. It must have been awkward for him, just steps away from the commander in chief, to listen to Lincoln's inaugural address, which contained statements obviously critical of the Taney Court. Sympathetic to the South, Taney nevertheless refused to resign his position on the High Court during the Civil War, unlike Justice John A. Campbell, who returned home to Alabama and joined the Confederacy. As the North and South waged war, Taney continued to collect his chief justice's salary from a government he did not support. When President Lincoln suspended the writ of habeas corpus in Taney's native state of Maryland early in the war, an increasingly angry and bitter Taney quickly began to regard Lincoln as a despot and tyrant. His southern loyalties combined with his opinion in the *Dred Scott* case to make him the special target of Republican venom. Loathed and despised by his political adversaries, Taney spited them by serving as chief justice right up to his death in October 1864 at the age of 87. "The Hon. Old Roger B. Taney has earned the gratitude of his country by dying at last," one Taney critic confided in his diary. "Better late than never."*

---

* Fehrenbacher, *Slavery, Law, and Politics*, 113; Horace Gray, *A Legal Review of the Case of Dred Scott, as Decided by the Supreme Court of the United States* (Boston: Crosby, Nichols and Company, 1857), 9; quoted in Fehrenbacher, *Slavery, Law, and Politics*, 298.

an 1813 statute stating who was eligible to serve on American ships distinguished between "citizens" and "persons of color." Satisfied that citizenship was confined to whites, Taney reported that "Dred Scott was not a citizen of Missouri within the meaning of the Constitution of the United States, and not entitled as such to sue in its courts." The majority opinion made no distinction between slaves and free blacks, conflating them into a single racial category denied the benefits of citizenship. By the *Dred Scott* ruling, no black American—no one of African descent—qualified as a citizen of the United States. The Taney Court thus stripped them of any rights they might have held or once enjoyed under the U.S. Constitution. (See "Chief Justice Roger B. Taney on Black Citizenship, 1857," on page 383 in the Primary Sources section.)

The Court next moved on to the question of whether Scott had been freed by virtue of his residence in a territory where slavery was outlawed. According to Article IV, Section 3, of the Constitution, "Congress shall have Power to dispose of and make all needful Rules and Regulations respecting the Territory or other Property belonging to the United States." The Supreme Court majority decision in *Dred Scott* defined this clause narrowly, giving Congress the power only to dispose of public lands but not to govern them or make their laws. As Justice Campbell explained in his concurring opinion, "the recognition of a plenary power in Congress to dispose of the public domain, or to organize a Government over it, does not imply a corresponding authority to determine the internal polity, or to adjust the domestic relations, or the persons who may lawfully inhabit the territory in which it is situated." Without offering any legal precedent, Taney contended that the "needful rules" clause applied only to those territories that belonged to the United States when the Constitution was ratified. The Louisiana Purchase was acquired 15 years later, in 1803. Therefore, the congressional law that prohibited slavery in the Wisconsin Territory where Scott was held as a slave—the Missouri Compromise of 1820—was unconstitutional. According to the Taney Court majority, Congress was powerless to impose any restrictions on slavery in any existing American territories.

Taney and the concurring justices also expressed concerns about the rights of Americans who settled the territories. "Citizens of the United States who migrate to a Territory belonging to the people of the United States, cannot be ruled as mere colonists, dependent upon the will of the General Government, and to be governed by any laws it may

Chief Justice Roger B. Taney wrote the majority opinion in the *Dred Scott v. Sandford* Supreme Court decision of 1857. (Library of Congress)

think proper to impose," Taney remarked. Congress may not infringe "upon the rights of person or rights of property of the citizen who might go there to reside." No less than the First Amendment rights to freedom of speech or freedom of the press, Taney explained, Fifth Amendment protections of "life, liberty, and property" extended to citizens in the territories. Taney adjudged "the right of property in a slave . . . distinctly and expressly affirmed in the Constitution." "This is done in plain words—too plain to be misunderstood," he stated. "And no word can be found in the Constitution which gives Congress a greater power over slave property, or which entitles property of that kind to less protection than property of any other description." Indeed, Justice Daniel insisted that the Constitution conferred special guarantees upon enslaved property. (See "Justice Peter V. Daniel on Property Rights, 1857," on page 385 in the Primary Sources section.) Although he did not go that far, Justice Catron observed that it made no more sense to forbid the South's slaves from entering a territory than the North's "cattle or horses." He feared the prohibition of "one species of property" might justify restrictions on other forms of property. For the *Dred Scott* majority, the Fifth Amendment protected masters' right to their slaves, regardless of where they lived. Although Taney did not explicitly declare the Missouri Compromise a violation of the Fifth Amendment, he did note that "an act of Congress which deprives a citizen of the United States of his liberty or property, merely because he came himself or brought his property into a particular Territory of the United States, . . . could hardly be dignified with the name of due process of law." Taney further reasoned that if Congress could not restrict slavery in the territories, neither could a territorial legislature established by Congress.

If Scott's residence in the free Wisconsin Territory gave him no constitutional claim to freedom, did his two years in the free state of Illinois? The majority of the Court said no. Taney cited as precedent *Strader v. Graham* (1851), a case in which slaves from Kentucky were sent to work temporarily in Ohio, then returned to Kentucky. The Supreme Court ruled that the slaves' "*status* . . . depended upon the laws of Kentucky, when they were brought back into that State, and not of Ohio." Likewise, by this doctrine of reversion, when Dr. Emerson conveyed Scott to Illinois, Scott's "*status*, as free or slave, depended on the laws of Missouri, and not of Illinois." Illinois laws against slavery did not enjoy extraterritoriality in Missouri and therefore did not entitle Scott to freedom. Justice Nelson and other concurring judges took a different path to the same destination. They distinguished between temporary and permanent residence. "The removal of Dr. Emerson from Missouri to the military posts was in the discharge of his duties as surgeon in the army, and under the orders of his Government. He was liable at any moment to be recalled," Nelson observed.

"In such a case, the officer goes to his post for a temporary purpose, to remain there for an uncertain time, and not for the purpose of fixing his permanent abode." Scott's domicile was in Missouri; he merely sojourned in Illinois, and therefore Missouri laws remained operable.

The Supreme Court might have dispensed with the *Dred Scott* case perfunctorily, concluding with its ruling that Scott was not a citizen capable of appearing before the Court. Responding to criticisms that the Court acted "extrajudicially" in declaring the Missouri Compromise unconstitutional, Justice Wayne defended the majority's actions. As he explained it, "The case involves private rights of value, and constitutional principles of the highest importance, about which there had become such a difference of opinion, that the peace and harmony of the country required the settlement of them by judicial decision." By this reasoning, the pressing political issues that plagued the country in 1857 and threatened the Union demanded the intervention of the High Court. The majority depicted its unabashedly proslavery ruling as a well-intentioned effort to grapple with the sectional crisis.

The Case that the *Dred Scott* Decision Was Not Legally Sound

The Supreme Court majority's sweeping judgment in favor of slavery was not unanimous. Justices John McLean of Ohio and Benjamin R. Curtis of Massachusetts each filed dissenting opinions. A number of contemporary politicians (typically but not exclusively Republicans), lawyers, and abolitionists echoed and elaborated upon the minority's criticisms of the *Dred Scott* ruling. They found the decision mistaken on several counts, historically inaccurate, and defiant of established precedents. The minority on the Court maintained that Scott was indeed a citizen, that Congress did exercise legislative authority over the territories, and that the Missouri Compromise did not violate the Constitution. In their view, Scott's residence in Illinois and the Wisconsin Territory should have made him a free man.

Justices McLean and Curtis determined that Scott was a citizen with the right to take his case to court. African ancestry was not an insurmountable obstacle to citizenship. The standard for citizenship did not require that one be a full member of the polity, with all the rights and privileges of white men, McLean argued. "Females and minors may sue in the Federal courts, and so may any individual who has a permanent domicil in the State under whose laws his rights are protected, and to which he owes allegiance." Scott was a citizen of Missouri, and any citizen of a state was, by extension, also a citizen of the United States. Moreover, Scott's birth in Virginia meant that he was not a foreigner who required naturalization to become a citizen. That "a colored citizen would not be an agreeable member of society," McLean observed, "is more a matter of taste than of law." Justice Curtis added that "color is not a necessary qualification for citizenship under the Constitution." Many states had in fact recognized free blacks as citizens. Curtis stressed that several states, including slaveholding North Carolina, had even permitted them to vote. In contrast to Chief Justice Taney, Curtis regarded the franchise as a solid indicator of U.S. citizenship. (See "Justice Benjamin R. Curtis on Black Citizenship, 1857," on page 386 in the Primary Sources section.)

Many contemporary observers opposed to the *Dred Scott* decision noted that, since the Taney Court majority determined Scott was not a citizen, the case should have been promptly dismissed. "Having so decided," wrote an anonymous "Kentucky lawyer" in a shrewdly argued pamphlet, "the Court should have stopped there, and not attempted to go any further into the case. All beyond that was extra-judicial, and entitled to no further respect than if the judges had expressed the same opinions in a debating club, or had published them in a newspaper for the undisguised purpose of aiding a political party." The Supreme Court's lack of jurisdiction to rule on the case should have made *Dred Scott* an uncontroversial ruling dispensed without trouble or fanfare. Instead, fumed former Missouri senator Thomas Hart Benton, a moderate Democrat and unionist disappointed in the outcome, the Supreme Court exploited the case and transformed it into an avenue through which to engage larger constitutional issues that a majority of its members were eager to discuss. Using Scott as "a bridge to get from a case of personal rights to a question of political power," the Court needlessly and improperly ruled on the Missouri Compromise. As one Massachusetts Republican congressman reasoned, if the Missouri state supreme court found the compromise constitutional, and the U.S. Supreme Court found it unconstitutional, but both courts ruled Scott a slave, the Missouri Compromise was obviously irrelevant to the case. The

Supreme Court insidiously employed the *Dred Scott* decision to rescind the power Congress had exercised over the territories for decades.[1]

Unlike their colleagues in the majority, Justices McLean and Curtis believed that Article IV, Section 3, of the Constitution granted Congress not only the ability to dispose of public lands but also extensive powers to govern American territories. "The power to make all needful rules and regulations is a power to legislate," McLean declared. "If Congress should deem slaves or free colored persons injurious to the population of a free Territory, . . . they have the power to prohibit them from becoming settlers in it" as a matter of "sound national policy." The very language of the Constitution, Curtis observed, gave Congress the power to make *all* needful rules and regulations for the territories. He found it curious that a majority of his fellow judges somehow believed slavery an exception, magically immune to congressional intervention. Curtis furthermore dismissed Taney's distinction between Congress's power over territories owned at the founding versus those acquired later as unfounded and frankly nonsensical, a gross misreading of the Constitution. If the "needful rules and regulations" clause applied only to territories in the country's possession in 1789, Curtis noted, the Constitution was a very limited document ill suited to the purposes for which it was created. (See "Justice Benjamin R. Curtis on Congressional Power over the Territories, 1857," on page 387 in the Primary Sources section and the sidebar "Benjamin R. Curtis" on page 368.)

Curtis pointed out as well that Congress had regulated slavery in the territories in the past, beginning with the limitation on slavery contained in the Northwest Ordinance of 1787. Chief Justice Taney's majority opinion acknowledged that fact but sidestepped it by indicating that

---

[1] A Kentucky Lawyer, *A Review of the Decision of the Supreme Court of the United States in the Dred Scott Case* (Louisville: Morton & Griswold, 1857), 3; Thomas Hart Benton, *Historical and Legal Examination of That Part of the Decision of the Supreme Court of the United States in the Dred Scott Case, Which Declares the Unconstitutionality of the Missouri Compromise Act, and the Self-Extension of the Constitution to Territories, Carrying Slavery Along with It* (New York: D. Appleton and Company, 1857; reprint, New York: Kraus Reprint, 1969), 11; *The Supreme Court and Dred Scott: Speech of Hon. Daniel W. Gooch, of Mass. Delivered in the U.S. House of Representatives, May 3, 1860* (Washington, D.C.: Republican Executive Congressional Committee, 1860), 6.

BENJAMIN R. CURTIS

Like fellow Supreme Court justice John McLean, Benjamin R. Curtis offered a dissent to the majority opinion in the *Dred Scott* decision. Members of the Republican Party applauded Curtis's masterful rejoinder to Chief Justice Taney, but he made for them an unlikely hero. Although personally opposed to slavery, Curtis was no antislavery champion, prioritizing instead the maintenance of relations among the states. A Whig, he favored the Compromise of 1850 signed into law by President Millard Fillmore. Curtis supported, defended, and urged obedience to its provision strengthening the Fugitive Slave Law. He endorsed the repeal of Massachusetts' personal liberty laws, which he considered unconstitutional, and, in the case of *Commonwealth v. Aves*, defended masters' right to take their slaves to the free states for brief, temporary visits. Curtis despised abolitionists and during the Civil War even railed against President Abraham Lincoln's Emancipation Proclamation.

Born in Massachusetts in 1809, Curtis graduated from Harvard Law School, where he was mentored by Supreme Court justice Joseph Story. Throughout most of his career, Curtis was an attorney with a private practice in Boston. But in 1851, with the endorsement of the longtime U.S. senator from Massachusetts and then–secretary of state Daniel Webster, President Fillmore appointed Curtis to the U.S. Supreme Court. In *Dred*

the United States owned the Northwest Territory when the Constitution was drafted. Furthermore, the state of Virginia had voluntarily surrendered its claims to land north of the Ohio River, explicitly agreeing to forbid slavery there in the process. Justice Curtis looked at the original states' land cessions to Congress differently. When North Carolina ceded its claims to the territory that became the state of Tennessee, for instance, the terms of the transfer expressly prevented Congress from emancipating slaves. Similarly, the government established for the Mississippi Territory mirrored that for the Northwest Territory, except for the 1787 provision prohibiting slavery. These agreements, Curtis argued, implied Congress's right to restrict slavery from the territories; absent that right, no exemptions for slavery were necessary. By Curtis's tally, between 1789 and 1848, Congress excluded slavery

Scott v. Sandford, Curtis's brother George aided Scott's lawyer, Montgomery Blair.

Although Benjamin Curtis sided with the minority, his dissent in the *Dred Scott* case is arguably the highlight of his unexpectedly brief tenure on the Supreme Court. After the High Court handed down its judgment, a dispute erupted between Curtis and Taney. Taney revised the majority opinion prior to publication, bolstering his position with 18 additional pages of text. He refused, however, to release a copy to Curtis, who thought revisions to his dissent might be in order as well. Taney brusquely informed Curtis that he had no right to a copy of the majority opinion prior to publication. An icy series of letters passed between the two men, but it was clear that Curtis would be granted no opportunity to refute Taney's expanded arguments as they would appear in print. Citing the time his Supreme Court duties took away from his family and the meager salary that he earned—but no doubt swayed by the hostile atmosphere on the Court—Curtis resigned after serving only six years on the bench.

Curtis regarded himself as apolitical. When the Whig Party dissolved in the 1850s, he could not find a home in the newly created Republican Party, given its strong and politically divisive stance against the extension of slavery into the territories. He instead gravitated increasingly toward the Democrats. His later legal career included defending President Andrew Johnson at his impeachment trial in 1868. Curtis died in 1874.

from a territory eight times and recognized it six times. According to the nameless Kentucky lawyer's count, Congress forbade slavery in territories a dozen times between 1790 and 1850, "with the sanction of nearly every President we have had." For the Supreme Court to negate a "settled" right of Congress "of more than sixty years," he warned, "the Constitution becomes a flimsy thing to be perverted and misapplied at any moment to serve the purposes of a political party or gratify the caprice of any judge." Justices Curtis and McLean both judged the Missouri Compromise constitutionally valid, no different from previous legislation against slavery in the territories.[2]

---

[2] Kentucky Lawyer, *A Review of the Decision,* 24, 29.

Not only had Congress traditionally maintained the right to restrict slavery, they continued, but the Missouri state supreme court had acknowledged that authority in the case of *Rachel v. Walker* (1836). Rachel's story seemed eerily similar to that of Dred Scott. A U.S. Army officer purchased Rachel, an enslaved woman, in Missouri and took her with him to the location where he was stationed in the free territory of Michigan. He later returned to St. Louis and sold her. At that point, in 1834, Rachel sued for her freedom on the grounds that she had lived in a free territory. After losing her case in the St. Louis Circuit Court, she appealed to the Missouri state supreme court, which granted her claim to freedom, arguing that masters surrendered their ownership rights when they ventured with their slaves into free territory. For Curtis and McLean, *Rachel v. Walker* established the applicable precedent for the *Dred Scott* case. Why did the Missouri state supreme court reverse itself in 1854 when the circumstances surrounding the two cases were virtually identical?

Justice Curtis raised a separate issue not discussed in any of the trials leading up to *Dred Scott v. Sandford*. He found Dred Scott's marriage to Harriet Robinson legally pertinent to his dissent. Scott was formally wed in the free territory of Wisconsin, and only free people could lawfully marry. Antebellum slave couples often married informally, in unofficial ceremonies typically conducted by a master, but their unions enjoyed no legal standing. Scott's marriage could only have been possible if he had been free. "If the laws of Congress governing the Territory of Wisconsin were constitutional and valid laws, there can be no doubt these parties were capable of contracting a lawful marriage, attended with all the usual civil rights and obligations of that condition," Curtis explained. "In that Territory they were absolutely free persons, having full capacity to enter into the civil contract of marriage." The Missouri Compromise had "operated directly on and changed the status" of Dred to that of a free man. Dr. Emerson's consent that his slave "enter into a lawful contract of marriage, attended with the civil rights and duties which belong to that condition" was tantamount to "an effectual act of emancipation."

Curtis's and McLean's dissenting opinions discounted the majority's lone constitutional argument against the Missouri Compromise that the Fifth Amendment protected masters' right to enslaved property in the territories. The majority of the Taney Court upheld "the equal right of all citizens to go with their property upon the public domain" and noted "the inequality of a regulation which would admit the property of some and exclude the property of other citizens." In that sense, limitations on slavery in the territories discriminated against slaveholders. "I agree" that the Louisiana Purchase was "acquired for the equal benefit of all the citizens of the United States," Curtis stated. "But it was acquired for their benefit in their collective, not their individual, capacities. It was acquired for their benefit, as an organized political society . . . to be administered justly and impartially, and as nearly as possible for the equal benefit of every individual citizen, according to the best judgment and discretion of the Congress." McLean took a different tack. His dissent showcased his antislavery principles. "A majority of the court have said that a slave may be taken by his master into a Territory . . . the same as a horse, or any other kind of property," he explained, but a slave is not "the same as other property which the master may own." No "mere chattel," the slave "bears the impress of his Maker, and is amenable to the laws of God and man." More practically, the "Kentucky lawyer" made the point that citizens were only deprived of their enslaved property if they voluntarily took their slaves unlawfully into a territory, in which case the slaveholder "is deprived of his property by *due process of law*": "So long as his slave remains outside the territory the law does not touch the property."[3]

Did Dred Scott's residence in a free state or a free territory liberate him from slavery? Justice McLean reasoned that since slavery existed by local law, where local law did not countenance slavery, the institution could not exist. The master should not expect to retain as a slave any bond person he took into a free territory because he did not "carry with him the law of the State from which he removes." Curtis agreed, stating that slaves "must cease to be available as property, when their owners voluntarily place them permanently within another jurisdiction, where no municipal laws on the subject of slavery exist." Curtis and McLean both believed Scott had domiciled outside Missouri, having spent sufficient time not to be considered a temporary resident or transient. As an army surgeon, Dr. Emerson relocated by order of the U.S. government, but for Curtis, even an indefinite stay in a free state or territory emancipated Scott. Moreover, argued the dissenting justices, freedom gained

---

[3] Kentucky Lawyer, *A Review of the Decision*, 26.

by living in a free state or territory could not be retracted upon reentry into a slave state. Emancipation was permanent and irrevocable. To argue otherwise gave Missouri law extraterritoriality.

McLean, in particular, cited the judicial opinion of Hamilton Rowan Gamble, chief justice of the Missouri state supreme court and dissenter in *Dred Scott v. Emerson*. Gamble had argued in favor of Dred Scott's freedom because, he said, the operable laws were the ones in the state in which the master and the slave presently lived. According to Gamble, a master who went from Missouri to Illinois automatically "dissolves the relation between him and his slave," as if he had voluntarily manumitted the slave. And if the former slave returned to Missouri, enslavement did not reattach. "The slave States have generally adopted the rule," explained Justice McLean, "that where the master, by a residence with his slave in a State or Territory where slavery is prohibited, the slave was entitled to freedom everywhere." South Carolina, Mississippi, Virginia, Louisiana, and other southern states agreed. As McLean noted, "This was [also] the settled doctrine of the Supreme Court of Missouri," until overturned by *Dred Scott v. Emerson* in 1852. In upholding the Missouri state supreme court verdict, the U.S. Supreme Court affirmed that heedless of the Northwest Ordinance, the constitution of Illinois, the territorial law of Wisconsin, and the Missouri Compromise, Missouri law was paramount.

If the Supreme Court hoped to quell the controversy over slavery in the territories, it failed miserably. "Far from settling the question," former Senator Benton related, "the opinion itself has become a new question, more virulent than the former!" Critics charged that the Taney Court acted foolishly in appointing itself arbiter of the slavery question. Its unwelcome excursion into the political arena seemed a gross example of judicial activism. The blatantly proslavery *Dred Scott* ruling usurped congressional power over the territories and, to paraphrase Benton, inserted invisible clauses into the Constitution. A defeated unionist, Benton asked incredulously, "why take the course which has been so serious to our Constitution? so contrary to seventy years' action of our government? so inflammatory to political parties? and so aggravating to the spirit of sectional division?" Passions ran high when the Supreme Court "rendered a *political and sectional instead of judicial decision.*"[4]

---

[4] Benton, *Historical and Legal Examination*, 4, 9; Kentucky Lawyer, *A Review of the Decision*, 44.

OUTCOME AND IMPACT

Word of the *Dred Scott v. Sandford* decision rippled across the country. It met with a mixed reception in the press as the public discussed the meaning and repercussions of the case. Although some midwestern newspapers applauded the decision, and a few border South papers criticized it, as a general rule, the southern press cheered the ruling while that in the North condemned it. Southern newspaper editors were gratified that the Supreme Court validated their proslavery views. On the losing side of the case, the northern Republican press overflowed with vituperative, indignant editorials. Spearheaded by editor Horace Greeley of the *New York Tribune,* Republican newspapers printed almost daily inflammatory pieces attacking the injustice of the *Dred Scott* decision. (See "Horace Greeley on the *Dred Scott* Decision, 1857," on page 389 in the Primary Sources section.) Republican members of Congress scored political points chastising the Taney Court. According to one New England congressman, the majority opinion seemed "the argument of some astute attorney, especially distinguished for his ability to ignore and reject all law and fact which make against him." He described the outcome in hyperbolic terms, "as one of the most direct and positive falsifications of the well-known facts of history to be found in the English language, and the greatest libel upon the men who framed the institutions under which we live, ever published to the world."[5] Abolitionists in the North such as Frederick Douglass struck the most defiant tone. Reflecting upon the *Dred Scott* case, Douglass urged continued agitation and found consolation in his belief that a higher, divine court would one day dispense justice. (See "Speech of Frederick Douglass, 1857," on page 390 in the Primary Sources section.) After the publication of the case, legal reviews—the vast majority critical of the *Dred Scott* decision—struck a somewhat more moderate if incredulous tone.

That seven of the nine justices ruled Scott a slave and six agreed on the unconstitutionality of the Missouri Compromise line was not surprising. The composition of the Supreme Court suggested such an outcome. Tainted by their interests, judges divided along sectional lines as well as by political affiliation. Of the seven justices in the majority, five hailed from southern, slaveholding states, and all of them were

---

[5] *The Supreme Court and Dred Scott: Speech of Hon. Daniel W. Gooch,* 3.

members of a Democratic Party that had no objections to the extension of slavery into the territories. The two dissenters, Justices Curtis and McLean, were northerners from Massachusetts and Ohio, respectively. By 1857, Curtis was a onetime Whig without a true political home, McLean an openly antislavery Republican. Divisions in the Supreme Court reflected those writ large throughout the country.

Among the most notorious of all Supreme Court decisions, the *Dred Scott* case, which coursed its way through state and federal court systems for more than a decade, began modestly with one man seeking freedom for himself and his enslaved family. Despite the Supreme Court ruling against them, the Scotts soon did gain their liberty. Their nominal master, John F. A. Sanford, had descended into madness by the mid-1850s, entered an asylum, and died on May 5, 1857, only two months after the *Dred Scott* decision. At the conclusion of the case, the Scotts were remanded to Sanford's sister, Eliza Irene Emerson. Dr. Emerson's widow, however, had remarried, uniting in matrimony with a prominent abolitionist, Massachusetts Republican congressman Calvin C. Chaffee. Having a slave family in his household was hypocritical and politically embarrassing for the congressman, who disclaimed any knowledge that his wife owned the most famous slave in the country until the proceedings had almost concluded. The Chaffees transferred ownership of the Scotts in late May 1857 to Taylor Blow, the son of Scott's original master and a childhood friend. The Blow family had remained very supportive of the Scotts, and Blow had aided them financially. Upon taking possession of the Scotts, Blow immediately manumitted them. Dred Scott lived as a free man, working as a hotel porter in St. Louis, for 16 months before his death of tuberculosis in September 1858. His wife Harriet, a laundress, reportedly outlived him by only a short few years.

Beyond its effects on one individual family, the *Dred Scott* case held implications for the nation's entire free black population. In ruling that black Americans were not citizens, the Supreme Court made life that much more difficult for the country's free people of color. Legally, states could now pass discriminatory legislation to take away rights concomitant with citizenship. Arkansas, for instance, passed a law in 1859 enslaving any free black individual who did not evacuate the state within a year. *Dred Scott* also posed the question of whether free blacks had the constitutional right to exercise the franchise in the few remaining northern states in which they were still allowed to vote.

The *Dred Scott* decision also had an explosive impact on national politics. In *Dred Scott*, the Supreme Court declared a law unconstitutional for only the second time, the first since the *Marbury v. Madison* decision of 1803. By invalidating the Missouri Compromise of 1820 (already partly legislated away by the Kansas-Nebraska Act of 1854), the High Court rescinded the authority of Congress to legislate with regard to slavery in the territories, a power it had exercised since the ratification of the Constitution. By implication, all territories were open to slavery, and the federal government was powerless to stop slavery's spread. Such a sweeping judgment could not help but exacerbate sectional strains and accelerate the crisis of Union already evident before 1857.

The Republican Party immediately felt the acute sting of the *Dred Scott* decision. The Taney Court obliterated any lingering faith in the impartiality of the Supreme Court by manipulating the law for overtly partisan purposes. In the estimation of the Republicans, overzealous, activist judges had improperly inserted their presence into the most controversial political question of the day. Most northerners proved less offended by the assault upon black citizenship than by the invalidation of the Missouri Compromise. The Republican Party had been created on a platform opposed to the extension of slavery into the territories. By removing the power of Congress to legislate in the territories, *Dred Scott v. Sandford* seemed to undermine the very foundation of the Republican Party. For Republicans, the case afforded further evidence of the slave-power conspiracy at work. By their reckoning, a Supreme Court composed of five devious southerners had not only opened all the territories to slavery but also paved the way for the nationalization of the peculiar institution, restoring slavery even in states where it had been abolished.

Devastated and disheartened Republicans united in opposition to the *Dred Scott* ruling needed to respond cautiously to the verdict, however. On the one hand, the Republican Party had to reject *Dred Scott's* outcome without appearing to dismiss the law. Republicans therefore declared the *Dred Scott* decision illegitimate and denied that it voided the Missouri Compromise. Since Scott lacked citizenship and the power to appear before the Court, there should have been no case. The majority decision enunciated by Chief Justice Taney was thus, in legal parlance, an obiter dictum, a mere opinion neither part of the decision nor legally binding. On the other hand, Republican critics had to distance themselves from the North's radical abolitionists. The Republican Party had a distinct "race problem." Although it advocated restricting slavery from the territories, it did not join in the abolitionists' demand to eradicate slavery in the South where it already existed. In an effort to sabotage the Republicans while the party was still in its infancy, Democrats such as Senator Stephen Douglas of Illinois leaped at the chance to distort their platform, charging that Republicans advocated racial equality and race mixing. (See "Speech of Senator Stephen Douglas, 1858," on page 391 in the Primary Sources section.) The Republican Party thus trod a thin and dangerous line as it sought to prevent the spread of slavery without ushering in racial equality. The Republicans could not be the party of social and political equality for black Americans and expect to survive. Abraham Lincoln's June 1857 speech in Springfield, Illinois, illustrated the delicate balance Republicans had to strike in criticizing *Dred Scott.* (See "Speech of Abraham Lincoln, 1857," on page 392 in the Primary Sources section.)

Although the Democrats escaped the immediate effects of *Dred Scott* that beset the Republicans, the case proved at least as significant to them in the long term as it contributed to a division within the party. Initially, the Democratic press impressed upon its readers that the Supreme Court had ruled and that disgruntled elements ought to acquiesce to the decision in deference to the High Court. Elated with the outcome of the *Dred Scott* case, southern Democrats advanced the position that the Taney Court prevented any restrictions on slavery in the territories. Northern Democrats such as Stephen Douglas accepted the *Dred Scott* decision but with an important qualification. The leading proponent of popular sovereignty, Douglas argued on June 12, 1857, that the ability to take slaves into a territory "necessarily remains a barren and a worthless right, unless sustained, protected and enforced by appropriate police regulations and local legislation, prescribing adequate remedies for its violation. These regulations and remedies must necessarily depend entirely upon the will and wishes of the people of the Territory, as they can only be prescribed by the local Legislatures. Hence, the great principle of popular sovereignty and self-government is sustained and firmly established by the authority of this decision."[6] In Douglas's reading, *Dred Scott v. Sandford* was perfectly compatible with the principle of popular sovereignty.

---

[6] Quoted in Maltz, Dred Scott *and the Politics of Slavery,* 149; and Fehrenbacher, *Slavery, Law, and Politics,* 246.

Interpretive differences within the Democratic Party over the meaning of *Dred Scott* remained latent until after the events in Kansas in 1857 and 1858. The proslavery legislature in Kansas developed the Lecompton Constitution, a document that would usher Kansas into the Union as a slave state if approved. Senator Douglas of Illinois, with reelection looming in a state opposed to the Lecompton Constitution, broke with President Buchanan and the South to lead those Democrats opposed to the admission of a slave Kansas. The proslavery Lecompton Constitution went down to defeat in August 1858. Joining the Republican Party to take a stand against it, Douglas alienated southern Democrats.

As the Lecompton drama unfolded in 1858, Douglas, the Democratic incumbent, and Republican challenger Abraham Lincoln stumped in a contest for a U.S. Senate seat from Illinois. The *Dred Scott* decision figured prominently in the seven official Lincoln-Douglas debates that began in August as well as in a series of speeches in the months preceding them. Lincoln understood *Dred Scott v. Sandford* to authorize slavery in all territories and to forbid territorial legislatures from imposing any restrictions on the institution. As such, he believed *Dred Scott* undermined popular sovereignty. Having explored the implications of the ruling, Lincoln repeatedly pressed Douglas in 1858 to reconcile popular sovereignty with the Court's opinion. Douglas continued to contend, as he had the previous year, that *Dred Scott* did not preclude territories from deciding for themselves whether or not to permit slavery. Even if Congress could not limit slavery in the territories, their respective legislatures retained authority over the slave question and could restrict it if they chose. Eventually labeled the Freeport doctrine, Douglas's response to Lincoln—that slavery could survive only where the citizenry wanted it—seemed a betrayal to southern Democrats, as well as their executive branch ally President Buchanan. (See "Third Annual Message of President Buchanan, 1859," on page 394 in the Primary Sources section.) They believed that Douglas and like-minded northern Democrats had united with the Republicans to deny them their clear-cut judicial victory in *Dred Scott v. Sandford*. Douglas's positions on the Lecompton Constitution and the *Dred Scott* decision ultimately split the Democratic Party into sectional factions. Whereas northern Democrats nominated Douglas for president in 1860, southern Democrats advanced Vice President John C. Breckinridge of Kentucky as their candidate.

With the victory of the Republican presidential candidate Abraham Lincoln in 1860, southern states began seceding from the United States. The Crittenden compromise, a last-ditch proposal to avert the sundering of the Union, featured a constitutional amendment that would have restored the Missouri Compromise line of 1820 and extended it westward to the Pacific. It would, in effect, have rescinded one piece of the Kansas-Nebraska Act and overturned *Dred Scott's* assurances that all territories were open to slavery. Legislators North and South rejected the Crittenden compromise, however, and secession continued.

With most slaveholding state representatives absent, Congress abolished slavery in the territories in June 1862 in complete defiance of the *Dred Scott* decision. After the Civil War, first the Civil Rights Act of 1866, then the Fourteenth Amendment ratified two years later, repudiated *Dred Scott* by affirming that black Americans were citizens of the United States. A little more than a decade after the Supreme Court handed down its judgment, the *Dred Scott* decision lay in tatters, even as the racial prejudice that shaped it persisted.

WHAT IF?

What if the Supreme Court had ruled in Dred Scott's favor?

The composition of the Supreme Court militated against a judgment in Dred Scott's favor. Justices Curtis and McLean offered well-reasoned arguments in their minority opinions, however. Had they managed to carry the day, Scott would have been legally declared free. As it happened, he gained his freedom soon after the conclusion of the case anyway. A ruling granting Scott his liberty would probably have had greater actual benefit to free blacks across the United States because it would have recognized the citizenship of black Americans and stemmed the passage of at least some discriminatory legislation. In terms of national politics, *Dred Scott* did not truly resolve the issue of slavery in the territories. Despite emerging from the nation's highest Court, the decision left enough interpretive wiggle room to argue, as President Buchanan and southern Democrats did, that slavery could not be restricted at all, *and*, as Douglas and other northern Democrats insisted, that territorial legislatures still maintained that right. When they rejected the Lecompton Constitution in 1858, the voters of Kansas in fact exercised popular sovereignty, despite the southern Democratic reading of the case. *Dred Scott v. Sandford* played a significant but not exclusive role in the fracture of the Democratic Party. The Lecompton controversy might have been sufficient in and of itself to divide the party into northern and southern flanks. Although seemingly a devastating blow to the Republican Party,

Dred Scott ultimately galvanized the Republicans and might have accelerated the party's growth somewhat. Its rise might have slowed negligibly without it. With or without the *Dred Scott* decision, sectional tensions were rising in the 1850s. Although the case exacerbated animosity between North and South, historians generally do not regard *Dred Scott v. Sandford* as a "cause" of the Civil War per se.

CHRONOLOGY

1787   The Confederation Congress prohibits slavery in the Northwest Territory.

1799   Dred Scott is born in Virginia.

1803   The United States acquires the Louisiana Purchase through treaty with France.

1820   Congress passes the Missouri Compromise.

1821   Missouri enters the Union as the 24th state.

1830   Dred Scott relocates with his master, Peter Blow, to Missouri.

1832   Peter Blow dies, prompting Scott's sale to Dr. John Emerson.

1834   Dr. Emerson takes Scott with him to Rock Island, Illinois.

1836   Dr. Emerson is transferred to Fort Snelling, taking Scott with him.

1838   Dred Scott and his wife serve Dr. Emerson briefly in Louisiana before returning to Fort Snelling.

1843   Dr. Emerson dies.

1846   Dred Scott sues Mrs. John Emerson for his and his wife's freedom in St. Louis Circuit Court.

The Wilmot Proviso proposes the prohibition of slavery in any territory acquired from Mexico.

1847   The circuit court rules against Scott but allows for a second trial.

1848   The Free-Soil Party platform endorses the Wilmot Proviso's restriction on slavery in the territories.

1850   The jury at the second trial finds in favor of Dred Scott.

1852   On appeal, the Missouri state supreme court reverses the lower court's decision.

1854   The U.S. Circuit Court upholds the Missouri state supreme court decision.

The Republican Party is founded.

President Franklin Pierce signs into law the Kansas-Nebraska Act, repealing the Missouri Compromise line.

1856   Blood is spilled in the territory of Kansas over the issue of slavery. Democrat James Buchanan is elected president.

1857   The U.S. Supreme Court issues its decision in the case of *Dred Scott v. Sandford.*

Mrs. Emerson returns Dred Scott and his family to the Blows, who free them.

1858   The Lincoln-Douglas debates take place across Illinois.

Dred Scott dies of tuberculosis.

1860   The Democratic Party splits into northern and southern factions.

1861   The Civil War begins.

1865   *Apr. 9:* Robert E. Lee surrenders to Ulysses S. Grant at Appomattox Court House, Virginia.

Dec. 18: The Thirteenth Amendment to the Constitution abolishes slavery in the United States.

1868   The Fourteenth Amendment to the Constitution makes black Americans citizens of the United States.

DISCUSSION QUESTIONS

1. What role did historical precedent play in the *Dred Scott* decision?
2. How pertinent was the Missouri Compromise to the *Dred Scott* case?
3. How did the national controversy over slavery affect the outcome of the trial?
4. Did the Supreme Court overstep its power in ruling on the *Dred Scott* case? Why or why not?
5. What is the proper role of the Supreme Court with respect to important social and political issues? Can the Supreme Court render an "impartial" judgment?

WEB SITES

FindLaw. "Scott v. Sandford," Landmark Decisions. Available online. URL: http://supreme.lp.findlaw.com/supreme_court/landmark/dred-scott.html. Accessed November 21, 2009.

Gilder Lehrman Institute of American History. "The Dred Scott Decision and Its Bitter Legacy," Online Exhibitions. Available online. URL:

http://www.gilderlehrman.org/collection/online/scott/index.html.
Accessed November 21, 2009.

Library of Congress. "Dred Scott v. Sandford," Primary Documents in
American History. Available online. URL: http://www.loc.gov/rr/pro-
gram/bib/ourdocs/DredScott.html. Accessed November 21, 2009.

Missouri Office of the Secretary of State, Missouri State Library, Missouri State Archives, The State Historical Society of Missouri. "Missouri's Dred Scott Case, 1846–1857," Missouri Digital Heritage Initiative, African American History Initiative. Available online. URL:
http://www.sos.mo.gov/archives/resources/africanamerican/scott/
scott.asp. Accessed November 21, 2009.

National Archives and Records Administration. "Dred Scott v. Sanford
(1857)," Our Documents: A National Initiative on American History,
Civics, and Service. Available online. URL: http://www.ourdocu-
ments.gov/. Accessed November 21, 2009.

Public Broadcasting Service. "Dred Scott's Fight for Freedom," Africans
in America, Resource Bank. Available online. URL: http://www.pbs.
org/wgbh/aia/part4/4p2932.html. Accessed November 21, 2009.

Street Law & the Supreme Court Historical Society. "Dred Scott v. Sandford," Landmark Supreme Court Cases. Available online. URL: http://
www.landmarkcases.org/dredscott/home.html. Accessed November
21, 2009.

United States Department of the Interior. "The Dred Scott Case,"
National Park Service. Available online. URL: http://www.nps.gov/
archive/jeff/dred_scott.html. Accessed November 21, 2009.

Washington University in St. Louis. University Libraries. Dred Scott
Case Collection. Available online. URL: http://library.wustl.edu/vlib/
dredscott/index.html. Accessed November 21, 2009.

BIBLIOGRAPHY

Allen, Austin. *Origins of the* Dred Scott *Case: Jacksonian Jurisprudence
and the Supreme Court, 1837–1857.* Athens: University of Georgia
Press, 2006. Examines the judicial lenses through which the Taney
Court viewed the *Dred Scott* decision. Suggests that the ruling represented the culmination of a convergence of legal concerns decades
in the making.

Ehrlich, Walter. *They Have No Rights: Dred Scott's Struggle for Freedom.* Westport, Conn.: Greenwood Press, 1979. A narrowly focused study of the legal history of the *Dred Scott* case, paying close attention to the lower court decisions that preceded the Supreme Court's judgment.

Fehrenbacher, Don E. *Slavery, Law, and Politics: The* Dred Scott *Case in Historical Perspective.* New York: Oxford University Press, 1981. The more manageable, abridged edition of Fehrenbacher's Pulitzer Prize–winning *The* Dred Scott *Case: Its Significance in American Law and Politics* (1978), the classic work on the decision. Highly critical of the verdict.

Finkelman, Paul. Dred Scott v. Sandford: *A Brief History with Documents.* Boston: Bedford Books, 1997. A classroom-friendly text that includes a thorough selection of primary sources.

Graber, Mark A. Dred Scott *and the Problem of Constitutional Evil.* New York: Cambridge University Press, 2006. Argues that the *Dred Scott* decision was constitutionally defensible and that the Taney Court was an arbiter of law rather than morals.

Maltz, Earl M. Dred Scott *and the Politics of Slavery.* Lawrence: University Press of Kansas, 2007. An even-handed account of the *Dred Scott* decision that argues that the Supreme Court overreached its power in rendering such an inherently political ruling.

Wong, Edlie L. *Neither Fugitive nor Free: Atlantic Slavery, Freedom Suits, and the Legal Culture of Travel.* New York: New York University Press, 2009. An interdisciplinary cultural study of slaves whose movement led to freedom suits.

PRIMARY SOURCES

1. Inaugural Address of President James Buchanan, 1857

Victorious presidential candidate James Buchanan took the oath of office on March 4, 1857. A Democrat, he endorsed the principle of popular sovereignty to resolve the status of slavery in the territories. In his inaugural address, Buchanan celebrated the virtues of popular sovereignty and alluded to the upcoming decision regarding Dred Scott.

What a happy conception . . . was it for Congress to apply this simple rule—that the will of the majority shall govern—to the settlement of the question of domestic slavery in the Territories! Congress is neither "to legislate slavery into any Territory or State, nor to exclude it therefrom; but to leave the people thereof perfectly free to form and regulate their domestic institutions in their own way, subject only to the Constitution of the United States." . . .

A difference of opinion has arisen in regard to the point of time when the people of a Territory shall decide this question for themselves. This is, happily, a matter of but little practical importance. Besides, it is a judicial question which legitimately belongs to the Supreme Court of the United States, before whom it is now pending, and will, it is understood, be speedily and finally settled. To their decision, in common with all good citizens, I shall cheerfully submit, whatever this may be. . . . Nothing can be fairer than to leave the people of a Territory free from all foreign interference to decide their own destiny for themselves, subject only to the Constitution of the United States.

The whole territorial question being thus settled upon the principle of popular sovereignty. . . . No other question remains for adjustment; because all agree that under the Constitution slavery in the States is beyond the reach of any human power except that of the respective States themselves wherein it exists. . . . Most happy will it be for the country when the public mind shall be diverted from this question to others of more pressing and practical importance. . . . The whole progress of this agitation . . . has alienated and estranged the people of the sister States from each other, and has even seriously endangered the very existence of the Union.

Source: Marion Mills Miller, ed., *Great Debates in American History: From the Debates in the British Parliament on the Colonial Stamp Act (1764–1765) to the Debates in Congress at the Close of the Taft Administration (1912–1913),* vol. 4 (New York: Current Literature Publishing Company, 1913), 375–376.

—∽∾∽—

2. Chief Justice Roger B. Taney on Black Citizenship, 1857

Chief Justice Roger B. Taney alleged in the Supreme Court's majority opinion in Dred Scott *in 1857 that blacks were not citizens of the United States.*

The plaintiff [Dred Scott] was not a citizen of the State of Missouri, as alleged in his declaration, being a negro of African descent, whose ancestors were of pure African blood, and who were brought into this country and sold as slaves. . . .

The question is simply this: Can a negro, whose ancestors were imported into this country, and sold as slaves, become a member of the political community formed and brought into existence by the Constitution of the United States, and as such become entitled to all the rights, and privileges, and immunities, guarantied by that instrument to the citizen? One of which rights is the privilege of suing in a court of the United States in the cases specified in the Constitution. . . .

The question before us is, whether the class of persons described in the plea in abatement compose a portion of this people, and are constituent members of this sovereignty? We think they are not, and that they are not included, and were not intended to be included, under the word "citizens" in the Constitution, and can therefore claim none of the rights and privileges which that instrument provides for and secures to citizens of the United States. On the contrary, they were at that time considered as a subordinate and inferior class of beings, who had been subjugated by the dominant race, and, whether emancipated or not, yet remained subject to their authority, and had no rights or privileges but such as those who held the power and the Government might choose to grant them.

It is not the province of the court to decide upon the justice or injustice, the policy or impolicy, of these laws. . . . The duty of the court is, to interpret the instrument they have framed, with the best lights we can obtain on the subject, and to administer it as we find it, according to its true intent and meaning when it was adopted. . . .

No State can, by any act or law of its own, passed since the adoption of the Constitution, introduce a new member into the political community created by the Constitution of the United States. It cannot make him a member of this community by making him a member of its own. . . .

It is true, every person, and every class and description of persons, who were at the time of the adoption of the Constitution recognized as citizens in the several States, became also citizens of this new political body; but none other; it was formed by them, and for them and their posterity, but for no one else. And the personal rights and privileges guarantied to citizens of this new sovereignty were intended to embrace those only who were then members of the several State communities, or who should afterwards by birthright or otherwise become members, according to the provisions of the Constitution and the principles on which it was founded. . . .

It becomes necessary, therefore, to determine who were citizens of the several States when the Constitution was adopted. . . . We must inquire who, at that time, were recognized as the people or citizens of a State. . . .

In the opinion of the court, the legislation and histories of the times, and the language used in the Declaration of Independence, show, that neither the class of persons who had been imported as slaves, nor their descendants, whether they had become free or not, were then acknowledged as a part of the people, nor intended to be included in the general words used in that memorable instrument. . . .

They had for more than a century before been regarded as beings of an inferior order, and altogether unfit to associate with the white race, either in social or political relations; and so far inferior, that they had no rights which the white man was bound to respect; and that the negro might justly and lawfully be reduced to slavery for his benefit. He was bought and sold, and treated as an ordinary article of merchandise and traffic, whenever a profit could be made by it. This opinion was at that time fixed and universal in the civilized portion of the white race. It was regarded as an axiom in morals as well as in politics, which no one thought of disputing, or supposed to be open to dispute; and men in every grade and position in society daily and habitually acted upon it in their private pursuits, as well as in matters of public concern, without doubting for a moment the correctness of this opinion.

Source: Dred Scott v. Sandford, 60 U.S. 393; 15 L. Ed. 691; 1856 U.S. Lexis 472; 19 How. 393.

—⚭—

3. Justice Peter V. Daniel on Property Rights, 1857

Justice Peter V. Daniel of Virginia, the most overtly proslavery judge on the Supreme Court in 1857, upheld slavery as a form of property uniquely protected by the Constitution. He denied the government had authority to pass laws that would separate masters from their enslaved property.

Upon every principle of reason or necessity, this power to dispose of and to regulate the territory of the nation could be designed to extend no farther than to its preservation and appropriation to the uses of those to whom it belonged, viz: the nation. Scarcely anything more illogical or extravagant can be imagined than the attempt to deduce from this provision in the Constitution a power to destroy or in any wise to impair the civil and political rights of the citizens of the United States, and much more so the power to establish inequalities amongst those citizens by creating privileges in one class of those citizens, and by the disfranchisement of other portions or classes, by degrading them from the position they previously occupied. . . .

Nothing can be more conclusive to show the equality of this with every other right in all the citizens of the United States, and the iniquity and absurdity of the pretension to exclude or to disfranchise a portion of them because they are the owners of slaves, than the fact that the same instrument, which imparts to Congress its very existence and its every function, guaranties to the slaveholder the title to his property, and gives him the right to its reclamation throughout the entire extent of the nation; and, farther, that the only private property which the Constitution has specifically recognized, and has imposed it as a direct obligation both on the States and the Federal Government to protect and enforce, is the property of the master in his slave; no other right of property is placed by the Constitution upon the same high ground, nor shielded by a similar guaranty.

Can there be imputed to the sages and patriots by whom the Constitution was framed, or can there be detected in the text of that Constitution, or in any rational construction or implication deducible therefrom, a contradiction so palpable as would exist between a pledge to the slaveholder of an equality with his fellow-citizens, and of the formal and solemn assurance for the security and enjoyment of his property, and a warrant given . . . to another, to rob him of that property, or to subject him to proscription and disfranchisement for possessing or for endeavoring to retain it? The injustice and extravagance necessarily implied in a supposition like this, cannot be nationally imputed to the patriotic or the honest, or to those who were merely sane.

Source: Dred Scott v. Sandford, 60 U.S. 393; 15 L. Ed. 691; 1856 U.S. Lexis 472; 19 How. 393.

—ɯ—

4. Justice Benjamin R. Curtis on Black Citizenship, 1857

In his dissenting opinion in the Dred Scott *case, Justice Benjamin R. Curtis found ample evidence in the historical record that black Americans qualified as citizens. Exercising the franchise seemed to him one of the best signifiers of their citizenship status.*

To determine whether any free persons, descended from Africans held in slavery, were citizens of the United States under the Confederation, and consequently at the time of the adoption of the Constitution of the United States, it is only necessary to know whether any such persons were citizens of either of the States under the Confederation, at the time of the adoption of the Constitution.

Of this there can be no doubt. At the time of the ratification of the Articles of Confederation, all free native-born inhabitants of the States of New Hampshire, Massachusetts, New York, New Jersey, and North Carolina, though descended from African slaves, were not only citizens of those States, but such of them as had the other necessary qualifications possessed the franchise of electors, on equal terms with other citizens. . . .

I can find nothing in the Constitution which . . . deprives of their citizenship any class of persons who were citizens of the United States at the time of its adoption. . . . And my opinion is, that, under the Constitution of the United States, every free person born on the soil of a State, who is a citizen of that State by force of its Constitution or laws, is also a citizen of the United States. . . .

Though . . . I do not think the enjoyment of the elective franchise essential to citizenship, there can be no doubt it is one of the chiefest attributes of citizenship under the American Constitutions. . . . All such persons as are allowed by the Constitution to exercise the elective franchise, and thus, to participate in the Government of the United States, must be deemed citizens of the United States.

I dissent, therefore, from that part of the opinion of the majority of the court, in which it is held that a person of African descent cannot be a citizen of the United States.

Source: Dred Scott v. Sandford, 60 U.S. 393; 15 L. Ed. 691; 1856 U.S. Lexis 472; 19 How. 393.

—∞—

5. Justice Benjamin R. Curtis on Congressional Power over the Territories, 1857

In his dissent in Dred Scott, *Justice Benjamin R. Curtis broadly interpreted the "needful rules and regulations" clause of the Constitution. He found no constitutional rationale for excluding certain territories or for exempting slavery from its force.*

No reason has been suggested why any reluctance should have been felt, by the framers of the Constitution, to apply this provision to all the territory which might belong to the United States, or why any distinction should have been made, founded on the accidental circumstance of the dates of the cessions; a circumstance in no way material as respects the necessity for rules and regulations, or the propriety of conferring on the Congress power to make them. . . .

I construe this clause, therefore, as if it had read, Congress shall have power to make all needful rules and regulations respecting those tracts of country, out of the limits of the several States, which the United States have acquired, or may hereafter acquire, by cessions, as well of the jurisdiction as of the soil, so far as the soil may be the property of the party making the cession, at the time of making it. . . .

But it is insisted [by the majority], that whatever other powers Congress may have respecting the territory of the United States, the subject of negro slavery forms an exception.

The Constitution declares that Congress shall have power to make "all needful rules and regulations" respecting the territory belonging to the United States.

The assertion is, though the Constitution says all, it does not mean all—though it says all, without qualification, it means all except such as allow or prohibit slavery. . . .

If it can be shown, by anything in the Constitution itself, that when it confers on Congress the power to make all needful rules and regulations respecting the territory belonging to the United States, the exclusion or the allowance of slavery was excepted; or if anything in the history of this provision tends to show that such an exception was intended by those who framed and adopted the Constitution to be introduced into it, I hold it to be my duty carefully to consider, and to allow just weight to such considerations in interpreting the positive text of the Constitution. But where the Constitution has said all needful rules and regulations, I must find something more than theoretical reasoning to induce me to say it did not mean all.

Source: Dred Scott v. Sandford, 60 U.S. 393; 15 L. Ed. 691; 1856 U.S. Lexis 472; 19 How. 393.

—ɯ—

6. Horace Greeley on the *Dred Scott* Decision, 1857

Horace Greeley, editor of the New York Tribune, *lamented the* Dred Scott *decision. On March 11, 1857, just five days after the Supreme Court issued its ruling, he expressed fears that slavery would now spread unimpeded.*

It is impossible to exaggerate the importance of the recent decision of the Supreme Court. The grounds and methods of that decision we have exposed elsewhere; and we now turn from them to contemplate the great fact which it establishes—the fact that *Slavery is National;* and that, until that remote period when different Judges, sitting in this same Court, shall reverse this wicked and false judgment, the Constitution of the United States is nothing better than the bulwark of inhumanity and oppression.

It is most true that this decision is bad law; that it is based on false historical premises and wrong interpretations of the Constitution; that it does not at all represent the legal or judicial opinion of the Nation; that it is merely a Southern sophism clothed with the dignity of our highest Court. Nevertheless there it is; the final action of the National Judiciary, established by the founders of the Republic to interpret the Constitution, and to embody the ultimate legal conclusions of the whole people—an action proclaiming that in the view of the Constitution *slaves are property.* The inference is plain. If slaves are recognized as property by the Constitution, of course no local or State law can either prevent property being carried through an individual State or Territory, or forbid its being sold as such wherever its owner may choose to hold it. This is all involved in the present decision; but let a single case draw from the Court an official judgment that slaves can be held and protected under National law, and we shall see men buying slaves for the New York market. There will be no legal power to prevent it. At this moment, indeed, any wealthy New York jobber connected with the Southern trade can put in his next orders: "Send me a negro cook, at the lowest market value! Buy me a waiter! Balance my account with two chambermaids and a truckman!" ...

We have been accustomed to regard Slavery as a local matter for which we were in no wise responsible. As we have been used, to say, it belonged to the Southern States alone, and they must answer for it before the world. We can say this no more. Now, wherever the stars and stripes wave, they protect Slavery and represent Slavery. The black and cursed stain is thick on our hands also. From Maine to the Pacific, over all future conquests and annexations, wherever in the islands of western seas, or in the South American Continent, or in the Mexican Gulf, the flag of the Union, by just means or unjust, shall be planted, there it plants the curse, and tears, and blood, and unpaid toil of this "institution." The Star of Freedom and the stripes of bondage are henceforth one. American Republicanism and American Slavery are for the future synonymous. This, then, is the final fruit.

Source: New York Tribune, 11 March 1857, in David A. Copeland, comp., *The Antebellum Era: Primary Documents on Events from 1820 to 1860* (Westport, Conn.: Greenwood Press, 2003), 378–379.

—⁓—

7. Speech of Frederick Douglass, 1857

In May 1857, the fugitive slave and abolitionist Frederick Douglass offered his assessment of the Dred Scott *case. "As a man, an American, a citizen, a colored man of both Anglo-Saxon and African descent," he said, "I denounce this representation as a most scandalous and devilish perversion of the Constitution, and a brazen misstatement of the facts of history."*

This last settlement must be called the Taney settlement. We are now told, in tones of lofty exultation, that the day is lost all lost and that we might as well give up the struggle. The highest authority has spoken. The voice of the Supreme Court has gone out over the troubled waves of the National Conscience, saying peace, be still. . . .

I have no fear that the National Conscience will be put to sleep by such an open, glaring, and scandalous tissue of lies as that decision is, and has been, over and over, shown to be.

The Supreme Court of the United States is not the only power in this world. It is very great, but the Supreme Court of the Almighty is greater. Judge Taney can do many things, but he cannot perform impossibilities. . . . He may decide, and decide again; but he cannot reverse the decision of the Most High. He cannot change the essential nature of things—making evil good, and good evil. . . .

Your fathers have said that man's right to liberty is self-evident. . . . To decide against this right in the person of Dred Scott, or the humblest and most whip-scarred bondman in the land, is to decide against God. It is an open rebellion against God's government. . . .

Such a decision cannot stand. God will be true though every man be a liar. We can appeal from this hell-black judgment of the Supreme Court, to the court of common sense and common humanity. We can appeal from man to God. If there is no justice on earth, there is yet justice in heaven. You may close your Supreme Court against the black man's cry for justice, but you cannot, thank God, close against him the ear of a sympathising world, nor shut up the Court of Heaven. All that is merciful and just, on earth and in Heaven, will execrate and despise this edict of Taney. . . .

In one point of view, we, the abolitionists and colored people, should meet this decision, unlooked for and monstrous as it appears, in a cheerful spirit. This very attempt to blot out forever the hopes of an enslaved people may be one necessary link in the chain of events preparatory to the downfall and complete overthrow of the whole slave system.

Source: Two Speeches, By Frederick Douglass, One on West India Emancipation, Delivered at Canandaigua, Aug. 4th, and the Other on the Dred Scott Decision, Delivered in New York, on the Occasion of the Anniversary of the American Abolition Society, May, 1857 (Rochester, N.Y.: C. P. Dewey, 1857), 30–32.

—⚬—

8. Speech of Senator Stephen Douglas, 1858

Illinois senator Stephen Douglas believed popular sovereignty consistent with the Dred Scott *decision. In the following speech he delivered in Chicago on July 9, 1858, Douglas expressed his respect for the Supreme Court and criticized the Republican Party (and its senatorial candidate Abraham Lincoln) for its imputed belief in racial equality.*

I regard the great principle of popular sovereignty as having been vindicated and made triumphant in this land as a permanent rule of public policy in the organization of territories and the admission of new states. . . .

I have no warfare to make on the Supreme Court of the United States, either on account of that or any other decision which they have pronounced from that bench. . . . What security have you for your property, for your reputation, and for your personal rights, if the courts are not upheld, and their decisions respected when once firmly rendered by the highest tribunal known to the Constitution? I do not choose, therefore, to go into any argument with Mr. Lincoln in reviewing the various decisions which the Supreme Court has made, either upon the Dred Scott case, or any other. . . .

The reason assigned by Mr. Lincoln for resisting the decision of the Supreme Court in the Dred Scott case does not in itself meet my approbation. He objects to it because that decision declared that a negro descended from African parents who were brought here and sold as slaves is not, and cannot be a citizen of the United States. He says it is wrong, because it deprives the negro of the benefits of that clause of the Constitution which says that citizens of one state shall enjoy all the privileges and immunities of citizens of the several states. . . . I am free to say to you that in my opinion this government of ours is founded on the white basis. It was made by the white man, for the benefit of the white man, to be administered by white men, in such manner as they should determine. . . .

Mr. Lincoln goes for a warfare upon the Supreme Court of the United States, because of their judicial decision in the Dred Scott case. I yield obedience to the decisions of that Court—to the final determination of the highest judicial tribunal known to our Constitution. He objects to the Dred Scott decision because it does not put the negro in the possession of the rights of citizenship on an equality with the white man. I am opposed to negro equality. I repeat that this nation is a white people . . . and I am in favor of preserving not only the purity of the blood, but the purity of the government from any mixture or amalgamation with inferior races.

Source: Paul M. Angle, ed., *Created Equal? The Complete Lincoln-Douglas Debates of 1858* (Chicago: University of Chicago Press, 1958), 14, 20–23.

—〰—

9. Speech of Abraham Lincoln, 1857

The following excerpts are abstracted from a speech Illinois Republican Abraham Lincoln delivered in the state capital of Springfield on June 26, 1857. In it, Lincoln countered Democrat Stephen Douglas's portrayal of Republican principles with his own nuanced view of the meaning of equality.

There is a natural disgust in the minds of nearly all white people, to the idea of an indiscriminate amalgamation of the white and black races . . .

[Stephen Douglas] finds the Republicans insisting that the Declaration of Independence includes ALL men, black as well as white; and forthwith he boldly denies that it includes negroes at all, and proceeds to argue gravely that all who contend it does, do so only because they want to vote, and eat, and sleep, and marry with negroes! He will have it that they cannot be consistent else. Now I protest against that counterfeit logic which concludes that, because I do not want a black woman for a *slave* I must necessarily want her for a *wife*. I need not have her for either, I can just leave her alone. In some respects she certainly is not my equal; but in her natural right to eat the bread she earns with her own hands without asking leave of any one else, she is my equal, and the equal of all others.

Chief Justice Taney, in his opinion in the Dred Scott case, admits that the language of the Declaration is broad enough to include the whole human family, but he and Judge Douglas argue that authors of that instrument did not intend to include negroes, by the fact that they did not at once, actually place them on an equality with the whites. . . . And this is the staple argument of both the Chief Justice and the Senator, for doing this obvious violence to the plain, unmistakable language of the Declaration. I think the authors of that notable instrument intended to include *all* men, but they did not intend to declare all men equal *in all respects*. They did not mean to say all were equal in color, size, intellect, moral developments, or social capacity. They defined with tolerable distinctness, in what respects they did consider all men created equal—equal in "certain inalienable rights, among which are life, liberty, and the pursuit of happiness." This they said, and this meant. They did not mean to assert the obvious untruth, that all were then actually enjoying that equality, nor yet, that they were about to confer it immediately upon them. In fact they had no power to confer such a boon. They meant simply to declare the *right*, so that the *enforcement* of it might allow as fast as circumstances should permit. They meant to set up a standard maxim for free society, which could be familiar to all, and revered by all; constantly looked to, constantly labored for, and even though never perfectly attained, constantly approximated, and thereby constantly spreading and deepening its influence, and augmenting the happiness and value of life to all people of all colors everywhere. . . .

But Judge Douglas is especially horrified at the thought of the mixing of blood by the white and black races: agreed for once—a thousand times agreed. There are white men enough to marry all the white women, and black men enough to marry all the black women; and so let them be married. On this point we fully agree with the Judge; and when he shall show that his policy is better adapted to prevent amalgamation than ours we shall drop ours, and adopt his.

Source: Abraham Lincoln, *Speeches and Writings 1832–1858: Speeches, Letters, and Miscellaneous Writings: The Lincoln-Douglas Debates* (New York: Library of America, 1989), 397–398, 400.

—ᴍ—

10. Third Annual Message of President Buchanan, 1859

Though from Pennsylvania, President James Buchanan consistently pursued political alliances with the South. He believed concessions to the South were necessary to preserve the Union. His Republican critics contemptuously labeled him a "doughface" for kowtowing to southern, proslavery interests. In his third annual message to Congress, delivered December 19, 1859, Buchanan spoke optimistically that the question of slavery in the territories was fully resolved. He also challenged the principle of popular sovereignty that Stephen Douglas upheld, arguing that not only Congress but also territorial legislatures were now powerless to restrict slavery.

I cordially congratulate you upon the final settlement, by the Supreme Court of the United States, of the question of slavery in the Territories, which had presented an aspect so truly formidable at the commencement of my administration. The right has been established of every citizen to take his property of any kind, including slaves, into the common Territories belonging equally to all the States of the confederacy, and to have it protected there under the Federal Constitution. Neither Congress, nor a territorial legislature, nor any human power, has any authority to annul or impair this vested right. The supreme judicial tribunal of the country, which is a coördinate branch of the government, has sanctioned and affirmed these principles of constitutional law, so manifestly just in themselves, and so well calculated to promote peace and harmony among the States. It is a striking proof of the sense of justice which is inherent in our people, that the property in slaves has never been disturbed, to my knowledge, in any of the Territories. . . . Had it been decided that either Congress or the territorial legislature possess the power to annul or impair the right to property in slaves, the evil would be intolerable. . . .

Thus has the status of a Territory, during the intermediate period from its first settlement until it shall become a State, been irrevocably fixed by the final decision of the Supreme Court. Fortunate has this been for the prosperity of the Territories, as well as the tranquillity of the States.

Source: John Bassett Moore, ed., *The Works of James Buchanan Comprising His Speeches, State Papers, and Private Correspondence,* vol. 10 (New York: Antiquarian Press, 1960), 341–342.

11

SLAVERY AND THE CIVIL WAR:
Should Northern Military Forces Accept Fugitive Slaves Who Flee to Union Lines?

—ɯ—

THE CONTROVERSY

The Issue

During the Civil War, thousands of African-American slaves escaped from their masters and sought refuge with northern (Union) military forces. Should northern armies accept fugitive slaves who flee to their lines or send them back to their masters?

- ♦ *Arguments in favor of accepting fugitive slaves who flee to Union lines:* Early in the Civil War, some military commanders for the North willingly accepted runaway slaves who sought refuge in their camps. Since the states of the Confederacy had seceded, they argued, the Fugitive Slave Act of 1850 requiring the return of runaways no longer applied. Slaves constituted a military resource exploited by the South that could be appropriated for Northern benefit. They could offer not only their labor but also valuable information about the enemy and the surrounding area. Furthermore, Union soldiers did not take to the battlefield for the purpose of restoring runaway slaves to their masters. Sending fugitives back would violate the humanitarian sensibilities of many Northerners participating in the conflict.

- ♦ *Arguments against accepting fugitive slaves who flee to Union lines:* Some Union military leaders shunned fugitive slaves who fled to their camps. They regarded the runaways as useless, burdensome, and potentially even subversive to the Union cause. Existing laws called for the return of fugitive slaves to their masters, and since the Civil War was not a war of liberation, Northern commanders ought to comply. At the very least, Northern forces should return the enslaved property of masters loyal to the Union. Politically, such a policy would serve to conciliate the border states, whose allegiance hung in the balance.

—ɯ—

INTRODUCTION

After the election of Abraham Lincoln as president in 1860, South Carolina led a parade of Southern states down the path to secession, forming the Confederate States of America in February 1861. Two months later, the Civil War broke out between North and South. As the Confederacy fought for its independence from the United States, the North, President Lincoln declared at the beginning of the war, was fighting to preserve the Union, to reunify the house divided. However much slavery contributed to the schism between North and South, Lincoln, early in the war, denied that the conflict was a war of liberation for American slaves. As late as August 22, 1862, he explained to editor Horace Greeley of the New York *Tribune*, "My paramount object in this struggle is to save the Union, and is *not* either to save or to destroy slavery. If I could save the Union without freeing *any* slave I would do it, and if I could save it by freeing *all* the slaves I would do it; and if I could save it by freeing some and leaving others alone, I would also do that."[1] Only one month later, however, Lincoln issued the preliminary Emancipation Proclamation, which redefined the war as a struggle over slavery.

The slaves themselves had contributed to the president's shifting political course. From the early days of the Civil War, slaves fled their masters to seek refuge with Union troops. Taking advantage of wartime opportunities, they used their feet to join the soldiers dressed in blue uniforms in an effort to liberate themselves. Slaves' agency demanded a response from the U.S. government, yet Congress proved slow to pass authoritative legislation concerning fugitive slaves to Union lines. As a result, Northern military commanders pursued their own individual preferences in dealing with runaways. The ad hoc decision-making process produced confusion within the ranks of the U.S. military.

Those Union officers who welcomed fugitive slaves into camp believed themselves justified. Since the states of the Confederacy had seceded from the Union, the Fugitive Slave Act of 1850 that mandated the restoration of runaways to their owners was inapplicable. Refusing to

---

[1] Abraham Lincoln, *Speeches and Writings, 1859–1865: Speeches, Letters, and Miscellaneous Writings, Presidential Messages, and Proclamations* (New York: Library of America, 1989), 358.

As the Civil War progressed, President Abraham Lincoln's Emancipation Proclamation transformed the conflict into a war of liberation for Southern slaves. (Library of Congress)

return fugitive slaves also stole an important source of labor away from the Confederacy while augmenting the Union's own human resources. Runaway slaves not only worked for the Union but also supplied useful information about local areas unfamiliar to invading Northern armies. As the war progressed, growing numbers of Northern soldiers objected to the return of fugitive slaves. Considerations of humanity demanded that they offer safe haven for runaways.

Other commanders preferred not to aid fugitive slaves who sought refuge with Union forces. For some, slaves seemed lazy, indolent, and unhelpful. They proved burdensome by depleting the army's provisions as well. More disconcerting still, some military leaders feared that blacks masquerading as fugitive slaves might be serving as Confederate spies. For them, it seemed wise to honor slaveholder property rights guaranteed in the Fifth Amendment to the U.S. Constitution, the Fugitive Slave Act of 1850, and various state laws. The Union army was not mustered in to free slaves but to follow through on President Lincoln's limited aim of preserving the Union. Strategically, pressing the slavery issue threatened to alienate the border states, drive them to the Confederacy, and undermine the Union cause.

BACKGROUND

The long-simmering tensions between North and South boiled over in the 1860s. In the presidential election of 1860, Republican candidate Abraham Lincoln defeated three challengers—Northern Democrat Stephen A. Douglas, Southern Democrat John C. Breckinridge, and Constitutional Union Party candidate John Bell—with less than 40 percent of the overall vote. Lincoln's electoral support was exclusively from the North, signifying to the South its political subjugation. Before the year was out, and months before Lincoln ever took office, South Carolina became the first state to sever its ties to the Union. By February 1861, six other Deep South states followed South Carolina's lead and seceded. Together, they formed the Confederate States of America, electing Mississippi's Jefferson Davis president. In April, the recently formed Confederate government resolved to prevent the resupply of Fort Sumter, a federal garrison in South Carolina, because the South could not tolerate a "foreign" military installation on Confederate soil. When Confederate guns fired on Fort Sumter on April 12, the Civil War began. By the middle of May, four additional Southern states cast their lot with the Confederacy.

Throughout the War Between the States, slaves fled to the invading Union forces. War was conducive to flight. Many slaves absconded from masters or overseers absent from the plantation while fighting in the

In May 1861, General Benjamin F. Butler declared runaway slaves to the Union camp at Fort Monroe, Virginia, "contraband of war." (Library of Congress)

Confederate army. The wartime breakdown of plantation discipline set the stage for the slaves' escape. Some fugitives were evading service for the Confederacy, such as driving teams or building fortifications. Some fled malnourishment. Amid the chaos and disruption of war, the proximity of Union troops made flight a risk worth taking. Whether they walked, ran, or arrived by canoe or small boat, fugitive slaves escaped to

Union lines seeking safety and protection and perhaps liberation. Desertions even preceded the firing on Fort Sumter. In March 1861, eight fugitives descended upon Fort Pickens, Florida, "entertaining the idea," reported Lieutenant Adam J. Slemmer, "that we were placed here to protect them and grant them their freedom."[2] In what must have been a crushing disappointment to the fugitives, Slemmer handed them over to the local authorities to return them to their owners. Two months later, however, three slaves belonging to Charles Mallory, a Confederate colonel, met with a different result when they sought asylum at the Union's Fort Monroe, near Hampton Roads, Virginia. General Benjamin F. Butler refused to restore the fugitives to their master. Thus, very early in the war, Union commanders in the field confronted the dilemma of runaway slaves fleeing to their encampments. As the contrasting actions of Slemmer and Butler reveal, they divided over the proper policy to pursue. From 1861 to 1862, as growing numbers of fugitives flocked to the men in blue uniforms, bond people themselves forced the question, Should Northern military forces accept fugitive slaves who fled to Union lines?

THE DEBATE

The Case that Northern Military Forces Should Accept Fugitive Slaves

General Benjamin F. Butler's pioneering refusal to return fugitive slaves to their masters set a precedent that others in the U.S. military followed. Like Butler, General Abner Doubleday, Colonel Harvey Brown, and Major George E. Waring, Jr., accepted fugitive slaves into their camps. Butler gave multiple reasons for retaining runaways. In addition to denying the applicability of the Fugitive Slave Act, he emphasized the theme of military necessity. Keeping fugitive slaves robbed the Confederacy of manpower as it augmented the Union's own. Doubleday valued the intelligence and knowledge that slaves supplied. Moral and ethical concerns also entered the discussion. Abolitionists in the North such as Frederick Douglass and Governor John A. Andrew of Massachusetts

---

[2] *The War of the Rebellion: A Compilation of the Official Records of the Union and Confederate Armies,* ser. 2, vol. 1 (Washington, D.C.: Government Printing Office, 1894), 750.

resented the use of Union troops to return fugitive slaves to bondage. Union commanders possessing antislavery sentiments recognized the injustice of delivering runaways to their masters and refused on humanitarian grounds to surrender them.

Although the Fugitive Slave Act of 1850 remained federal law at the beginning of the Civil War, General Butler argued that it no longer applied in Virginia and the other Southern states that had seceded from the Union. In his mind, the Confederacy qualified as "a foreign country." When fugitive slaves from Virginia arrived at Butler's camp, therefore, he felt no "constitutional obligation" to return the runaways to their master. Such was the consequence of Virginia's defection to the Confederacy. Butler noted that fugitives from Maryland had been returned to their owners, but that was because Maryland, unlike Virginia, had remained loyal to the Union. The Fugitive Slave Act could only be considered valid within the United States. Butler offered to return the slaves who had fled to his camp, but only "if their master would come to the fort and take the oath of allegiance to the Constitution of the United States."[3]

More practically, Butler viewed the retention of fugitive slaves in Union camps as a means to deprive the Confederacy of a valuable source of labor. When questioned, the three fugitives to Butler's camp in May 1861 informed him that they "were about to be taken to Carolina for the purpose of aiding the secession forces there." One had fled "from fear that he would be called upon to take part in the rebel armies." Southern forces often employed slaves at constructing fortifications. According to Butler, "the negroes in this neighborhood are now being employed in the erection of batteries and other works by the rebels which it would be nearly or quite impossible to construct without their labor." Just days later, Butler reported from Fort Monroe that a dozen fugitive slaves in his camp "escaped from the batteries on Sewall's Point. . . . Without them the batteries could not have been erected, at least for many weeks." Consequently, the general concluded, "it would seem to be a measure of necessity to deprive their masters of their services." Military "necessity," in short, justified Butler's refusal to return fugitive slaves.[4] (See "Letter, Benjamin F. Butler to Winfield Scott, 1861," on page 422 in the Primary Sources section.)

---

[3] *War of the Rebellion*, ser. 2, vol. 1, 752.
[4] *War of the Rebellion*, ser. 2, vol. 1, 752, 754.

The corollary of not surrendering fugitive slaves to their rebel masters was the appropriation of their labor by Union forces. "Shall they [the Confederates] be allowed the use of this property against the United States and we not be allowed its use in aid of the United States?" Butler asked. The general confessed a "great need of labor in my quartermaster's department" and, recognizing runaway slaves' military value, welcomed their services. Cleverly, Butler declared the fugitives "contraband of war," turning the term *contraband* into a synonym for a

Early in the Civil War, Northern commanders did not abide by a uniform or consistent policy toward fugitive slaves who fled their masters to Union lines. (Library of Congress)

runaway slave. Defining runaways as property the Confederacy could use to wage war against the North permitted him to retain possession of the fugitives and work them instead for the benefit of the Union. Contraband slaves—human property—satisfied the Union's desperate need for labor. Butler's policy toward fugitive slaves gained the support of Secretary of War Simon Cameron, who stated that the Union could not "afford to send them forward to their masters to be by them armed against us or used in producing supplies to sustain the rebellion." Runaway slaves, Cameron continued, "constitute a military resource," and "their labor may be useful to us": "that they should not be turned over to the enemy is too plain to discuss."[5] (See the sidebar "Black soldiers in the Union Army" on page 404.)

Fugitive slaves offered the Union advantages other than labor. As General Abner Doubleday explained, they supplied information unavailable from other sources. Contraband slaves revealed the locations and strength of enemy forces, pinpointed Confederate hideouts, and identified "traitors" and "rebel organizations." Union officials sometimes credited slaves for sharing the intelligence that prevented ambushes and defeats. Fugitives also gave the Union knowledge of the

---

[5] *War of the Rebellion,* ser. 2, vol. 1, 752, 783.

BLACK SOLDIERS IN THE UNION ARMY

For President Lincoln, officials in his cabinet, and a number of his military commanders, employing fugitive slaves in Union camps and arming them to fight the Confederacy were two starkly different matters. In a letter written on October 14, 1861, Secretary of War Simon Cameron permitted General Thomas W. Sherman to work slaves for the Union cause. "This, however," he added, "[is] not to mean a general arming of them for military service." Lincoln and others feared that any weapons placed in the hands of slaves would soon fall into the possession of the rebel army. The president's reluctance to wage war with black troops failed to stop General David Hunter, in command of the Department of the South. Hunter created an uproar in May 1862 when, without authorization, he began arming fugitive slaves, organizing the First South Carolina Colored Regiment of black Union troops to compensate for a shortage of manpower. With slaveholding constituents alarmed at the potentially liberating implications of Hunter's scheme, border-state representative Charles A. Wickliffe of Kentucky pressed the new secretary of war, Edwin M. Stanton, for information about government policy on arming blacks. When Stanton demanded an explanation of Hunter, the general replied sardonically that the blacks he had armed were not fugitive slaves; rather, their masters were "fugitive rebels" who had fled the Union advance, leaving their slaves behind. Amusing to some and infuriating to others, Hunter's reply to the secretary of war did not persuade the administration, and his experiment with black soldiers abruptly ended.

Nevertheless, by mid-1862, the North's use of black troops was gradually becoming a legitimate possibility. On August 25, 1862, Secretary of

local terrain, roads, paths, and byways, making them able guides for Yankee forces in unfamiliar territory. For Doubleday, it seemed foolish to cast aside such a potentially valuable resource as runaway slaves to Union lines. (See "Letter, E. P. Halsted to John D. Shaul, 1862," on page 423 in the Primary Sources section.)

Northern abolitionists pointed out that Union troops were not fighting for the purpose of returning fugitive slaves. Frederick Douglass condemned the way in which some in the U.S. military "performed the disgusting duty of slave dogs to hunt down slaves for rebel masters."

War Stanton granted formal permission to Rufus Saxton, Hunter's replacement in the Department of the South, to arm blacks in South Carolina. Lincoln was slow to approve the use of black soldiers but by early 1863, desperate for soldiers, welcomed them into Union service. As he explained in March to Andrew Johnson, military governor of Tennessee, the mere sight of armed and trained black soldiers was the stuff of Southern white nightmares. By August 1863, Lincoln was crediting U.S. colored troops with contributing to Union military successes. By that point, black soldiers had played significant roles at the Battles of Port Hudson, Milliken's Bend, and especially Fort Wagner. The most famous black regiment of the Civil War, the 54th Massachusetts, fought valiantly at the unsuccessful assault upon Fort Wagner, South Carolina, in July 1863. The 54th's heroics became the basis for the movie *Glory* (1989), starring actor Matthew Broderick as Robert Gould Shaw, the white colonel who died leading the 54th Massachusetts into battle. (Two sons of runaway slave and abolitionist Frederick Douglass also fought in the 54th.) By December 1863, some 100,000 black troops fought for the Union. At war's end, approximately 180,000 African Americans had donned Union blue; of them, roughly 110,000 were former slaves. Responding to those opposed to the emancipation of slaves, Lincoln pointedly reminded his critics, "You say you will not fight to free negroes. Some of them seem willing to fight for you."*

* *War of the Rebellion,* ser. 2, vol. 1, 773; Lincoln quoted in Phillip Shaw Paludan, *The Presidency of Abraham Lincoln* (Lawrence: University Press of Kansas, 1994), 222.

Abolitionist and Massachusetts governor John A. Andrew shared Douglass's outrage. In November 1861, "several negroes" in Maryland innocently "selling cakes, pies, &c., to the soldiers" one Sunday morning were arrested and escorted back to their owners. In response, Andrew fired off an irate letter to Secretary of War Cameron to decry the "dirty and despotic work" his state's soldiers were required to do in restoring the slaves to their masters. "Massachusetts does not send her citizens forth," Andrew fumed, "to become the hunters of men or to engage in the seizure and return to captivity of persons claimed to be fugitive slaves." He considered the order to deliver runaways to their masters an affront to the honor and dignity of Yankee troops.[6]

Humanitarian considerations forbade some in the military to become accessories to slavery. They could not stomach fugitive slaves' return to bondage. As Colonel Harvey Brown declared in June 1861, "I shall not send the negroes back as I will never be voluntarily instrumental in returning a poor wretch to slavery." Navy Secretary Gideon Welles agreed: "It is not the policy of the Government to invite or encourage . . . desertions, and yet, under the circumstances, no other course . . . could be adopted without violating every principle of humanity." Returning fugitive slaves, he wrote, "would be impolitic as well as cruel." "Humanity," echoed General John E. Wool, "requires that they should be taken care of." Not all high-ranking officials agreed, but after General Henry W. Halleck issued a decree excluding fugitive slaves from Union lines in his department, a resolution introduced in the U.S. House of Representatives—ultimately tabled on December 11, 1861—condemned the order as "cruel and inhuman" and requested its repeal. Commenting on Halleck's order, Major George E. Waring, Jr., wrote bluntly, "my private feelings revolt."[7]

Waring's objections to Halleck's refusal to accept fugitive slaves into Union camps were not entirely humanitarian. Although concerned about the "hardship" slaves would suffer if turned away from Union lines, like others, he understood that Northern armies would suffer in the absence of their labor. At the very least, contraband slaves' value to the Union military effort promoted "an interest" in the fugitives' "welfare." Waring thus suggested a mutuality in the relationship between Northern troops and runaway slaves. Each needed the other. Fugitive slaves benefited from Union protection, while the Union benefited from contraband labor. In just one brief letter, Waring succinctly recapitulated the many reasons for welcoming fugitive slaves into Union camps. (See "Letter, George E. Waring, Jr., to Alexander Asboth, 1861," on page 424 in the Primary Sources section.)

---

[6] John W. Blassingame, ed., *The Frederick Douglass Papers*, ser. 1, vol. 3 (New Haven, Conn.: Yale University Press, 1985), 595; *War of the Rebellion*, ser. 2, vol. 1, 784.

[7] *War of the Rebellion*, ser. 2, vol. 1, 755; *Official Records of the Union and Confederate Navies in the War of the Rebellion*, ser. 1, vol. 6 (Washington, D.C.: Government Printing Office, 1896), 10; *War of the Rebellion*, ser. 2, vol. 1, 771, 784, 790.

The Case that Northern Military Forces Should Not Accept Fugitive Slaves

Some Union commanders had no intention of entangling Northern armies with the thorny problem of runaway slaves. On July 17, 1861, Joseph K. Mansfield of the Department of Washington issued General Order No. 33, stating, "Fugitive slaves will under no pretext whatever be permitted to reside or be in any way harbored in the quarters and camps of the troops serving in this department. Neither will such slaves be allowed to accompany troops on the march." In the Department of the Missouri, General Halleck's General Order No. 3, of November 20, declared that no fugitive slave shall "be hereafter permitted to enter the lines of any camp or of any forces on the march." Furthermore, he added, "any now within such lines [must] be immediately excluded therefrom." In August 1862, General John A. Dix, commanding the Department of Virginia, explained to a captain under his command, "You are under no obligation to receive negroes within your lines, indeed they should be kept out," having "no business" there.[8] Generals Thomas W. Sherman, George B. McClellan, and others likewise cautioned against aiding fugitive slaves.

General Sherman disputed the claim that fugitive slaves positively augmented the Union labor force; rather, he characterized them as virtually useless. The experiment in "negro labor," he declared in December 1861, "is so far almost a failure." Sherman discerned the reasons why: "They [fugitive slaves] are disinclined to labor and will evidently not work to our satisfaction without those aids to which they have ever been accustomed, viz, the driver and the lash." In Sherman's estimation, for lazy blacks, the "sudden change of condition from servitude to apparent freedom is more than their intellects can stand." He elaborated upon his point in a letter dated December 15, predicting that the slaves would not work until forced by desperate circumstances. Finally, Sherman added, "for every able-bodied male" among the fugitive slave population there were also a number of women, children, and "decrepit" slaves entirely unsuitable for labor.[9] (See "Letter of Thomas W. Sherman, 1861," on page 424 in the Primary Sources section.)

---

[8] *War of the Rebellion*, ser. 2, vol. 1, 760, 778; *War of the Rebellion*, ser. 2, vol. 4, 359.

[9] *War of the Rebellion*, ser. 2, vol. 1, 785–786.

Some military leaders considered fugitive slaves not a blessing for the Union cause but an unwelcome burden. Generals John A. Dix and Alexander McD. McCook each called them an "annoyance." The stampede of runaways to Union forces created logistical problems and interfered with the completion of military objectives. Fugitive slaves' drain on the North's rations proved acute not only on land but also aboard Union vessels. O. S. Glisson, commanding the USS *Mount Vernon* in Virginia's Rappahannock River, reported in August 1861 that the fugitive slaves onboard were "consuming our provisions and water faster than I think is desirable." William A. Parker of the USS *Cambridge* likewise complained that the "large number of contrabands on board" his ship "are rapidly consuming the provisions of this vessel, and it is very inconvenient to keep them here any longer, most of them being dirty, ragged, and lousy." With more than 40 contrabands under his command in need of rations, Lieutenant A. D. Harrell of the USS *Union* confessed that "it is becoming very embarrassing to me, short of provisions as I am. . . . I think it would be a good stroke of policy to return these negroes to their owners. It would tend to put a stop to the wholesale desertion that is now going on, and relieve us of a most unpleasant difficulty." Space constraints aboard Union ships compounded the difficulties posed by fugitive slaves. Off Roanoke Island, North Carolina, L. M. Goldsborough declared that "it is absolutely impossible for us to accommodate more contrabands on board of our already crowded little vessels." In February 1862, he ordered "that no more of them are to be received on board any vessel of the Navy now in these waters."[10]

More than a mere inconvenience, however, fugitive slaves might seriously undermine the Union war effort. Military leaders needed to exercise caution in their dealings with runaways to Union lines. Fugitives sometimes gave Union forces news that was not always reliable or trustworthy, and in the context of wartime, acting on misinformation could produce tragic results. When a fugitive slave related intelligence to William Budd of the USS *Resolute* in August 1861, the commander smelled deception. "I am of the opinion that he is a spy or trap of some kind," Budd wrote.

---

[10] *War of the Rebellion*, ser. 2, vol. 4, 359; *War of the Rebellion*, ser. 2, vol. 1, 776; *Official Records of the Union and Confederate Navies*, ser. 1, vol. 6, 107, 424; *Official Records of the Union and Confederate Navies in the War of the Rebellion*, ser. 1, vol. 4 (Washington, D.C.: Government Printing Office, 1896), 748; *Official Records of the Union and Confederate Navies*, ser. 1, vol. 6, 650.

The fear that ostensible fugitives might in fact be serving as Confederate spies informed General Halleck's General Order No. 3, which excluded runaways from Union camps in the Department of the Missouri. As Halleck explained, "important information respecting the numbers and condition of our forces is conveyed to the enemy by means of fugitive slaves who are admitted within our lines." The general also resented masters snooping around in Union camps in search of fugitive slaves. General Order No. 3 put a stop to a practice that Halleck considered disruptive for the troops and detrimental to the broader Northern cause.[11]

At the start of the Civil War, the law favored Southern masters' claims to their fugitive slaves. First, the Fifth Amendment protected slaveholders' property in human beings, and many Union soldiers were ordered "to respect private property" and "send back to the farm the negroes . . . troops brought away." Second, the Fugitive Slave Act of 1850 remained in force. Obedience to the law mandated that the North return runaways on the master's claim. And third, state laws regarding the return of fugitive slaves also applied. As General William Tecumseh Sherman wrote while in Louisville in October 1861, "The laws of the United States and of Kentucky all of which are binding on us compel us to surrender a runaway negro on application of negro's owner or agent." Referring to his General Order No. 3 from November, General Halleck explained his opposition to Union soldiers serving as either "negro-catchers" or "negro-stealers." By "keeping fugitive slaves out of our camps," refusing to interfere in the master-slave relationship, and leaving questions concerning slavery for civil authorities, Halleck believed he was avoiding a host of complications.[12] (See "Letter, Henry W. Halleck to Alexander Asboth, 1861," on page 425 in the Primary Sources section.)

Generals John A. Dix and George B. McClellan each emphasized repeatedly in 1861 that the North's exclusive war aim was to preserve the Union. "Our mission is to uphold the Government against treasonable attempts to subvert it," Dix declared, and nothing more. Only those suffering under "delusions" believed the war was about slavery. Hence, Dix explained, "We would not meddle with the slaves even of secessionists . . . We have nothing to do with slaves; . . . we are neither negro-stealers nor negro-catchers, and . . . we should send them away if they

---

[11] *Official Records of the Union and Confederate Navies,* ser. 1, vol. 4, 629; *War of the Rebellion,* ser. 2, vol. 1, 778.

[12] *War of the Rebellion,* ser. 2, vol. 1, 760, 774, 796.

came to us." Accordingly, when three runaway slaves from Anne Arundel County, Maryland, reached Fort McHenry, Dix "declined to receive them into the fort on the ground that I could neither harbor them as fugitives from service nor arrest them for the purpose of restoring them to their masters." Dix authorized taking into custody only blacks accused of crimes, and even then they would be handed over to civilian authorities.[13] (See "Letter, John A. Dix to George B. McClellan, 1861," on page 425 in the Primary Sources section.)

Whereas Dix preferred the wholesale exclusion of fugitive slaves from Union camps, other military leaders drew finer distinctions. Many discriminated between slaves of disloyal Confederate masters and those belonging to slaveholders still faithful to the Union. They promised loyal masters that, with evidence or proof of ownership, their enslaved property would be restored to them. At Camp Upton, Virginia, where slaves had fled from Rockville, Maryland, General Robert C. Schenck vowed that his "camp will not be permitted . . . to be made a harbor for escaping slaves": "persons owing labor or service to loyal citizens of loyal States if they resort to us shall always be surrendered when demanded on proper order or authority by the lawful owner or his representatives." General McClellan likewise assured "the Union men of Western Virginia" in May 1861 that his army would not interfere with their slaves.[14]

The willingness of some Union commanders to return runaways of loyal masters was a strategic decision. "You should not let them [fugitive slaves] take refuge in camp," General William Tecumseh Sherman wrote General McCook in November 1861. "It forms a source of misrepresentation by which Union men are estranged from our cause." Halleck similarly feared that the act of admitting fugitive slaves into Union camps was "liable to be misrepresented and misunderstood" as an attack upon slavery itself and consequently push loyal slaveholders to the Confederacy. Most Unionist slaveholders lived in the critical border states of Maryland, Kentucky, and Missouri. Though home to slaveholders, those states had not joined the Confederacy, and President Lincoln wanted it to remain that way. Union commanders in the border states therefore frequently returned fugitive slaves to loyal masters in order to cultivate sentiment favorable to the Union and keep them within the fold. Refusing

---

[13] *War of the Rebellion,* ser. 2, vol. 1, 775, 763, 766.
[14] *War of the Rebellion,* ser. 2, vol. 1, 756, 753.

to harbor fugitive slaves helped prevent the alienation of the border states from the Union. General Dix's policy of turning away fugitive slaves in the Department of Virginia was intended "to avoid all cause of complaint on the part of the citizens of Maryland in regard to any interference with their rights of property especially in slaves knowing how sensitive they are on this subject." McClellan's major concern was Kentucky, a Southern-leaning state with only tenuous ties to the Union. Agitating the slavery issue there might embolden Confederate sympathizers and prompt Kentucky's secession. (See "Letter, George B. McClellan to D. C. Buell, 1861," on page 426 in the Primary Sources section.) General Ulysses S. Grant ordered that any fugitive slaves found in camp at Kentucky's Fort Holt be "expelled" and their accomplices in the army punished.[15]

As Grant explained, Union soldiers' "private views" on the subject of slavery were irrelevant.[16] For a variety of reasons, the Union army could not offer safe haven for runaways. Their value as laborers was exaggerated, they consumed scarce rations needed by Northern troops, and they might even infiltrate camp as covert agents of the Confederacy. The U.S. Constitution, the Fugitive Slave Act, and various state laws all required the return of runaway slaves. Furthermore, slavery was incidental to the war itself, so the Union had no authority to withhold bond people from their masters, especially those siding with the North. Politically, the border states merited special consideration. Any Union agitation on the slavery issue might drive them to the Confederacy.

OUTCOME AND IMPACT

Fugitive slaves inundated Union lines throughout the Civil War. By late summer 1861, some 1,500 runaways had arrived at Fort Monroe, Virginia, alone. At Port Royal, South Carolina, 150 contrabands showed up in only two days in November of the same year. Historian Allen C. Guelzo estimates that somewhere between 60,000 and 200,000 contrabands and runaways—as much as 5 percent of the total slave population—were in possession of the Union by September 1862. By the time the war drew to a close in 1865, several hundred thousand slaves, perhaps one-fifth of the whole, had sought refuge with Union troops.

---

[15] *War of the Rebellion*, ser. 2, vol. 1, 777, 799, 772–773, 794.
[16] *War of the Rebellion*, ser. 2, vol. 1, 794.

Union forces divided, however, over the advisability of accepting fugitive slaves into their camps.[17]

Benjamin F. Butler's contraband policy met with the approval of Secretary of War Simon Cameron on May 30, 1861. Rather than surrender fugitive slaves to rebellious masters, Cameron saw the wisdom in putting them to work for the Union. He instructed Butler to keep accounts for each runaway. Butler's bookkeeping listed the fugitives' names, documented the value of their labor, and deducted expenses for the clothing and rations they consumed. Other Union officers followed Butler's lead. Although they were supposed to pay wages to their contraband laborers, in various places, runaways received little compensation or were unpaid. Under the Butler plan, fugitive slaves' ultimate fate remained murky. "The question of their final disposition," wrote Secretary Cameron of the fugitives, "will be reserved for future determination."[18]

Although Butler declared fugitive slaves contraband of war in May 1861, the Union adopted no firm, consistent, or uniform military policy early in the war. The U.S. government instead left the fate of fugitive slaves to the discretion of individual military commanders. Depending upon their personal political views, Union leaders might opt to send runaways back to their masters, as they commonly did in 1861 and early 1862. The lack of government direction resulted in a patchwork, haphazard, and improvised series of decisions rather than a formal policy per se. Even then, Union soldiers whose attitudes toward slavery conflicted with those of their superiors sometimes disobeyed orders. One pro-Union civilian in Missouri commended Henry Halleck's order prohibiting fugitives from Union camps but informed the general that "your orders are not obeyed here." Defiantly, some soldiers under Halleck's command secreted runaways and made the recovery of fugitive slaves difficult if not impossible, physically threatening masters or uncooperatively giving them the runaround when they searched Union camps.[19]

Congress at last weighed in on the issue of fugitive slaves in Union camps in summer 1861. In July, the House of Representatives adopted a resolution introduced by abolitionist Owen Lovejoy of Illinois stating that "it is no part of the duty of the soldiers of the United States

---

[17] Allen C. Guelzo, *Lincoln's Emancipation Proclamation: The End of Slavery in America* (New York: Simon & Schuster, 2004), 212.

[18] *War of the Rebellion*, ser. 2, vol. 1, 755.

[19] *War of the Rebellion*, ser. 2, vol. 1, 780.

to capture and return fugitive slaves." The measure passed by a vote of 93 to 55 but was nonbinding and did not establish policy.[20] On August 6, however, Congress passed the First Confiscation Act, which at last authorized Union forces to protect fugitive slaves who had absconded from Confederate masters and validated Butler's designation of them as contraband. The law belatedly affirmed the months-old practice of confiscating slaves as property of the enemy. Slaves who proved they had been employed in service to the Confederacy could legally find asylum with the Union military. The First Confiscation Act left unresolved the question of how to handle runaways escaped from loyal masters, although the Lincoln administration continued to enforce the Fugitive Slave Act in the border states in an effort to maintain their allegiance to the Union. Commanders in the field thus faced the daunting task of distinguishing between fugitive slaves fleeing from Confederate service and those intending to escape slavery altogether.

Despite the passage of the First Confiscation Act, Union generals continued to decide for themselves whether or not to return runaways until late winter 1862. Then, on March 13, Congress passed an article of war that explicitly forbade Union commanders to return fugitive slaves to their masters, regardless of the slaveholder's Union or Confederate sympathies. According to the new mandate, "All officers or persons in the military or naval service of the United States are prohibited from employing any of the forces under their respective commands for the purpose of returning fugitives from service or labor." Any officers who violated the law by returning runaway slaves to their masters were subject to court martial.[21]

More than a narrow military question, however, the flood of fugitive slaves to Union lines had political ramifications. By deserting their masters, streaming into Union camps, and contributing to the Northern war effort, slaves exerted pressure for their own emancipation. General Butler resisted it. His contraband policy did not interfere with slaves' status as property or attempt to emancipate runaways. Butler, in fact, wrote Colonel Mallory a receipt assuring his slaves' return after

---

[20] *The Congressional Globe: Containing the Debates and Proceedings of the First Session of the Thirty-seventh Congress* (Washington, D.C.: Congressional Globe Office, 1861), 32.

[21] Roy P. Basler, ed., *The Collected Works of Abraham Lincoln*, vol. 5 (New Brunswick, N.J.: Rutgers University Press, 1953), 435.

the war. General John C. Frémont was another story. Commanding the Department of the West, Frémont had imposed martial law in Missouri on August 30, 1861, and declared free the slaves of Confederate sympathizers. On September 2, President Lincoln requested that Frémont modify his order to conform to the First Confiscation Act, but the general demurred. Defending his action, he explained to Lincoln that "I acted with full deliberation and . . . the conviction that it was . . . right and necessary." At Frémont's own urging, Lincoln ordered him to alter his decree, and Frémont complied.[22] (See the sidebar "John C. Frémont" on page 416.)

The Union's judge advocate general Joseph Holt complained to Lincoln that Frémont, in emancipating slaves, overstepped the bounds of the First Confiscation Act. Frémont's action, Holt wrote, provoked "alarm and condemnation" among "the Union-loving citizens of Kentucky." Holt preferred a more "conservative policy" toward fugitive slaves because "the loyal men of the border slave States" feared "any attempt on the part of the Government of the United States to liberate suddenly in their midst a population unprepared for freedom and whose presence could not fail to prove a painful apprehension if not a terror to the homes and families of all." By the time Lincoln received Holt's missive, the president had already acted. Lincoln, conscious of public opinion in Kentucky and aware that the Union maintained only a precarious grip on the state, agreed with Holt, remarking to Frémont that "the confiscation of property, and the liberating slaves of traiterous [sic] owners, will alarm our Southern Union friends, and turn them against us—perhaps ruin our rather fair prospect for Kentucky." In addition to his concerns about border-state loyalty, Lincoln explained in September 1861 to Senator Orville H. Browning of Illinois that "military necessity" could not justify Frémont's emancipation decree. To seize and liberate a master's slaves, Lincoln argued, amounted to "dictatorship." He stated that the power to emancipate slaves stood outside the president's authority, residing instead with Congress.[23] (See "Letter, Abraham Lincoln to Orville H. Browning, 1861," on page 426 in the Primary Sources section.)

---

[22] Basler, *Collected Works of Abraham Lincoln*, vol. 4, 507.
[23] *War of the Rebellion*, ser. 2, vol. 1, 769, 768; Lincoln, *Speeches and Writings, 1859–1865*, 266.

Lincoln reined in another of his military commanders in May 1862. After declaring martial law in the Department of the South on April 25, General David Hunter issued General Order No. 11 on May 9, liberating slaves in South Carolina, Georgia, and Florida. Denying Hunter's authority to emancipate slaves, Lincoln rescinded the order on May 19. No "indispensable necessity" yet justified liberation, he wrote. In revoking Hunter's proclamation, Lincoln added that "I reserve to myself"—"as Commander-in-Chief of the Army and Navy"—the right to emancipate slaves. Whereas Lincoln had ceded emancipation to the legislative branch when he reversed Frémont's order freeing bond people in Missouri, the president now claimed for himself the power to liberate slaves.[24]

To the frustration of abolitionists, who immediately recognized the Civil War as an opportunity to eradicate slavery, Lincoln was not yet prepared to free slaves. William Lloyd Garrison, Frederick Douglass, and other abolitionists were outraged at the president's handling of the Frémont and Hunter decrees. "Generals who are on the ground where slavery exists, and see what effects emancipation would produce, are the best judges when to strike the blow," insisted editor Philip A. Bell of the *Pacific Appeal,* a black newspaper published in San Francisco. Bell urged Lincoln to "grant them unrestricted power." Lincoln opposed emancipation by the military, however, and now claimed control over slavery for the executive. Disappointed and increasingly impatient abolitionists could only watch as Lincoln continued to promote a program of gradual, compensated emancipation and colonization well into 1862.[25]

Immediate emancipation would have been unthinkable at the start of the Civil War. The Northern public vehemently opposed the liberation of slaves, fearing a mass migration of freed people northward to take whites' jobs. Northern hostility to emancipation helped explain the dogged persistence of colonization schemes in the public discourse, despite their obvious impracticality. In 1862, however, pressure on Lincoln to emancipate slaves grew. On April 16, he signed a law abolishing slavery in Washington, D.C., where the Constitution gave Congress the unquestionable authority to legislate. On July 17, Congress passed the Second Confiscation Act, which freed any slaves who fell into Union

---

[24] Lincoln, *Speeches and Writings, 1859–1865,* 586, 319, 318.

[25] C. Peter Ripley, ed., *The Black Abolitionist Papers,* vol. 5 (Chapel Hill: University of North Carolina Press, 1992), 145–146.

JOHN C. FRÉMONT

Without authorization from President Lincoln, John C. Frémont, in 1861, became the first of two Union generals in the field to liberate slaves well in advance of the president's own Emancipation Proclamation. Although neither order was allowed to stand, the generals anticipated the major consequence of the Civil War for Southern slaves: the freedom eventually guaranteed them by ratification of the Thirteenth Amendment in 1865.

Born in Georgia, Frémont gained renown as a frontier explorer and mapmaker. His exploits earned him the nickname "Pathmarker of the West." During the Mexican-American War, he fought in California. He briefly served as military governor of that state before becoming one of California's first two U.S. senators. With well-known antislavery credentials, Frémont was chosen as the first presidential nominee of the Republican Party in 1856 but went on to lose a three-way election to Democrat James Buchanan of Pennsylvania.

Early in the Civil War, Frémont commanded the Department of the West, headquartered in St. Louis, Missouri. It was in that capacity that Frémont, without consulting anyone in the Lincoln administration, issued his order freeing slaves. At the same time, to quell guerrilla warfare in Missouri and help repel a Confederate invasion in the state, he proclaimed martial law in Missouri and declared that civilians who took up arms against the U.S. government could be court-martialed and, if convicted, shot. Lincoln disapproved of both measures, which Frémont resented. To plead his case personally to the president, Frémont sent his outspoken wife, Jessie Benton Frémont, daughter of the powerful former Missouri senator Thomas Hart Benton, to Washington, D.C. Arriving on September 10, 1861, Jessie Frémont requested a meeting with the president. Lincoln obliged but arranged to have her meet him at the White House at 9 P.M., the same evening of her

hands if their owner was a rebel. In contrast to the First Confiscation Act, the slaves need not have labored for the Confederacy. (See "Second Confiscation Act, 1862," on page 428 in the Primary Sources section.) Just days later, on July 22, Lincoln read a draft of the Emancipation Proclamation to members of his cabinet. Citing military necessity, he disclosed his intention to free, on January 1, 1863, "all persons held as arrival. Tired and disheveled from her long travels, Frémont found the president brusque. Lincoln, obviously perturbed with her husband, did not even offer her a seat during their brief meeting. After hearing Frémont out, he commented, "You are quite a female politician" and informed her that "General Frémont should not have dragged the Negro into it." Despite his meeting with Jessie Frémont, Lincoln rescinded her husband's decree. Frémont's unauthorized order, combined with his knack for making political enemies of important people and the various scandals that took place under his watch, prompted the president to remove him from command on November 2.

In early 1862, General Frémont was put in charge of the newly created Mountain Department, operating in portions of Virginia, Kentucky, and Tennessee. In the Shenandoah Valley of Virginia, Confederate general Stonewall Jackson repeatedly outfoxed Frémont's troops, and Frémont resigned by the middle of the year after his underwhelming—or, as some might argue, incompetent—performance as a military leader. Lincoln later asked Frémont to gather black troops in the South for the Union cause, but the general declined the offer.

In the presidential election of 1864, Frémont emerged as a possible Republican challenger to the incumbent Lincoln. Certainly, he felt personal animosity toward the president, and, although Frémont's 1861 order freeing slaves purportedly undermined Unionist sentiment in the border states, it was popular in the Northern press and gained Frémont the support of radical Republicans and abolitionists disenchanted with Lincoln. In 1864, they nominated him for president on a platform calling for a constitutional amendment to abolish slavery. But Frémont's base of political support was always rather narrow, and as the North's prospects for victory brightened and the political winds shifted, Frémont withdrew his name from the contest. Frederick Douglass and other African Americans who had backed his candidacy turned then to Lincoln.

slaves within any state or states, wherein the constitutional authority of the United States shall not then be practically recognized."[26] Although Lincoln was confident the public would willingly accept emancipation, Secretary of State William H. Seward advised the president to postpone

---

[26] Basler, *Collected Works of Abraham Lincoln,* vol. 5, 336–337.

publicizing the proclamation until after a Union military victory or risk the measure implying Northern desperation. Days after the nominal Union triumph at the Battle of Antietam, Lincoln issued his preliminary Emancipation Proclamation on September 22, 1862, and signed the second Emancipation Proclamation on the first day of 1863. Slaves belonging to those actively in rebellion and not under Union control were freed, but loyal slaveholders in the border states were unaffected.

Emancipation was a wartime measure with many purposes. It sought to reinvigorate support for the war in the North, where public opinion had shifted in favor of liberation. Redefining the war as a moral struggle against slavery had diplomatic advantages as well, gaining European support for the North and deterring Great Britain from aiding the Confederacy. Militarily, the Emancipation Proclamation encouraged more slaves than ever to run away from their masters. Without the benefit of slave labor, the Confederacy was weakened. That the Civil War had been transformed into a war of liberation also inspired blacks to support the Union cause, some 180,000 as Union troops. With the Union's victory over the Confederacy and the passage of the Thirteenth Amendment in 1865, the institution of slavery in the United States was legally dead.

Within a week of Confederate general Robert E. Lee's surrender to the Union's Ulysses S. Grant in April 1865, actor and Confederate sympathizer John Wilkes Booth assassinated President Lincoln in Washington, D.C. As Frederick Douglass argued in 1876 at the unveiling of a monument to the slain president, Lincoln's journey toward the emancipation of slaves was slow and halting. (See "Speech of Frederick Douglass, 1876," on page 429 in the Primary Sources section.) Lincoln did not agitate for liberation early in the war as he struggled to maintain Northern unity and prevent border states from defecting to the Confederacy, and he rejected attempts by his military leaders to free Southern slaves. He nevertheless became known as the Great Emancipator, thanks in no small part to the slaves who asserted their presence by fleeing to Union lines.

WHAT IF?

What if Northern military forces had acted differently toward fugitive slaves?
Had Union generals uniformly welcomed fugitive slaves from the beginning of the Civil War, the conflict might have more quickly morphed into the war of liberation it ultimately became. But whereas radical abolitionists would have been pleased

with the most direct possible path to emancipation, the Northern masses in 1861 possibly would have recoiled at the Union army's aggressive pursuit of slaves' freedom. President Lincoln's fears of alienating the border states might also have come to fruition, driving Missouri, Kentucky, and Maryland from the Union to grow and strengthen the Confederacy.

If Northern military leaders consistently turned away slaves who fled to their camps, they would have undermined their own strategic interests. It was well known that the Confederacy had put slaves to work building fortifications and defenses to benefit the cause of their masters. Failure to take in runaway slaves would therefore have been self-defeating. Each slave the Union invited into camp was another slave not in the employ of the enemy.

But what if Southern slaves had not fled to Union lines at all? This would certainly have been out of character. Running away had been well established in the repertoire of slave resistance for centuries. To be sure, most slaves could be more accurately described as truants, temporarily absenting themselves from the home plantation for only a few days or weeks at a time, but some—younger, male slaves in particular—occasionally struck out in bids for freedom. In 1838 Frederick Douglass had disguised himself as a free black sailor and ridden a train to freedom. Ten years later, the enslaved woman Ellen Craft took advantage of her remarkably white skin to masquerade as a free white person, while her enslaved husband William pretended to be her servant. Together, they traveled to freedom in the North. In 1849, Henry "Box" Brown had himself mailed to freedom in a wooden crate. Wartime lent added danger to already risky attempts at flight, but for many slaves, the opportunity presented by passing Northern armies was too great to relinquish.

With time, Lincoln grew to support emancipation for several overlapping reasons, including the needs to reinvigorate support for the war in the North, to dissuade foreign intervention on the Confederacy's behalf, and to bolster Union forces militarily. But slaves themselves pressed the issue. Rather than passively awaiting freedom, they inundated Union lines and probably accelerated the transformation of the war into a war of liberation.

CHRONOLOGY

1850 Congress passes the Fugitive Slave Act.
1860 Abraham Lincoln is elected the nation's 16th president.
1861 *Mar. 4:* Abraham Lincoln is inaugurated.
      Apr. 14: Fort Sumter falls to the Confederacy.

May 24: Union general Benjamin F. Butler resolves to appropriate the labor of fugitive slaves belonging to disloyal masters.

Aug. 6: Congress passes the First Confiscation Act.

Aug. 30: Union general John C. Frémont declares martial law in Missouri and liberates slaves there.

Sept. 2: Lincoln requests that Frémont rescind his order to free slaves.

Sept. 11: Lincoln orders Frémont to rescind his decree.

Nov. 20: Union general Henry W. Halleck issues General Order No. 3, barring fugitive slaves from military camps in the Department of the Missouri.

1862 *Mar. 13:* Congress passes an article of war instructing Union forces not to capture or return fugitive slaves.

Apr. 16: Slavery is abolished in the District of Columbia, with compensation for masters.

May 9: Union general David Hunter declares martial law in South Carolina, Georgia, and Florida and declares slaves free in the Department of the South.

May 19: Lincoln revokes Hunter's proclamation of freedom.

July 17: Congress passes the Second Confiscation Act.

July 22: Lincoln reads a first draft of the Emancipation Proclamation to his cabinet.

Sept. 17: The North and South fight the bloody Battle of Antietam.

Sept. 22: Lincoln issues his preliminary Emancipation Proclamation.

1863 *Jan. 1:* The Emancipation Proclamation frees slaves in areas still waging war against the United States.

1864 *June 28:* Lincoln signs the repeal of the Fugitive Slave Act.

1865 *Apr. 9:* Confederate general Robert E. Lee surrenders to Union general Ulysses S. Grant.

Apr. 14: John Wilkes Booth assassinates Lincoln.

Dec. 18: The Thirteenth Amendment abolishes slavery in the United States.

DISCUSSION QUESTIONS

1. How consistent over time was Union policy toward fugitive slaves? How did it differ from one place to another?

2. What accounts for Union generals' differing opinions on what to do with fugitive slaves fleeing to Union lines?
3. Which argument for accepting slaves into Union camps seems to you most persuasive? Why?
4. Which argument against accepting slaves into Union camps seems to you most persuasive? Why?
5. President Abraham Lincoln, the U.S. Congress, Union generals, or the fugitive slaves: Who do you believe was most responsible for bringing about the eventual emancipation of American slaves? Why?

WEB SITES

Burton, Vernon. "The Age of Lincoln." Available online. URL: http://www.ageoflincoln.com/. Accessed June 29, 2010.

Cornell University. Making of America. *The War of the Rebellion: A Compilation of the Official Records of the Union and Confederate Armies.* Available online. URL: http://digital.library.cornell.edu/m/moawar/waro.html. Accessed June 30, 2010.

Library of Congress. "Abraham Lincoln Papers," American Memory. Available online. URL: http://memory.loc.gov/ammem/alhtml/malhome.html. Accessed June 29, 2010.

Public Broadcasting Service. "The Civil War," Africans in America, Resource Bank. Available online. URL: http://www.pbs.org/wgbh/aia/part4/4narr5.html. Accessed June 29, 2010.

BIBLIOGRAPHY

Carwardine, Richard. *Lincoln: A Life of Purpose and Power.* New York: Alfred A. Knopf, 2006. Chapter 5 credits Lincoln's knack for accurately assessing public opinion with helping him successfully navigate the issues of slavery and emancipation in the context of wartime.

Escott, Paul D. *"What Shall We Do with the Negro?" Lincoln, White Racism, and Civil War America.* Charlottesville: University of Virginia Press, 2009. An account of the wartime opportunities missed by Lincoln and white Americans to pursue enlightened racial principles.

Fredrickson, George M. *Big Enough to Be Inconsistent: Abraham Lincoln Confronts Slavery and Race.* Cambridge, Mass.: Harvard University Press, 2008. A collected series of lectures that explore Lincoln's complex views on slavery and race, his struggles over slavery and constitutionalism, and the effect of wartime on his willingness to free slaves.

Guelzo, Allen C. *Lincoln's Emancipation Proclamation: The End of Slavery in America.* New York: Simon & Schuster, 2004. Thoroughly contextualizes the Emancipation Proclamation while portraying Lincoln as the last Enlightenment president.

Neely, Jr., Mark E. *The Last Best Hope of Earth: Abraham Lincoln and the Promise of America.* Cambridge, Mass.: Harvard University Press, 1993. Chapter 4 examines President Lincoln's shifting attitudes toward emancipation in 1861 and 1862.

Paludan, Phillip Shaw. *The Presidency of Abraham Lincoln.* Lawrence: University Press of Kansas, 1994. Stresses Lincoln's commitment to constitutionalism and the law.

Siddali, Silvana R. *From Property to Person: Slavery and the Confiscation Acts, 1861–1862.* Baton Rouge: Louisiana State University Press, 2005. A detailed examination of the legal and constitutional questions raised by the Confiscation Acts.

PRIMARY SOURCES

1. Letter, Benjamin F. Butler to Winfield Scott, 1861

Writing from Fort Monroe, Virginia, on May 24–25, 1861, General Benjamin F. Butler informed General Winfield Scott of the circumstances that prompted him to declare fugitive slaves to Union camps "contraband of war."

On Thursday night three negroes, field hands belonging to Col. Charles K. Mallory now in command of the secession forces in this district, delivered themselves up to my picket guard and as I learned from the report of the officer of the guard in the morning had been detained by him. I immediately gave personal attention to the matter and found satisfactory evidence that these men were about to be taken to Carolina for the purpose of aiding the secession forces there; that two of them left wives and children (one a free woman) here; that the other had left his master from fear that he would be called upon to take part in the rebel armies. Satisfied of these facts from cautious examination of each of the negroes apart from the others I determined for the present and until better advised as these men were very serviceable and I had great need of labor in my quartermaster's department to avail myself of their services, and that I would send a receipt to Colonel Mallory that I had so taken them as I would for any other property of a private citizen which the exigencies of the service seemed to require to be taken by me, and especially property that was designed, adapted and about to be used against the United States.

As this is but an individual instance in a course of policy which may be required to be pursued with regard to this species of property I have detailed to the lieutenant-general this case and ask his direction. I am credibly informed that the negroes in this neighborhood are now being employed in the erection of batteries and other works by the rebels which it would be nearly or quite impossible to construct without their labor. Shall they be allowed the use of this property against the United States and we not be allowed its use in aid of the United States?

Source: The War of the Rebellion: A Compilation of the Official Records of the Union and Confederate Armies, ser. 2, vol. 1 (Washington, D.C.: Government Printing Office, 1894), 752.

—⁓—

2. Letter, E. P. Halsted to John D. Shaul, 1862

Acting Assistant Adjutant General E. P. Halsted wrote to Lieutenant Colonel John D. Shaul of the 76th Regiment New York Volunteers on April 6, 1862, discussing General Abner Doubleday's thoughts on the military value of fugitive slaves to the Union cause. According to legend, Doubleday invented the sport of baseball, but this myth is false.

The question has been asked whether it would not be better to exclude negroes altogether from the lines. The general [Doubleday] is of the opinion that they bring much valuable information which cannot be obtained from any other source. They are acquainted with all the roads, paths, fords and other natural features of the country and they make excellent guides. They also know and frequently have exposed the haunts of secession spies and traitors and the existence of rebel organizations. They will not therefore be excluded.

Source: The War of the Rebellion: A Compilation of the Official Records of the Union and Confederate Armies, ser. 2, vol. 1 (Washington, D.C.: Government Printing Office, 1894), 815.

—⚏—

3. Letter, George E. Waring, Jr., to Alexander Asboth, 1861

On December 19, 1861, Major General George E. Waring, Jr., wrote to Acting Major General Alexander Asboth, questioning how to enforce Henry W. Halleck's General Order No. 3. Waring's letter makes evident his overlapping concerns for fugitive slaves, as both objects of humanitarian sympathy and sources of labor.

These negroes all claim and insist that they are free. Some of them I have no question are so; others I have as little doubt have been slaves but no one is here to prove it and I hesitate to take so serious a responsibility as to decide arbitrarily in the absence of any direct evidence that they are such. If I turn them away I inflict great hardship upon them as they would be homeless and helpless; furthermore such a course would occasion much personal inconvenience and sincere regret to other officers no less than to myself. These people are mainly our servants and we can get no others. They have been employed in this capacity for some time—long enough to like them as servants, to find them useful and trustworthy and to feel an interest in their welfare.

Source: The War of the Rebellion: A Compilation of the Official Records of the Union and Confederate Armies, ser. 2, vol. 1 (Washington, D.C.: Government Printing Office, 1894), 789–790.

—⚏—

4. Letter of Thomas W. Sherman, 1861

General Thomas W. Sherman reflected the racist attitudes prevalent among many Union soldiers when he explained in a letter of December 15, 1861, why blacks were not a valuable source of labor in northern camps.

First. They are naturally slothful and indolent and have always been accustomed to the lash, an aid we do not make use of.

Second. They appear to be so overjoyed with the change of their condition that their minds are unsettled to any plan.

Third. Their present ease and comfort on the plantations as long as their provisions will last will induce most of them to remain there until compelled to seek our lines for subsistence.

Source: The War of the Rebellion: A Compilation of the Official Records of the Union and Confederate Armies, ser. 2, vol. 1 (Washington, D.C.: Government Printing Office, 1894), 785–786.

—⁂—

5. Letter, Henry W. Halleck to Alexander Asboth, 1861

General Henry W. Halleck wrote to General Alexander Asboth on December 26, 1861, explaining his General Order No. 3. The congressional exception he notes is a reference to the First Confiscation Act's approval of the harboring of slaves formerly employed by the Confederacy.

The object of those orders is to prevent any person in the army from acting in the capacity of negro-catcher or negro-stealer. The relations between the slave and his master is not a matter to be determined by military officers except in the single case provided for by Congress. This matter in all other cases must be decided by the civil authorities. One object in keeping fugitive slaves out of our camps is to keep clear of all such questions.

Source: The War of the Rebellion: A Compilation of the Official Records of the Union and Confederate Armies, ser. 2, vol. 1 (Washington, D.C.: Government Printing Office, 1894), 796.

—⁂—

6. Letter, John A. Dix to George B. McClellan, 1861

In a letter dated August 21, 1861, General John A. Dix discussed with General George B. McClellan the dangers of receiving fugitive slaves.

I expressed the desire that no officer in this department should take negroes into custody unless they were detected in committing some criminal act in which case they might be arrested and turned over to the civil authority. . . . We as a part of the military establishment of the country had nothing to do with fugitives from service; that we had no ministerial powers for their capture or surrender, and that their masters must resort to the measures provided by law for their recovery. . . .

Unless we abstain from the reception or the capture of fugitive slaves I think we shall involve ourselves in the most serious difficulty. Their numbers will increase rapidly if it is understood that they are to be received and fed especially as we advance into Virginia; and we shall not only be oppressed by a useless burden but we shall expose ourselves to the imputation of intermeddling with a matter entirely foreign to the great questions of political right and duty involved in the civil strife which has been brought upon us by disloyal and unscrupulous men. Our cause is a holy one and should be kept free from all taint.

Source: The War of the Rebellion: A Compilation of the Official Records of the Union and Confederate Armies, ser. 2, vol. 1 (Washington, D.C.: Government Printing Office, 1894), 764–765.

—⚉—

7. Letter, George B. McClellan to D. C. Buell, 1861

General George B. McClellan wrote to General D. C. Buell on November 7, 1861, stressing the need to hold Kentucky for the Union.

It is absolutely necessary that we shall hold all the State of Kentucky. . . .

The inhabitants of Kentucky may rely upon it that their domestic institutions will in no manner be interfered with and that they will receive at our hands every constitutional protection. I have only to repeat that you will in all respects carefully regard the local institutions of the region in which you command allowing nothing but the dictates of military necessity to cause you to depart from the spirit of these instructions.

Source: The War of the Rebellion: A Compilation of the Official Records of the Union and Confederate Armies, ser. 2, vol. 1 (Washington, D.C.: Government Printing Office, 1894), 776–777.

—⚉—

8. Letter, Abraham Lincoln to Orville H. Browning, 1861

President Abraham Lincoln wrote to his friend and Illinois senator Orville H. Browning on September 22, 1861, explaining why he rescinded General John C. Frémont's emancipation order.

Yours of the 17th is just received; and coming from you, I confess it astonishes me. That you should object to my adhering to a law, which you had assisted in making, and presenting to me, less than a month before, is odd enough. But this is a very small part. Genl. Fremont's proclamation, as to confiscation of property, and the liberation of slaves, is *purely political,* and not within the range of *military* law, or necessity. If a commanding General finds a necessity to seize the farm of a private owner, for a pasture, an encampment, or a fortification, he has the right to do so, and to so hold it, as long as the necessity lasts; and this is within military law, because within military necessity. But to say the farm shall no longer belong to the owner, or his heirs forever; and this as well when the farm is not needed for military purposes as when it is, is purely political, without the savor of military law about it. And the same is true of slaves. If the General needs them, he can seize them, and use them; but when the need is past, it is not for him to fix their permanent future condition. That must be settled according to laws made by law-makers, and not by military proclamations. The proclamation in the point in question, is simply "dictatorship." It assumes that the general may do *anything* he pleases—confiscate the lands and free the slaves of *loyal* people, as well as of disloyal ones. And going the whole figure I have no doubt would be more popular with some thoughtless people, than that which has been done! But I cannot assume this reckless position; nor allow others to assume it on my responsibility. You speak of it as being the only means of *saving* the government. On the contrary it is itself the surrender of the government. Can it be pretended that it is any longer the government of the U.S.—any government of Constitution and laws,—wherein a General, or a President, may make permanent rules of property by proclamation?

I do not say Congress might not with propriety pass a law, on the point, just such as General Fremont proclaimed. I do not say I might not, as a member of Congress, vote for it. What I object to, is, that I as President, shall expressly or impliedly seize and exercise the permanent legislative functions of the government.

So much as to principle. Now as to policy. No doubt the thing was popular in some quarters, and would have been more so if it had been a general declaration of emancipation. The Kentucky Legislature would not budge till that proclamation was modified; and Gen. Anderson telegraphed me that on the news of Gen. Fremont having actually issued deeds of manumission, a whole company of our Volunteers threw down their arms and disbanded. I was so assured, as to think it probable, that the very arms we had furnished Kentucky would be turned against us. I think to lose Kentucky is nearly the same as to lose the whole game. Kentucky gone, we can not hold Missouri, nor, as I think, Maryland. These all against us, and the job on our hands is too large for us. We would as well consent to separation at once, including the surrender of this capitol. On the contrary, if you will give up your restlessness for new positions, and back me manfully on the grounds upon which you and other kind friends gave me the election, and have approved in my public documents, we shall go through triumphantly.

You must not understand I took my course on the proclamation *because* of Kentucky. I took the same ground in a private letter to General Fremont before I heard from Kentucky. . . .

There has been no thought of removing Gen. Fremont on any ground connected with his proclamation.

Source: Abraham Lincoln, *Speeches and Writings, 1859–1865: Speeches, Letters, and Miscellaneous Writings Presidential Messages and Proclamations* (New York: Library of America, 1989), 268–270.

—⚭—

9. Second Confiscation Act, 1862

On July 17, 1862, the Second Confiscation Act became law. It passed by a vote of 28 to 13 in the Senate and 82 to 42 in the House of Representatives. Officially, slaves could only gain their freedom in federal court.

"An Act to suppress Insurrection, to punish Treason and Rebellion, to seize and confiscate property of rebels, and for other purposes," July 17, 1862. . . .

SEC. 9. *And be it further enacted,* That all slaves of persons who shall hereafter be engaged in rebellion against the government of the United States, or who shall in any way give aid or comfort thereto, escaping from such persons and taking refuge within the lines of the army; and all slaves captured from such persons or deserted by them and coming under the control of the government of the United States; and all slaves of such persons found *on* (or) being within any place occupied by rebel forces and afterwards occupied by the forces of the United States, shall be deemed captives of war, and shall be forever free of their servitude and not again held as slaves.

SEC. 10. *And be it further enacted,* That no slave escaping into any State, Territory, or the District of Columbia, from any other State, shall be delivered up, or in any way impeded or hindered of his liberty, except for crime, or some offence against the laws, unless the person claiming said fugitive shall first make oath that the person to whom the labor or service of such fugitive is alleged to be due is his lawful owner, and has not borne arms against the United States in the present rebellion, nor in any way given aid and comfort thereto; and no person engaged in the military or naval service of the United States shall, under any pretence whatever, assume to decide on the validity of the claim of any person to the service or labor of any other person, or surrender up any such person to the claimant, on pain of being dismissed from the service.

Source: Roy P. Basler, ed., *The Collected Works of Abraham Lincoln,* vol. 5 (New Brunswick, N.J.: Rutgers University Press, 1953), 435.

—◊◊◊—

10. Speech of Frederick Douglass, 1876

On April 14, 1876, the 11th anniversary of Abraham Lincoln's assassination, Frederick Douglass delivered an oration in honor of the slain president in Washington, D.C., at the unveiling of the Freedmen's Monument in memory of Lincoln. Douglass offered an ultimately laudatory but remarkably blunt and honest assessment of the former president. Douglass catalogued Lincoln's accomplishments only after the prefatory remarks excerpted here.

Truth is proper and beautiful at all times and in all places, and it is never more proper and beautiful in any case than when speaking of a great public man whose example is likely to be commended for honor and imitation long after his departure to the solemn shades, the silent continents of eternity. It must be admitted, truth compels me to admit, even here in the presence of the monument we have erected to his memory, Abraham Lincoln was not, in the fullest sense of the word, either our man or our model. In his interests, in his associations, in his habits of thought, and in his prejudices, he was a white man.

He was preeminently the white man's President, entirely devoted to the welfare of white men. He was ready and willing at any time during the first years of his administration to deny, postpone, and sacrifice the rights of humanity in the colored people to promote the welfare of the white people of this country. In all his education and feeling he was an American of the Americans. He came into the Presidential chair upon one principle alone, namely, opposition to the extension of slavery. His arguments in furtherance of this policy had their motive and mainspring in his patriotic devotion to the interests of his own race. To protect, defend, and perpetuate slavery in the states where it existed Abraham Lincoln was not less ready than any other President to draw the sword of the nation. He was ready to execute all the supposed guarantees of the United States Constitution in favor of the slave system anywhere inside the slave states. He was willing to pursue, recapture, and send back the fugitive slave to his master, and to suppress a slave rising for liberty, though his guilty master were already in arms against the Government. The race to which we belong were not the special objects of his consideration. . . .

Our faith in him was often taxed and strained to the uttermost, but it never failed. When he tarried long in the mountain; when he strangely told us that we were the cause of the war; when he still more strangely told us that we were to leave the land in which we were born; when he refused to employ our arms in defence of the Union; when, after accepting our services as colored soldiers, he refused to retaliate our murder and torture as colored prisoners; when he told us he would save the Union if he could with slavery; when he revoked the Proclamation of Emancipation of General Fremont; when he refused to remove the popular commander of the Army of the Potomac, in the days of its inaction and defeat, who was more zealous in his efforts to protect slavery than to suppress rebellion; when we saw all this, and more, we were at times grieved, stunned, and greatly bewildered; but our hearts believed while they ached and bled. . . . Despite the mist and haze that surrounded him; despite the tumult, the hurry, and confusion of the hour, we were able to take a comprehensive view of Abraham Lincoln, and to make reasonable allowance for the circumstances of his position. We saw him, measured him, and estimated him; . . . we came to the conclusion that the hour and the man of our redemption had somehow met in the person of Abraham Lincoln.

Source: Philip S. Foner, ed., *Frederick Douglass: Selected Speeches and Writings* (Chicago: Lawrence Hill Books, 1999), 618–619.

๛๛๛๛๛๛๛๛๛๛๛ INDEX ๛๛๛๛๛๛๛๛๛๛๛

Italic page numbers indicate illustrations; page numbers followed by *c* indicate chronology entries; page numbers followed by *m* indicate maps.

A

AASS. *See* American Anti-Slavery Society

Ableman v. Booth 291, 298*c*

abolitionists/abolitionism
American Revolution 16
Bible and slavery 235–239, 246–247, 250, 251, 254, 257–258, 258*c*
colonization 114, 115, 132, 134–135, 141*c*
Dred Scott decision 375–376
fugitive slaves in Civil War 401–402, 415
gag rule 252–253
slavery in Virginia after Turner rebellions 198, 220*c*
three-fifths clause 55

"Abolition of Negro Slavery" (Dew) 218, 237

Abraham 241

ACS. *See* American Colonization Society

Act of 1807 89, 98–99, 101, 103*c*

Adams, John Quincy 252, *253*

AFASS. *See* American and Foreign Anti-Slavery Society

Africa, return to. *See* colonization

African Church of Philadelphia 15

African Repository 135

Alabama 172, 177*c*

Allen, Richard 12, *12*, 14

American and Foreign Anti-Slavery Society (AFASS) 254, 258*c*

American Anti-Slavery Society (AASS) 134–135, 238, 254, 258*c*

American Colonization Society (ACS) 114, 120–121, 123, 127, 132–134, 136, 137, 139–141, 141*c*

American Revolution xviii, 1–43, *5*
background 2–5
chronology 24*c*–25*c*
colonization 115–116, 141*c*
debate over Revolution's effect on status/condition of black Americans 1–2, 6–19
outcome and impact 21–24
primary source documents 27–43
transatlantic slave trade 79

"American System" 120

Andrew, James 255

Andrew, John A. 405–406

Anti-Federalists 60

"Appeal of the Independent Democrats in Congress to the People of the United States" (Chase) 330–331, 347–349

Appeal to the Coloured Citizens of the World (Walker) 197–198, 236, 258*c*

Appomattox Court House, Virginia 380*c*

Arkansas Territory 173, 340*c*

Articles of Confederation
American Revolution 16
and Constitution 44–45, 54, 56, 66*c*
weaknesses of 45–47

Atchison, David Rice 316

Attucks, Crispus 5

B

back-to-Africa movement 140

Bacon, Nathaniel xv

Bacon's Rebellion 102c

Badger, George 278–280, 320–323, 325–326

Baldwin, Roger 282, 283, 303

Banneker, Benjamin 11, 36–39

Baptists 251, 254, 258c

Barbé Marbois, François de 39

Barbour, James 167, 168, 170–172, 192

Barbour, Philip P. 167–170

Bard, David 83–85, 90, 106–107

Barnes, Albert
   Bible and slavery 245–247, 249
   on equality 269–270
   An Inquiry into the Scriptural Views of Slavery 265–266
   on slavery and polygamy 267–268

Bedinger, George M. 92

Beecher, Charles 246, 307

Bell, John 318, 327, 333, 399

Bell, Philip A. 415

Benton, Thomas Hart
   Dred Scott decision 366, 372
   Fugitive Slave Bill of 1850 296
   Kansas-Nebraska Bill 319

Berry, Henry 206–207, 218–219

Berry Plan 218–219

the Bible, slavery and 235–270
   background 237–240
   chronology 258c–259c
   debate over proslavery/antislavery stance in Bible 235–236, 240–250
   outcome and impact of debate 250–251, 254–255, 257–258
   primary source documents 261–270

"The Bible Argument on Slavery" (Hodge) 263

Bidwell, Barnabas 88, 97

Birney, James G. 251, 254, 258c

Black Codes xxii

black regiments 10

Black Star Line 140

Bledsoe, Albert Taylor 241–243

Bleeding Kansas 337–339, 380c

"Bleeding Sumner" 338, *339*

Blow, Peter 356, 374, 379c, 380c

Booth, John Wilkes 418, 420c

Booth, Sherman M. 290

border states 396, 399, 410–411

Boston, Massachusetts 22, 292–293

Bourne, George 247–248

Bradley, Stephen Row 95–97

Breckinridge, John C.
   Dred Scott decision 377
   fugitive slaves in Civil War 399
   Kansas-Nebraska Bill 319

Brodnax, William Henry 210, 212–213, 215, 219, 231–233

Brooks, Preston 321, 326–327, 338, 341c

Broom, James Madison 84–87, 90, 106, 108

Brown, Harvey 406

Brown, Henry "Box" 419

Brown, John 217, 220c, 338, 341c

Brown, John Thompson 210, 214

Bruce, James 212

Buchanan, James
   Dred Scott decision 358, 377, 378, 380c, 382–383
   Fugitive Slave Bill of 1850 290
   gag rule 252
   on slavery in territories 394–395

Budd, William 408

Burgess, Ebenezer 121, 126, 130, 131, 145–146, 149

Burns, Anthony 292–293

Butler, Andrew P.
   "Bleeding Sumner" 338
   Fugitive Slave Bill of 1850 277, 297
   Kansas-Nebraska Bill 320–322

Butler, Benjamin F. *400*, 401–403, 412–414, 420c, 422–423

Butler, Pierce 52

C

Cain, curse of 240

Calhoun, John C. xxi
   Bible and slavery 238
   Fugitive Slave Bill of 1850 272, 274
   gag rule 252

California 275, 287, 315, 325

Cameron, Simon 403, 412

Campbell, John A. 362

Canaan, curse of. *See* Ham/Canaan, curse of

Canada 123

Cartwright, Samuel A. 256

Cary, Lott 121

Cass, Lewis 274–275, 317, 321

Catron, John 364

Chaffee, Calvin C. 374

Chambers, Ezekiel 121, 125, 127, 141*c*

Chase, Salmon P.
   Fugitive Slave Bill of 1850 281
   Kansas-Nebraska Bill 327, 328, 330–332, 334, 347–349

Chesapeake region xiv–xvii

"Christian abolitionists" 251, 254

Christianity. *See also* the Bible, slavery and
   colonization 113, 115, 128–130, 141
   race laws in 1660s xvi

Cilley, Jonathan 319

citizenship 365–366, 383–385, 387

Civil Rights Act of 1866 378

Civil Rights movement 140

Civil War 396–430
   background 399–401
   Bible and slavery 259*c*
   chronology 419*c*–420*c*
   colonization 138, 140
   debate over accepting fugitive slaves who fled to Union lines 396, 401–411
   Dred Scott decision 380*c*
   Fugitive Slave Bill of 1850 291–293
   outcome and impact 411–419
   primary source documents 422–430

Clay, Henry *175*
   colonization 120, 121, 123, 126, 127, 130
   Fugitive Slave Bill of 1850 278, 280, 287, 295
   gag rule 252
   Kansas-Nebraska Bill 323
   slavery in Missouri 174
   speech on colonization 148

Clay, Joseph 97

Clinton, Sir Henry 9

colonization 113–153, 139*m*
   background 115–121
   chronology 141*c*–142*c*
   debate 113–114, 121, 124–137
   forfeiture 89
   Rufus King and 165
   outcome and impact 137–141
   primary source documents 143–153

compensated emancipation 22–24, 142*c*, 258*c*

Compromise of 1850 286*m*
   Fugitive Slave Bill of 1850 272, 287, 288, 295–296, 297*c*
   Kansas-Nebraska Bill 312, 314, 315, 317, 321, 323–325, 330–332, 340, 341*c*, 345–346

Confederation Congress 48, 170–171, 177*c*, 379*c*

The Confessions of Nat Turner 198–199

Confiscation Act, First 413, 414, 420*c*, 425

Confiscation Act, Second 415–416, 420*c*, 428–429

Congress, U.S. *See also* House of Representatives, U.S.; Senate, U.S.
   Fugitive Slave Bill of 1850 271–311
   gag rule 252–253
   slavery in Missouri 154–158, 161–163, 168–169, 174
   transatlantic slave trade 81–98, 102*c*, 103*c*

Connecticut 10, 25*c*

Constitutional Convention (1787) xxi
American Revolution 25*c*
and Constitution 44–45, 47–54, 66
excerpt from debates at 69, 71
transatlantic slave trade 79, 102*c*
George Washington and 62–63

Constitution of the United States
44–76
antislavery aspects 57–60
background 45–54
chronology 66*c*–67*c*
debate over Constitution as proslavery document 44, 54–60
Dred Scott decision 367
Fugitive Slave Bill of 1850 297*c*
Kansas-Nebraska Bill 328
outcome and impact 60–66
passages concerning slavery 69–71
passages with bearing on Missouri
controversy 180–181
primary source documents 69–76
proslavery aspects 54–57
slavery in Missouri 161–163, 166
South Carolina ratification debate
72–73
transatlantic slave trade 77–80

Continental army 10

Continental Congress, First 7, 24*c*

Continental Congress, Second 45

"contraband of war" policy 403, 412,
413, 422–423

Coolidge, Calvin 140

Cornwallis, Charles, Lord 21, 24*c*

cotton gin 21, 159

Craft, Ellen 419

"Crime Against Kansas" speech (Sumner) 338, 341*c*, 352–353

Crittenden compromise 378

Cuba 336–337

Cuffee, Paul 12, 118, 119, 121, *188*

Cullom, William 327, 329, 330, 334,
346–347

curse of Ham. *See* Ham/Canaan, curse
of

Curtis, Benjamin R. 368–369
on black citizenship 386–387
on Congressional power over the
territories 387–388
Dred Scott decision 365–371, 374,
378

Cutting, Francis B. 319

D

Daniel, Peter V. 364, 385–386

Davis, Jefferson 275, 277, 315

Davis, John 282

Dayton, William L. 281–283, 285

death penalty 100–101

Declaration of Independence 2, 4–5,
24*c*, 27–28, 66*c*, 102*c*

Declaration of Rights (Vermont, 1777)
28–29

Deep South
colonization 114
Fugitive Slave Bill of 1850 272
slave trade 50–51
transatlantic slave trade 79–80

Delany, Martin R. 138

Delaware 66*c*

Democratic Party
Dred Scott decision 374, 376–378,
380*c*
Kansas-Nebraska Bill 335–337

Dew, Thomas Roderick 218, 237

Dickinson, John 66*c*

discrimination 19, 115, 140

Dix, John A. 407–411, 425–426

Dixon, Archibald 317

Dodge, Augustus C. 316

Doubleday, Abner 401, 403, 404

Douglas, Stephen A. *316*
Dred Scott decision 376–378,
391–392
ethnology and polygenesis 256
Fugitive Slave Bill of 1850 295
fugitive slaves in Civil War 399

Kansas-Nebraska Bill 312–318,
320–326, 328–330, 333, 334, 336,
340, 343–346
Douglass, Frederick
colonization 133
Dred Scott decision 373, 390–391
fugitive slaves in Civil War 401, 404,
415, 418, 419
oration in honor of Lincoln
429–430
Dred Scott case *(Dred Scott v. Sandford)*
341*c*, 354–396
background 356–358
chronology 379*c*–380*c*
debate over legal soundness of decision 354–355, 358–372
outcome and impact 373–379
primary source documents 382–395
Dred Scott v. Emerson 372
Dunmore, Lord 9, 24*c*

E

Early, Peter 88, 91–94, 101
election of 1860 377–378, 399
election of 1864 417
Electoral College 54–55
Elliott, Charles 249
Elmer, Ebenezer 84, 100
emancipation xx
after American Revolution 17
colonization 127–128
dates of, in Northeast 3*m*
slavery in Missouri 172
slavery in Virginia after Turner
rebellions 193, 219
Emancipation Act of 1833 (Britain)
22–23
Emancipation Proclamation 368,
416–418, 420*c*
Emerson, John 356, 364, 370, 371, 379*c*
England xvi
equality 4–5
ethnology 256
Everett, Edward 327, 329

Exodus (biblical book) 100, 240, 243,
246, 247

F

Faulkner, Charles James 207
Federalist 54 60–64, 73–76
Federalist Papers 60–64
excerpt from Federalist No. 42
71–72
excerpt from Federalist No. 54
73–76
Federalist Party 60, 164–165
federal number/ratio 47–50. *See also*
three-fifths clause
"Females of the County of Augusta"
225–227
Fifth Amendment
Dred Scott decision 355, 363–364,
370–371
Fugitive Slave Bill of 1850 274
fugitive slaves in Civil War 399
slavery in Virginia after Turner
rebellions 211, 214
Fillmore, Millard 287, 288, 290, 358
Findley, William 84–87, 89
Finley, Robert 120, 126
First Congress of the United States 80
Fitzhugh, George 240, 257
Fitzsimmons, Thomas 80
Florida 123
Floyd, John 198–199, 223–225
forfeiture 88–89
Forten, James *133*
address objecting to colonization
149–151
American Revolution 11
colonization 133, 134
Paul Cuffee and 119
Fourteenth Amendment 378, 380*c*
France 154, 156, 158, 159
Franklin, Benjamin 63
Free African Society 14
free blacks
after American Revolution 10–11

colonization 113, 114, 116, 120,
125–128, 131–133, 135, 136, 140
Dred Scott decision 362
Fugitive Slave Bill of 1850
282–283
slavery in Missouri 174
slavery in Virginia after Turner
rebellions 216
Freedom's Journal 137
Freeport doctrine 377
Free-Soil Party 341*c*, 379*c*
Frémont, John C. 414, 416–417, 420*c*
French and Indian War 3, 24*c*, 158
fugitive slave(s)
during American Revolution 9
as Constitutional issue 52, 56
status during Civil War 396–430,
403
Fugitive Slave Act of 1793 xix, 271, 272,
275–276, 278–280, 297*c*, 300–301
Fugitive Slave Bill of 1850 271–311
background 273–277
chronology 297*c*–298*c*
debate over passage of 271, 277–285
fugitive slaves in Civil War 396, 397,
402, 409, 419*c*, 420*c*
outcome and impact 285–297
primary source documents
300–311
fugitive slave clause (U.S. Constitution)
59
Fuller, Richard 242, 262
Fuller, Timothy 161–164, 166, 185

G

Gabriel slave conspiracy 103*c*, 116,
141*c*, 197, 220*c*
Gadsden Purchase 315, 341*c*
gag rule 252–253
Gamble, Hamilton Rowan 372
Garrison, William Lloyd *200*
Bible and slavery 236–239, 257,
258*c*
colonization 134, 141*c*

on Constitution 54
fugitive slaves in Civil War 415
slavery in Virginia after Turner
rebellions 198, 220*c*
three-fifths clause 55
Garrisonians 251, 254, 258*c*
Garvey, Marcus 139–140
General Order No. 3 407, 409, 420*c*,
424
General Order No. 11 415
George III (king of England) 3, 4, 7, 22,
24*c*
Georgia
American Revolution 25*c*
proslavery provisions in Constitu-
tion 57, 65, 66
slave trade 15, 50
transatlantic slave trade 79–81,
103*c*
Gholson, James 210–216
Giddings, Joshua R. 281, 282, 284, 288
Glisson, O. S. 408
Glory (movie) 405
Glover, Joshua 290
Golden Rule 237, 244, 248
Goldsborough, L. M. 408
Goode, William O. 202, 203, 210, 228
Goodwyn, James 229
gradual abolition 195
gradual emancipation
American Revolution 7–8, 17–18,
24*c*
colonization 142*c*
Fugitive Slave Bill of 1850 297
Pennsylvania law 29–31
Rhode Island law 31–32
slavery in Virginia after Turner
rebellions 220*c*
Grant, Ulysses S. 380*c*, 411, 418, 420*c*
Graves, William J 319
Gray, Thomas R. 198–199
Great Britain
in 1780s 46
American Revolution 9–10, 22–23

colonization 117, 141c, 142c
transatlantic slave trade 79
Great Compromise 47, 66c
Greeley, Horace 373, 389–390
Gregg, Andrew 92–94, 102, 110
Guadalupe Hidalgo, Treaty of 273,
   297c, 340c

H

Haiti 18, 159
Halleck, Henry W. 406, 407, 409, 412,
   420c, 425
Halsted, E. P. 423–424
Ham/Canaan, curse of 235, 236, 240
Hamilton, Alexander 60
Hamlet, James 287
Hammond, James Henry
   Bible and slavery 240
   Fugitive Slave Bill of 1850 296
   gag rule 252
   "Slavery in the Light of Political Sci-
      ence" 264–265
Harper, Robert Goodloe 121, 124–128,
   131, 144–147
Harpers Ferry Raid 217, 220c
Harrell, A. D. 408
Hayne, Robert Y. 136, 141c, 152–153
Hemings, Sally 17
Hemphill, Joseph 161, 162
Hepburn, John B. 121
"higher law" 271, 279, 284–285,
   302–310
Hodge, Charles 240, 242, 263
Holland, James 93, 94, 100, 101
honor, in debates over Kansas-Nebraska
   Bill 318–319
Hopkins, Samuel 116, 121, 126–128,
   147–148
Hosmer, William 246, 247
House of Representatives, U.S.
   and anti-slavery petitions 202
   and Constitution 47, 49, 54–55

Fugitive Slave Bill of 1850 285–286,
   293
fugitive slaves in Civil War 406,
   412–413
gag rule 252–253
Kansas-Nebraska Bill 319, 321, 323,
   326–328, 335–336, 338, 340
   slavery in Missouri 156, 157, 161,
      162, 172, 173, 176
   transatlantic slave trade 78, 84, 95,
      97, 100, 102, 103c
Houston, Sam 327, 333, 336, 349
How, Samuel Blanchard 243
Huger, Benjamin 91, 93–95, 108–109,
   111–112
Hunter, David 404, 415, 420c
Hunter, Robert M. T. 320, 321

I

Illinois 158, 364
importation, migration vs. 59, 163,
   167–168
indentured servitude xiv–xv, xvi, xvii
Indian Removal Act of 1830 332–333,
   340c
An Inquiry into the Character and Tendency of the American Colonization,
   and American Anti-Slavery Societies
   (Jay) 151–152
An Inquiry into the Scriptural Views of
   Slavery (Barnes) 265–266
interstate slave trade 58–59

J

Jackson, Andrew 340c
Jamestown, Virginia xiv, xv, 79, 102c
Jay, John 60
Jay, William 135, 151–152
Jefferson, Thomas 129
   colonization 121–124, 130, 141c
   Declaration of Independence 4–5, 7
   drafts of emancipation laws 16–17

equality in Declaration of Independence 2
forfeiture 88–89
Rufus King and 165
law prohibiting transatlantic slave trade 58
letter from Benjamin Banneker on slavery 36–39
letter to John Holmes on Missouri Compromise 190–191
Louisiana Purchase 159
Notes on the State of Virginia 18, 39–43
slavery in Missouri 175
transatlantic slave trade 97, 98
Jerry (slave) 288
Jesus Christ 235–237, 243–244, 248
Johnson, Jane 294–295
Johnson, Samuel 6
Jones, Absalom 12, 14–15, *15*, 98
Julian, George W. 282, 287, 296, 304, 308–310

K

Kansas
Dred Scott decision 377
Kansas-Nebraska Bill 337–339, 341*c*
Kansas-Nebraska Bill 312–353
background 315–320
chronology 340*c*–341*c*
debate over repeal of Missouri Compromise of 1820 312–313, 320–335
Dred Scott decision 379*c*
Fugitive Slave Bill of 1850 290
honor in the debates 318–319
Kansas-Nebraska Bill 317, 320
organization by territory 324*m*
outcome and impact 335–340
primary source documents 343–353
slavery in Missouri 176
text of bill 343
Keitt, Laurence M. 338
Kentucky 411, 414, 426
Key, Francis Scott 120

King, Rufus 161, 162, 164–165, 183–185
Know-Nothing Party 337
Knox, Alexander 214, 215, 219, 233–234

L

Leavitt, Joshua 251
Lecompton Constitution 377, 378
Lee, Robert E. 217, 380*c*, 418, 420*c*
Lee, William 63
Leviticus (biblical book) 243
Lexington and Concord, Battles of 24*c*
Liberator (newspaper)
Bible and slavery 236, 237, 258*c*
colonization 134, 141*c*
slavery in Virginia after Turner rebellions 198, 220*c*
Liberia 89, 121, 123, 137, 139, 139*m*, 140, 141*c*, 142*c*
Liberty Party 254, 258*c*
Lincoln, Abraham *398*
colonization 138
Dred Scott decision 376, 377, 392–394
John C. Frémont 416–417
Fugitive Slave Bill of 1850 291–292
fugitive slaves in Civil War 397, 399, 404, 405, 410, 413–417, 419*c*
Kansas-Nebraska Bill 334, 340
letter to Orville H. Browning on rescinding of Frémont's emancipation order 426–428
speech on popular sovereignty 349–350
Lincoln-Douglas debates 377, 380*c*
Livermore, Arthur 166
Livingston, Robert R. 159
Lloyd, Edward 100
Locke, John 4–5
Lord, John C. 306
Louisiana 162, 220*c*
Louisiana Purchase 160*m*
Dred Scott decision 379*c*

Kansas-Nebraska Bill 313–315, 324, 340c
  slavery in Missouri 156, 158–159, 170, 177c
  transatlantic slave trade 82, 87, 103c
Lovejoy, Elijah 258c
Lovejoy, Owen 412–413
Lower South 277
Lowndes, Thomas 91–94, 109–110
Lucas, John Baptiste Charles 84, 86, 105–107

M

Macon, Nathaniel 88, 91, 93, 95, 110–111
Madison, James 61
  colonization 120, 121, 123–125, 127, 128, 141c
  Paul Cuffee and 119
  on divide between North and South 47
  Federalist Papers 60, 71–72
  letter to Robert J. Evans on colonization 143–144
  notes on Constitutional Convention 53–54
  on slave trade and Constitution 57–58
  three-fifths clause 48
Maine 172–174, 177c
Mansfield, Joseph K. 407
manumission 8, 17, 115
Marion, Robert 93
Marshall, Thomas 219
Martin, Luther 52–53, 71
Maryland
  Articles of Confederation 66c
  colonization 116
  fugitive slaves in Civil War 411
  manumission 8
  race laws in 1660s xvi
  slave trade 50
Mason, James 278, 285

Massachusetts 24c, 119. *See also* Boston, Massachusetts
McClellan, George B. 407, 409–411, 426
McCook, Alexander McD. 408
McDowell, James, Jr. 205, 206, 230–231
McLane, Louis 173
McLean, John 358, 365–367, 369–372, 374, 378
Mennonites 251
Mercer, Charles Fenton 118, 120
Methodists 251, 254, 258c
Mexican-American War 272, 273, 317
Mexican Cession 273, 274m, 297c, 323, 340c
Mexico, U.S. acquisitions from (1848) 274m
Middle Passage 83
migration, importation *vs.* 59, 163, 167–168
Mississippi River 46
Missouri, slavery in 154–192
  background 156–161
  chronology 177c
  debate over restriction of slavery 154–155, 161–171
  outcome and impact 172–177
  primary source documents 179–192
Missouri Compromise of 1820
  debate over repeal of. *See* Kansas-Nebraska Bill
  Dred Scott decision 354, 355, 357, 362, 364–366, 369, 373, 375, 378, 379c
  Fugitive Slave Bill of 1850 275, 290
  slavery in Missouri 173–177, 177c
Mitchill, Samuel Latham 84–87
Monroe, James 120, 121, 177c
Monrovia 121
Moore, Samuel 206, 227–228
Moore, Thomas 91, 92, 102
Morris, Gouverneur 49, 52

Mosaic law 236, 242, 243, 246
Moseley, Jonathan Ogden 101
Moses (biblical figure) 235, 237, 242
Mott, Lucretia 295

N

Napoléon Bonaparte (emperor of
France) 159
Nash, Gary 12–13
Nashville Convention 296
Native Americans 333
natural rights 8–9
Navy, U.S. 93
Nebraska Territory 316, 317, 320
"necessary evil" 171
Nelson, Samuel 359, 364–365
New England 50, 79
New England Anti-Slavery Society
238
New Hampshire 24c, 66c
New Jersey 18, 25c
New Mexico Territory 287, 317, 325
New Testament 235, 236, 243–244,
248–250
New York State 25c, 66c
Noah (biblical figure) 240
nonintervention 312, 314, 318, 321,
325–328, 330, 333
northeastern U.S., dates of emancipa-
tion in 3m
Northwest Ordinance
American Revolution 7, 16, 20m,
21, 25c
Dred Scott decision 357
Kansas-Nebraska Bill 332
slavery in Missouri 162–163, 170–
171, 177c
U.S. Constitution 56–57
Northwest Territory 20m, 177c
Notes on the State of Virginia (Jefferson)
18, 39–43, 122, 124
Nott, Josiah C. 256
Nova Scotia 117, 141c
nullification xxi

O

Old Testament 235–237, 240–242, 244,
246, 247
Oregon Territory 323
Ostend Manifesto 336–337, 341c

P

Paris, Peace of (1763) 24c
Paris, Treaty of (1783) 21, 24c
Parker, Josiah 81, 82, 102c
Parker, William A. 408
Parrish, John 124
parus sequitur ventrem 213
Paterson, William 49
Paul (apostle) 244, 249
Pennsylvania 8, 24c, 29–31
petitions, anti-slavery
American Revolution 8–9, 16
Fugitive Slave Bill of 1850 288
gag rule 252–253
slavery in Virginia after Turner
rebellions 200, 202
transatlantic slave trade 102c
Petitions of Black Americans to State
Legislatures (1779, 1791) 32–36
Philadelphia, Pennsylvania
colonization 133
Paul Cuffee and 119
free black population after Ameri-
can Revolution 11–12
Absalom Jones in 14–15
Phipps, Benjamin *203*
Piedmont region, Virginia 201
Pierce, Franklin
Dred Scott decision 379c
Fugitive Slave Bill of 1850 290
Kansas-Nebraska Bill 335, 336,
341c
Pinckney, Charles 50–51
Pinckney, Charles Cotesworth 50–52
Pitkin, Timothy 89
Plessy v. Ferguson xxiii
Plumer, William 161, 162, 165–166

Polk, James Knox 273
polygenesis 256
popular sovereignty
 Dred Scott decision 376, 377
 Fugitive Slave Bill of 1850 274–275
 Kansas-Nebraska Bill 314, 317, 326, 333, 334
 "positive good" 161, 238
Pottawatomie Massacre 338, 341*c*
Pratt, Thomas 296–297
Preliminary Emancipation Proclamation 397
Presbyterians 255, 258*c*, 259*c*
Preston, William Ballard 204, 217
Prigg v. Pennsylvania 276–277, 279, 291, 297*c*, 301–302
Prince (slave) 10
Proclamation Line of 1763 4, 16, 24*c*
property rights
 Dred Scott decision 363–364, 370–371, 385–386
 Fugitive Slave Bill of 1850 274
 fugitive slaves in Civil War 399
 slavery in Missouri 169

Q

Quakers xviii, 16
 Bible and slavery 251
 Paul Cuffee and 119
 Fugitive Slave Bill of 1850 288
 Kansas-Nebraska Bill 335
 slavery in Virginia after Turner rebellions 200
 transatlantic slave trade 80, 81
Quincy, Josiah 89

R

race mixing 124, 138
Rachel v. Walker 370
Radical Reconstruction xxii, 138
Randolph, John 120
Randolph, Thomas Jefferson 193, 202–203, 206, 208, 228

Randolph Plan 193–194, 203, 206–209, 211–212, 214–216
Rankin, John 249
ratification of the Constitution 66*c*, 72–73
Raymond, Daniel 132
Reid, Robert W. 171, 188–189
religion. *See also* the Bible, slavery and; Christianity
 background 237–240
 chronology 258*c*–259*c*
 debate over proslavery/antislavery stance in Bible 235–236, 240–250
 Absalom Jones and 14–15
 letter from Chicago clergy opposing Kansas-Nebraska Bill 351–352
 outcome and impact of debate 250–251, 254–255, 257–258
 primary source documents 261–270
representation 47, 54–55, 61, 64
Republican Party
 colonization 138
 Dred Scott decision 375–376, 378–379, 379*c*
 Kansas-Nebraska Bill 337, 340, 341*c*
revolts/resistance. *See* slave resistance; *specific revolts, e.g.:* Turner, Nat, revolt
Revolutionary War. *See* American Revolution
Rhett, Robert Barnwell 288, 308
Rhode Island
 American Revolution 10
 gradual emancipation 25*c*, 31–32
 ratification of Constitution 66*c*
rice xvii
Richardson, William A. 321
Richmond Enquirer 222–223
Roane, William 200
Roberts, Jonathan 161, 163
Robinson, Harriet 356–357, 370
Ross, Fred A. 242
runaway slaves. *See* fugitive slave(s)
Rush, Benjamin 15

Russwurm, John Brown 121, 127, 137
Rutledge, John 50, *51*, 55–56, 71

S

Saint-Domingue 18, 82, 103*c*, 123, 159
Sanford, John F. A. 374
Schenck, Robert C. 410
science 256
Scott, Dred 355–358, *357*, 370, 379*c*.
  See also Dred Scott case
Scott, John 167–170
Second Missouri Compromise 174
segregation xxiii
Senate, U.S.
  Constitution 56
  Fugitive Slave Bill of 1850 278,
    285–286, 293
  Kansas-Nebraska Bill 316–319, 321,
    323, 335, 336, 338, 341*c*
  Rufus King and 164–165
  slavery in Missouri 157–158, 161,
    162, 172–173, 176
  transatlantic slave trade 81, 95–97,
    141*c*
"separate but equal" xxiii
Sergeant, John 161, 162
Seward, William H.
  Fugitive Slave Bill of 1850 284–285,
    304–305
  fugitive slaves in Civil War
    417–418
  Kansas-Nebraska Bill 320, 327,
    330–332, 335
Shadrack (slave) 288
sharecropping xxiii
Sharp, Granville 117
Shays's Rebellion 47, 62, 66*c*
Sherman, Thomas W. 407, 424–425
Sherman, William Tecumseh 409, 410
Sierra Leone 9, 114, 117, 119, 121,
    139*m*, 141*c*
slave resistance xvii–xviii, 193–234,
    196
  background 195–204

chronology 220*c*
The Confessions of Nat Turner
    198–199
  debate over abolition of slavery in
    Virginia following Turner revolt
    193–194, 204–216
  outcome and impact 216–219
  primary source documents 222–234
  in Saint-Domingue 18
  transatlantic slave trade 90
"Slavery in the Light of Political Sci-
    ence" (Hammond) 264–265
Slavery: Its Origin, Nature, and History
    (Stringfellow) 261–262
Slavery Ordained of God (Ross) 242
slave trade, transatlantic 7, 25*c*,
    77–112, 96*m*
  antislavery interpretation of Consti-
    tution 57–59
  background 79–83
  chronology 102*c*–103*c*
  colonization 130, 131
  Constitution 55–56
  Constitutional Convention 49–52,
    71
  death penalty and 100–101
  debate over taxation of slave imports
    77, 83–87, 90–95
  in *Federalist Papers* 60, 71–72
  forfeiture 88–89
  Luther Martin's opposition to
    52–53
  outcome and impact 95–99, 102
  outlawing of 66*c*
  primary source documents 105–112
Sloan, James 88, 95, 97
Smilie, John 89, 90, 100
Smith, Truman 329
Smyth, Alexander 125, 167, 169–171,
    186–188
Society for Effecting the Abolition of
    the Slave Trade 5
Society of Friends. *See* Quakers
Southard, Henry 86, 90, 95

South Carolina xvii, xxi, xxii, 103*c*
  colonization 136
  Fugitive Slave Bill of 1850 282–283
  ratification of Constitution 72–73
  slavery in Missouri 176–177
  slavery provisions in Constitution
    57, 65, 66
  slave trade 15–16, 50–52
  slave trade provisions in Constitution 56
  transatlantic slave trade 78–87,
    90–95, 98–99
Southern Baptist Convention 254–255,
  258*c*
southwestern U.S. 272, 273
Spain 46, 158, 159
Stamp Act 4
Stanton, Edwin M. 404–405
Stanton, Joseph, IV 87, 100–101
states' rights
  Articles of Confederation 45
  Fugitive Slave Bill of 1850 272
  slavery in Missouri 154, 155
Stephens, Alexander H. 321
Stevens, Thaddeus 292–293
Stono Rebellion 82, 102*c*, 197, 220*c*
Story, Joseph 301–302
Stowe, Harriet Beecher 288–290, 297*c*,
  310–311
Strader v. Graham 364
Stringfellow, Thornton 236, 240, 242,
  245, 261–264
Summers, George 206, 207–208
Sumner, Charles
  "Crime Against Kansas" speech 338,
    339, 352–353
  Fugitive Slave Bill of 1850 293
  Kansas-Nebraska Bill 327, 330, 331,
    334–335, 341*c*
Sunderland, LaRoy 239, 246–248, 250,
  269
Supreme Court, U.S.
  Dred Scott decision 354–373, 375,
    380*c*

Fugitive Slave Bill of 1850 276, 291,
  297*c*, 298*c*
Kansas-Nebraska Bill 341*c*

T

Taliaferro, Lawrence 356
Tallmadge, Benjamin 97, 100
Tallmadge, James, Jr. 160–161, 167,
  177*c*. *See also* Tallmadge Amendments
Tallmadge Amendments 154–157,
  163–164, 167–172, 174, 176, 177*c*,
  179–180
Taney, Roger B. *363*
  biography 360–361, *363*
  on citizenship status of blacks
    383–385
  Dred Scott decision 358–364, 367–
    369, 375
  Fugitive Slave Bill of 1850 291
Tappan, Arthur and Lewis 238, 251
taxation
  in *Federalist Papers* 64
  slaves as taxable goods 48–49
  three-fifths clause 48, 54, 55
  transatlantic slave trade 77–112
Taylor, John W. 161, 162, 164, 173,
  181–183
Taylor, Zachary 275
The Testimony of God Against Slavery
  (Sunderland) 269
Texas 287, 328, 340*c*
Thirteenth Amendment xxii, 59, 66*c*
  Bible and slavery 259*c*
  colonization 138
  Dred Scott decision 380*c*
  fugitive slaves in Civil War 418, 420*c*
  slavery in Virginia after Turner
    rebellions 220*c*
Thomas, Jesse B. 173, 177*c*. *See also*
  Thomas Amendment
Thomas Amendment 173, 189–190
Thornton, William 116
three-fifths clause

as antislavery provision in Constitution 57, 58
in Constitution 45, 47–50, 54–55,
66c
in *Federalist Papers* 60, 61, 64,
73–76
Kansas-Nebraska Bill 340
Rufus King and 164
Tidewater region, Virginia 201
tobacco xvii, 79
Toombs, Robert 318
transatlantic slave trade. *See* slave trade,
transatlantic
transcontinental railroad 315–316
Turner, Nat *203,* 220c
Turner, Nat, revolt
Bible and slavery 237, 258c
colonization 138, 142c
The Confessions of Nat Turner
198–199
effect on debate over slavery in Virginia 193–234
history of revolt xx, 193–197, *196, 203*
Tyler, John 167, 171

U

Uncle Tom's Cabin (Stowe) 288–290,
289, 297c, 310–311
Underwood, Joseph R. 277, 279,
302–303
Union Army, black soldiers in 404–405
Upham, Charles W. 332
Upper South 272, 277
U.S. Constitution. *See* Constitution of
the United States
Utah Territory 324, 325, 332

V

Van Dyke, Nicholas 168–171
Vermont Declaration of Rights (1777)
7, 24c, 28–29
Vesey, Denmark 220c
Virginia xxi–xxii
colonization 116, 136, 138
drafts of emancipation laws 16–17
early slavery in xiv–xv
free black expulsion 25c, 116
fugitive slaves in Civil War 402
increase in slaves after American
Revolution 15
manumission 8, 17, 18, 24c
race laws in 1660s xvi–xvii
ratification of Constitution 66c
slavery after Turner rebellion
193–234
slave trade 50
Virginia House of Delegates 142c,
193–220, 222–234, 258c
voting rights 19, 366

W

Wade, Benjamin 327, 328, 335,
350–351
Walker, David 197–198, 236, 258c
Waring, George E., Jr. 406, 424
Washington, Bushrod 120
Washington, George, and
administration
American Revolution 21, 25c
biography 62–63
Constitutional Convention
62–63
crossing of Delaware 10
election as president 67c
Fugitive Slave Act of 1793 300
Louisiana Purchase 158
Wayland, Francis 247, 266–267
Welles, Gideon 406
Wentworth, Tappan 327, 328, 334
West Virginia 220c
westward expansion
American Revolution 16
Kansas-Nebraska Bill 315–317
Louisiana Purchase 158
Missouri controversy 154–192
slavery in Missouri 164

Wheatley, Phillis 22–23
Wheeler, John Hill 294, 295
Whig Party 335–337, 340
Whipple, Charles K. 251
Whitefield, George 22
Whitney, Eli 21
Williams, David Rogerson 95
Williams, Peter, Jr. 98

Williamson, Passmore 294, 295
Wilmot Proviso 273, 274, 297c, 340c,
    341c, 379c
Wilson, James 48
Winthrop, Robert Charles 282
Wisconsin Territory 356, 362, 364
Wool, John E. 406
Wright, Elizur, Jr. 135